W9-BNX-015

INVESTMENT UNDER UNCERTAINTY, COALITION SPILLOVERS AND MARKET EVOLUTION IN A GAME THEORETIC PERSPECTIVE

THEORY AND DECISION LIBRARY

General Editors: W. Leinfellner (*Vienna*) and G. Eberlein (*Munich*)

Series A: Philosophy and Methodology of the Social Sciences

Series B: Mathematical and Statistical Methods

Series C: Game Theory, Mathematical Programming and Operations Research

Series D: System Theory, Knowledge Engineering an Problem Solving

SERIES C: GAME THEORY, MATHEMATICAL PROGRAMMING AND OPERATIONS RESEARCH

VOLUME 35

Scope: Particular attention is paid in this series to game theory and operations research, their formal aspects and their applications to economic, political and social sciences as well as to socio-biology. It will encourage high standards in the application of game-theoretical methods to individual and social decision making.

INVESTMENT UNDER UNCERTAINTY, COALITION SPILLOVERS AND MARKET EVOLUTION IN A GAME THEORETIC PERSPECTIVE

by

JACCO THIJSSEN

Department of Economics,
Trinity College Dublin, Ireland

KLUWER ACADEMIC PUBLISHERS
BOSTON / DORDRECHT / LONDON

A C.I.P. Catalogue record for this book is available from the Library of Congress.

ISBN 1-4020-7877-3 (HB)
ISBN 1-4020-7944-3 (e-book)

Published by Kluwer Academic Publishers,
P.O. Box 17, 3300 AA Dordrecht, The Netherlands.

Sold and distributed in North, Central and South America
by Kluwer Academic Publishers,
101 Philip Drive, Norwell, MA 02061, U.S.A.

In all other countries, sold and distributed
by Kluwer Academic Publishers,
P.O. Box 322, 3300 AH Dordrecht, The Netherlands.

Printed on acid-free paper

Printed in the Netherlands

Contents

List of Figures

Acknowledgments

No research can be the outcome of an entirely solitary process. The research that is presented in this book is the product of four and a half years of research. Most of it has been conducted during a four years stay at the Department of Econometrics & Operations Research, and the CentER for Economic Research at Tilburg University, Tilburg, The Netherlands. The last six months have been spent at the Department of Economics at Trinity College Dublin, Dublin, Ireland. I would like to thank both institutions for creating the atmosphere in which I could write this book.

Furthermore, I want to thank my co-authors Kuno Huisman and Peter Kort (Chapters 3, 4, and 5), Dolf Talman (Chapters 8 and 10), and Peter Borm and Ruud Hendrickx (Chapter 6) for the pleasant and fruitful cooperation. Furthermore, Dolf Talman and Peter Kort are especially thanked for many valuable discussions and for reading a previous version of the entire manuscript.

Finally, I thank my family and friends for their love and support over the past years.

Jacco Thijssen
January 2004
Dublin

Chapter 1

INTRODUCTION

> *Both economists and popular writers*
> *have once more run away with some*
> *fragments of reality they happened*
> *to grasp.*

Joseph A. Schumpeter,
Capitalism, Socialism, and Democracy, 1942.

1.   Rational Behaviour and Economics

Never in the history of mankind has there been such unlimited belief in the abilities of the human mind as in the Age of Reason in the first half of the eighteenth century. The likes of Mozart, Goethe, and Rousseau ensured a new era of optimism and creativity in both the arts and the sciences. In mathematics, the theory of probability was refined and its laws were believed to be good descriptions of human reasoning and decision making.[1] The French Revolution was the logical conclusion of the Age of Reason and Enlightenment. It also brought about its political and social downfall, ending in an age of terror; a victim of its own success. In the early nineteenth century, however, most fields of science abandoned many ideas from the era of Enlightenment. Nevertheless, in psychology and economics the probabilistic approach to describing a human being as a fully rational *homo economicus* remained popular as ever.

---

[1] In Rousseau (1762, p. 97), for example, one finds: *"Calculateurs, c'est maintenant votre affaire; comptez, mesurez, comparez"*.

1

Most of contemporary economics still uses the axiom of rational economic agents, where agents are believed to maximise expected utility. Expectations are often assumed to be based on objective probabilities. Expected utility with objective probabilities has been axiomatised by Von Neumann and Morgenstern (1944). Also, if one replaces objective probabilities with subjective ones, expected utility can still be axiomatised, see, for example, Savage (1954). Along the way some doubts were cast on the rational economic agent, notably by Allais (1953), Ellsberg (1961), and Tversky and Kahneman (1981), who showed by means of experiments that in decision-making people often violate the axioms underlying (subjective) expected utility theory. What consequences do these experimental results have on economic science?

If one considers economics to be a positive science, describing what *actually* happens, experimental violations of basic behavioural axioms should be met with a willingness to adapt the behavioural assumptions underlying economic analysis. If, however, one takes the point of view that economics is a normative science, which tries to find how people *should* behave, one could argue that these violations might not pose a problem. In this case, the *homo economicus* can survive as the cornerstone of economic science.

The validity of the (subjective) expected utility paradigm can be questioned, moreover, from a methodological point of view as well. For example, Laville (2000) argues that optimisation is rhetorically inconsistent. In another contribution Hermann-Pillath (2001) points at ontological problems in the standard neoclassical paradigm. He also argues that rivalling theories (to the standard neoclassical paradigm) do not survive empirical validation tests simply because these theories are tested using neoclassical ways of measurement. Hence, the neoclassical paradigm validates itself, because the methods to do so are based on it. Therefore, a Popperian falsification of neoclassical economics is impossible.

Furthermore, one of the ontological issues underlying all human sciences is that they deal with human beings and their own view of the world and individual beliefs. The human mind is therefore an integral part of economic science. Hence, to simply discard the experimental evidence that human minds do not work as machines calculating optima by stating that economics is a normative science, is an invalid argument. Any normative issue should fall under the constraints of the human mind. Thus, economic theory needs to take into account the cognitive, emotional, social and cultural aspects of their basic ingredient: people.

Numerous contributions have been made in the literature to adapt the rationality assumption and replace it with the concept of *bounded rationality*, a notion introduced in psychology by Herbert Simon (cf. Simon (1957)). The concept of bounded rationality has extended to fields like macroeconomics (e.g. Sargent (1993), Bomfim and Diebold (1997)), microeconomics (e.g. Radner (1996), Conlisk (1996), Vega–Redondo (1997)), and game theory (Samuelson (1996), Rubinstein (1998)).

Many different approaches have been used to model bounded rationality. In the field of evolutionary game theory (cf. Weibull (1995), Samuelson (1997)), one usually stays close to the biological concept of (Darwinian) evolution. In this literature, players are assumed to behave like machines, using pre-programmed strategies.[2] The growth rate of the population playing the most successful strategy is assumed to increase. In such models there is, however, no explicit learning. Modelling learning has been done using several different approaches (cf. Fudenberg and Levine (1998) for an excellent overview). One way is by assuming that players use some probability distribution over their opponents' strategies based on past observations. Each player uses this assessment to choose the action which maximises his own payoff in the next period. This is called fictitious play (cf. Young (1998)). Less elaborate learning processes are, for example, models based on heuristic behaviour like the imitation of successful opponents. Another approach to bounded rationality is case-based decision theory (cf. Gilboa and Schmeidler (2001)). Here, agents are assumed to make decisions on the basis of similarities with cases from past experience. Another recent idea can be found in Kosfeld (1999), who uses interacting particle systems to model boundedly rational decision making.

In analysing the performance of decision rules, an important component is the cognitive and computational burden it imposes on the decision maker. It has been argued by, for example, Gigerenzer and Goldstein (1996) that heuristic decision-making algorithms may even outperform rational inference, taking into account computational speed and accuracy.[3] So, bounded rationality may not be so "bounded" as the name suggests.[4]

Most models that apply boundedly rational decision making are used to analyse frequently recurring strategic or economic situations, like, for

---

[2]So, this literature strips every form of rationality, thinking, and learning from human beings.
[3]In economics, not only individual-decision making is subject to bounded rationality because of people's limited cognitive possibilities, but also the organisation of economic activity is limited by computational requirements. A formal computational analysis to economic behaviour and organisations has recently been advocated by Mount and Reiter (2002).
[4]The above shows that the standard approach to bounded rationality is mainly focussed on cognitive limitations of human beings. Other authors, however, have argued that for a substantial part human decision making is culturally and sociologically determined (cf. Hofstede (1984)) and that human emotions play an important role as well (Hanoch (2002)).

example, coordination problems. This is to be expected, since humans learn most from frequent interaction and assign less cognitive abilities to solve these problems. One can argue, however, that for infrequently occurring decisions economic agents assign more cognitive abilities to the decision-making process. As an illustration, an individual will think through the consequences of getting a mortgage to buy a house much more than she does in deciding to walk either on the right-hand or left-hand side of the pavement. This is, loosely speaking, the approach that is used in this book to analyse some aspects of firm behaviour.

The main point can easily be illustrated by means of an arm-chair analysis of a firm. The firm is frequently confronted with changes on its output markets, to which it has to react with a change in its production or price policy. This kind of decision has to be made on a regular basis, implying that managers get so much experience that they develop a "gut-feeling", resulting in behavioural routines and rules of thumb. However, once in a while the firm's management needs to make an important investment decision that determines its medium- or long-run capacity and strategic capabilities. This kind of decision needs to be thoroughly analysed. Large firms have entire divisions employed to perform this task. The rationality assumption might not be such a bad proxy for analysing these decisions.

Due to the above it can be argued that it is reasonable to say that important and large scale investment decisions are analysed by assuming rationality on the side of the firms, whereas frequent interaction situations should be modelled using a boundedly rational approach, as is done in this book. In Part I, models are presented to analyse the option to invest in a project with an uncertain payoff stream in the future. In Part II, the attention is focussed on strategic aspects of cooperation and its implications on a specific investment decision: mergers. Both parts use the rationality assumption as the starting point of the analysis. The purpose is to construct models that take as many crucial aspects of the investment problems into account as possible. We analyse the economic effects of uncertainty, strategic consideration, and cooperative possibilities due to the actions of rational (in the neoclassical sense) agents.

In Part III, the bounded rationality approach is used to analyse a single market where firms repeatedly compete in quantities.[5] For this

---

[5]The formal analysis of quantity competition dates back to Cournot (1838). His idea of equilibrium in quantities appears to be the same as the famous Nash equilibrium for non-cooperative games (cf. Nash (1950b)). It is interesting to point out that Cournot already assumes firms to be rational, profit maximising entities. We read (Cournot (1838, p. 83)): "*Nous n'invoquerons qu'une seule hypothèse, savoir que chacun cherche à tirer de sa chose ou de son travail la plus grande valeur possible*".

particular kind of market interaction we study the impact of different kinds of behaviour on the evolution of the market. Furthermore, a model is developed where boundedly rational price formation on financial markets is modelled. This model replaces the omnipresent "invisible hand" of Adam Smith with a market-maker who has limited knowledge about the preferences and endowments of consumers.

2. Introduction to Part I

The investment in new markets, products and technologies by firms is an important part of its competitive edge. In fact, Schumpeter (1942) argues that it is the most important part of competition in a capitalist system. According to him, a capitalist economic structure should be viewed as an evolutionary process. Capitalism is by definition a form or method of economic change and can never be viewed as static.

A firm that introduces a new product, uses a new technology, or enters a new market, is therewith creating new forms of industrial organisation. Schumpeter calls this a process of *creative destruction*. Any economic analysis should have this dynamic process as a starting point. The standard neoclassical theory is therefore regarded as fundamentally wrong by Schumpeter. The text-book analysis of oligopoly theory, for example, tries to explain the well-known moves of firms to set quantities or prices such as to maximise profits. That is, one accepts the momentary situation as it is and does not take into account the changing environment. Even in the case of a repeated game analysis, this is essentially the case. One can read in Schumpeter (1942, p. 84):

> But in capitalist reality [...] it is not that kind of competition which counts but the competition from the new commodity, the new technology, the new source of supply, the new type of organisation [...] – competition which commands a decisive cost or quality advantage and which strikes not at the margins of the profits and outputs of the existing firms but at their foundations and their very lives. This kind of competition is as much more effective than the other as a bombardment is in comparison with forcing a door[.]

Schumpeter's view was empirically supported by Solow (1957), who found that only a small fraction of per-capita growth (10% for the U.S. non-farm sector over the period 1909–1949) was associated with an increase in the ratio of capital to labour. Hence, technological progress plays an important role.

In macroeconomics the idea of creative destruction has been used extensively in the literature on endogenous growth (cf. Aghion and Howitt (1998)). Firms engage in Research and Development (R&D) and once in a while one firm (randomly) succeeds in introducing a new and better technology. This yields the firm monopoly rents until another firm takes over. The process that evolves in this way is called leap-frogging. The quality increments in the technology, due to R&D, are the engine of economic growth. Since the R&D expenditures are determined endogenously, the growth rate is endogenous as well.

In his seminal contribution, Arrow (1962) started the microeconomic analysis of incentives for R&D investments. In general, one considers two distinct areas in this literature. The first deals with the question of the pure benefits of innovation, like, for example, monopoly rents due to patents. This problem has been addressed notably by, e.g., Dasgupta and Stiglitz (1980), Lee and Wilde (1980), Loury (1979), and Reinganum (1982). The second strand concerns the strategic timing of the adoption of new technologies. For an overview of this literature see e.g. Tirole (1988). The literature that is reviewed there consists of deterministic models of the timing of adoption. In the past decades there has evolved a substantial literature on investment under uncertainty. For an overview, see the excellent book by Dixit and Pindyck (1996).

There are four basic characteristics of investment projects: (partly) irreversibility of investment, the possibility of delay of the investment, uncertainty about the profit stream generated by the investment and the presence of competitors who can make a similar investment. Irreversibility can arise simply because of technical conditions. For example, marketing and advertisement costs can not be recovered if a new market entry fails. Furthermore, due to the lemons problem (cf. Akerlof (1970)) many investments are worthless if one tries to reverse them. Secondly, most investment decisions can be postponed. A firm can buy a machine today or it can buy one tomorrow. In a deterministic world the possibility of postponement has no value since it is known from the start what the cash flows generated by an investment will be. However, most investment projects exhibit uncertainty about this flow of cash streams. This is the third characteristic of investment. The uncertainty induces an *option value* of postponing the investment. One can distinguish between two kinds of uncertainty, namely intrinsic uncertainty and uncertainty that is resolved upon investment. The former type of uncertainty will always exist, regardless whether the firm has invested in the project or not. As an example, there will always be uncertainty about the demand for the firm's output, depending on, for example, the business cycle, the unemployment rate, and so on. The latter kind of uncertainty refers to aspects of the investment that can not be foreseen until the investment actually takes place. Often one can obtain information on these aspects so that the uncertainty reduces over time. A key feature of this latter kind of information is that it is usually imperfect. For example, consider the introduction of a new communication technology by a telecom firm. The level of structural demand for the new service is unknown *a priori* and will only be revealed upon introduction. However, because of marketing research, the firm can gain some insight in the level of structural demand, thus reducing the uncertainty involved in the investment decision. Since a marketing survey consists of a sample and not the entire population, however, the signals that it provides on the profitability of the investment are imperfect. The last characteristic of investment is the presence of competitors, which has an influence on the investment decision. If a firm postpones investment longer than its competitors, it may loose the battle for customers, have less experience, no benefits from patents, and so on. On the other hand, it has the time to gain more information and adopt when it is very well prepared, maybe even with a superior technology. In short, a firm has to take into account the option value of waiting, the costs of waiting due to discounting, and strategic effects in determining its optimal time of investment.

The real options literature considers the investment problem of a monopolistic firm that faces only intrinsic uncertainty. In this literature, investment is seen as closely linked to an American call option (cf. Merton (1990)). The basic continuous time real options model is developed in McDonald and Siegel (1986). It assumes that the profit stream generated by the investment project follows a geometric Brownian motion and that the optimal time for investment is determined by solving an optimal stopping problem. The main conclusion is that the investment threshold (the value that needs to be attained for investment to be optimal) is significantly higher than when one applies the net present value rule. Applications of the real options approach can be found in, for example, Trigeorgis (1996) and Pennings (1998).

The basic model for the strategic timing of investment is given in Fudenberg and Tirole (1985). It is a deterministic model in continuous time of a duopoly with a first mover advantage of investment. It is shown that in equilibrium both firms will try to preempt each other, to the point where equilibrium rents are equalised. This implies that, in expectation, firms get the same value as if they are the second firm to invest. Recent contributions to this literature have been made by, for example, Stenbacka and Tombak (1994), who introduce experience effects and Hoppe (2000), who analyses the effect of second mover advantages on the strategic timing of investment. The literature combining both the real options and the strategic investment literature first started with the paper by Smets (1991). Recent contribution to the game theoretic real options literature can be found in, for example, Nielsen (2002) who shows that competition does not lead to greater delay in investment than does monopoly, or Weeds (2002) who shows that investment is delayed more when firms act non-cooperatively, because of the fear of preemption. Huisman (2001) extends the standard model to asymmetric firms and analyses the case where there are two consecutive investment projects, the latter having lower sunk costs than the former, but the point in time at which the superior technology becomes available is uncertain. More recent game theoretic real options models can be found in Pawlina (2003), who analyses, for example, strategic quality choice and issues regarding debt renegotiations for firms in financial distress, or in Murto (1999) who gives applications in energy markets. For an overview of the literature on game theoretic real option models see e.g. Grenadier (2000) or Huisman et al. (2004).

The literature on the timing of investment under uncertainty reducing over time due to information streams can be dated back to Wald (1947). He considers the, in essence statistical, problem of how much (costly) data to collect before taking a decision on a project with uncertain pay-off based on this information. A well-known example is the introduction of a new drug; the question is, how many experiments to conduct before deciding upon introduction of the drug. Wald proposes using a Bayesian updating procedure to make statistically sound decisions and then determining the optimal number of observations. For an exposition on this problem see, for example, Berger (1985). Wald's problem has proven to be notoriously hard to solve.

In Jensen (1982) a model is considered where signals are costless and the project can either be profitable or not. He shows that there exists an optimal threshold concerning the belief in a profitable project, but no analytical solution is provided. Recently, the paper by Décamps and Mariotti (2000) solves Wald's problem by making some simplifying assumptions on the structure of the uncertainty. The literature on the strategic effects of this kind of uncertainty is limited. The most notable contribution is made by Mamer and McCardle (1987). In that paper, the impact on the timing of innovation of costs, speed and quality of information arriving over time is studied for a one-firm model as well as for a duopoly. However, due to an elaborate information structure, Mamer and McCardle (1987) do not provide explicit results.

The contribution of Part I is twofold. On the one hand, it analyses the problem of strategic investment under uncertainty with imperfect information streams. As such, it complements papers like Jensen (1982) and Mamer and McCardle (1987). On the other hand, it gives a formal game theoretic underpinning for game theoretic real option models in general. In Chapter 3, which is based on Thijssen et al. (2004), a monopolistic firm that has the opportunity to invest in a project with uncertain profitability is considered. It is assumed that the project can lead to either high or low profits. Randomly over time, imperfect signals arrive that give an indication of the profitability of the investment project. After each arrival of a signal, the firm adjusts its belief on the profitability in a Bayesian way. An analytic expression for the threshold belief at which investment becomes optimal is attained. Furthermore, some measures to assess the probability of making a wrong investment decision by applying this threshold are given and a comparative statics analysis is conducted. It is shown that the threshold need not be monotonic in the quality and quantity of the signals.

Chapter 4 introduces the tools that are needed to analyse game theoretic real option models. It is partly based on Thijssen et al. (2002). It is shown that for preemption games like the one studied in Fudenberg and Tirole (1985), the stochastic counterpart leads to a similar kind of equilibrium. This equilibrium need not be unique, however. Furthermore, it is shown by means of simulations that the standard game theoretic real options model as presented in Smets (1991) leads to significantly different predictions than the one-firm real options model and the deterministic timing game model. The welfare implications of strategic considerations and uncertainty are also assessed. In the standard model there are situations where both the preemption equilibrium and a joint investment (collusion) equilibrium are optimal (see Huisman (2001, Chapter 7)). It is well-known that the collusion equilibrium is Pareto dominant. Here it is shown that it is also risk dominant (cf. Harsanyi and Selten (1988)). This is additional theoretical evidence that (tacit) collusion is likely to arise in some industries.

In Chapter 5 a duopoly version of the model presented in Chapter 3 is analysed using the methods developed in Chapter 4. That is, two competing firms which have the opportunity to invest in a project that can lead to either a high or a low profit stream are considered. Both firms have the same prior belief in the project yielding a high profit stream. At random points in time, signals arrive that indicate the profitability of the project. Both firms can observe these signals without costs. It is assumed that there is a first mover advantage in the sense that the firm that invests first has a (temporary) Stackelberg advantage. Furthermore, it is assumed that after a firm has invested the true state of the project immediately becomes common knowledge. Hence, there is an information spillover from the firm that invests first to its competitor, yielding a second mover advantage. It is shown that if the first mover advantage dominates, competition leads to a preemptive equilibrium where rents are equalised. If the second mover advantage dominates, a war of attrition occurs. If no investment takes place during the war of attrition (which happens with positive probability), a preemption equilibrium might arise. So, both types of interaction – preemption and war of attrition – can occur intermittently. Welfare effects are ambiguous in the case of preemption. It can be higher in duopoly, but there are also cases in which monopoly leads to higher welfare. This chapter is based on Thijssen et al. (2003).

Although a step is made in Part I towards a dynamic analysis of capitalist economies, in order to build a theory that is really in line with Schumpeter (1942), one should consider models that take both the intrinsic and the vanishing parts of uncertainty into account. Furthermore, the main shortcoming of the present literature is that it considers only one, or at most two, investment projects at a time. In order to build a truly dynamic model of capitalist economic interaction, one needs to consider a recurrent pattern of investment opportunities as well as an integration of the adoption literature and the R&D literature.

3.   Introduction to Part II

Game theory has traditionally been divided in non-cooperative theory and cooperative theory. Roughly one can say that non-cooperative theory is the micro branch of game theory and cooperative theory is its macro branch, as has been remarked by Aumann (1997). In non-cooperative theory, the play of a game is described in great detail. The strategies of all players are specified as well as the rules of the game, the payoffs and the order of play. The purpose is to make predictions on the outcome of the game. It is assumed that players cannot make binding agreements. Therefore, any prediction on the outcome of a game should be internally stable. That is, no player should have an incentive to deviate. This has been formalised by Nash (1950b) in the famous *Nash equilibrium*.

In cooperative theory, one abstracts from the specifics of the strategic interaction. The emphasis lies on the possibilities of cooperation between agents. It is therefore assumed that agents can make binding agreements. Furthermore, it is assumed that agents use the same unit of account for payoffs so that utility is transferable. A cooperative model assumes the payoff to a coalition as a given input. The question is, how the value that the grand coalition (all players together) can achieve should be divided over all players. The cooperative approach has been used, for example, for operations research problems (see Borm et al. (2001) for an overview).

One of the important questions cooperative theory deals with is how to divide a surplus or cost between the players. This naturally leads to the study of bargaining problems. The first cooperative bargaining model has been developed by Nash (1950a), who proposes a solution concept. Rubinstein (1982) developed a non-cooperative alternating offer game for two players and showed that it has a unique subgame perfect equilibrium. It is shown in Binmore (1987) that this subgame perfect equilibrium corresponds to the Nash solution for a certain cooperative bargaining problem. This is an important result in the so-called "Nash program". This program aims at underpinning cooperative solution concepts with non-cooperative games. For an overview of the Nash program in bargaining theory, see e.g. Bolt and Houba (2002).

Just as in transferable utility games, (cooperative) bargaining assumes that the grand coalition forms. If players disagree, the coalition breaks down and all players get their so-called "disagreement payoff". However, in most situations it is not *necessary* that the grand coalition forms. Think about a group of scientists that want to conduct a research project. There is no *a priori* reason to impose that they all work together. It is perfectly viable for one or more scientists to leave the group and pursue their own agenda. Hence, an important part of cooperative behaviour deals with the question of how coalitions form and, as a result, which coalitions form. Also the literature on coalition formation can be divided into a non-cooperative and a cooperative part. For an overview of the literature, see, for example, Montero (2000). Non-cooperative models of endogenous coalition formation can often be traced back to Rubinstein (1982). The result is a partition of the set of players in coalitions. The partition that forms depends crucially on the specifics of the model. One of these specifics is the exact payoff division between players. For coalition formation, the most important question for a player is what he gains by joining one coalition over another.

One important aspect that is usually ignored in the coalition formation literature is that the payoff to a player not only depends on her own action, but is also influenced by what other players do. In other words, the payoff of a player is influenced by the coalition structure that eventually arises. Consequently, there may be spillovers attached to coalition formation. Think, for example, about government formation. The payoff to the parties *outside* the government coalition is influenced by the parties in the coalition that actually forms the government. Cooperative models of coalition formation abstract entirely from the underlying specifics of the bargaining procedure and address questions like stability of certain partitions. However, an assessment of the stability of certain coalitions should be partly based on an assessment of the underlying spillovers, simply because these spillovers largely determine a player's willingness to join a coalition. Furthermore, if one wants to find a "fair" division of the surplus of a coalition among its members, one has to take these spillovers into account. Namely, if the spillovers are such that given a certain division the value of the *outside option* to one of its members (namely leaving the coalition) is greater than the part of the surplus that the division assigns to this player, the coalition will break down. In such cases, a player can successfully claim that the division is not fair because of the value of her outside option. Therefore, a division of a coalition's surplus has to take into account both *internal* as well as *external* fairness. Cooperative theory is only concerned with internal fairness, since players are not allowed to leave the grand coalition.

In Chapter 6, a class of cooperative games called *spillover games*, is therefore introduced that explicitly includes coalitional spillovers. It is shown that spillover games can naturally arise from non-cooperative games. Therefore, spillover games are especially suited to study situations where cooperation in an essentially non-cooperative (strategic) situation is desired. For example, consider a group of countries that wants to find a solution to environmental externalities. Each country has its own economic and political agenda which yields a non-cooperative game. All these strategic considerations influence the payoffs that coalitions can achieve together as well as the payoff of the outside option of not joining a coalition. The resulting spillover game can be used to find division rules that take into account both the cooperative as well as the non-cooperative aspects of the problem. In the case of the Kyoto treaty for example, the US find the outside option of not joining the coalition apparently more valuable than joining the coalition.

Some basic properties of spillover games are developed and some applications are introduced, like government situations, public-private connection problems and mergers between firms. Two solution concepts are proposed based on well-known solutions for TU games, namely the Shapley value and the compromise value. Furthermore, a criterion is derived by which the stability of each possible coalition can be assessed. Chapter 6 is for a large part based on Thijssen et al. (2002).

In Chapter 7, we elaborate on the merger example first introduced in Chapter 6. Mergers play an important role in modern capitalist economies. A reason for this is that economic growth and development are mainly supply driven in the sense of Say's observation that all supply leads to its own demand. Therefore, firms constantly seek new worlds to explore in the hope that consumers want to buy their products, giving them a competitive edge and higher rents. In order to achieve this in capitalist reality, firms seek to control their economic environment so that they can exploit it.[6]

---

[6]So, firms will not accept the role of one price-taking firm among many equals as they would do in the utopian description of fully competitive markets. Hence, a capitalist economy seems incompatible with perfect competition. In a perfectly competitive market, firms are price-takers. However, by obtaining and exercising market power, firms can increase shareholder

One of the ways to get market power is by innovation. It can also be accomplished by merging with other firms, thereby reducing competition. Mergers can be seen as investments with an uncertain future profit stream. So, the decision to merge resembles the investment decisions analysed in Part I of the book. One additional and essential feature of mergers, however, is that the should be strategically viable. In other words, the value of the merged firms should be larger than the outside options of the firms. These outside options are just simply the stand-alone values of the firms, i.e. the merger (a coalition between two firms) should be stable in the sense of Chapter 6. Chapter 7 analyses the interplay between the economic and strategic aspects of merger decisions in uncertain economic environments. As such it combines the ideas presented in Part I and Chapter 6. The chapter is based on Thijssen (2004).

4.   Introduction to Part III

The concept of Nash equilibrium has firmly established itself as one of the most important work-horse tools in non-cooperative game theory. However, multiplicity of Nash equilibria in most games poses a considerable conceptual problem, because it is not *a priori* clear how and why players should coordinate on a particular Nash equilibrium. In the literature it has been argued (cf. Kohlberg and Mertens (1986)) that the equilibrium selection problem is outside the scope of non-cooperative game theory. Others have devoted themselves to the introduction of ever more refinements of the Nash equilibrium concept to bring down the number of equilibria (see Van Damme (1991) for an excellent overview). The main problem with most refinements is that they assume an extreme level of rationality on the side of the players. In his foreword to Weibull (1995), Ken Binmore remarks that the number of refinements has become so large that almost any Nash equilibrium can be supported by some refinement or another.

A more explicit dynamic and behavioural approach to equilibrium selection seems to be needed. In biology, game theory has been used to

---

value (the ultimate goal in a capitalist system). Since most economists and policy-makers believe that fully competitive markets lead to a socially optimal allocation of resources (one of the greatest results of general equilibrium theory), legal instruments and institutions like competition authorities are needed to block the natural tendency of firms to obtain market power. This observation extends to society as a whole. In liberal states the individual is the focal point of society. Paradoxically, this leads to a political and economic structure where the individual is reduced to an anonymous entity (a "price-taker"). As a reaction, groups of people try to regain influence by forming unions, pressure groups, NGOs and so on. As such, the anti-globalisation movement has exactly the same motives as the multinationals they are fighting (cf. Klein (1999) or Hertz (2002)).

model the evolution of species. This literature started with the paper by Maynard Smith and Price (1973). In Maynard Smith (1974, 1982) a population is considered in which members are randomly matched to play a bimatrix game. A mixed strategy is interpreted as the share of the population playing a certain (pure) strategy. Basically, it is assumed that players are programmed to play a certain strategy from which they cannot deviate. To analyse this model, one can use the concept of evolutionary stable strategy (ESS) as introduced by Taylor and Jonker (1978). In short, a strategy is an ESS if it is stable against small perturbations. The biological story behind it is as follows. Suppose that the entire population plays an ESS. If the population is invaded by a small group of mutants that plays a different strategy, then the player with the ESS gets a higher payoff if this player is matched with a mutant player. One can show that the set of ESS is a (possibly empty) subset of the set of pure Nash equilibria.

The question of how evolution selects an ESS cannot be answered by using the ESS concept as such, since it is essentially a static concept. Evolutionary selection is the dynamics of fractions of players playing a certain strategy within a population. Usually, evolutionary selection is based on the payoffs that players obtain from repeated play of the game. In a biological setting, payoffs can be seen as an indication of fitness. The higher the payoff to playing a certain strategy relative to the average payoff in the population, the higher the growth rate of the fraction of the population that is programmed with this strategy. If one models this process in continuous time, the so-called *replicator dynamics* is obtained (cf. Taylor and Jonker (1978)). It has been shown that every evolutionary stable strategy is asymptotically stable for the replicator dynamics.

In economics, the replicator dynamics has been widely applied. Excellent overviews can be found in, e.g. Van Damme (1994), Weibull (1995) and Samuelson (1997). There are, however, several problems in translating results from biology readily to economics. Firstly, natural selection by fitness should be replaced by a good concept of learning (cf. Crawford (1989)). Secondly, in the replicator dynamics the frequencies of all strategies that have a higher payoff than average are increasing, even if they are not a best reply. In general, models of learning assume that only best-reply actions are played. It has been shown by e.g. Matsui (1992) and Samuelson and Zhang (1992) that also under weak monotonicity of the replicator dynamics most results are preserved. Furthermore, several researchers addressed the question whether it is possible to find a learning or imitation process that leads to the replicator dynamics. See, for example, Björnstedt and Weibull (1996), Gale et al. (1995) and Schlag (1998).

Part of the development of explicit learning models has been the use of the concept of stochastic stability, which is introduced in Foster and Young (1990). Kandori et al. (1993) consider a model that is close to a discrete time version of the replicator dynamics. This dynamics is perturbed by stochastic noise, i.e. with a small but strictly positive probability that a player chooses a strategy at random. To stay close to the biological roots, this is called *mutation*. This yields a dynamic process that can be shown to be an ergodic Markov chain which has a unique invariant (limit) probability measure. The stochastically stable states are the strategies that are in the support of the invariant probability measure when the probability of a mutation converges to zero. It is shown in Kandori et al. (1993), that for 2×2 symmetric games with two symmetric pure Nash equilibria, the risk-dominant equilibrium is selected (cf. Harsanyi and Selten (1988)). Young (1993) obtains a similar result for 2×2 symmetric games where players choose optimal strategies based on a sample of information about what other players have done in the past. For an overview of the literature on stochastic stability see Vega–Redondo (1996) or Young (1998).

As Mailath (1992) already noticed, most evolutionary selection mechanisms assume players to be quite stupid. They are assumed to stick to their behaviour even if it is not profitable. One of the purposes of this part of the book is to construct models that allow players to change their behaviour if they experience that it performs poorly relative to the behaviour of other players. As such, it has links with the literature on indirect evolution (cf. Güth and Yaari (1992)), or with papers like Ok and Vega-Redondo (2001) where evolution works directly on preferences. Another strand of literature where agents can switch between different behavioural modes uses non-linear switching rules that are based on the results of the respective behavioural rules. When applied to economic markets this can lead to chaotic price patterns, as has been shown in, for example, Brock and Hommes (1997) and Droste and Tuinstra (1998).

In a stochastic stability setting, the presence of multiple behavioural rules has been analysed by e.g. Kaarbøe and Tieman (1999) and Schipper (2003). In these papers, however, behavioural change is exogenous. In this part of the book, some models are presented that make the choice between different kinds of behaviour endogenous. The models are applied to an oligopolistic market. The seminal paper by Vega–Redondo (1997) shows that profit imitation (which has, as a behavioural rule, already been advocated by Alchian (1950)), leads to the Walrasian equilibrium[7] being the unique stochastically stable state. This is in contrast with the standard analysis that predicts the Cournot-Nash outcome[8]. However, some experiments as reported in Offerman et al. (2002) suggest that not only the Walrasian equilibrium, but also the cartel (collusion) equilibrium[9] arises during a significant amount of time.

There is a vast literature on the sustainability of collusion in oligopolistic markets. One approach is, for example, to assume incomplete information in a static setting. If one allows for side payments and information sharing it has been shown that collusion can be a Bayesian equilibrium, see Roberts (1983, 1985). Kihlstrom and Vives (1989, 1992) show that an efficient cartel (i.e. a cartel where the firms with the lowest costs produce) is possible in a duopoly. An efficient cartel can also be sustained as an equilibrium when there is a continuum of firms and costs can be of only two types. Crampton and Palfrey (1990) show that collusion is still possible without side payments but with a continuum of cost types, provided that the number of firms is not too large.

In a dynamic repeated game context cooperative behaviour can be sustained under a wide variety of assumptions by means of trigger strategies. The sustainability of cartels in repeated games, however, is often the result of Folk Theorem-like results. This reduces the applicability of these results since under a Folk Theorem almost any outcome can be sustained as an equilibrium by choosing appropriate strategies. First consider a finite horizon. In general, only the Cournot-Nash equilibrium is a Subgame Perfect Equilibrium (SPE) in the repeated Cournot game. If one allows for ε-optimising behaviour (cf. Radner (1980)) by agents, one may obtain a folk theorem saying that there is a trigger strategy that sustains cooperation as an ε-SPE. A second approach is that one models the market in such a way that there are multiple single-stage equilibria. This approach has been followed by e.g. Friedman (1985) and Fraysseé and Moreau (1985). Benoit and Krishna (1985) show that if there are two equilibria that can be Pareto ranked, a folk theorem holds: if the (finite) time horizon is long enough and firms are patient enough then almost any outcome can be sustained as an SPE. In particular, the trigger strategy where firms play the Pareto superior strategy (i.e. the cartel quantity) as long as the competitors do the same and otherwise switch

---

[7]The Walrasian equilibrium arises when all firms behave as competitive price takers. Firms produce a quantity such that the price equals their marginal costs. In the absence of fixed costs, this implies that all firms have zero profits.

[8]In the Cournot-Nash outcome, each firm produces the quantity that maximises its profit given that the other firms produce their Cournot-Nash quantity.

[9]In the collusion equilibrium, each firm produces the quantity that maximises total industry profits. That is, it is the equilibrium that arises if all firms behave cooperatively.

to the Pareto inferior quantity, is an SPE supporting the cartel outcome. A third approach is assuming a market with a unique one-shot equilibrium, but allowing for a small amount of incomplete information or "craziness". Here too, a folk theorem applies: any outcome can be supported as a subgame perfect Bayesian equilibrium, given that firms are patient enough (Fudenberg and Maskin (1986)). With an infinite horizon too, a Folk Theorem can be obtained stating that any outcome can be sustained if firms are patient enough (Friedman (1971)). In an infinite horizon setting, asymmetries make collusion more difficult as has been shown by Sherer and Ross (1990, Chapter 8). Finally, the possibility of communication, possibly cheap talk, makes collusion possible (cf. Compte (1998) and Kandori and Matsushima (1998)).

In Chapter 8, which is based on Thijssen (2001), a model is developed where firms can choose between two types of behaviour. A firm can either imitate the quantity of the firm that made the highest profit in the previous period, or it can imitate the quantity of the firm that would generate the highest industry profit if all firms were to set this quantity. The former kind of behaviour is called profit imitation and the latter kind exemplary imitation. It is clear that profit imitation is competitive behaviour while exemplary imitation constitutes cooperative behaviour. So, at each point in time there is a group of firms that behaves competitively and a group that behaves cooperatively. It is assumed that within the market there is a tendency to collusion since all firms realise that collusion yields higher profits for all. As long as the difference between the cartel profit and the realised industry profit stays within a certain bound, firms behave cooperatively. It is shown that if behaviour adaptation occurs sufficiently less often than quantity adaptation, then either the Walrasian or the collusion equilibrium is the unique stochastically stable state.

In Chapter 9 a model is considered where firms are myopic profit maximisers. In setting their quantity they use a conjecture on how the competitors react to their change in quantity. At the behavioural level, firms imitate the conjecture of the firm that makes the highest profit. So, as in Chapter 8, a dynamic system is obtained with evolution on two levels: quantity and behaviour. If behavioural adaptation occurs with a sufficiently low frequency, the Walrasian equilibrium is the unique stochastically stable state. This chapter is based on Thijssen (2003).

In both chapters, the technique of nearly-complete decomposability is used to aggregate over the quantity level and to obtain results on the behavioural dynamics therewith. This technique was introduced in the economics literature in the 1960s, notably by Simon and Ando (1961) and Ando and Fisher (1963). The technique was used to aggregate large input-output models so that these models could be analysed using the limited computational power of the time.

Chapters 8 and 9 show that profit imitation is very robust to other behavioural rules. If one wants to obtain a sustainable cartel it is necessary to drop, or at least greatly relax, the profit imitative behaviour. For example, if one does not assume an exogenous inclination to cooperative behaviour in Chapter 8, even the presence of another behavioural rule can not lead the market away from the Walrasian equilibrium. This is partly due to the aggregation technique that is used in these chapters to obtain analytical results on the stochastically stable states. First, the limit behaviour of the quantity dynamics is determined for each behavioural configuration. These results are then used to aggregate over the quantity dynamics and obtain results on the behavioural dynamics. This implies that in determining the equilibrium at the behavioural level only the equilibria in quantities for any (fixed) behavioural pattern among the players is relevant. Since Vega–Redondo (1997) already showed that the Walrasian equilibrium yields the highest relative profit, any profit-based imitation rule at the behavioural level will lead to the Walrasian equilibrium. This should not be a reason to discard the aggregation method, since even simulations that are not using the aggregation procedure show a strong tendency towards the Walrasian equilibrium as is shown in Chapter 9. It merely points to a fundamental difficulty in this kind of model, namely the crucial dependence of the results on specific behavioural assumptions. For example, it might be the case that if learning is modelled via neural networks, as is often done in the psychological literature, strong results that support cooperation can be obtained.

Furthermore, the results that are obtained are long-run results. The "long-run" in these models can be unconvincingly long, since "in the long-run we are all dead", as has already been astutely remarked by Keynes. Especially in an oligopolistic market with fixed demand and cost functions, learning should take place at a relatively high speed. Therefore, this kind of evolutionary analysis might be more appropriate to analyse large scale social phenomena on different levels. It has been argued, for example, in Binmore (1994, 1998) that the evolution of social norms has a short-run, a medium-run and a long-run component. Using the aggregation technique that is used in this part together with different levels of sophistication, one might be able to analyse in one coherent framework the evolution of social norms. As an example, on the lowest level agents might behave as myopic optimisers. This models their day to day social behaviour in the short-run, which is based on their preferences, which change over the medium- and long-run. On the second level, the evolution of preferences takes place, whereby people might imitate the behaviour of the successful. Since they are cognitively less aware of this behaviour, modelling it as imitative can be justified. Over the long-run, preferences are influenced on the level of the genes, which could be modelled by a replicator dynamics approach.

In Chapter 10, a general equilibrium model with incomplete markets is considered. An attempt is made to use globally convergent adjustment processes to model a boundedly rational route to equilibrium. For non-cooperative games, such an adjustment process can be found in Van den Elzen and Talman (1991). For general equilibrium models, many price adjustment processes have been proposed. See for an overview e.g. Van der Laan and Talman (1987), Herings (1996), and Yang (1999). In the current chapter, an algorithm developed in Talman and Yamamoto (1989) for stationary point problems on polytopes is used to follow a path of price adjustments that are made by a boundedly rational market-maker who myopically maximises the value of excess demand on the asset markets. The algorithm generates a piece-wise linear path on a triangulation of the set of no-arbitrage asset prices. The chapter is based on Talman and Thijssen (2003).

Chapter 2

MATHEMATICAL PRELIMINARIES

1. Basic Concepts from Topology and Calculus

In this section we review some basic concepts from topology and calculus. Some primitives are assumed knowledge. For more details the reader is referred to e.g. Jänich (1984).

Let $(X, \boldsymbol{T})$ be a topological space. A subset $A \subset X$ is *closed* if its complement is open, i.e. if $A^c \in \boldsymbol{T}$. The set A is *compact* if every open covering of A has a finite subcovering. The topological space $(X, \boldsymbol{T})$ is said to be *connected* if there do not exist two disjoint, non-empty, open sets whose union is X. A subset $A \subset X$ is connected if the induced topological space is connected. The *closure* of a set $A \subset X$, $cl(A)$, is the smallest closed set containing A. The set A is *dense* in X if $cl(A) = X$.

Let $(X, \boldsymbol{T})$ and $(Y, \boldsymbol{U})$ be topological spaces. A function $f : X \to Y$ is *continuous* if for all $U \in \boldsymbol{U}$ it holds that $f^{-1}(U) \in \boldsymbol{T}$, i.e. if the inverse of an open set is open. A correspondence $\varphi : X \to Y$ is *upper semi-continuous* (USC) if for all $U \in \boldsymbol{U}$ it holds that $\{x \in X | \varphi(x) \subset U\} \in \boldsymbol{T}$. The correspondence is lower semi-continuous (LSC) if for all $U \in \boldsymbol{U}$ it holds that $\{x \in X | \varphi(x) \cap U \neq \emptyset\} \in \boldsymbol{T}$. The correspondence is continuous if it is both USC and LSC.

THEOREM 2.1 (BERGE'S MAXIMUM THEOREM) *Let $(X, \boldsymbol{T})$ and $(Y, \boldsymbol{U})$ be topological spaces. Let $\varphi : X \to Y$ be a compact-valued, continuous correspondence. Let $f : X \times Y \to \mathbb{R}$ be a continuous function. Then*

1 The function $m : X \to \mathbb{R}$, defined by

$$m(x) = \sup_{y \in \varphi(x)} f(x, y),$$

is continuous;

2 The correspondence $M : X \to Y$, defined by

$$M(x) = \arg\sup_{y \in \varphi(x)} f(x, y),$$

is USC.

Let (X, d) be a metric space. The *open ball* around $x \in X$ with radius $r > 0$, $B(x, r)$, is defined by

$$B(x, r) = \{y \in X | d(x, y) < r\}.$$

A set $A \subset X$ is *bounded* if there is an open ball containing A, i.e. if there exist an $x \in X$ and $r > 0$ such that $A \subset B(x, r)$.

Let $\mathbb{R}^n$ denote the n-dimensional Euclidian space for $n \in \mathbb{N}$. The nonnegative orthant of $\mathbb{R}^n$ is defined by $\mathbb{R}^n_+ = \{x \in \mathbb{R}^n | \forall_{i=1,\dots,n} : x_i \geq 0\}$ and the positive orthant is denoted by $\mathbb{R}^n_{++} = \{x \in \mathbb{R}^n | \forall_{i=1,\dots,n} : x_i > 0\}$. The inner product of two n-dimensional vectors x and y is denoted by xy. The Euclidian norm of $x \in \mathbb{R}^n$ is denoted by $\|x\|$. A set $X \in \mathbb{R}^n$ is *convex* if for all $x, y \in X$ and all $\lambda \in (0, 1)$ it holds that $\lambda x + (1-\lambda)y \in X$. A subset of $\mathbb{R}^n$ is compact if and only if it is closed and bounded.

A sequence $(x_k)_{k \in \mathbb{N}}$ in X *converges* to $x \in X$ if for all $\varepsilon > 0$ there exists a $k_0 \in \mathbb{N}$ such that for all $k \geq k_0$ it holds that $d(x_k, x) < \varepsilon$. In $\mathbb{R}^n$ any bounded sequence has a convergent subsequence.

A set $A \subset X$ is closed in the topology induced by the metric d if the limit of all convergent sequences in A are in A. A *boundary point* of A is a point $a \in A$ such that for all $r > 0$ it holds that $B(a, r) \cap A \neq \emptyset$ and $B(a, r) \cap A^c \neq \emptyset$. The *boundary* of A, ∂A, is the set of all boundary points of A.

Let X be a connected subset of $\mathbb{R}^n$ that is endowed with the standard topology, i.e. the topology induced by the Euclidian norm. Let $f : X \to \mathbb{R}$ be a function. The point $d \in \mathbb{R}$ is the *limit* of f when x converges to $c \in X$, denoted by $\lim_{x \to c} f(x) = d$, if

$$\forall_{\varepsilon > 0} \exists_{\delta > 0} \forall_{x \in X} : \|x - c\| < \delta \Rightarrow |f(x) - d| < \varepsilon.$$

The function f is *continuous* in $c \in X$ if it holds that $\lim_{x \to c} f(x) = f(c)$. The function f is continuous if it is continuous in all $c \in X$.

Let $X \subset \mathbb{R}$ and let $f : X \to \mathbb{R}$ be a function. The point $d \in \mathbb{R}$ is called the *left limit* of f when x converges to $c \in X$, denoted by $\lim_{x \uparrow c} f(x) = d$, if

$$\forall_{\varepsilon > 0} \exists_{\delta > 0} \forall_{x < c} : |x - c| < \delta \Rightarrow |f(x) - d| < \varepsilon.$$

For simplicity, we denote $d = f(c-)$. Similarly, the point $d \in \mathbb{R}$ is called the *right limit* of f when x converges to $c \in X$, denoted by $\lim_{x \downarrow c} f(x) = d$, if

$$\forall_{\varepsilon > 0} \exists_{\delta > 0} \forall_{x > c} : |x - c| < \delta \Rightarrow |f(x) - d| < \varepsilon.$$

For simplicity we denote $d = f(c+)$. The function f is *left-continuous* in $c \in X$ if it holds that $f(c-) = f(c)$ and it is *right-continuous* in $c \in X$ if $f(c+) = f(c)$ for all $c \in X$. The *derivative* of f in $c \in X$, $f'(c)$, is defined by

$$f'(c) = \lim_{x \to c} \frac{f(x) - f(c)}{x - c},$$

provided that the limit exists. The *right-derivative* of f in $c \in X$, $f'(c+)$, is defined by

$$f'(c+) = \lim_{x \downarrow c} \frac{f(x) - f(c)}{x - c},$$

provided that the limit exists. If the (right-) derivative exists for all $c \in X$ we say that f is *(right-) differentiable*. In the same way the *left-derivative* of f in $c \in X$, $f'(c-)$, can be defined. For a function $f : X \to \mathbb{R}$ with $X \subset \mathbb{R}^n$ the *partial derivative* of f in $c \in X$ with respect to x_i, $i = 1, \ldots, n$, is denoted by $\frac{\partial f(c)}{\partial x_i}$ and defined by

$$\frac{\partial f(c)}{\partial x_i} = \lim_{x_i \to c_i} \frac{f(c_1, \ldots, c_{i-1}, x_i, c_{i+1}, \ldots, c_n) - f(c)}{x_i - c_i}.$$

For a function $f : X \to \mathbb{R}^m$ continuity and differentiability are defined component-wise.

Let X and Y be subsets of $\mathbb{R}^n$. A *stationary point* of a function $f : X \to Y$ is a point $x^* \in X$ such that for all $x \in X$ it holds that $xf(x^*) \leq x^* f(x^*)$. Existence of a stationary point is established in the following theorem, which is due to Eaves (1971).

THEOREM 2.2 (STATIONARY POINT THEOREM) *Let $X \subset \mathbb{R}^n$ and let $f : X \to \mathbb{R}^n$ be a continuous function. If C is a compact and convex subset of X, then f has a stationary point on C.*

A *fixed point* of a function $f : X \to Y$ is a point $x \in X$ such that $x = f(x)$. Existence of a fixed point of a continuous function $f : C \to C$, where C is a non-empty, convex and compact subset of $\mathbb{R}$ is established by Brouwer (1912).

Let $X \subset \mathbb{R}^n$ and $Y \subset \mathbb{R}^m$ and let $f : X \to Y$ and $g : X \to Y$ be functions. A *homotopy* is a function $h : X \times [0, 1] \to Y$ such that for all $x \in X$ it holds that $h(x, 0) = f(x)$ and $h(x, 1) = g(x)$. The following result is due to Browder (1960).

THEOREM 2.3 (BROWDER'S FIXED POINT THEOREM) *Let S be a non-empty, compact and convex subset of $\mathbb{R}^n$ and let $f : S \times [0,1] \to S$ be a function. Then the set $F_f = \{(x, \lambda) \in S \times [0,1] | x = f(x, \lambda)\}$ contains a connected set F_f^c such that $(S \times \{0\}) \cap F_f^c \neq \emptyset$ and $(S \times \{1\}) \cap F_f^c \neq \emptyset$.*

2.   Convex Analysis

This section reviews some of the main definitions and results from convex analysis. For a concise treatment the reader is referred to Rockafellar (1970).

From Section 1 we know that a set $C \subset \mathbb{R}^n$ is convex if for all $x, y \in C$ and all $\lambda \in (0,1)$ it holds that $\lambda x + (1 - \lambda)y \in C$. That is, a set is convex if the line segment between any two points of the set lies entirely in the set as well. The intersection of an arbitrary number of convex sets is convex as well.

Let $b \in \mathbb{R}^n \backslash \{0\}$ and $\beta \in \mathbb{R}$. A *closed half space* is a set of the form

$$\{x \in \mathbb{R}^n | xb \leq \beta\} \quad \text{or} \quad \{x \in \mathbb{R}^n | xb \geq \beta\}.$$

If the inequalities are strict we speak of an *open half space*. The set $\{x \in \mathbb{R}^n | xb = \beta\}$ is called a *hyperplane*. The intersection of finitely many closed half spaces is called a *polyhedron*.

Let $x^1, \ldots, x^m$ be a sequence of vectors in $\mathbb{R}^n$ and let $\lambda^1, \ldots, \lambda^m$ be a sequence of non-negative scalars such that $\sum_{i=1}^m \lambda^i = 1$. The vector sum

$$\lambda^1 x^1 + \cdots + \lambda^m x^m,$$

is called a *convex combination* of $x^1, \ldots, x^m$. The intersection of all the convex sets containing a set $S = \{s^1, \ldots, s^m\} \subset \mathbb{R}^n$ is called the *convex hull* of S and is denoted by $conv(S)$. It can be shown that

$$conv(S) = \{x \in \mathbb{R}^n | \exists_{\lambda^1 \geq 0, \ldots, \lambda^m \geq 0, \lambda^1 + \cdots + \lambda^m = 1} : x = \sum_{i=1}^m \lambda^i s^i\}.$$

A set that is the convex hull of finitely many points is called a *polytope*. Note that each polytope is a bounded polyhedron.

A subset C of $\mathbb{R}^n$ is a *cone* if it is closed under positive scalar multiplication, i.e. $\lambda x \in C$ for all $x \in C$ and $\lambda > 0$. Such a set is the union of half-lines emanating from the origin (which need not be included). It can be shown that a subset of $\mathbb{R}^n$ is a convex cone if and only if it is closed under addition and positive scalar multiplication. Let $S = \{y_1, \ldots, y_m\}$ be a finite set of directions in $\mathbb{R}^n$. The convex cone generated by S, $cone(S)$, equals the set

$$cone(S) = \{x \in \mathbb{R}^n | x = \sum_{i=1}^m \lambda_i y^i, \lambda_i \geq 0, y_i \in S, i = 1, \ldots, m\}.$$

Let $C \subset \mathbb{R}^n$ be a convex set. A vector $y \in \mathbb{R}^n \backslash \{0\}$ with the property that $c + \lambda y \in C$ for all $c \in C$ and all $\lambda \geq 0$ is called a *direction* of C. The *recession cone* of C is denoted by $re(C)$ and equals

$$re(C) = \{y \in \mathbb{R}^n | \forall_{x \in C} \forall_{\lambda \geq 0} : x + \lambda y \in C\}.$$

Let S_0 be a set of points in C and let S_1 be a set of directions of C such that
$$C = conv(S_0) + cone(S_1).$$
The set C is *finitely generated* if both S_0 and S_1 are finite sets.

THEOREM 2.4 (CARATHÉODORY'S THEOREM) *Let $C \subset \mathbb{R}^n$ be a finitely generated convex set and let S_0 be a finite set of points in C and let S_1 be a finite set of directions of C, such that $C = conv(S_0) + cone(S_1)$. Then $x \in C$ if and only if*

$$x = \lambda^1 x^1 + \cdots + \lambda^k x^k + \lambda^{k+1} x^{k+1} + \cdots + \lambda^{n+1} x^{n+1},$$

for some non-negative scalars $\lambda^1, \ldots, \lambda^{n+1}$ such that $\lambda^1 + \cdots + \lambda^k = 1$ where $x^1, \ldots, x^k$ are (not necessarily distinct) elements of S_0 and $x^{k+1}, \ldots, x^{n+1}$ are (not necessarily distinct) elements of S_1.

An important implication of this theorem is that a convex set C is a polyhedron if and only if it is finitely generated.

3. Triangulations

This section briefly reviews the main concepts needed for the simplicial algorithm described in Chapter 10. For a more extensive treatment see e.g. Yang (1999). For affinely independent vectors $x^1, \ldots, x^{t+1}$ in $\mathbb{R}^n$, the convex hull of these points is called a *t-dimensional* *simplex*, denoted by $\sigma(x^1, \ldots, x^{t+1})$. The vectors $x^1, \ldots, x^{t+1}$ are called the *vertices* of σ. A simplex τ is a *face* of σ if all the vertices of τ are vertices of σ. A $(t-1)$-dimensional face of a t-dimensional simplex is called a *facet*. A facet τ of the simplex σ is called the facet *opposite* the vertex x if x is a vertex of σ but not of τ.

A *triangulation*, or simplicial subdivision, of a convex set C is a collection of simplices whose union is C and that "nicely" fit together.

DEFINITION 2.1 *Let C be a t-dimensional convex set in $\mathbb{R}^n$. A collection $\mathcal{T}$ of t-dimensional simplices is a triangulation of C if the following conditions hold.*

1 *C is the union of all simplices in $\mathcal{T}$;*

2 *for any $\sigma_1, \sigma_2 \in \mathcal{T}$ it holds that $\sigma_1 \cap \sigma_2$ is either the empty set or a common face of both;*

3 for each element x in C there is an open ball around x which intersects only a finite number of simplices in $\mathcal{T}$.

Let σ_1 and σ_2 be faces of simplices in $\mathcal{T}$. The simplices σ_1 and σ_2 are *adjacent* if they share a common facet or if one of them is a facet of the other. A triangulation of a compact and convex subset of $\mathbb{R}^n$ contains a finite number of simplices.

Let $\mathcal{T}$ be a triangulation of a convex set in $\mathbb{R}^n$. The *diameter* of a simplex $\sigma \in \mathcal{T}$ is given by

$$diam(\sigma) = \max\{\|x - y\| | x, y \in \sigma\}.$$

The *mesh* of the triangulation $\mathcal{T}$ is defined by

$$mesh(\mathcal{T}) = \sup_{\sigma \in \mathcal{T}}\{diam(\sigma)\}.$$

Let a t-dimensional compact and convex subset S of $\mathbb{R}^m$, a subset T of $\mathbb{R}^n$, a triangulation $\mathcal{T}$ of S and a function $f : S \to T$ be given. A function $\bar{f} : S \to \mathbb{R}^n$ is a *piece-wise linear approximation* of f with respect to $\mathcal{T}$ if for every vertex w of any simplex $\sigma \in \mathcal{T}$ it holds that $\bar{f}(w) = f(w)$ and for every element x of S it holds that

$$\bar{f}(x) = \sum_{i=1}^{t+1} \lambda_i f(w^i),$$

whenever $x \in \sigma(w^1, \ldots, w^{t+1})$ for some simplex $\sigma \in \mathcal{T}$ and some $\lambda_i \in \mathbb{R}_+$, $i = 1, \ldots, t + 1$, with $\sum_{i=1}^{t+1} \lambda_i = 1$, such that $x = \sum_{i=1}^{t+1} \lambda_i w^i$. One can find in e.g. Munkres (1975) that when S is compact, for any continuous function $f : S \to T$ and $\varepsilon > 0$ there exists a $\delta > 0$ such that for all $x, y \in S$ with $\|x - y\|_\infty < \delta$ it holds that $\|f(x) - f(y)\|_\infty < \varepsilon$. This implies that a piece-wise linear approximation of a continuous function can be made arbitrarily precise by choosing the mesh size of the triangulation small enough.

4.   Game Theory

Game theory is a mathematical theory that is used to model strategic interaction between several (economic) agents, called *players*. Usually, a distinction is made between non-cooperative and cooperative theory. This distinction dates back to the ground-breaking contribution of Von Neumann and Morgenstern (1944). In non-cooperative theory it is assumed that players cannot make binding agreements, whereas in cooperative theory it is assumed that agents can. The implication of this distinction is that in non-cooperative theory the emphasis is on the strategies of players and the consequences of the interaction of strategies on payoffs. In cooperative theory one tries to find ways of dividing a certain surplus (or cost) among a group of players. Ideally, various division rules satisfy different sets of properties (axioms). In applications, the modeler can then decide on a division rule by judging the desirability of the different axioms.

This section describes some concepts from both branches of game theory. For a mathematically oriented text-book exposition of non-cooperative game theory the reader is referred to Osborne and Rubinstein (1994). Fudenberg and Tirole (1991) devote much attention to applications in economics. A good introduction to cooperative game theory can be found in Peleg and Sudhölter (2003).

4.1 Non-Cooperative Theory

A game in *strategic form* is a model of a strategic situation where players make one strategy choice simultaneously. Formally, it is a tuple $G = \left(N, (A_i)_{i \in N}, (u_i)_{i \in N} \right)$, where N is the set of players and A_i, $i \in N$, is the set of pure actions for player i. Denote the cartesian product of all A_i by A. The function $u_i : A \to \mathbb{R}$ is the *utility function* of player i. That is, $u_i(a)$ is the payoff to player i if the actions played by all players are given by $a \in A$.

It is assumed that there is no external agency that can enforce agreements between the players. Therefore, rational players will choose their actions such that it is unprofitable for each of them to deviate. Any prediction for the outcome of a game in strategic form should have this property. The most well-known equilibrium concept is the *Nash equilibrium*. This equilibrium states that players will choose their actions such that unilateral deviations are not beneficial. Formally, a Nash equilibrium is a tuple of actions $a^* \in A$ such that for each player $i \in N$ and for all $a_i \in A_i$ it holds that

$$u_i(a^*) \geq u_i(a_i, a^*_{-i}),$$

where $(a_i, a^*_{-i}) = (a^*_1, \ldots, a^*_{i-1}, a_i, a^*_{i+1}, \ldots, a^*_n)$.

A Nash equilibrium in pure actions may not exist for every game in strategic form. Let G be a game in strategic form. The *mixed extension* of G is the strategic game $G^m = \left(N, (\Delta(A_i))_{i \in N}, (U_i)_{i \in N} \right)$, where $\Delta(A_i)$ is the set of probability distributions over A_i and $U_i : \prod_{j \in N} \Delta(A_j) \to \mathbb{R}$ is the *Von Neumann-Morgenstern* (vNM) utility function, defined for all

$\alpha \in \prod_{j \in N} \Delta(A_j)$ by

$$U_i(\alpha) = \sum_{a \in A} \left(\prod_{j \in N} \alpha_j(a_j) \right) u_i(a).$$

A mixed strategy is a probability distribution over a player's pure actions. It describes the probabilities with which a player plays each of her pure actions. A *mixed Nash equilibrium* of a game in strategic form G is a Nash equilibrium of its mixed extension G^m. The following theorem establishes existence of a mixed Nash equilibrium for finite games in strategic form.

THEOREM 2.5 (NASH (1950B)) *Every finite game in strategic form has a mixed strategy Nash equilibrium.*

The interpretation of mixed strategy Nash equilibrium is not straightforward. The reader is referred to Osborne and Rubinstein (1994, Section 3.2) for a discussion.

In Parts I and II of this book, substantial attention is paid to timing games in continuous time. The concept of subgame perfectness is introduced for stochastic versions of timing games. Subgame perfectness is best understood in the context of games that have a straightforward dynamic structure. An *extensive form game* is a tuple $\mathcal{G} = \left(N, H, P, (u_i)_{i \in N} \right)$, where N is the set of players, H is the set of histories, P is the player function and for each $i \in N$, u_i denotes the utility function.

The set of histories, H, satisfies the following conditions:

- $\emptyset \in H$;

- if $(a^k)_{k=1,...,K} \in H$ and $L < K$, then $(a^k)_{k=1,...,L} \in H$;

- if a sequence $(a^k)_{k=1}^{\infty}$ satisfies $(a^k)_{k=1,...,L} \in H$ for all $L \in \mathbb{N}$, then $(a^k)_{k=1}^{\infty} \in H$.

Each element of H is a history and each component of a history is an action taken by a player. A history $(a^k)_{k=1,...,K} \in H$ is *terminal* if $K = \infty$ or if there is no a^{K+1} such that $(a^k)_{k=1,...,K+1} \in H$. The set of terminal histories is denoted by Z.

The player correspondence $P : H \backslash Z \to N$ assigns to each nonterminal history a set of players. That is, $P(h)$ are the players who take an action after history h from the set $A(h) = \{a | (h, a) \in H\}$. Finally, the domain of the utility function is the set of terminal histories Z.

A strategy of player $i \in N$ in an extensive form game $\mathcal{G}$ is a function $s_i : H \backslash Z \rightarrow A$ that assigns an action in $A(h)$ to each non-terminal history $h \in H \backslash Z$ for which $i \in P(h)$. For each strategy profile $s = (s_i)_{i \in N}$, the *outcome*, $O(s)$, is defined to be the terminal history that results when each players $i \in N$ plays s_i. A Nash equilibrium for the extensive form game $\mathcal{G}$ is a tuple of strategies s^* such that for all $i \in N$ and all $s_i \neq s_i^*$ it holds that

$$u_i(O(s^*)) \geq u_i(O(s_i, s_{-i}^*)).$$

The *subgame* of an extensive form game $\mathcal{G}$ that follows the history $h \in H$ is the reduction of $\mathcal{G}$ to h. This implies that we take a particular history and look at the game along this path. For a Nash equilibrium of $\mathcal{G}$ it might hold that if the game actually ends up in a particular history h, that the prescribed equilibrium play is not optimal any more. That means that the Nash equilibrium contains incredible threats since the other players know that player i will not stick to her Nash equilibrium strategy. For extensive form games we therefore need an extra stability requirement. We focus on *subgame perfectness*. For a strategy s_i and a history $h \in H$ define $s_{i|h} = s_i(h, h')$ for each $h' \in \{(h, h') \in H\}$. A *subgame perfect equilibrium* (SPE) for an extensive form game $\mathcal{G}$ is a strategy profile s^* such that for each player $i \in N$ and every non-terminal history $h \in H \backslash Z$ for which $i \in P(h)$ we have

$$u_i(O(s_{|h}^*)) \geq u_i(O(s_i, s_{-i|h}^*)),$$

for every strategy s_i of player i in the subgame that follows the history h. In discrete time, any finite game in extensive form has a subgame perfect equilibrium.

4.2 Cooperative Theory

A *transferable utility* (TU) game is a tuple (N, v), where N is the set of players and $v : 2^N \rightarrow \mathbb{R}$ is a function, assigning to each coalition $S \in 2^N$ a real number $v(S)$ such that $v(\emptyset) = 0$. The function v is called the *characteristic function* of the game and $v(S)$ is the value of coalition S. The idea is that $v(S)$ is the value that coalition S can attain by cooperating. In TU games one assumes that the value $v(S)$ can be transferred among the players in S, i.e. they can make binding agreements and they attach the same utility to $v(S)$.

A TU game is *superadditive* if for all $S, T \in 2^N$ with $S \cap T = \emptyset$ it holds that

$$v(S \cup T) \geq v(S) + v(T).$$

So, in superadditive games, larger coalitions have a higher value. A TU game is *convex* if for all $i, j \in N$ and $S \subset N \backslash \{i, j\}$ it holds that

$$v(S \cup \{i\}) - v(S) \leq v(S \cup \{i\} \cup \{j\}) - v(S \cup \{j\}).$$

Hence, in a convex game, the marginal contribution of a player to a coalition is less than her marginal contribution to a larger coalition.

The *imputation set* of a TU game (N, v) is the set of all individual rational and Pareto efficient allocations, i.e.

$$I(v) = \{x \in \mathbb{R}^n | \forall_{i \in N} : x_i \geq v(\{i\}), \sum_{i \in N} x_i = v(N)\}.$$

The *core* of a TU game is the set of all imputations that can not be blocked by any coalition of players, i.e.

$$C(v) = \{x \in I(v) | \forall_{S \in 2^N \backslash \emptyset} : \sum_{i \in S} x_i \geq v(S)\}.$$

The main issue in cooperative game theory is to find ways to divide $v(N)$. This is usually done by using the *axiomatic method*, which boils down to defining a rule that divides $v(N)$ and showing that this division rule is the only one that satisfies certain properties (axioms). We describe two of these solutions below.

Let G^n denote the set of all n-person TU games. A *solution* to $G \in G^n$ is a map $f : G^n \to \mathbb{R}^n$. A function $\sigma : N \to N$ is a *permutation* if for all $i \in N$ there exists exactly one $j \in N$ such that $\sigma(i) = j$. So, $\sigma(1)$ is the first player in the permutation, $\sigma(2)$ is the second and so on. The set of all permutations on N is denoted by $\Pi(N)$. For $\sigma \in \Pi(N)$, the *marginal vector* of $(N, v) \in G^n$, $m^\sigma(v) \in \mathbb{R}^n$, has as $\sigma(k)$-th entry

$$m^\sigma_{\sigma(k)}(v) = \begin{cases} v(\{\sigma(1)\}) & \text{if } k = 1, \\ v(\{\sigma(1), \ldots, \sigma(k)\}) - v(\{\sigma(1), \ldots, \sigma(k-1)\}) & \text{otherwise.} \end{cases}$$

The permutation σ describes the order in which players arrive and the marginal vector m^σ gives for each player her marginal contribution to the coalition that is already present. The *Shapley value* (Shapley (1953)), $\Phi(v)$, is the average of all marginal vectors, i.e.

$$\Phi(v) = \frac{1}{n!} \sum_{\sigma \in \Pi(N)} m^\sigma(v).$$

The Shapley value can be seen as the expected marginal value given that each permutation is equally likely.

The *compromise* or *τ-value* is introduced in Tijs (1981) for quasi-balanced games. It is based on the *utopia vector* and the *minimum right vector*. For each TU game (N, v), the utopia vector is an n-dimensional vector, $M(v)$, with i-th coordinate

$$M_i(v) = v(N) - v(N\backslash\{i\}),$$

which is the marginal contribution of player i to the grand coalition. In a sense it is the utopia payoff of player i: if she asks more it is beneficial for the other players to exclude her from the grand coalition. The minimum right vector, $m(v)$, has i-th coordinate

$$m_i(v) = \max_{\{S|i\in S\}} \left(v(S) - \sum_{j\in S\backslash\{i\}} M_j(v) \right).$$

Player i can make a case to at least receive $m_i(v)$, because he can argue that he can always get together with a coalition S in which all the other players get their utopia payoff and he gets $m_i(v)$.

A TU game (N, v) is *quasi-balanced* if it holds that

1 $m(v) \leq M(v)$;

2 $\sum_{i=1}^{n} m_i(v) \leq v(N) \leq \sum_{i=1}^{n} M_i(v)$.

The set of n-person quasi-balanced games is denoted by Q^n. For quasi-balanced games, the compromise value is defined to be the unique vector $\tau(v)$ on the closed interval $[m(v), M(v)]$ in $\mathbb{R}^n$, such that $\sum_{i=1}^{n} \tau_i(v) = v(N)$.

To characterise the Shapley and compromise values we introduce the following axioms:

- $f : G^n \to \mathbb{R}^n$ satisfies *efficiency* (EFF) if $\sum_{i\in N} f_i(v) = v(N)$ for all $v \in G^n$;

- $f : G^n \to \mathbb{R}^n$ satisfies *anonymity* (AN) if $f(v^\sigma) = \sigma^*(f(v))$ for all $\sigma \in \Pi(N)$, where $v^\sigma(S) = v(\sigma^{-1}(S))$ and σ^* is such that $(\sigma^*(x))_{\sigma(k)} = x_k$ for all $x \in \mathbb{R}^n$ and $k \in N$;

- $f : G^n \to \mathbb{R}^n$ satisfies the *dummy player* property (DUM) if $f_i(v) = v(\{i\})$ for all dummy players $i \in N$, i.e. players $i \in N$ such that $v(S \cup \{i\}) = v(S) + v(\{i\})$ for all $S \in 2^{N\backslash\{i\}}$;

- $f : G^n \to \mathbb{R}^n$ satisfies *additivity* (ADD) if $f(v + w) = f(v) + f(w)$ for all $v, w \in \mathcal{G}^n$;

- $f : G^n \to \mathbb{R}^n$ satisfies *weak proportionality* (wPROP) if $f(v)$ is proportional to $M(v)$ if $v \in \{v \in G^n | m(v) = 0\}$;

- $f : G^n \to \mathbb{R}^n$ satisfies the *minimum right property* (MIN) if $f(v) = m(v) + f(v - m(v))$, for all $v \in G^n$.

The following axiomatisations have been obtained in the literature.

THEOREM 2.6 (SHAPLEY (1953)) *There is a unique solution $f : G^n \to \mathbb{R}^n$ that satisfies EFF, AN, DUM, and ADD. This solution is the Shapley value.*

THEOREM 2.7 (TIJS (1987)) *There is a unique solution $f : Q^n \to \mathbb{R}^n$ that satisfies EFF, wPROP, and MIN. This solution is the compromise value.*

5. Basic Concepts from Probability Theory

In this section we review some basic concepts from probability theory. Some basic measure and integration theory is assumed knowledge. Readers that are interested in a more detailed account are referred to e.g. Williams (1991) or Billingsley (1995).

Let $(\Omega, \mathcal{F}, P)$ be a probability space, where Ω is the sample space, $\mathcal{F}$ is a σ-algebra of events on Ω and P is a probability measure on $(\Omega, \mathcal{F})$. A probability space is called *complete* if for all subsets A of a null-set $F \in \mathcal{F}$ it holds that $A \in \mathcal{F}$. A *statement* about outcomes is a function $S : \Omega \to \{0, 1\}$. A statement is said to be true for $\omega \in \Omega$ if $S(\omega) = 1$. A statement S about outcomes is true *almost surely* (a.s.) if

$$F := \{\omega \in \Omega | S(\omega) = 1\} \in \mathcal{F} \text{ and } P(F) = 1.$$

Let $\mathcal{B}$ denote the Borel σ-algebra on $\mathbb{R}$. A *random variable* on $(\Omega, \mathcal{F}, P)$ is a function $X : \Omega \to \mathbb{R}$ such that for all Borel sets $B \in \mathcal{B}$ it holds that $X^{-1}(B) \in \mathcal{F}$. If there can be no confusion about the underlying probability space we will simply speak about "the random variable X". The *σ-algebra generated by* a random variable X is the σ-algebra that is generated by the set $\{\omega \in \Omega | X(\omega) \in B, B \in \mathcal{B}\}$. A sequence of random variables is *independent* if the generated σ-algebras are independent.

Let X be a random variable. The *law of X*, $\mathcal{L}_X$, is defined by $P \circ X^{-1}$. One can show that $\mathcal{L}_X$ is the unique extension to $\mathcal{B}$ of the probability measure $F_X : \mathbb{R} \to [0, 1]$ defined on $\{(-\infty, x] | x \in \mathbb{R}\}$ by[1]

$$F_X(x) = \mathcal{L}_X((-\infty, x]) = P(\{\omega \in \Omega | X(\omega) \le x\}), \qquad x \in \mathbb{R}.$$

---

[1] This stems from the fact that $\mathcal{B}$ is the σ-algebra generated by $\{(-\infty, x] | x \in \mathbb{R}\}$, which implies that F_X can be uniquely extended to the Borel σ-algebra.

The measure $F_X(\cdot)$ is called the *cumulative distribution function* (cdf).

Let μ and ν be two measures on a measurable space $(S, \mathcal{A})$ and let $f : S \to [-\infty, \infty]$ be an $\mathcal{A}$-measurable function. The measure ν has a *density* f with respect to μ if for all $A \in \mathcal{A}$ it holds that

$$\nu(A) = \int_A f(s)d\mu(s),$$

where $\mathbb{1}_A$ denotes the identity map on A. The measure ν is *absolutely continuous* with respect to μ if the null-sets of μ and ν coincide. According to the Radon-Nikodym theorem it follows that if P is absolutely continuous with respect to the Borel measure, then there exists a density $f : \mathbb{R} \to [0, 1]$, i.e. for all $F \in \mathcal{F}$ it holds that

$$P(F) = \int_F f(x)d\lambda(x),$$

where λ denotes the Lebesgue measure. The function $f(\cdot)$ is called the *probability density function* (pdf). The density $f(\cdot)$ has an *atom* or *positive probability mass* at $x \in \mathbb{R}$ if $f(x) - f(x-) > 0$. Let f and g be two density functions. The density function h is the *convolution* of f and g if for all $x \in \mathbb{R}$ it holds that

$$h(x) = \int_{-\infty}^{\infty} f(x - y)g(y)dy.$$

Let F be the distribution function on $[0, \infty)$ of a random variable X. The *Laplace transform* ϕ of F is defined for all $\lambda \geq 0$ by

$$\phi(\lambda) = \int_0^{\infty} e^{-\lambda x}dF(x).$$

Some well-known distribution functions are given below.

1 A random variable X on $\{0, 1, 2, \ldots\}$ is *Poisson* distributed with parameter $\mu > 0$, denoted by $X \sim \mathcal{P}(\mu)$ if the pdf for X is given by

$$f(x) = \frac{e^{-\mu}\mu^x}{x!}.$$

2 A random variable X on $(0, \infty)$ is *exponentially* distributed with parameter $\lambda > 0$, denoted by $X \sim \mathcal{E}(\lambda)$, if the pdf for X is given by

$$f(x) = \frac{1}{\lambda}e^{-x/\lambda}.$$

3 A random variable X on $[a, b]$, $a < b$, is *uniformly* distributed, denoted by $X \sim \mathcal{U}(a, b)$, if the pdf for X is given by

$$f(x) = \frac{1}{b - a}.$$

4 A random variable X on $\mathbb{R}$ is *normally* distributed with parameters μ and σ, denoted by $X \sim \mathcal{N}(\mu, \sigma)$, if the pdf for X is given by

$$f(x) = \frac{1}{\sigma\sqrt{2\pi}} e^{-\frac{(x-\mu)^2}{2\sigma^2}}.$$

5 A random variable X on $(0, \infty)$ is *chi-squared* distributed with ν degrees of freedom, denoted by $X \sim \chi_\nu^2$, if the pdf for X is given by

$$f(x) = \frac{1}{\Gamma(\nu/2)2^{\nu/2}} x^{\frac{\nu}{2}-1} e^{-\frac{1}{2}x},$$

where $\Gamma(x) = \int_0^\infty t^{x-1}e^{-t}dt$ denotes the Gamma function.

Let $Z_1, \ldots, Z_n$ be a sequence of independent and identically distributed (iid) random variables distributed according to $\mathcal{N}(0, 1)$. Then $\sum_{i=1}^n Z_i^2 \sim \chi_n^2$.

Let X be a random variable with cdf $F(\cdot)$. The *expectation* of X, $\mathbb{E}(X)$, is defined as

$$\mathbb{E}(X) = \int_\Omega X(\omega)dP(\omega) = \int xdF(x).$$

If $f : \mathbb{R} \to \mathbb{R}$ is a function, the expectation of $f(X)$ is defined by

$$\mathbb{E}(f(X)) = \int f(x)dF(x).$$

The *variance* of X, $Var(X)$, is defined as

$$Var(X) = \int (x - \mathbb{E}(X))^2 dF(x).$$

Let X and Z be random variables and let the σ-algebra generated by Z be denoted by $\sigma(Z)$. According to Kolmogorov's theorem there exists a random variable Y that is $\sigma(Z)$-measurable with $\mathbb{E}(|Y|) < \infty$ and that satisfies for all $G \in \sigma(Z)$,

$$\int_G Y(\omega)dP(\omega) = \int_G X(\omega)dP(\omega).$$

The random variable Y is called a *conditional expectation*, $\mathbb{E}(X|Z)$, of X given Z. If Y_1 and Y_2 are both conditional expectations of X given Z it holds that $Y_1 = Y_2$ a.s.

Let $(X_n)_{n \in \mathbb{N}}$ be a sequence of independent and identically distributed (iid) random variables with distribution functions $(F_n)_{n \in \mathbb{N}}$. The sequence *converges in probability* to a random variable X with distribution F, denoted by $X_n \overset{p}{\to} X$ if for all $\varepsilon > 0$ it holds that

$$\lim_{n \to \infty} P(|X_n - X| > \varepsilon) = 0.$$

The sequence *converges in distribution* to X, denoted by $X_n \overset{d}{\to} X$ if for every set A with $F(\partial A) = 0$ it holds that $F_n(A)$ converges to $F(A)$. The *sample mean* of a finite sequence $(X_1, \ldots, X_n)$, $\bar{X}$, is defined by $\bar{X} = \frac{1}{n} \sum_{i=1}^{n} X_i$ and the *sample variance*, $\hat{\sigma}_X^2$, is defined by $\hat{\sigma}_X^2 = \frac{1}{n} \sum_{i=1}^{n} (X_i - \bar{X})^2$.

THEOREM 2.8 (CENTRAL LIMIT THEOREM) *If $(X_n)_{\nu \in \mathbb{N}}$ is a sequence of iid random variables with mean μ and variance σ^2, then it holds that*

$$\sqrt{n}(\bar{X} - \mu) \overset{d}{\to} \mathcal{N}(0, \sigma^2).$$

Suppose that σ^2 is not known, but that we have an estimator $\hat{\sigma}^2$ such that $\hat{\sigma}^2 \overset{p}{\to} \sigma^2$. Then it follows that

$$\frac{\sqrt{n}(\bar{X} - \mu)}{\hat{\sigma}} \overset{d}{\to} \mathcal{N}(0, 1).$$

6.   Markov Chains

In this section we briefly review some basic facts concerning Markov chains. For a thorough treatment the reader is referred to e.g. Billingsley (1995) or Tijms (1994). In the two subsections that follow we introduce two topics that are extensively used in Part III of the book, namely stochastic stability and nearly-complete decomposability.

Let S be a finite set. Suppose that to each pair $(i, j) \in S \times S$ a nonnegative number, p_{ij}, is attached such that for all $i \in S$ it holds that

$$\sum_{j \in S} p_{ij} = 1.$$

Let $X_0, X_1, X_2, \ldots$ be a sequence of random variables on a probability space $(\Omega, \mathcal{F}, P)$ whose ranges are contained in S. The sequence is a *Markov chain* if for all $n \geq 1$ and for all sequences $i_0, \ldots, i_n$ for which $P(X_0 = i_0, \ldots, X_n = i_n) > 0$ it holds that

$$P(X_{n+1} = j | X_0 = i_0, \ldots, X_n = i_n)$$
$$= P(X_{n+1} = j | X_n = i_n) = p_{i_n j}.$$

The p_{ij}'s are called *transition probabilities*. The *initial probabilities* are for all $i \in S$, $\alpha_i = P(X_0 = i)$.

A *stochastic matrix* is a non-negative matrix whose row totals equal unity. The following theorem shows that a Markov chain can be constructed for any stochastic matrix combined with a vector of initial probabilities.

THEOREM 2.9 *Suppose that $P = [p_{ij}]$ is an $S \times S$ stochastic matrix and that for all $i \in S$, α_i is a non-negative number such that $\sum_{i \in S} \alpha_i = 1$. Then on some probability space $(\Omega, \mathcal{F}, P)$ there is a Markov chain with initial probabilities $(\alpha_i)_{i \in S}$ and transition probabilities p_{ij}, $i, j \in S$.*

Let ΔS denote the set of probability measures on S. A probability measure $\mu \in \Delta(S)$ is called an *invariant probability measure* if μ satisfies $\mu = \mu P$. That is, if a Markov chain is in state μ at time $t \in \mathbb{N}$, then it is in state μ at time $t + 1$ as well a.s. An invariant probability measure is often called a limit distribution since it describes the long-run behaviour of a Markov chain.

A matrix A is *irreducible* if there exists a $t \in \mathbb{N}$ such that $I + A + A^2 + \cdots + A^t > 0$, where I is the identity matrix. A Markov chain is *ergodic* if the transition matrix P is irreducible. That is, a Markov chain is ergodic if with positive probability there exists a path from each state to any other state, such that the connection takes place in finite time. An important theorem is the so-called ergodicity theorem.

THEOREM 2.10 *Let $(X_t)_{t \in \mathbb{N}}$ be a finite state ergodic Markov chain. Then there exists a unique invariant probability measure.*

The importance of the ergodicity theorem lies in the fact that if a Markov chain is ergodic, then irrespective of the starting point, the chain converges to the unique invariant probability measure.

A set of states $A \subset S$ is called a *recurrent class* if the transition matrix $[p_{aa'}]_{a,a' \in A}$ is irreducible and if for all $a \in A$ and for all $s \in S \backslash A$ it holds that $p_{a,s} = 0$.

6.1   Stochastic Stability

The notion of stochastic stability was first introduced in Foster and Young (1990). A stochastically stable strategy is a strategy that is robust against small random perturbations. We will formalise this notion, drawing heavily on Young (1998) and Freidlin and Wentzell (1984). In the remainder, let Ω be a finite set and let T_0 be a – possibly non-ergodic – transition matrix on Ω.

DEFINITION 2.2 *Let T_0 be the transition matrix of a Markov chain and let $\varepsilon^* > 0$. A set of Markov chains with transition matrices T_ε, $0 < \varepsilon \leq$*

ε^*, *is a family of* regular perturbed Markov chains *of the Markov chain with transition matrix* T_0 *if the following conditions hold:*

1. T_ε *is irreducible for all* $0 < \varepsilon \le \varepsilon^*$;

2. *for all* $\omega, \omega' \in \Omega$ *it holds that* $\lim_{\varepsilon \to 0} T_\varepsilon(\omega, \omega') = T_0(\omega, \omega')$;

3. *if* $T_\varepsilon(\omega, \omega') > 0$ *for some* $\varepsilon > 0$, *then* $\lim_{\varepsilon \to 0} \frac{T_\varepsilon(\omega, \omega')}{\varepsilon^{r(\omega, \omega')}} \in (0, \infty)$ *for some* $r(\omega, \omega') \ge 0$.

Note that $r(\omega, \omega')$ is uniquely defined, since there cannot be two distinct exponents that satisfy the last condition in Definition 2.2. Furthermore, it holds that $r(\omega, \omega') = 0$ if $T_0(\omega, \omega') > 0$. So, transitions that are possible under T_0 have $r(\omega, \omega') = 0$. The transitions with a non-zero value for $r(\cdot)$ are those that depend crucially on the perturbation part of the chain. Note that the last two conditions of Definition 2.2 require that $T_\varepsilon(\omega, \omega')$ converges to $T_0(\omega, \omega')$ at an exponential rate. Furthermore, each perturbed chain has a unique invariant probability measure due to the irreducibility of T_ε.

The results in this section rely heavily on the concept of *trees*.

DEFINITION 2.3 *Given* $\omega \in \Omega$, *an* ω-tree H_ω *is a collection of ordered pairs in* $\Omega \times \Omega$ *such that:*

1. *every* $\omega' \in \Omega \backslash \{\omega\}$ *is the first element of exactly one pair;*

2. *for all* $\omega' \in \Omega \backslash \{\omega\}$ *there exists a path* $(\omega', \omega^1), (\omega^1, \omega^2), \ldots, (\omega^{s-1}, \omega^s)$, (ω^s, ω) *in* H_ω.

The set of all ω-trees is denoted by $\mathcal{H}_\omega$, $\omega \in \Omega$.

Given any $\omega \in \Omega$ and $\varepsilon > 0$, define

$$r_\varepsilon(\omega) = \sum_{H \in \mathcal{H}_\omega} \prod_{(\omega', \omega'') \in H} T_\varepsilon(\omega', \omega''), \qquad (2.1)$$

which is called the ε-*resistance* of state $\omega \in \Omega$. Using Freidlin and Wentzell (1984, Lemma 6.3.1, p. 177) we obtain that for all $0 < \varepsilon \le \varepsilon^*$ the unique invariant distribution $\mu_\varepsilon \in \Delta(\Omega)$ is given by,

$$\mu_\varepsilon(\omega) = \frac{r_\varepsilon(\omega)}{\sum_{\omega' \in \Omega} r_\varepsilon(\omega')}.$$

Since $r_\varepsilon(\omega)$ is a polynomial in ε, the limit distribution $\mu := \lim_{\varepsilon \downarrow 0} \mu_\varepsilon$ is well-defined. Note that the states in the support of $\mu(\cdot)$ are precisely those states that have the lowest rate of convergence to zero if $\varepsilon \downarrow 0$, i.e. they have the lowest resistance. The *stochastically stable states* are defined to be the states in the support of $\mu(\cdot)$.

Define $d(\omega, \omega')$ to be the number of coordinates which differ between ω and ω', i.e. $d(\omega, \omega') = |\{i | \omega_i \neq \omega'_i\}|$. Consider the function $c : \Omega \times \Omega \to \mathbb{N}$, defined by

$$c(\omega, \omega') = \min_{\omega'' \in \Omega} \{d(\omega, \omega'') | T_0(\omega'', \omega') > 0\}.$$

If $T_0(\omega, \omega') = 0$ one needs the random perturbations to reach ω' from ω. Since the concept of stochastic stability originates from the biological literature, any transition due to a random perturbation is called a *mutation*. It describes the change of strategy of an animal or a species that cannot be explained by the model. The function $c(\cdot)$ gives the minimum number of entries of ω that need to be changed by random perturbations to get to ω'. Hence, it gives the minimum number of mutations. Therefore, $c(\omega, \omega')$ is also called the cost of the transition form ω to ω'.

Define for each ω-tree H_ω, the function $c(H_\omega) = \sum_{(\omega', \omega'') \in H_\omega} c(\omega', \omega'')$ and the function $S(\omega) = \min_{H \in \mathcal{H}_\omega} c(H)$. The latter is called the *stochastic potential* and it gives the minimum number of mutations along any possible ω-tree. From (2.1) one can see that

$$r_\varepsilon(\omega) = O\left(\varepsilon^{S(\omega)}\right).$$

Hence, the stochastically stable states are those states whose minimum cost trees are minimal across all states, that is, denoting the set of stochastically stable states by S^*,

$$S^* = \arg\min_{\omega \in \Omega} \{S(\omega)\}.$$

So, the stochastically stable states are the states with minimal stochastic potential. To simplify the task of finding the stochastically stable states, Young (1993) shows that one only needs to find the classes that have minimum stochastic potential among the recurrent classes of the mutation free dynamics, i.e. of T_0. The intuition behind this result is that for any state outside a recurrent class of T_0 there is a path of zero resistance to one of the recurrent classes. Therefore, the states that are not in a recurrent class do not add to the stochastic potential.

Summarising, we get the following theorem.

THEOREM 2.11 (YOUNG (1993)) *Let $(T_\varepsilon)_{0 < \varepsilon \leq \varepsilon^*}$ be a family of regular perturbed Markov chains of T_0, and let μ^ε be the unique invariant probability measure of T_ε for each $\varepsilon \in (0, \varepsilon^*]$. Then $\mu = \lim_{\varepsilon \to 0} \mu^\varepsilon$ exists and μ is* *an invariant probability measure of T_0. The stochastically stable states are those states that are contained in the recurrent classes of T_0 having minimum stochastic potential.*

6.2 Nearly-Complete Decomposability

This subsection is based on Courtois (1977). Intuitively, a nearly-complete decomposable system is a Markov chain where the matrix of transition probabilities can be divided into blocks such that the interaction *between* blocks is small relative to interaction *within* blocks. In the remainder let Q be an $n \times n$ irreducible stochastic matrix. The dynamic process $(y_t)_{t \in \mathbb{N}}$, where $y_t \in \mathbb{R}^n$ for all $t \in \mathbb{N}$, is then given by

$$(y_{t+1})^\top = (y_t)^\top Q. \tag{2.2}$$

Note that Q can be written as follows:

$$Q = Q^* + \varepsilon C, \tag{2.3}$$

where Q^* is of order n and given by

$$Q^* = \begin{bmatrix} Q_1^* & & & & \\ & \ddots & & 0 & \\ & & Q_I^* & & \\ & 0 & & \ddots & \\ & & & & Q_N^* \end{bmatrix}.$$

The matrices Q_I^*, $I = 1, \ldots, N$, are irreducible stochastic matrices of order $n(I)$. Hence $n = \sum_{I=1}^N n(I)$. Therefore the sums of the rows of C are zero. We choose ζ and C such that for all rows k_I, $I = 1, \ldots, N$, $k = 1, \ldots, n$, it holds that

$$\sum_{J \neq I} \sum_{l=1}^{n(J)} C_{k_I l_J} = \sum_{J \neq I} \sum_{l=1}^{n(J)} Q_{k_I l_J}$$

and

$$\zeta = \max_{k_I} \left(\sum_{J \neq I} \sum_{l=1}^{n(J)} Q_{k_I l_J} \right),$$

where the k_I denotes the k-th element in the I-th block. The parameter ζ is called the *maximum degree of coupling* between subsystems Q_I^*.

It is assumed that all elementary divisors[2] of Q and Q^* are linear. Then the spectral density composition of the t-step probabilities – Q^t – can be written as

$$Q^t = \sum_{I=1}^{N} \sum_{k=1}^{n(I)} \lambda^t(k_I) Z(k_I), \qquad (2.4)$$

where

$$Z(k_I) = s(k_I)^{-1} v(k_I) v(k_I)^\top,$$

$\lambda(k_I)$ is the k_I-th maximal eigenvalue in absolute value of Q, $v(k_I)$ is the corresponding eigenvector normalised to one using the vector norm $\| \cdot \|_1$, and $s(k_I)$ is the condition number $s(k_I) = v(k_I)^\top v(k_I)$. Since Q is a stochastic matrix, the Perron-Frobenius theorem gives that the maximal eigenvalue of Q equals 1. Therefore, (2.4) can be rewritten as

$$Q^t = Z(1_1) + \sum_{I=2}^{N} \lambda^t(1_I) Z(1_I) + \sum_{I=1}^{N} \sum_{k=2}^{n(I)} \lambda^t(k_I) Z(k_I). \qquad (2.5)$$

If one defines for each matrix Q_I^* in a similar way $Z^*(k_I)$, $s^*(k_I)$, $\lambda^*(k_I)$, and $v^*(k_I)$, e.g. $\lambda^*(k_I)$ is the k-th maximal eigenvalue in absolute value of Q_I^*, then one can find a similar spectral decomposition for Q^*, i.e.

$$(Q^*)^t = \sum_{I=1}^{N} Z^*(1_I) + \sum_{I=1}^{N} \sum_{k=2}^{n(I)} (\lambda^*)^t(k_I) Z^*(k_I), \qquad (2.6)$$

using the fact that $v_{k_I}^*(1_I) = n(I)^{-1}$ for all k_I. The behaviour through time of y_t and y_t^*, where the dynamics of $(y_t)_{t \in \mathbf{N}}$ is described by (2.2) and the process $(y_t^*)_{t \in \mathbf{N}}$ is defined by

$$(y_{t+1}^*)^\top = (y_t^*)^\top Q^*, \qquad (2.7)$$

are therefore also specified by (2.5) and (2.6). The behaviour of y_t can be seen as long-run behaviour whereas y_t^* describes short-run behaviour. The comparison between both processes follows from two theorems as proven by Simon and Ando (1961).

---

[2]See e.g. Lancaster and Tismentetsky (1985).

THEOREM 2.12 *For an arbitrary positive real number ξ, there exists a number ζ_ξ such that for $\zeta < \zeta_\xi$,*

$$\max_{p,q}|Z_{pq}(k_I) - Z^*_{pq}(k_I)| < \xi,$$

for any $2 \le k \le n(I)$, $1 \le I \le N$, where $1 \le p, q \le n$.

THEOREM 2.13 *For an arbitrary positive real number ω, there exists a number ζ_ω such that for $\zeta < \zeta_\omega$,*

$$\max_{k,l}|Z_{k_I l_J}(k_I) - v^*_{l_J}(1_J)\alpha_{IJ}(1_K)| < \omega,$$

for any $1 \le k \le n(I)$, $1 \le l \le n(J)$, $1 \le K, I, J \le N$, and where $\alpha_{IJ}(1_K)$ is given by

$$\alpha_{IJ}(1_K) = \sum_{k=1}^{n(I)} \sum_{l=1}^{n(J)} v^*_{k_I} z_{k_I l_J}(1_K).$$

It can be shown that for all $I = 1, \ldots, N$, $\lambda(1_I)$ is close to unity. Therefore $\lambda^t(1_I)$ will also be close to unity for small t. Hence, the first two terms on the right-hand side of eq. (2.5) will not vary much for $t < T_2$, for some $T_2 > 0$. The first term of the right-hand side of (2.6) does not change at all. Hence, for $t < T_2$ the behaviour through time of y_t and y^*_t is determined by the last terms of Q^t and $(Q^*)^t$, respectively. Also, if $\varepsilon \to 0$ it can be shown that $\lambda(k_I) \to \lambda^*(k_I)$ and from Theorem 2.12 it follows that $Z(k_I) \to Z^*(k_I)$, for all $k = 2, \ldots, n(I)$ and $I = 1, \ldots, N$. This means that for ζ small and $t < T_2$ the paths of y_t and y^*_t are very close.

The eigenvalues $\lambda^*(k_I)$ are strictly less than unity in absolute value for all $k = 2, \ldots, n(I)$, and $I = 1, \ldots, N$. For any positive real number ξ_1 we can therefore define a smallest time T^*_1 such that

$$\max_{1 \le p,q \le n}\left|\sum_{I=1}^{N} \sum_{k=2}^{n(I)}(\lambda^*)^t(k_I)Z^*_{pq}(k_I)\right| < \xi_1 \qquad \text{for } t > T^*_1.$$

Similarly we can find a T_1 such that

$$\max_{1 \le p,q \le n}\left|\sum_{I=1}^{N} \sum_{k=2}^{n(I)}\lambda^t(k_I)Z_{pq}(k_I)\right| < \xi_1 \qquad \text{for } t > T_1.$$

Theorem 2.12 plus convergence of the eigenvalues with ζ then ensures that $T_1 \to T^*_1$ as $\zeta \to 0$. We can always choose ζ such that $T_2 > T_1$.

As long as ζ is not identical to zero it holds that $\lambda(1_I)$ is not identical to unity for $I = 2, \ldots, N$.[3] Therefore, there will be a time $T_3 > 0$ such that for sufficiently small ξ_3,

$$\max_{1 \le p,q \le n} \left| \sum_{I=1}^{N} \sum_{k=2}^{n(I)} \lambda^t(1_I) Z_{pq}(1_I) \right| < \xi_3 \qquad \text{for } t > T_3.$$

This implies that for $T_2 < t < T_3$, the last term of Q^t is negligible and the path of y_t is determined by the first two components of Q^t. According to Theorem 2.13 it holds that for any I and J the elements of $Z(1_K)$,

$$Z_{k_I 1_J}(1_K), \ldots, Z_{k_I l_J}(1_K), \ldots, Z_{k_I n(J)_J}(1_K),$$

depend essentially on I, J and l, and are almost independent of k. So, for any I and J they are proportional to the elements of the eigenvector of Q_J^* corresponding to the largest eigenvalue. Since Q^* is stochastic and irreducible, this eigenvector corresponds to the unique invariant probability measure μ_J^* of the Markov chain with transition matrix Q_J^*. Thus, for $T_2 < t < T_3$ the elements of the vector y_t, $(y_{l_J})_t$, will approximately have a constant ratio that is similar to that of the elements of μ_J^*. Finally, for $t > T_3$ the behaviour of y_t is almost completely determined by the first term of Q^t. So, y_t evolves towards $v(1_1)$, which corresponds to the unique invariant probability measure μ of the Markov chain with transition matrix Q. Summarising, the dynamics of y_t can be described as follows.

1 Short-run dynamics: $t < T_1$. The predominant terms in Q^t and $(Q^*)^t$ are the last ones. Hence, y_t and y_t^* evolve similarly.

2 Short-run equilibrium: $T_1 < t < T_2$. The last terms of Q^t and $(Q^*)^t$ have vanished while for all I, $\lambda^t(1_I)$ remains close to unity. A similar equilibrium is therefore reached within each subsystem of Q and Q^*.

3 Long-run dynamics: $T_2 < t < T_3$. The predominant term in Q^t is the second one. The whole system moves to equilibrium, while the short-run equilibria in the subsystems are approximately maintained.

4 Long-run equilibrium: $t > T_3$. The first term of Q^t dominates. Therefore, a global equilibrium is attained.

The above theory implies that one can estimate $\mu(\cdot)$ by calculating μ_I^* for $I = 1, \ldots, N$, and the invariant measure $\tilde{\mu}$ of the process

$$(\tilde{y}_{t+1})^\top = (\tilde{y}_t)^\top P, \qquad (2.8)$$

---

[3]If $\zeta = 0$, all blocks Q_I are irreducible and then we would have $\lambda(1_I) = \lambda^*(1_I) = 1$ for all I.

where $(\tilde{y}_I)_t = \sum_{k=1}^{n(I)} (y_{k_I})_t$ for all $I = 1, \ldots, N$, and some transition matrix P. For $t > T_2$ we saw that $\frac{(y_{k_I})_t}{(\tilde{y}_I)_t} \approx \mu_{I,k}^*$. Hence, the probability of a transition from group I to group J is given by

$$(p_{IJ})_{t+1} = (\tilde{y}_I)_t^{-1} \sum_{k=1}^{n(I)} (y_{k_I})_t \sum_{l=1}^{n(J)} Q_{k_I l_J}.$$

For $t > T_2$ this can be approximated by

$$(p_{IJ})_{t+1} \approx \sum_{k=1}^{n(I)} \mu_{I,k}^* \sum_{l=1}^{n(J)} Q_{k_I l_J} \equiv p_{IJ}.$$

So, by taking $P = [p_{IJ}]$, the process in (2.8) gives a good approximation for $t > T_2$ of the entire process $(y_t)_{t \in \mathbb{N}}$. It is shown in Courtois (1977, Section 2.1) that the error of this approximation is of order $O(\zeta)$.

Until now we have not been concerned by how large ζ can be. It was stated that for $T_1^* < t < T_2$, the original system Q is in a short-run equilibrium close to the equilibrium of the completely decomposable system Q^*. If this is to occur it must hold that $T_1^* < T_2$. Every matrix Q can be written in the form of eq. (2.3), but not for all matrices it holds that $T_1^* < T_2$. Systems that satisfy the condition $T_1^* < T_2$ are called *nearly-complete decomposable* systems (cf. Ando and Fisher (1963)). Since T_1^* is independent of ζ and T_2 increases with $\zeta \to 0$, the condition is satisfied for ζ sufficiently small. It is shown in Courtois (1977, Section 3.2) that a sufficient condition for nearly-complete decomposability is given by

$$\zeta < \tfrac{1}{2} \left[1 - \max_{I=1,\ldots,N} |\lambda^*(2_I)| \right]. \tag{2.9}$$

7. Stochastic Processes in Continuous Time

In this section the most important concepts for stochastic processes in continuous time are introduced. First, the general concept of a semi-martingale, the notions of stochastic integral and stochastic differential equation, and the change of variables formula (also known as Ito's lemma) are presented. Then, some basic stochastic processes (semi-martingales) that are used in the book are discussed. Finally, some notions related to dynamic programming and optimal stopping are described. This section is based on Protter (1995), Karatzas and Shreve (1991) and Øksendal (2000). For an exposition that is oriented on the theory of financial markets the reader is referred to Dana and Jeanblanc (2003).

In continuous time the time index, t, is such that $t \in [0, \infty)$.

DEFINITION 2.4 *A filtration,* $(\mathcal{F}_t)_{0 \le t \le \infty}$ *is a family of σ-algebras such that $\mathcal{F}_s \subset \mathcal{F}_t$ if $s \le t$. A filtered probability space, $(\Omega, \mathcal{F}, (\mathcal{F}_t)_{0 \le t \le \infty}, P)$ is a complete probability space augmented with a filtration.*

In the remainder, it will always be assumed that a filtered probability space satisfies the *usual hypotheses,* i.e.

1   $\mathcal{F}_0$ contains all the P-null sets of $\mathcal{F}$;

2   the filtration $(\mathcal{F}_t)_{0 \le t \le \infty}$ is right-continuous, i.e. $\mathcal{F}_t = \bigcap_{u > t} \mathcal{F}_u$, all t, $0 \le t < \infty$.

In parts I and II of this book an important role is played by stopping times.

DEFINITION 2.5 *A random variable $T : \Omega \to [0, \infty]$ is a stopping time if the event $\{\omega \in \Omega | T(\omega) \le l\} \in \mathcal{F}_t$ for all $t \in [0, \infty]$.*

A *stochastic process* X on $(\Omega, \mathcal{F}, (\mathcal{F}_t)_{0 \le t \le \infty}, P)$ is a collection of random variables $(X_t)_{0 \le t \le \infty}$. The process X is *adapted* if for all $t \in [0, \infty)$ it holds that $X_t \in \mathcal{F}_t$. The stochastic processes X and Y are *modifications* if $X_t = Y_t$ a.s. for all $t \ge 0$. They are *indistinguishable* if a.s. for all $t \ge 0$ it holds that $X_t = Y_t$. For all $\omega \in \Omega$, the *sample path* is the mapping $t \mapsto X_t(\omega)$ from $[0, \infty)$ into $\mathbb{R}$. For indistinguishable processes, the sample paths are a.s. identical. For modifications this need not be the case. This arises from the fact that $[0, \infty)$ is an uncountable set. For all $t \ge 0$, let N_t be a null set. If X is a modification of Y this implies that for $\omega \notin N_t$ it holds that $X_t(\omega) = Y_t(\omega)$. We cannot guarantee, however, that $N = \bigcup_{t \ge 0} N_t$ is a null set. If two processes are indistinguishable, there is just one null set. One can show that if X is a modification of Y and both have right-continuous sample paths a.s., then X and Y are indistinguishable. A stochastic process is called *cadlag* if its sample paths are right-continuous with left limits.[4] The following theorem plays an important role.

THEOREM 2.14 *Let X be an adapted cadlag stochastic process and let $A \subset \mathbb{R}$ be a closed set. Then the function $T : \Omega \to [0, \infty]$, which for all $\omega \in \Omega$ is defined by*

$$T(\omega) = \inf\{t > 0 | X_t(\omega) \in A \text{ or } X_{t-}(\omega) \in A\},$$

is a stopping time, where $t- = \lim_{\Delta t \uparrow 0} t + \Delta t$. If A is open, then

$$T(\omega) = \inf\{t > 0 | X_t(\omega) \in A\},$$

---

[4]The term "cadlag" is an acronym from the French *"continu à droite, limites à gauche"*.

is a stopping time.

A real-valued, adapted stochastic process $X = (X_t)_{0 \leq t \leq \infty}$ is called a *martingale* with respect to the filtration $(\mathcal{F}_t)_{0 \leq t \leq \infty}$ if $\mathbb{E}(|X_t|) < \infty$ for all $0 \leq t \leq \infty$ and if for all $0 \leq s \leq t \leq \infty$ it holds that $\mathbb{E}(X_t|\mathcal{F}_s) = X_s$, a.s. A martingale is said to be *closed* by a random variable Y if $\mathbb{E}(|Y|) < \infty$ and $X_t = \mathbb{E}(Y|\mathcal{F}_t)$, for all $0 \leq t < \infty$. If X is a martingale, then there exists a unique cadlag modification. We will always implicitly assume that we use this cadlag modification.

Let A be a set. A family of random variables $(U_\alpha)_{\alpha \in A}$ is *uniformly integrable* if

$$\lim_{n \to \infty} \sup_{\alpha \in A} \int_{\{|U_\alpha| \geq n\}} |U_\alpha| dP = 0.$$

Uniform integrability is a sufficient condition for a martingale to be closed.

Let X be a stochastic process and let T be a stopping time. The *stopped process*, $(X_t^T)_{0 \leq t < \infty}$ is defined for all $0 \leq t < \infty$ by

$$X_t^T = X_t \mathbb{1}_{\{t < T\}} + X_T \mathbb{1}_{\{t \geq T\}}.$$

An adapted cadlag process X is a *local martingale* if there exists a sequence of increasing stopping times $T_1, T_2, \ldots$, with $\lim_{n \to \infty} T_n = \infty$ a.s. such that $X^{T_n} \mathbb{1}_{\{T_n > 0\}}$ is a uniformly integrable martingale for all n.

For $\omega \in \Omega$, the path $(X_t(\omega))_{t \geq 0}$ is of finite variation if for all $t \geq 0$ it holds that $X_t - X_{t-} < \infty$. X is called a *finite variation process* (FV) if almost all paths of X are of finite variation.

Now, the concept of a semimartingale can be introduced. A process H is said to be *simple predictable* if H has a representation

$$H_t = H_0 \mathbb{1}_{\{0\}}(t) + \sum_{i=1}^{n} H_i \mathbb{1}_{(T_i, T_{i+1}]}(t), \qquad t \geq 0,$$

where $0 = T_1 \leq \cdots \leq T_{n+1} < \infty$, a.s., is a finite sequence of stopping times, $H_i \in \mathcal{F}_{T_i}$, with $|H_i| < \infty$ a.s., $i \in \{1, 2, \ldots, n\}$. The collection of simple predictable processes is denoted by $\boldsymbol{S}$.

It is said that a sequence of process $X^1, X^2, \ldots$ converges *uniformly* to X if $\sup_t |X_t^n - X_t| \xrightarrow{p} 0$. Let $\boldsymbol{S}_u$ denote the topological space induced by uniform convergence.[5] Let $\boldsymbol{L}^0$ denote the set of finite-valued

---

[5]In this topology a set $S \subset \boldsymbol{S}$ is closed if for all uniformly convergent sequences in S it holds that the limit is in S.

random variables topologised by convergence in probability. Let X be a stochastic process. Define the linear mapping $I_X : \boldsymbol{S}_u \to \boldsymbol{L}^0$ by

$$I_X(H) = H_0 X_0 + \sum_{i=1}^{n} H_i (X_{T_{i+1}} - X_{T_i}).$$

DEFINITION 2.6 *A process X is a* semimartingale *if for all $t \in [0, \infty)$ it holds that X^t is cadlag, adapted and $I_{X^t} : \boldsymbol{S}_u \to \boldsymbol{L}_0$ is continuous.*

It can be shown that X is a semimartingale if and only if for all $t \geq 0$ it holds that,

$$X_t = X_0 + N_t + B_t,$$

where N is a local martingale and B is a finite variation (FV) process.

Semimartingales turn out to be good integrators. For simple predictable processes this is easy to be seen. Let X be a semimartingale. Then the mapping I_X can be seen as the integral of a simple predictable process H with respect to X. The standard (deterministic) Stieltjes integral is defined as a limit of sums. For FV processes, one could extend the Stieltjes integral to a meaningful stochastic equivalent. Famous processes like for example the Brownian motion, however, have paths of infinite variation on compacts. The semimartingale seems to be an alternative way to define a stochastic integral that comprises some processes of infinite variation on compacts. Let $\mathbb{D}$ denote the space of adapted processes with cadlag paths. The set $\mathbb{L}$ denotes the set of adapted processes with caglad (left-continuous with right-limits) paths. A sequence of processes $H^1, H^2, \ldots$ is said to converge to a process H *uniformly on compacts in probability* (ucp) if for all $t > 0$ it holds that $\sup_{0 \leq s \leq t} |H^n_s - H_s| \xrightarrow{p} 0$. If $\mathbb{D}$ is topologised under ucp one can show that this gives a complete metric space. Furthermore, the space $\boldsymbol{S}$ is dense in $\mathbb{L}$ under the ucp topology. For $H \in \boldsymbol{S}$ and X a cadlag process define the linear mapping $J_X : \boldsymbol{S} \to \mathbb{D}$ by

$$J_X(H) = H_0 X_0 + \sum_{i=1}^{n} H_i (X^{T_{i+1}} - X^{T_i}).$$

If X is a semimartingale the mapping J_X is continuous (under the ucp topology).

DEFINITION 2.7 *Let X be a semimartingale. The continuous linear mapping $J_X : \mathbb{L} \to \mathbb{D}$ obtained as the extension of $J_X : \boldsymbol{S} \to \mathbb{D}$ is the* stochastic integral *with respect to X, i.e.*

$$J_{X_t}(H) = \int_0^t H_s dX_s.$$

One of the most useful results on stochastic integration with respect to semimartingales is Ito's lemma. Let X be a semimartingale. The *quadratic variation process* of X, denoted by $[X, X]$, is defined by

$$[X, X] = X^2 - 2 \int X_- dX.$$

The path by path continuous part is denoted by $[X, X]^c$.

THEOREM 2.15 (ITO'S LEMMA) *Let X be a semimartingale and let f be a C^2 real valued function. Then $f(X)$ is again a semimartingale and for all $t > 0$ it holds that*

$$f(X_t) - f(X_0) = \int_{(0,t]} f'(X_{s-}) dX_s + \frac{1}{2} \int_{(0,t]} f''(X_{s-}) d[X, X]_s^c$$
$$+ \sum_{0 < s \leq t} \left(f(X_s) - f(X_{s-}) - f'(X_{s-}) \Delta X_s \right).$$

An operator F mapping $\mathbb{D}^n$ to $\mathbb{D}$ is *functional Lipschitz* if for any X, Y in $\mathbb{D}^n$ the following two conditions are satisfied:

1 for any stopping time T, $X^{T-} = Y^{T-}$ implies $F(X)^{T-} = F(Y)^{T-}$;

2 there exists an increasing (finite) process $K = (K_t)_{t \geq 0}$ such that

$$|F(X)_t - F(Y)_t| \leq K_t \|X - Y\|_t^* \quad \text{a.s.,} \ \forall t \geq 0,$$

   where $\|X\|_t^* = \sup_{0 \leq u \leq t} \|X_u\|$.

For functional Lipschitz mappings we have the following result that underlies the theory of Chapter 4 and which can be found in Protter (1995).

THEOREM 2.16 *Let $\mathbf{Z} = (Z^1, \ldots, Z^d)$ be a vector of semimartingales, $\mathbf{Z}_0 = 0$ a.s. and let $J \in \mathbb{D}$ be an adapted cadlag process. Furthermore, let for all $j = 1, \ldots, d$, the mappings $F_j : \mathbb{D} \to \mathbb{D}$ be functional Lipschitz. Then, for all $t > 0$ the equation*

$$X_t = J_t + \sum_{j=1}^{d} \int_0^t Fj(X)_{s-} dZ_s^j, \tag{2.10}$$

has a unique solution in $\mathbb{D}$. Moreover, if J is a semimartingale, then so is X.

An equation of the form (2.10) is called a *stochastic differential equation* and is often written in differential form:

$$dX_t = dJ_t + \sum_{j=1}^{d} F_j(X)_t dZ_t^j.$$

A process X is a *strong Markov* process if for any subset A, any stopping time T with $P(T < \infty) = 1$ and all $t > 0$ it holds that

$$P(X_{T+t} \in A|\mathcal{F}_t) = P(X_{T+t} \in A|X_T).$$

A strong Markov process satisfies the *reflection principle*, that is it "starts afresh" at stopping time T. If the process B is strong Markov this means that the process $(B_{T+t} - B_T)_{t \geq 0}$ is independent of the σ-algebra $\mathcal{F}_T$. This property turns out to be useful in calculating some expected values in Chapter 4.

7.1   Basic Stochastic Processes

In this subsection two basic stochastic processes are introduced that are used in this book, namely the Poisson process and the geometric Brownian motion.

Let $T_0, T_1, \ldots$ be a strictly increasing sequence of positive random variables with $T_0 = 0$, a.s. Associated with this sequence one can define the *counting process*, $N = (N_t)_{0 \leq t \leq \infty}$, which is for all $t \geq 0$ given by

$$N_t = \sum_{n \geq 1} \mathbb{1}_{\{t \geq T_n\}}.$$

Let $T = \sup_n T_n$ be the explosion time of N. If $T = \infty$, a.s., we say that N is a counting process without explosions.

DEFINITION 2.8 *An adapted counting process N without explosions is a Poisson process if*

1 *for all $0 \leq s < t < \infty$ it holds that $N_t - N_s$ is independent of $\mathcal{F}_s$ (independent increments);*

2 *for all $0 \leq s < t < \infty$, $0 \leq u < v < \infty$, $t - s = v - u$ it holds that the distribution of $N_t - N_s$ is the same as the distribution of $N_v - N_u$ (stationary increments).*

If N is a Poisson process then there exists a $\mu \geq 0$ such that for all $t > 0$ it holds that $N_t \sim \mathcal{P}(\mu t)$. We will therefore speak of the Poisson process with parameter μ.

DEFINITION 2.9 *An adapted process $B = (B_t)_{0 \leq t < \infty}$ taking values in $\mathbb{R}$ is a* Brownian motion *or* Wiener process *if*

1 *for all $0 \leq s < t < \infty$ it holds that $B_t - B_s$ is independent of $\mathcal{F}_s$;*

2 *for all $0 \leq s < t < \infty$ it holds that $B_t - B_s \sim \mathcal{N}(0, t - s)$.*

Existence of Brownian motion is proved in e.g. Karatzas and Shreve (1991). If B is a Brownian motion there exists a modification that has continuous sample paths a.s. We will always assume to use this modification. Both the Poisson process and the Brownian motion are examples of semimartingales. Furthermore, the Brownian motion is strong Markov.

A *diffusion*, or *Ito process* is a stochastic differential equation of the form

$$X_t = X_0 + \int_0^t b(X_s, s)ds + \sum_{j=1}^r \int_0^t \sigma_j(X_s, s)dW_s^r, \qquad (2.11)$$

where for all r, W^r is a Wiener process (Brownian motion).

For diffusions with $r = 1$, one can show that Ito's lemma becomes (in differential form)

$$df(x, t) = \left[\frac{\partial f(x,t)}{\partial t} + b(x,t)\frac{\partial f(x,t)}{\partial x} + \tfrac{1}{2}\sigma^2(x,t)\frac{\partial^2 f(x,t)}{\partial x^2} \right] dt$$
$$+ \sigma(x,t)\frac{\partial f(x,t)}{\partial x}dW_t,$$

where f is a C^2 function. The diffusion that is used in this book is called the *geometric Brownian motion* and is in differential form given by

$$dX_t = \alpha X_t dt + \sigma X_t dW_t.$$

An n-dimensional Ito process is a vector $X = (X^1, X^2, \ldots, X^n)$ driven by an n-dimensional Wiener process $W = (W^1, W^2, \ldots, W^n)$, where for all $i = 1, \ldots, n$, it holds that there exist functions $b^i : \mathbb{R}^n \times [0, \infty) \to \mathbb{R}$ and $\sigma^i : \mathbb{R}^n \times [0, \infty) \to \mathbb{R}^n$, such that (in differential form)

$$dX_t^i = b^i(X_t, t)dt + \sum_{j=1}^n \sigma_j^i(X_t, t)dW_t^j.$$

For an n-dimensional Ito process it holds for all $i, j = 1, \ldots, n$ that $dW^i dW^i = dt$, $dW^i dt = 0$, and $dW^i dW^j = \rho_{ij}dt$, where ρ_{ij} is the *instantaneous correlation* between the Wiener processes W^i and W^j. Note that if W^i and W^j are independent it holds that $dW^i dW^j = 0$. Let Y be a stochastic process such that $Y_t = f(X_t, t)$, where $f(\cdot)$ is a C^2 function and X is an n-dimensional Ito process. Then Ito's lemma reads

$$dY_t = \frac{\partial f(X_t, t)}{\partial t}dt + \sum_{i=1}^n \frac{\partial f(X_t, t)}{\partial x_i}dX_t^i + \frac{1}{2}\sum_{i=1}^n \sum_{j=1}^n \frac{\partial^2 f(X_t, t)}{\partial x_i \partial x_j}dX_t^i dX_t^j.$$

7.2   Optimal Stopping

This subsection describes the basic concepts involved in optimal stopping problems. For a more elaborate, heuristic introduction the interested reader can consult Dixit (1993). For a rigorous analysis of optimal stopping problems the reader is referred to Shiryaev (1978) or Øksendal (2000, Chapter 10).

Let X_t be a Poisson process or a diffusion. An expected value maximising decision maker has the opportunity to execute a project (e.g. investment in a new machine or early exercise of an American call option) in an uncertain environment. The uncertainty is governed by X. Let $\Pi(X)$ denote the payoff that the decision maker gets when he decides to undertake the project in state X. Before the project is undertaken, the decision maker gets a payoff flow governed by the function $\pi : \mathbb{R} \to \mathbb{R}$. The problem is to determine the optimal time to undertake the project, i.e. to find a stopping time T^* such that

$$\mathbb{E}\left(\int_0^{T^*} e^{-rt}\pi(X_t)dt + e^{-rT^*}\Pi(X_{T^*}) \right)$$

$$= \sup_T \mathbb{E}\left(\int_0^T e^{-rt}\pi(X_t)dt + e^{-rT}\Pi(X_T)dt \right). \tag{2.12}$$

The value of the project at time t is denoted by $V(X_t)$. Suppose that the decision maker has not stopped before time t. Then the value of the project is given by the maximum of the value of undertaking the project and the value of waiting, i.e.

$$V(X_t) = \max\left\{ \Pi(X_t), \pi(X_t)dt + e^{-rdt}\mathbb{E}(X_{t+dt}|X_t) \right\}. \tag{2.13}$$

This is called *Bellman's principle* of optimality. It can be shown that there exists a differentiable solution that simultaneously satisfies (2.12) and (2.13). Hence, we can use (2.13) to find a solution to (2.12).

If the second argument in (2.13) is larger it is optimal to wait. This is called the *continuation region*. Using a Taylor expansion and Ito's lemma, working out the Bellman principle for the continuation region yields

$$V(X_t) = \pi(X_t)dt + e^{-rdt}\Big(V(X_t) + \mathbb{E}(dV|X_t) \Big)$$

$$= \pi(X_t)dt + (1 - rdt + o(dt))\Big(V(X_t) + \mathbb{E}(dV|X_t) \Big)$$

$$\Longleftrightarrow rdtV(X_t) = \pi(X_t)dt + \mathbb{E}(dV|X_t) - rdt\mathbb{E}(dV|X_t) + o(dt)$$

$$= \pi(X_t)dt + \mathbb{E}(dV|X_t) - rdt\mathbb{E}\Big[V'(X_t)dX_t$$

$$+ \tfrac{1}{2}V''(X_t)(dX_t)^2|X_t \Big] + o(dt).$$

If X is a Poisson process we have

$$\mathbb{E}(dX_t) = \mu dt,$$
$$\mathbb{E}((dX_t)^2) = \mu dt - 2(\mu dt)^2.$$

For a geometric Brownian motion we get

$$\mathbb{E}(dX_t) = \alpha X_t dt$$
$$\mathbb{E}((dX_t)^2) = \sigma^2 X_t^2 dt.$$

Therefore, after dividing by dt, the value function in the continuation region should – for these two stochastic processes – satisfy

$$rV(X_t) = \pi(X_t) + \frac{1}{dt}\mathbb{E}(dV|X_t) + \frac{1}{dt}o(dt).$$

By taking $dt \downarrow 0$ we obtain the *Bellman equation*

$$rV(X_t) = \pi(X_t) + \lim_{dt \downarrow 0} \frac{1}{dt}\mathbb{E}(dV|X_t).$$

If the termination payoff Π is increasing in X_t and if the payoff flow is constant one can show that there exists a unique threshold x^* such that undertaking the project is optimal for $X_t > x^*$ and waiting is optimal for $X_t < x^*$. Since there exists a differentiable solution to (2.13) it should hold that at the optimal stopping time T^*,

$$V(x^*) = \Pi(x^*).$$

This is called the *value matching* condition. Furthermore, one can show that for strong Markov processes with continuous sample paths a.s. the so-called *smooth pasting* condition,[6]

$$V'(x^*) = \Pi'(x^*),$$

holds. These two conditions are often used to calculate the optimal threshold x^*.

---

[6]The smooth pasting condition is also known as the *high contact* or *smooth fit* principle.

I

INVESTMENT, STRATEGY, AND UNCERTAINTY

Chapter 3

THE EFFECT OF INFORMATION STREAMS ON CAPITAL BUDGETING DECISIONS

1. Introduction

In this chapter a firm is considered that faces the decision whether or not to invest in a project. The project's profitability is not known beforehand. However, imperfect signals arrive over time indicating the project either to be good or bad. These signals cause the firm to update its valuation of the project. The aim is to determine the timing of investment as well as the effects of the quantity and the quality of the signals on the investment decision.

The problem can for example be the adoption of a technological innovation whose effectiveness is unknown. One can also think of a firm having the opportunity to enter a new market which involves sunk investment costs. The uncertainty can then for instance be caused by unknown consumer interest, e.g. demand can be favourable or not. Consider for instance the telecommunication sector where there is one company that can supply a new service to its customers. However, the company is uncertain about the possible success of the new service. Occasionally, the firm receives signals from which it can deduce information concerning the profitability of the new service. Here we can think of market performance of related products and also of more general economic indicators that may influence the market performance of the new service. Another example is given by a pharmaceutical firm that is developing a new drug. Test results are coming in indicating whether the drug is effective or not.

This situation is modelled by considering a project that can be either good or bad. If the project is bad, the optimal strategy is to refrain from investment. Since the firm incurs sunk costs when investing in

55

the project, a loss is suffered in case the project is bad and the firm invests. At irregular intervals, however, the firm receives a signal about the quality of the project. The signals indicate whether the project is good or bad, but it is known to the firm that the signals are imperfect. The points in time at which signals arrive are unknown beforehand. Every time the firm receives a signal, it updates its belief that the project is good in a Bayesian way. Therefore, by delaying investment and waiting for more signals to arrive, the firm can predict with higher accuracy whether the market is good or bad. This induces an option value of waiting. The question is how many good signals relative to bad signals the firm needs to observe, to justify investment in the project. We show that this is equivalent to finding a critical level for the belief that the project is good, given the available signals. This belief turns out to depend critically on the quality of the signal, i.e. the probability with which the signals reflect the true state of the world, as well as the frequency at which signals occur over time. The signals are modelled as two correlated binomially distributed random variables. The first one models the arrival of signals while the latter models its type, i.e. indicating that the project is good or bad. As soon as the firm has invested, the true state of the world is revealed.

This chapter is related to several strands of literature. First of all, the model has strong similarities with the standard real options model as developed by McDonald and Siegel (1986) and for which Dixit and Pindyck (1996) develop the basic framework. It is important to note that the way we deal with uncertainty in our model differs crucially from this literature. Within our framework more information becomes available over time, whereas in the standard real-options literature uncertainty is constant over time caused by, for instance, price uncertainty in an existing market. In other words, whereas our model is a decision problem with incomplete information where nature determines the state of the world only at the beginning with information arriving to resolve uncertainty, the framework typically used in the literature is a decision problem with complete information, where nature determines the state of the world at each consecutive point in time. More formally, the stochastic processes in these models have stationary increments that are independent of the past. Examples of processes that are often used are Brownian motion, Poisson process, and Lévy processes. In contrast, the increments of the stochastic process that we consider are path-dependent and non-stationary. We allow for the variance of the stochastic process to decrease over time. This implies that the standard tools (cf. Øksendal (2000)) cannot be used in our framework.

A second branch of literature to which our chapter is related is the R&D literature. In her seminal paper, Reinganum (1981) develops a model of dynamic R&D competition. In that model technological innovations arrive via a Poisson process and the influence of patents is analysed. Again, the stochastic process driving the innovation process has stationary increments that are independent of the past. The paper by Malueg and Tsutsui (1997) introduces learning into the Reinganum framework and is therefore more closely related to this chapter. In the endogenous growth literature, Aghion and Howitt (1992) use a similar framework as Reinganum to model Schumpeterian growth.

The contributions mentioned above all consider a stream of technological innovations where there is uncertainty about when these innovations become available. Moscarini and Smith (2001) consider a situation where a single decision maker faces a project whose future stream of cash flows is uncertain. Information is modelled by a geometric Brownian motion that serves as a continuous time approximation of discrete time information in the sense that the diffusion process can be interpreted as a running sample mean of observations. The diffusion has an unknown mean that depends on the (unknown) state of nature and a variance that, at some costs, can be controlled by the decision maker. So the decision maker faces an optimal stopping problem, i.e. when to invest (if at all), as well as an optimal control problem, i.e. how much to invest in R&D. The main difference with our approach is the way uncertainty is modelled. Due to the higher complexity of the stochastic process used here, we assume, in contrast to Moscarini and Smith (2001), that information is obtained without costs.

The way we model uncertainty is closely related to Jensen (1982). The main difference is that in Jensen's model, signals only give information on the probability of the project being good. This probability is considered to be an unknown parameter. In each period one receives a signal about its true value. This signal is used to update the beliefs, just as in our model, i.e. the belief is a conditional probability based on past information. In short, one forms a belief on the belief in a good project. However, in Jensen's model, a good signal not only increases the belief in a good project, but it also increases the firm's probabilistic belief in receiving a good signal in the next period. In other words, the firm not only updates its belief but also the odds of the coin nature flips to determine the project's profitability. In our model it holds that the quality of the signal is independent of past realisations, i.e. the investor exactly knows the odds of the coin that nature flips. Due to this simplification the analysis of our framework provides an explicit expression for the critical value of the belief in a good project at which investing is optimal, contrary to Jensen (1982) who could only show existence. Furthermore, it allows us to simulate the investment problem and the effects of the model parameters on the investment timing. We show that the probability of investment within a certain time interval not necessarily increases in the quantity and the quality of signals. Another counterintuitive result we obtain is that, given that the project is good, the expected time before investment need not be monotonous in the parameter governing the Poisson arrivals of signals. In other words, it is possible that investment is expected to take place later when the expected number of signals per time unit is higher.

The chapter is organised as follows. In Section 2 the formal model is described. After that, the optimal investment decision will be derived in Section 3. In Section 4 an error measure for analysing the performance of capital budgeting rules in this model of investment under uncertainty is introduced. The decision rule from Section 3 will be interpreted using some numerical examples in Section 5. In the final section some conclusions are drawn and directions for future research are discussed.

2.   The Model

Consider a firm that faces the choice of investing in a certain project. The project can be either good (denoted by H), leading to high revenues, U^H, or bad (denoted by L), leading to low revenues U^L.[1] Without loss of generality we assume that $U^H > 0$ and $U^L = 0$. The sunk costs involved in investing in the project are given by $I > 0$. Furthermore, it is assumed that there is a constant discount rate, $0 < r < 1$.

When the firm receives the option to invest, it has a prior belief about the investment project being good or bad. The *ex ante* probability of high revenues is given by

$$\mathbb{P}(H) = p_0,$$

for some $p_0 \in (0, 1)$.

Occasionally, the firm receives a signal indicating the project to be good (an h-signal) or a signal indicating the project to be bad (an l-signal). The probabilities with which these signals occur depend on the true state of the project. It is assumed that a correct signal always occurs with probability $\lambda > \frac{1}{2}$, see Table 3.1. In this table, the first row (column) lists the probabilities in case of a good project (good signal) and the second row (column) in case of a bad project (bad signal).

As soon as the firm invests in the project, the state of the market is revealed. In reality this may take some time, but we abstract from that.

---

[1] The revenues represent an infinite discounted cash flow.

	h	l
H	λ	$1-\lambda$
L	$1-\lambda$	λ

Table 3.1. Probability of a signal indicating a good or bad market, given the true state of the project.

The signals' arrivals are modelled via a Poisson process with parameter $\mu > 0$ (see Section 7.1 of Chapter 2). The Poisson assumption is made to make the model analytically tractable when using dynamic programming techniques as described in Section 7.2 of Chapter 2. Hence, denoting the number of signals that have arrived before time t by $n(t)$, $t \geq 0$, this boils down to

$$dn(t) = \begin{cases} 1 & \text{with probability } \mu dt, \\ 0 & \text{with probability } 1 - \mu dt, \end{cases}$$

with

$$n(0) = 0.$$

Denoting the number of h-signals by g, the dynamics of g is then given by

$$dg(t) = u dn(t),$$

with

$$u = \begin{cases} 1 & \text{with probability } \lambda \text{ if } H \text{ and } 1-\lambda \text{ if } L, \\ 0 & \text{with probability } 1-\lambda \text{ if } H \text{ and } \lambda \text{ if } L, \end{cases}$$

and

$$g(0) = 0.$$

It is assumed that the firm knows the values of μ and λ. For notational convenience the time index will be suppressed in the remainder of the chapter. The belief that revenues are high, i.e. that the project is good, given the number of signals n and the number of h-signals, $g \leq n$, is denoted by $p(n,g)$. Now, the conditional expected payoff of the firm if it invests can be written as,

$$\mathbb{E}(U|n,g) = p(n,g)(U^H - I) - (1 - p(n,g))I.$$

The structure of the model is such that with respect to the signals there are two main aspects. The first one is the parameter which governs the arrival of the signals, μ. This parameter is a measure for the quantity of the signals, since $1/\mu$ denotes the average time between two signals. The other component is the probability of the correctness of the signal, λ. This parameter is a measure for the quality of the signals. For the model to make sense, it is assumed that $\lambda > \frac{1}{2}$.[2] In this chapter learning – or belief updating – takes place by using the Bayesian approach. This, together with the condition $\lambda > \frac{1}{2}$, implies that in the long-run the belief in high revenues converges to one or to zero if the market is good or bad, respectively. As will be shown in Section 3, quantity and quality together determine the threshold belief in a good project the firm needs to have in order for investment to be optimal.

3.   The Optimal Investment Decision

The uncertainty about the true state of the project and the irreversibility of investment induce an option value of waiting for more signals. In this section we will show how to find the critical level for $p(n,g)$ at which the firm is indifferent between investing and waiting, while taking into account the option value of waiting. After having determined the critical level we know that it is optimal to invest as soon as $p(n,g)$ exceeds this level.

First, we explicitly calculate $p(n,g)$. To simplify matters considerably, define $k := 2g - n$, the number of good signals in excess of bad signals, and $\zeta := \frac{1-p_0}{p_0}$, the unconditional odds of the project being bad. By using Bayes' rule we obtain that:

$$
\begin{aligned}
p(n,g) &= \frac{\mathbb{P}(n,g|H)\mathbb{P}(H)}{\mathbb{P}(n,g|H)\mathbb{P}(H) + \mathbb{P}(n,g|L)\mathbb{P}(L)} \\
&= \frac{\lambda^g(1-\lambda)^{n-g}p_0}{\lambda^g(1-\lambda)^{n-g}p_0 + (1-\lambda)^g\lambda^{n-g}(1-p_0)} \\
&= \frac{\lambda^g}{\lambda^g + \zeta(1-\lambda)^{2g-n}\lambda^{n-g}} \qquad\qquad (3.1) \\
&= \frac{\lambda^{2g-n}}{\lambda^{2g-n} + \zeta(1-\lambda)^{2g-n}} \\
&= \frac{\lambda^k}{\lambda^k + \zeta(1-\lambda)^k} \equiv p(k), \qquad k \in \mathbb{Z}.
\end{aligned}
$$

---

[2]This assumption is not as strong as it seems, for if $\lambda < \frac{1}{2}$ the firm can perform the same analysis replacing λ with $1 - \lambda$. If $\lambda = \frac{1}{2}$ the signals are not informative at all and the firm would do best by making a now-or-never decision, using its *ex ante* belief $p(0,0) = p_0$.

For further reference, we extend the domain of $p(k)$ in a natural way to the real line. The critical level of k where the firm is indifferent between investing and not investing in the project is denoted by $k^* \in \mathbb{R}$. Note that at any arrival of an h-signal k increases with unity and at any arrival of an l-signal k decreases with unity. Hence, enough h-signals must arrive to reach the critical level. The critical level of the conditional belief in high revenues is denoted by $p^* = p(k^*)$.

Suppose that the state of the process at a particular point in time is given by k. For the moment assume that k is a continuous variable. Then there are three possibilities. First, k might be such that $k \geq k^*$ and hence, $p(k) \geq p^*$. Then it is optimal for the firm to directly invest in the project. In this case the value of the project for the firm, denoted by Π, is given by

$$\Pi(k) = U^H p(k) - I. \tag{3.2}$$

A second possibility is that, even after a new h-signal arriving, it is still not optimal to invest, i.e. $k < k^* - 1$. We assume that pricing with respect to the objective probability measure implies risk-neutrality concerning the information gathering process. Then the value function of the opportunity to invest for the firm, denoted by $V_1(\cdot)$, must satisfy the following Bellman equation[3]:

$$rV_1(k) = \tfrac{1}{dt}\mathbb{E}(dV_1(k)), \qquad k < k^*. \tag{3.3}$$

Departing from this equation the following second order linear difference equation can be constructed:

$$rV_1(k) = \mu\big[p(k)(\lambda V_1(k+1) + (1-\lambda)V_1(k-1)) +$$
$$+ (1-p(k))(\lambda V_1(k-1) + (1-\lambda)V_1(k+1)) - V_1(k)\big]$$
$$\Longleftrightarrow (r+\mu)V_1(k) = \mu\big[(2p(k)\lambda + 1 - \lambda - p(k))V_1(k+1) +$$
$$+ (p(k) + \lambda - 2p(k)\lambda)V_1(k-1)\big], \qquad k < k^* - 1. \tag{3.4}$$

Eq. (3.4) states that the value of the option at state k must equal the discounted expected value an infinitesimal amount of time later. Using eq. (3.1) it holds that

$$2p(k)\lambda + 1 - \lambda - p(k) = \frac{\lambda^{k+1} + \zeta(1-\lambda)^{k+1}}{\lambda^k + \zeta(1-\lambda)^k} \tag{3.5}$$

and

$$p(k) + \lambda - 2p(k)\lambda = \frac{\lambda(1-\lambda)(\lambda^{k-1} + \zeta(1-\lambda)^{k-1})}{\lambda^k + \zeta(1-\lambda)^k}. \tag{3.6}$$

---

[3]See Section 7.2 of Chapter 2.

Substituting eqs. (3.5) and (3.6) in (3.4), and defining $F(k) := (\lambda^k + \zeta(1-\lambda)^k)V_1(k)$, yields

$$(r + \mu)F(k) = \mu F(k+1) + \mu\lambda(1-\lambda)F(k-1). \qquad (3.7)$$

Eq. (3.7) is a second order linear homogeneous difference equation which has as general solution

$$F(k) = A_1\beta_1^k + A_2\beta_2^k,$$

where A_1 and A_2 are constants and β_1 and β_2 are the roots of the homogeneous equation

$$\mathcal{Q}(\beta) \equiv \beta^2 - \frac{r+\mu}{\mu}\beta + \lambda(1-\lambda) = 0. \qquad (3.8)$$

Eq. (3.8) has two real roots,[4] namely

$$\beta_{1,2} = \frac{r+\mu}{2\mu} \pm \tfrac{1}{2}\sqrt{(\tfrac{r}{\mu}+1)^2 - 4\lambda(1-\lambda)}. \qquad (3.9)$$

Note that $\mathcal{Q}(0) = \lambda(1-\lambda) > 0$ and $\mathcal{Q}(1-\lambda) = -\frac{r}{\mu}(1-\lambda) \le 0$. Since the graph of $\mathcal{Q}$ is an upward pointing parabola we must have $\beta_1 \ge 1-\lambda$ and $0 < \beta_2 < 1-\lambda$ (see Figure 3.1). The value function $V_1(\cdot)$ is then

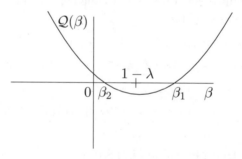

Figure 3.1.   Graph of $\mathcal{Q}$.

given by

$$V_1(k) = \frac{F(k)}{\lambda^k + \zeta(1-\lambda)^k} = \frac{A_1\beta_1^k + A_2\beta_2^k}{\lambda^k + \zeta(1-\lambda)^k}, \qquad (3.10)$$

---

[4]It should be noted that for all λ it holds that $4\lambda(1-\lambda) \le 1$. Since equality holds iff $\lambda = 1/2$, the homogeneous equation indeed has two real roots for any $\lambda \in (1/2, 1]$.

where A_1 and A_2 are constants. Here it is important to note that when the number of l-signals relative to h-signals tends to infinity the value of the firm converges to zero, i.e. $\lim_{k\to-\infty} V_1(k) = 0$. This implies that we only need to consider the larger root β_1, so that $A_2 = 0$.[5]

In the final case, $k^* - 1 \leq k < k^*$. Here, the value of k is such that it is not optimal to invest in the project right away. However, if the following signal is an h-signal, it will be optimal to invest. In this region the value function is denoted by $V_2(\cdot)$. Analogous to eq. (3.3) it follows that

$$rV_2(k) = \mu\big[p(k)(\lambda\Pi(k+1) + (1-\lambda)V_1(k-1)) + (1-p(k))$$
$$(\lambda V_1(k-1) + (1-\lambda)\Pi(k+1)) - V_2(k)\big] \iff$$
$$V_2(k) = \frac{\mu}{r+\mu}\big[(2p(k)\lambda + 1 - \lambda - p(k))\Pi(k+1) +$$
$$+ (p(k) + \lambda - 2p(k)\lambda)V_1(k-1)\big], \quad k^* \leq k < k^*. \tag{3.11}$$

Substituting eqs. (3.2), (3.5), (3.6) and (3.10) into eq. (3.11) yields

$$V_2(k) = \frac{\mu}{r+\mu}\Big(\lambda U^H p(k) - (\lambda p(k) + (1-\lambda)(1-p(k)))I$$
$$+ \lambda(1-\lambda)\frac{A_1\beta_1^{k-1}}{\lambda^k + \zeta(1-\lambda)^k}\Big). \tag{3.12}$$

If an h-signal arrives, the process jumps to the region where $k \geq k^*$ and if an l-signal arrives the process jumps to the region where $k < k^*$. Therefore the value V_2 is completely determined by $V_1(k-1)$ and $\Pi(k+1)$. The value function $V(\cdot)$ then equals

$$V(k) = \begin{cases} V_1(k) & \text{if } k < k^* - 1 \\ V_2(k) & \text{if } k^* - 1 \leq k < k^* \\ \Pi(k) & \text{if } k \geq k^*, \end{cases} \tag{3.13}$$

where $V_1(k)$, $V_2(k)$ and $\Pi(k)$ are given by (3.10), (3.12) and (3.2), respectively.

To determine A_1 and k^* we solve the continuity condition $\lim_{k\to k^*-1} V_1(k)$ $= V_2(k^*-1)$ and the value-matching condition $\lim_{k\to k^*} V_2(k) = \Pi(k^*)$.[6] The

---

[5]This stems from the fact that $0 < \beta_2 < 1 - \lambda$, so in $V_1(k)$ the term β_2^k dominates $(1-\lambda)^k$ if $k \to -\infty$. Hence, if $A_2 \neq 0$, then $V_1(k) \to \infty$ if $k \to -\infty$.
[6]Note that, despite the fact that k is an integer variable, the continuity and the value matching conditions should hold because the critical level k^* can be any real number. Since the realisations of k are discrete, the firm invests as soon as $k = \lceil k^* \rceil$.

latter equation yields

$$A_1 = \frac{1}{\beta_1^{k^*-1}\mu\lambda(1-\lambda)}[U^H\lambda^{k^*}(r+\mu(1-\lambda))$$
$$- rI(\lambda^{k^*} + \zeta(1-\lambda)^{k^*}) - \mu I(\lambda\zeta(1-\lambda)^{k^*} + (1-\lambda)\lambda^{k^*})].$$

Substituting A_1 in the former equation leads to an expression for $p^* \equiv p(k^*)$:

$$p^* = \frac{1}{\Psi(U^H/I - 1) + 1}, \tag{3.14}$$

where

$$\Psi = \frac{\beta_1(r+\mu)(r+\mu(1-\lambda)) - \mu\lambda(1-\lambda)(r+\mu(1+\beta_1-\lambda))}{\beta_1(r+\mu)(r+\mu\lambda) - \mu\lambda(1-\lambda)(r+\mu(\beta_1+\lambda))}. \tag{3.15}$$

The threshold number of h-signals relative to l-signals is then given by

$$k^* = \frac{\log(\frac{p^*}{1-p^*}) + \log(\zeta)}{\log(\frac{\lambda}{1-\lambda})}. \tag{3.16}$$

From eq. (3.16) it is obtained that k^* decreases with p_0. Hence, less additional information is needed when the initial belief in high revenues is already high.

Next, we check whether the optimal belief p^* is a well-defined probability. The following proposition establishes this result, which is proved in Appendix A. It furthermore shows the link between this approach and the traditional net present value rule (NPV). Note that the critical belief under the latter approach is obtained by solving $\mathbb{E}(U|k) = 0$, which yields $p_{NPV} = \frac{I}{U^H}$.

PROPOSITION 3.1 *For $U^H \geq I$ it holds that $p^* \leq 1$. Furthermore, $p^* > p_{NPV}$.*

So, the result that is obtained in the standard real option model, namely that the criterion for investment to be undertaken is less tight under NPV than under the real option approach, carries over to this model. The reason is the existence of a value of waiting for more information to arrive that reduces uncertainty.

Using eq. (3.14), one can obtain comparative static results. These are stated in the following proposition, the proof of which is given in Appendix B.

PROPOSITION 3.2 *The threshold belief in a good project, p^*, increases with I, r and λ and decreases with U^H.*

The fact that p^* increases with r is caused by the so-called net present value effect. If r increases, future income is valued less so that the net present value decreases. Therefore, the firm is willing to wait longer with investment until it has more information about the actual state of the project. An increase in λ leads to an increase in p^*, which can be explained by the fact that λ is a measure for the informativeness of the signal. Therefore, it is more worthwhile to wait for another signal, which implies a higher level of p^*. This does not necessarily imply that one should wait for more signals to arrive, a point which we elaborate upon in Section 5. It is impossible to get a knife-edged result on the comparative statics with respect to μ, although simulations suggest that in most cases p^* increases with μ, which confirms intuition.[7] The partial derivative of p^* with respect to μ is negative if $r \approx \mu\sqrt{2\lambda - 1}$.

4. Error Analysis

An important question the firm faces is how likely it is that it makes a wrong decision, in the sense that it invests while the project is bad. This question can be answered quantitatively by calculating the probability that k^* is reached while the project is bad. In order to do so, define

$$P^{(k^*)}(k) := \mathbb{P}(\exists_{t \geq 0} : k_t \geq k^* | k_0 = k, L) \tag{3.17}$$

Of course, for $k \geq k^*$ it holds that $P^{(k^*)}(k) = 1$. A second order linear difference equation can be obtained governing $P^{(k^*)}(k)$. Notice that starting from k, the process reaches either $k-1$ or $k+1$ with probabilities λ and $1 - \lambda$, respectively, given that the project is bad. Therefore, one obtains

$$P^{(k^*)}(k) = (1 - \lambda)P^{(k^*)}(k + 1) + \lambda P^{(k^*)}(k - 1). \tag{3.18}$$

Using the boundary conditions $P^{(k^*)}(k^*) = 1$ and $\lim_{k \to -\infty} P^{(k^*)}(k) = 0$, one can solve eq. (3.18), yielding

$$P^{(k^*)}(k) = \left(\frac{\lambda}{1 - \lambda}\right)^{k-k^*}. \tag{3.19}$$

Hence, the probability of a wrong decision decreases when the quality of the signals increases. Since $k_0 = 0$, the *ex ante* probability of a wrong decision is given by $P^{(k^*)}(0)$.

---

[7]See also Appendix B.

The error measure $P^{(k^*)}(\cdot)$ gives a worst-case scenario: the probability that a firm engages in an investment that has low profitability. Another error measure would be given by the probability that the firm forgoes an investment that would have generated a high profit stream, i.e. the probability that k^* is not reached within a certain time T given that the project is good. Note however that since $\lambda > \frac{1}{2}$ this probability converges to zero for $T \to \infty$. For any finite time T it is possible to calculate the probability that the firm has not invested before T given that the project is good. In order to calculate this probability, denote for all k the probability density function of the distribution of the first passage time through k by $f_k(\cdot)$, given that $k_0 = 0$. From Feller (1971, Section 14.6) one obtains that

$$f_k(t) = \left(\frac{1-\lambda}{\lambda}\right)^{-\frac{k}{2}} \frac{k}{t} I_k\left(2\mu\sqrt{\lambda(1-\lambda)}t\right)e^{-\mu t}, \qquad (3.20)$$

where $I_k(\cdot)$ denotes the modified Bessel function with parameter k. This is the *unconditional* density of first passage times. Given the first passage time distribution it holds for all $0 < T < \infty$ and $k^* > 0$ that

$$\tilde{P}^{(k^*)}(T) := \mathbb{P}(\neg\exists_{t\in[0,T]} : k_t \geq k^*|k_0 = 0, H)$$
$$= \mathbb{P}(\forall_{t\in[0,T]} : k_t < k^*|k_0 = 0, H)$$
$$= 1 - \int_0^T f_{k^*}(t)dt.$$

Since there is a positive probability mass on the project being bad, the expectation of the time of investment does not exist. However, conditional on the project being good, one can calculate the expected time of investment using the *conditional* density of first passage times, which is obtained in a similar way as eq. (3.20) and given by[8]

$$\tilde{f}_k(t) = \frac{\lambda^k + \zeta(1-\lambda)^k}{1+\zeta} \left(\lambda(1-\lambda)\right)^{-k/2} \frac{k}{t} I_k(2\mu\sqrt{\lambda(1-\lambda)}t)e^{-\mu t}. \qquad (3.21)$$

5. Economic Interpretation

As an example to see how U^H and U^L arise, consider a market where inverse demand is assumed to be given by the following function,

$$P(q) = \begin{cases} Y - q & \text{if } q \leq Y \text{ and } H \\ 0 & \text{otherwise,} \end{cases}$$

---

[8]See also Appendix D of Chapter 5.

where q is the quantity supplied. There is only one supplier so that the firm is a monopolist. The costs of producing q units are given by the cost function

$$C(q) = cq, \qquad c \geq 0.$$

The profit of producing q units is then equal to

$$\pi(q) = P(q)q - C(q).$$

Suppose for a moment that the project is good, i.e. that demand is high. Then the maximal revenue to the firm is given by,

$$R_g = \max_q \left\{ \int_0^\infty e^{-rt} \pi(q) dt \right\}$$

$$= \max_q \{ \pi(q) \tfrac{1}{r} \}.$$

Solving for q using the first order condition yields the optimal output level $q^* = \frac{Y-c}{2}$, leading to the maximal profit stream

$$U^H = \tfrac{1}{r}[P(q^*)q^* - C(q^*)]. \tag{3.22}$$

If the project is bad it is optimal not to produce at all. Hence, the revenue if demand is zero, U^L, equals,

$$U^L = 0. \tag{3.23}$$

In Proposition 3.2 comparative statics results are given. To get some feeling for the magnitude of several effects we consider some numerical examples. Consider a market structure as described above with parameter values as denoted in Table 3.2. So, the discount rate r is set at 10%.

$Y = 8$	$r = 0.1$
$c = 5$	$\mu = 4$
$I = 12$	$\lambda = 0.8$
$p_0 = \frac{1}{2}$	

Table 3.2.   Parameter values

The probability of a correct signal is 0.8 and on average four signals arrive every period.

Based on these parameter values the value function is calculated as function of k and depicted in Figure 3.2.[9] From this figure one can

---

[9]In interpreting Figure 3.2, notice that realisations of k are discrete, although k^* can be any real number (see Footnote 6).

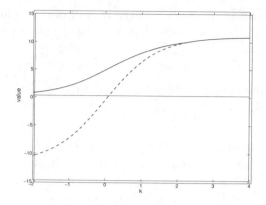

Figure 3.2.   Value function. The dashed line denotes the NPV.

see that the NPV rule prescribes not to invest at the moment the option becomes available ($k = 0$). In fact, in order to invest, the NPV rule demands that the NPV must be positive so that the belief of the firm in high market demand should at least be approximately 0.53 ($k_{NPV} \approx 0.10$). However, our approach specifies that the firm's belief should exceed $p^* \approx 0.96$. This may seem an extremely high threshold, but it implies that the firm invests as soon as $k = 3$, since $k^* \approx 2.23$. The NPV rule prescribes that, in absence of l-signals, only one h-signal is needed, while under our approach the firm invests after three h-signals (net from l-signals). From eq. (3.19) it is obtained that

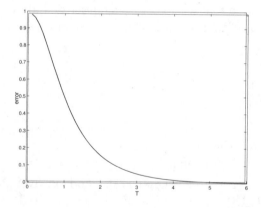

Figure 3.3.   Probability that investment has not taken place before time T given that the project is good.

the probability of investing in a bad project while using the optimal approach equals $P^{(k^*)}(0) = 0.00156$. Application of the NPV rule gives

$P^{(k_{NPV})}(0) = 0.25$. Hence, the probability of making a wrong decision using the optimal approach is negligible, while it is reasonably large when the NPV rule is used. The other error measure, $\tilde{P}^{k^*}(\cdot)$, is depicted in Figure 3.3 for different values of T. One observes that the error of the second type converges rapidly to zero. The probability of not having invested by period 6 given that the project is good is already negligible.

Using the same parameters we can determine how the critical value k^* changes with λ. From Proposition 3.2 we can conclude that the critical level for the believe in a good project increases with the quality of the signal λ, as one can also see in the left-hand panel of Figure 3.4. If λ

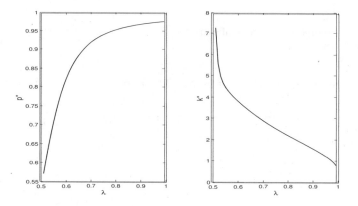

Figure 3.4. Comparative statics of p^* and k^* for λ.

is higher, then the informativeness of a signal is higher. So, it is more attractive for the firm to demand a higher certainty about the goodness of the market. This belief however, is reached after fewer signals as can be seen from the right-hand panel of Figure 3.4.

If one takes $Y = 50$, $c = 10$, $I = 500$, $p_0 = 0.5$, $\lambda = 0.8$, $r = 0.1$ and $\mu = 7$, one obtains $p_{NPV} = 0.125$. Since $p_0 = 1/2$ this implies $k_{NPV} < 0$. Hence, the firm invests immediately at time 0 if it applies the NPV rule. So, if the project is bad, the firm invests in the bad project with probability 1. Applying our decision rule gives $p^* = 0.842$, implying that the firm invests if $k = 2$. The probability of a wrong decision then becomes $P^2(0) = 0.06$. Again, our approach greatly reduces this probability compared to the NPV rule.

Consider an example where the demand and cost parameters are such that $U^H = 50$, $I = 30$, $r = 0.1$ and $p_0 = 0.5$. First, we consider the situation where the project is good. Using the conditional first passage time density in eq. (3.21) one can calculate the expected time until investment takes place as a function of μ and λ, cf. Figures 3.5 and 3.6.

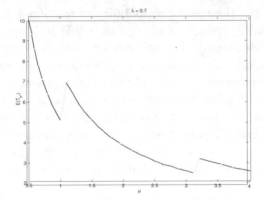

Figure 3.5. Comparative statics of expected time of investment given a good project for μ with $\lambda = 0.7$ fixed.

One can see that both functions are not continuous and the expected

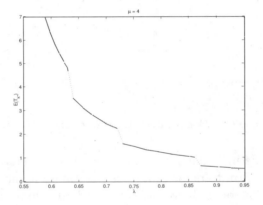

Figure 3.6. Comparative statics of expected time of investment given a good project for λ with $\mu = 4$ fixed.

time of investment is not monotonic with respect to μ. This stems from the fact that the realisations of k are discrete. Hence, for certain combinations of μ and λ, the threshold jumps from $\lceil k^* \rceil$ to $\lceil k^* \rceil + 1$. If p^* increases in μ (as it usually does), k^* is also increasing in μ. If, as a result, $\lceil k^* \rceil$ increases with unity, one additional good signal (in excess of bad signals) is needed before it is optimal to undertake the project. This implies that the expected time before investment jumps upwards. Immediately after a jump, the expected time decreases continuously with μ, as intuition suggests, until the threshold jumps again.

Concerning the comparative statics with respect to λ we already observed that an increase in p^* can lead to a decrease in k^*. This implies that for certain values of λ the threshold $\lceil k^* \rceil$ decreases with unity. As soon as this happens, there is a downward jump in the expected time of investment. So, for λ the discreteness of k works in the same direction as the increase of the quality of the signals.

We also analyse the comparative statics of the probability of investment before time $T = 20$ with respect to the parameters μ and λ using the unconditional first passage time density in eq. (3.20), cf. Figure 3.7. One can see that this probability is not monotonically increasing in μ

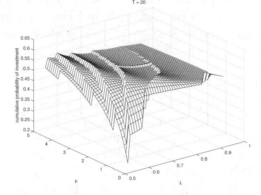

Figure 3.7. Comparative statics of the probability of investment before $T = 20$ for λ and μ.

and λ. Particularly, one can see from Figure 3.8 that, taking $\lambda = 0.7$, the comparative statics for μ are both non-continuous and non-monotonic. The explanation for this behaviour is the same as for the comparative

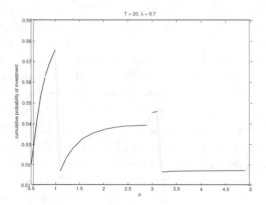

Figure 3.8. Comparative statics of the probability of investment before $T = 20$ with $\lambda = 0.7$ for μ.

statics of the expected time of investment given a good project. Note, however, that the increase in the probability of investment after each jump increases less fast. This is due to the fact that a higher threshold needs to be reached.

6. Conclusions

In this chapter a situation was analysed where a firm has the opportunity to invest in a project. Initially, the profitability of the project is unknown, but as time passes the firm receives signals about the profitability of the investment. There are two types of signals: one type indicating the project to be profitable and the other type indicating it to be unprofitable. The present chapter differs from the standard literature on investment under uncertainty (see Dixit and Pindyck (1996)) in that uncertainty diminishes in the course of time. The firm has a – subjective – a priori belief about the profitability of the project. A posterior belief about the profitability is obtained in a Bayesian way each time a signal arrives. It turns out that it is optimal for the firm to invest as soon as its belief in a profitable project exceeds a certain critical level. An analytical expression for this critical level is provided and it is seen that this level depends crucially on the reliability and the quantity of the signals and the firm's discount rate. Given the initial belief in a good project the critical level can be translated in a number of signals indicating a good project net from signals indicating a bad project. In other words, from the critical belief it can be derived how many "good" signals in excess of "bad" signals are needed before it is optimal for the firm to invest.

An interesting extension of the present model is to look at what happens when the firm is not a monopolist, but if there are rivalling firms to invest in the same project. This requires using game theoretic concepts in the present setting. In the standard real options framework such an analysis has been carried out by e.g. Huisman (2001), Lambrecht and Perraudin (2003) and Boyer et al. (2001). For the framework presented in this chapter, the necessary strategy and equilibrium concepts are presented in Chapter 4. In Chapter 5 a duopoly setting is analysed.

Another topic for further research is to include costs for receiving the signals. In this way one obtains a model for optimal sampling, closely related to statistical decision theory. For the standard real options model this has been done by Moscarini and Smith (2001). An interpretation of such a model could be that a firm can decide once about the intensity and quality of R&D, leading to a combination of μ and λ. If one assumes a cost function for μ and λ one can solve a two stage decision problem where the first stage consists of determining R&D intensity and quantity, while the second stage consists of the timing of investment. In fact, this chapter solves the second stage. With simulations one could solve the first stage, using our analysis as an input. Since the value stream depends on the (rather complicated) first passage density of the threshold, analytical results can probably not be found. One could even try to extend the model to a situation where the firm can continuously adjust its R&D intensity and quality, adding again to the complexity of the problem.

Finally, one could extend the idea of diminishing uncertainty. For instance, one could consider a market where two firms are competing in quantities or prices, with imperfect information about each each other's cost functions. Gradually, firms receive signals on each other's behaviour from which they infer the opponent's cost function, which then influences their strategies.

Appendix
A. Proof of Proposition 3.1

Denote the denominator of Ψ by $d(\Psi)$. Analogously, we denote the numerator of Ψ by $n(\Psi)$. Using $\beta_1 \geq 1 - \lambda$, we obtain that

$$
\begin{aligned}
n(\Psi) &= \beta_1(r + \mu)(r + \mu\lambda) - \mu\lambda(1 - \lambda)(r + \mu(\beta_1 + \lambda)) \\
&\quad - \mu(2\lambda - 1)[\beta_1(r + \mu) - \mu\lambda(1 - \lambda)] \\
&\leq \beta_1(r + \mu)(r + \mu\lambda) - \mu\lambda(1 - \lambda)(r + \mu(\beta_1 + \lambda)) \quad\quad (3.24) \\
&\quad - \mu(2\lambda - 1)[r(1 - \lambda) + \mu(1 - \lambda)^2] \\
&< d(\Psi).
\end{aligned}
$$

Hence, $\Psi < 1$.

If $r = 0$, it holds that $\beta_1 = \lambda$. Therefore,

$$
n(0) = \lambda\mu^2(1 - \lambda) - \mu\lambda(1 - \lambda)\mu = 0.
$$

Furthermore, using that $\beta_1 \geq 1 - \lambda$ and $\frac{\partial \beta_1}{\partial r} > 0$, it can be obtained that

$$
\begin{aligned}
\frac{dn(\Psi)}{dr} &= 2\beta_1 r - \mu\lambda(1 - \lambda) + \beta_1\mu(2 - \lambda) \\
&\quad + \frac{\partial \beta_1}{\partial r}\left(r(\mu(2 - \lambda) + r) + \mu^2(1 - \lambda)^2\right) \\
&\geq 2r(1 - \lambda) + 2\mu(1 - \lambda)^2 + \frac{\partial \beta_1}{\partial r}\left(r(\mu(2 - \lambda) + r) + \mu^2(1 - \lambda)^2\right) \\
&> 0.
\end{aligned}
$$

So, $\Psi > 0$ and p^* is a well-defined probability. Furthermore, since $U^H > I$ and $\Psi < 1$, it holds that

$$p^* = \frac{1}{\Psi(\frac{U^H}{I} - 1) + 1}$$

$$> \frac{I}{U^H} = p_{NPV}.$$

$\square$

B.   Proof of Proposition 3.2

Simple calculus gives the result for U^H and I. To prove the proposition for r, μ, and λ, let us first derive the comparative statics of β_1 for these parameters. First, take r. The total differential of Q with respect to r is given by

$$\frac{\partial Q}{\partial \beta_1}\frac{\partial \beta_1}{\partial r} + \frac{\partial Q}{\partial r} = 0.$$

From Figure 3.1 one can see that $\frac{\partial Q}{\partial \beta_1} > 0$. Furthermore, $\frac{\partial Q}{\partial r} = -\frac{\beta_1}{\mu} < 0$. Hence, it must hold that $\frac{\partial \beta_1}{\partial r} > 0$. In a similar way one obtains $\frac{\partial \beta_1}{\partial \mu} < 0$ and $\frac{\partial \beta_1}{\partial \lambda} > 0$.

The numerator and denominator of Ψ can be written in the following form:

$$n(\Psi) = \eta(r, \mu, \lambda) - 2\mu(1 - \lambda)\zeta(r, \mu, \lambda),$$
$$d(\Psi) = \eta(r, \mu, \lambda) - 2\mu(1 - \lambda)\nu(r, \mu, \lambda),$$

where

$$\eta(r, \mu, \lambda) = \beta_1(r + \mu)(r + \mu\lambda) - \mu\lambda(1 - \lambda)(r + \mu(\beta_1 + \lambda)),$$
$$\zeta(r, \mu, \lambda) = \beta_1(r + \mu) - \mu\lambda(1 - \lambda),$$
$$\nu(r, \mu, \lambda) = r(1 - \lambda) + \mu(1 - \lambda)^2.$$

Since $\Psi > 0$, this implies that to determine the sign of the derivative of Ψ with respect to one of the parameters, one only needs to compare the respective derivatives of $\zeta(\cdot)$ and $\nu(\cdot)$. Note that

$$\frac{\partial \zeta(\cdot)}{\partial r} = \beta_1 + \frac{\partial \beta_1}{\partial r}r > \beta_1$$

$$\geq 1 - \lambda = \frac{\partial \nu(\cdot)}{\partial r}.$$

Hence, $\frac{\partial \Psi}{\partial r} < 0$ and $\frac{\partial p^*}{\partial r} > 0$.

For λ a similar exercise can be done, yielding

$$\frac{\partial \zeta(\cdot)}{\partial \lambda} = \mu(2\lambda - 1) + (r + \mu)\frac{\partial \beta_1}{\partial \lambda} > 0$$

$$> -\left(r + 2\mu(1 - \lambda)\right) = \frac{\partial \nu(\cdot)}{\partial \lambda}.$$

Hence, $\frac{\partial p^*}{\partial \lambda} > 0$.   □

To prove a comparative statics result on μ, one needs to calculate $\frac{\partial \beta_1}{\partial \mu}$ explicitly. This yields

$$\frac{\partial \beta_1}{\partial \mu} = -r \frac{\beta_1}{\mu^2 \sqrt{(\frac{r}{\mu} + 1)^2 - 4\lambda(1 - \lambda)}}.$$

Furthermore, using this result, one can show that

$$\frac{\partial \zeta(\cdot)}{\partial \mu} = \frac{\partial \beta_1}{\partial \mu}(r + \mu) + \beta_1 - \lambda(1 - \lambda)$$

$$= \beta_1 \frac{\mu^2 \sqrt{(\frac{r}{\mu} + 1)^2 - 4\lambda(1 - \lambda)} - r(r + \mu)}{\mu^2 \sqrt{(\frac{r}{\mu} + 1)^2 - 4\lambda(1 - \lambda)}} - \lambda(1 - \lambda),$$

$$\frac{\partial \nu(\cdot)}{\partial \mu} = (1 - \lambda)^2.$$

Hence, substituting for β_1 using eq. (3.9), one obtains that

$$\frac{\partial \zeta(\cdot)}{\partial \mu} \geq \frac{\partial \nu(\cdot)}{\partial \mu}$$

$$\Leftrightarrow \left(\frac{r + \mu}{2\mu} + \tfrac{1}{2}\sqrt{(\frac{r}{\mu} + 1)^2 - 4\lambda(1 - \lambda)}\right)$$

$$\frac{\mu^2 \sqrt{(\frac{r}{\mu} + 1)^2 - 4\lambda(1 - \lambda)} - r(r + \mu)}{\mu^2 \sqrt{(\frac{r}{\mu} + 1)^2 - 4\lambda(1 - \lambda)}} \geq 1 - \lambda$$

$$\Leftrightarrow \left(\mu^2(r + \mu) - \mu r(r + \mu)\right)\sqrt{(\frac{r}{\mu} + 1)^2 - 4\lambda(1 - \lambda)}$$

$$- r(r + \mu)^2 + \mu^3\left((\frac{r}{\mu} + 1)^2 - 4\lambda(1 - \lambda)\right)$$

$$\geq 2\mu^3(1 - \lambda)\sqrt{(\frac{r}{\mu} + 1)^2 - 4\lambda(1 - \lambda)}$$

$$\Leftrightarrow \sqrt{(\frac{r}{\mu} + 1)^2 - 4\lambda(1 - \lambda)}$$

$$\geq \frac{r(r + \mu)^2 - \mu^3\left((\frac{r}{\mu} + 1)^2 - 4\lambda(1 - \lambda)\right)}{\mu(\mu^2 - r^2) - 2\mu^3(1 - \lambda)}.$$

Since the last inequality does not always hold, a knife-edged result for μ cannot be obtained. A computational study, however, shows that the inequality is virtually never violated.

Chapter 4

SYMMETRIC EQUILIBRIA IN GAME THEORETIC REAL OPTION MODELS

1.   Introduction

The timing of an investment project is an important problem in capital budgeting. Many decision criteria have been proposed in the literature, the net present value (NPV) rule being the most famous one. In the past twenty years the real options literature emerged (cf. Dixit and Pindyck (1996)) in which uncertainty about the profitability of an investment project is explicitly taken into account. In the standard real option model the value of the investment project is assumed to follow a geometric Brownian motion. By solving the resulting optimal stopping problem one can show that it is optimal for the firm to wait longer with investing than when the firm uses the NPV approach.

A natural extension of the one firm real option model is to consider a situation where several firms have the option to invest in the same project. Important fields of application of the game theoretic real options approach are R&D competition, technology adoption and new market models. Restricting ourselves to a duopoly framework, the aim of this chapter is to propose a method that solves the coordination problems which arise if there is a first mover advantage that creates a preemptive threat and, hence, erodes the option value. In the resulting preemption equilibrium, situations can occur where it is optimal for one firm to invest, but not for both. The coordination problem then is to determine which firm will invest. This problem is particularly of interest if both firms are *ex ante* identical. In the literature, several contributions (see Grenadier (2000) for an overview) solve this coordination problem by making explicit assumptions which are often unsatisfactory. In this chapter, we propose a method, based on Fudenberg and Tirole (1985), to solve the coordination problem endogenously.

The basic idea of the method is that one splits the game into a timing game where the preemption moment is determined and a game that is played either as soon as the preemption moment has been reached, or when the starting point is such that it is immediately optimal for one firm to invest but not for both. The outcome of the latter game determines which firm is the first investor. The first game is a game in continuous time where strategies are given by a cumulative distribution function. The second game is analogous to a repeated game in which firms play a fixed (mixed) strategy (invest or wait) until at least one firm invests.

As an illustration a simplified version of the model of Smets (1991) that is presented in Dixit and Pindyck (1996, Section 9.3), is analysed. In the preemption equilibrium situations occur where it is optimal for one firm to invest, but at the same time investment is not beneficial if both firms decide to do so. Nevertheless, contrary to e.g. Smets (1991) and Dixit and Pindyck (1996), we find that there are scenarios in which both firms invest at the same time, which leads to a low payoff for both of them. We obtain that such a coordination failure can occur with positive probability at points in time where the payoff of the first investor, the leader, is strictly larger than the payoff of the other firm, the follower. From our analysis it can thus be concluded that Smets' statement that "if both players move simultaneously, each of them becomes leader with probability one half and follower with probability one half" (see Smets (1991, p. 12) and Dixit and Pindyck (1996, p. 313)) need not be true.

The point we make here extends to other contributions that include the real option framework in duopoly models. These papers, such as Grenadier (1996), Dutta et al. (1995), and Weeds (2002), make unsatisfactory assumptions with the aim to be able to ignore the possibility of simultaneous investment at points of time that this is not optimal. Grenadier (1996, pp. 1656-1657) assumes that "if each tries to build first, one will randomly (i.e., through the toss of a coin) win the race", while Dutta et al. (1995, p.568) assume that "If both [firms] i and j attempt to enter at any period t, then only one of them succeeds in doing so".

In a recent paper, Weeds (2002) uses Markov strategies resulting in two different investment patterns, where in one of them the firms invest sequentially. In these asymmetric preemption equilibria one of the firms is the first mover with probability one. This implies that the probability of a coordination failure is always zero. In that paper, this result holds because of the assumption that the value of the starting point of the geometric Brownian motion is lower than the value corresponding to the preemption point. For more general stochastic processes and arbitrary starting points this claim needs not be true. In our framework the two different outcomes that Weeds (2002) reports can be obtained by one pair of symmetric strategies, thereby solving the coordination problem endogenously. Furthermore, we show our result for more general stochastic processes.

In this chapter we extend the strategy spaces and equilibrium concepts as introduced in Fudenberg and Tirole (1985) to a stochastic framework. In a recent paper, Boyer et al. (2001) make a similar attempt. Their adaptation however is less suitable to model war of attrition situations as could arise in stochastic analogues of e.g. Hendricks et al. (1988) or models in which both preemption and war of attrition equilibria can arise (see Chapter 5).

Furthermore, we provide some evidence that supports the simultaneous modelling of uncertainty and strategic interaction. Since game theoretic real option models lead to more conceptual and analytical complexities than both one-firm real option models and deterministic investment timing games, it is necessary to provide some evidence of its usefulness. We do so by making several comparisons using the basic game theoretic real option model by Smets (1991). Firstly, we analyse the different equilibrium scenarios that arise from deterministic models and the model with uncertainty. By using simulations we show that in a substantial number of cases the stochastic model predicts a different equilibrium *type* than its deterministic counterpart. Secondly, we analyse the option value under competition. Theoretically it is clear that competition erodes the option value. Huisman (2001) shows that the option value can even become negative in a preemption equilibrium. However, for the model to be of interest it should be the case that the option value is significantly different from zero. Furthermore, the option value should be significantly different from the option value in the monopoly case. We show that in preemption equilibria this is indeed the case. Finally, we analyse welfare effects in game theoretic real option models. To do so, we first introduce an appropriate welfare concept. Then, again by using simulations, we show that the stochastic model leads to significantly different welfare predictions as opposed to the deterministic model. In fact, we show that welfare is significantly higher in the deterministic model. Again, this is some evidence that game theoretic real option models are worth studying.

The contents of the chapter is as follows. In Section 2 the equilibrium concept is presented and a symmetric equilibrium is derived, which is applied to the Dixit and Pindyck (1996, Section 9.3) model in Section 3.

In Section 4 we perform a simulation study to show that game theoretic real option models lead to substantially different results than simpler models. Section 5 concludes.

2.   The General Model

The setting of the game is as follows. Two identical firms[1] $i = 1, 2$ both have access to an identical investment project. In the market there is some idiosyncratic risk or uncertainty about for example the profitability of the investment project. This creates an option value for the firms to postpone investment. On the other hand, strategic considerations push firms not to wait too long.

This section introduces the equilibrium notions and accompanying strategy spaces for timing games under uncertainty. We follow the approach that was introduced in Fudenberg and Tirole (1985) for the deterministic counterpart.

In most contributions to the literature, uncertainty is modelled by means of a geometric Brownian motion. We use a more general approach which has a geometric Brownian motion as a special case. Let $(\Omega, \mathcal{F}, (\mathcal{F}_t)_{0 \leq t \leq \infty}, P)$ be a filtered probability space satisfying the usual hypotheses.[2] With respect to the filtration $(\mathcal{F}_t)_{0 \leq t \leq \infty}$ on $(\Omega, \mathcal{F}, P)$, let $(J_t)_{0 \leq t < \infty}$ be an adapted cadlag process and let $(Z^1, \ldots, Z^d)$ be a vector of semimartingales with for all $j = 1, \ldots, d$, $Z_0^j = 0$ a.s. Furthermore, let for all $j = 1, \ldots, d$, $F_j : \mathbb{D} \to \mathbb{D}$ be mappings that are functional Lipschitz. Then we know from Theorem 2.16 that there is a unique semimartingale $(Y_t)_{0 \leq t < \infty}$, which, for all $\omega \in \Omega$, is the solution to the stochastic differential equation[3]

$$Y_t(\omega) = J_t(\omega) + \sum_{j=1}^{d} \int_0^t F_j(Y(\omega))_{s-} dZ_s^j(\omega). \qquad (4.1)$$

In the remainder, Y will be the stochastic process that governs the uncertainty about the profitability of the investment project. Examples of stochastic processes that can be used are the geometric Brownian motion or the more general Lévy process.

Given the stochastic process $(Y_t)_{t \geq 0}$ we can define the payoff functions for the firms. If there is a firm that invests first while the other firm does not, the firm that moves first is called the leader. When it invests at time

---

[1] Even with non-identical firms, the coordination problem that is analysed in this chapter can arise as is shown in Pawlina and Kort (2001).
[2] For technical details, see Section 7 of Chapter 2.
[3] In the remainder, let for $t \in [0, \infty)$, $t-$ be defined by $t- = \lim_{\Delta t \uparrow 0} (t + \Delta t)$.

t its discounted profit stream is given by $L(Y_t)$. The other firm is called the follower. When the leader invests at time t the optimal investment strategy of the follower leads to a discounted profit stream $F(Y_t)$. If both firms invest simultaneously at time t, the discounted profit stream for both firms is given by $M(Y_t)$. It is assumed that $L(\cdot)$, $F(\cdot)$ and $M(\cdot)$ are continuous and differentiable functions.

2.1   The Equilibrium Concept

As in Fudenberg and Tirole (1985), the aim is to find an equilibrium that is the continuous time analogue of a subgame perfect equilibrium.[4] To define the strategy spaces and equilibrium concept we extend and slightly adapt the concepts introduced in Fudenberg and Tirole (1985) in a path-wise way, i.e. we consider the paths $(Y_t)_{t \geq 0}$ that arise for each $\omega \in \Omega$.[5] First we define a simple strategy for the subgame starting at $t_0 \geq 0$.

DEFINITION 4.1 *A simple strategy for player* $i \in \{1,2\}$ *in the sub-game starting at* $t_0 \in [0,\infty)$ *is given by a tuple of real-valued functions* $(G_i^{t_0}, \alpha_i^{t_0}) : [t_0, \infty) \times \Omega \to [0,1] \times [0,1]$*, such that for all* $\omega \in \Omega$

1 $G_i^{t_0}(\cdot, \omega)$ is non-decreasing and right-continuous with left limits;

2 $\alpha_i^{t_0}(\cdot, \omega)$ is right-continuous with left limits;

3 if $\alpha_i^{t_0}(t, \omega) = 0$ and $t = \inf\{u \geq t_0 | \alpha_i^{t_0}(u, \omega) > 0\}$, then the right-derivative of $\alpha_i^{t_0}(t, \omega)$ exists and is positive.

Denote for given $\omega \in \Omega$ the set of simple strategies of player i in the subgame starting at t_0 by $S_i^s(t_0, \omega)$. Furthermore, define the strategy space by $S^s(t_0, \omega) = \prod_{i=1,2} S_i^s(t_0, \omega)$ and denote the strategy at $t \in [t_0, \infty)$ by $s^{t_0}(t, \omega) = \left(G_i^{t_0}(t, \omega), \alpha_i^{t_0}(t, \omega) \right)_{i=1,2}$.

Given $t_0 \geq 0$ and $\omega \in \Omega$, for $i = 1, 2$, $G_i^{t_0}(t, \omega)$ is the probability that firm i has invested before or at time $t \geq t_0$. The function $\alpha_i^{t_0}(\cdot, \omega)$ describes a sequence of atoms which describes the intensity of a firm to invest at time t, and is therefore called the *intensity function*. The intensity function gives firms the opportunity to coordinate in cases where investment by at least one firm is optimal. Let $t \geq t_0$ be the first point in time for some $\omega \in \Omega$ and $t_0 \geq 0$, at which investment is profitable for

---

[4]For a description of subgame perfect equilibrium in discrete time, see Section 4.1 in Chapter 2.

[5]The equilibrium concept of Fudenberg and Tirole (1985) is also linked to the concept used by Simon (1987a) and Simon (1987b).

exactly one of the two firms. $G_i^{t_0}(t,\omega) - G_i^{t_0}(t-,\omega) = 1$ for $i = 1, 2$ leads to investment by both firms a.s. which is suboptimal. Hence, if one only uses the cumulative distribution function (as in Dutta and Rustichini (1995) for example) symmetric strategies will lead to a suboptimal outcome a.s. In discrete time this problem does not exist because one can model a procedure in which a game is repeated just until one firm invests. In continuous time this cannot be done, basically because it is not known what is meant by "last period" and "next period". See Simon and Stinchcombe (1989) for an extensive discussion.

The intensity function replicates discrete time results that are lost by modelling in continuous time (see Fudenberg and Tirole (1985, p. 390)). To see this, we leave the continuous time setting for a moment, fixing the value of the stochastic process for some $t \geq t_0$ and consider the following game in discrete time, as depicted in Figure 4.1. Suppose that

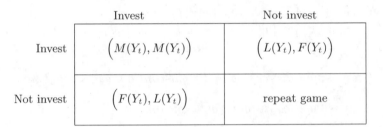

	Invest	Not invest
Invest	$\left(M(Y_t), M(Y_t)\right)$	$\left(L(Y_t), F(Y_t)\right)$
Not invest	$\left(F(Y_t), L(Y_t)\right)$	repeat game

Figure 4.1. Payoffs and actions in the bimatrix game. Firm 1 is the row player and firm 2 the column player.

in each round firm $i \in \{1, 2\}$ invests with probability α_i and does not invest with probability $1 - \alpha_i$ until at least one of the firms has invested, given that the realisation of the stochastic process remains constant. Let Δt be the size of a period and let T_Δ be such that for some constant $T \in \mathbb{N}, T_\Delta/\Delta t = T$. Then if we take $\Delta t = 1$ we get for instance that the probability that both firms invest simultaneously before time T, denoted by $\mathbb{P}(1, 2|T)$, is given by

$$\mathbb{P}(1, 2|T)$$
$$= \alpha_1\alpha_2 + (1 - \alpha_1)(1 - \alpha_2)\alpha_1\alpha_2 + \cdots + (1 - \alpha_1)^{T-1}(1 - \alpha_2)^{T-1}\alpha_1\alpha_2.$$

Letting $\Delta t \downarrow 0$ we get a result that is independent of T and that represents the probability that firms invest simultaneously at any time $\tau \geq t_0$

in our continuous time model,

$$
\begin{aligned}
\mathbb{P}(1,2|\tau) &= \lim_{\Delta t \downarrow 0} \sum_{t=0}^{T_\Delta/\Delta t - 1} (1-\alpha_1)^t (1-\alpha_2)^t \alpha_1 \alpha_2 \\
&= \alpha_1 \alpha_2 \sum_{t=0}^{\infty} \left((1-\alpha_1)(1-\alpha_2) \right)^t \\
&= \frac{\alpha_1 \alpha_2}{\alpha_1 + \alpha_2 - \alpha_1 \alpha_2} < 1.
\end{aligned}
\tag{4.2}
$$

Returning to the continuous time model, define for all $\omega \in \Omega$ the time of the first "sequence of atoms" in player i's strategy in the subgame starting at $t_0 \geq 0$ by

$$
\tau_i(t_0; \omega) = \begin{cases} \infty & \text{if } \alpha_i(t, \omega) = 0, \forall t \geq t_0, \\ \inf\{t \geq t_0 | \alpha_i(t, \omega) > 0\} & \text{otherwise}, \end{cases}
$$

and $\tau(t_0, \omega) = \min\{\tau_1(t_0, \omega), \tau_2(t_0, \omega)\}$. In the continuous time setting it is assumed that at time $\tau(t_0, \omega)$, the game depicted in Figure 4.1 is played, where firm i invests with probability $\alpha_i^{t_0}(\tau, \omega) > 0$. The value of the intensity function therefore measures the intensity of the firm's willingness to invest. Furthermore, it is assumed that playing the game consumes no time[6] and if firm 1 chooses row 2 and firm 2 chooses column 2 the game is repeated instantaneously. As soon as at least one firm has invested this game is over and time continues. So, at time τ at least one firm invests. It can be the case that only one firm invests, but it is also possible that both firms invest simultaneously. Note that from eq. (4.2) it follows that with symmetric strategies $\alpha_1^{t_0}(\tau, \omega) = \alpha_2^{t_0}(\tau, \omega) = \alpha$ we get

$$
\mathbb{P}(1,2|\tau) = \frac{\alpha^2}{2\alpha - \alpha^2} = \frac{\alpha}{2-\alpha} \geq 0.
\tag{4.3}
$$

Hence, if $\alpha > 0$ the probability that both firms invest simultaneously is strictly positive. This is not in accordance with many contributions in the literature where (unsatisfactory) assumptions are made to sustain the claim that only one firm invests (e.g. Weeds (2002) and Grenadier (1996)).

To summarise, simple strategies allow for several investment strategies of firm $i \in \{1, 2\}$. Firstly, the cumulative distribution function $G_i^{t_0}(\cdot, \omega)$ allows for continuous investment strategies (used in war of attrition models). Secondly, it allows for isolated atoms that are used for

---

[6]This implies that $Y_t(\omega)$ remains constant and that there is no discounting.

example in Chapter 5. Finally, via the intensity function $\alpha^{t_0}(\cdot, \omega)$, there is the possibility of a sequence of atoms that results in investment by at least one firm a.s. The intensity function plays an important role in preemption games as will be clear from the next subsection.

Our definition of simple strategies differs from Fudenberg and Tirole (1985). Firstly, the cumulative distribution function in Fudenberg and Tirole (1985) is conditional on the fact that no firm has invested yet. This implies that in their approach simple strategies do not describe the behaviour of each firm for the entire range of time. As soon as firm i has invested, the simple strategy cannot describe firm j's strategy anymore. Furthermore, it implies that the strategy of a firm depends on the strategy of the other firm which is conceptually undesirable, because each firm must in principle be able to choose its strategy without taking into account the strategy of its competitor. Secondly, Fudenberg and Tirole (1985) take the following restriction on the intensity function in their definition of simple strategies: $\alpha_i^{t_0}(t, \omega) > 0 \Rightarrow G_i^{t_0}(t, \omega) = 1$, which results from $G_i^{t_0}(\cdot, \omega)$ being the cumulative distribution function of a conditional distribution. However, it is not guaranteed that firm i invests with probability one if its intensity function is strictly positive. This requirement also implicates that the investment strategy of firm i cannot be described by simple strategies if firm j has invested. The analysis in Fudenberg and Tirole (1985) uses the $(G_i^{t_0}(\cdot, \omega), \alpha_i^{t_0}(\cdot, \omega))_{i=1,2}$ pair to describe a preemption situation in a deterministic analogue to our stochastic model. They conclude that at the preemption moment (to be made precise later) one firm invests and the other waits. However, since $G_i^{t_0}(\cdot, \omega)$ is based on the condition that no firm has invested yet, the $(G_i^{t_0}(\cdot, \omega), \alpha_i^{t_0}(\cdot, \omega))_{i=1,2}$ pair cannot describe the strategy of the firm that has not invested at the preemption moment. In our model, the cumulative distribution $G_i^{t_0}(\cdot, \omega)$ is unconditional and hence can describe a firm's strategy for the entire time span.[7]

Let $\omega \in \Omega$. The expected discounted value for firm $i = 1, 2$ of the subgame starting at $t_0 \geq 0$, given strategy $s^{t_0}(\omega) \in S^s(t_0, \omega)$, is denoted

---

[7]The strategies might seem far removed from everyday business practise. Of course, we do not assume that firms actually employ a probability distribution and an intensity function to determine when to invest. The construction should be merely thought of as clear and concise way to come to logically consistent and useful predictions on a firm's investment behaviour, taking into account uncertainty and strategic interaction.

by $V_i(t_0, s^{t_0}(\omega))$ and equals,[8]

$$V_i(t_0, s^{t_0}(\omega)) =$$
$$\Bigg[\int_{t_0}^{\tau(t_0,\omega)-} L(Y_t(\omega))(1 - G_j^{t_0}(t,\omega))dG_i^{t_0}(t,\omega)$$
$$+ \int_{t_0}^{\tau(t_0,\omega)-} F(Y_t(\omega))(1 - G_i^{t_0}(t,\omega))dG_j^{t_0}(t,\omega)$$
$$+ \sum_{t<\tau(t_0,\omega)} \lambda_i(t,\omega)\lambda_j(t,\omega)M(Y_t(\omega)) \Bigg]$$
$$+ \big(1 - G_i^{t_0}(\tau(t_0,\omega)-)\big)\big(1 - G_j^{t_0}(\tau(t_0,\omega)-)\big)W_i(\tau(t_0,\omega), s^{t_0}(\omega)),$$

where $\lambda_i(t,\omega) = G_i^{t_0}(t,\omega) - G_i^{t_0}(t-,\omega)$ and

$$W_i(\tau, s^{t_0}(\omega)) = \left(\frac{\lambda_j(\tau,\omega)}{1 - G_j^{t_0}(\tau-,\omega)} \right)$$
$$\times \big((1 - \alpha_i^{t_0}(\tau,\omega))F(Y_\tau(\omega)) + \alpha_i^{t_0}(\tau,\omega)M(Y_\tau(\omega))\big)$$
$$+ \left(\frac{1 - G_j^{t_0}(\tau,\omega)}{1 - G_j^{t_0}(\tau-,\omega)} \right) L(Y_\tau(\omega)),$$

if $\tau_j(t_0,\omega) > \tau_i(t_0,\omega)$;

$$W_i(\tau, s^{t_0}(\omega)) = \left(\frac{\lambda_i(\tau,\omega)}{1 - G_i^{t_0}(\tau-,\omega)} \right)$$
$$\times \big((1 - \alpha_j^{t_0}(\tau,\omega))L(Y_\tau(\omega)) + \alpha_j^{t_0}(\tau,\omega)M(Y_\tau(\omega))\big)$$
$$+ \left(\frac{1 - G_i^{t_0}(\tau,\omega)}{1 - G_i^{t_0}(\tau-,\omega)} \right) F(Y_\tau(\omega)),$$

if $\tau_i(t_0,\omega) > \tau_j(t_0,\omega)$; and

$$W_i(\tau, s^{t_0}(\omega)) =$$

---

[8]See Fudenberg and Tirole (1985).

$$
\begin{cases}
M(Y_\tau(\omega)) \quad \text{if } \alpha_i^{t_0}(\tau,\omega) = \alpha_j^{t_0}(\tau,\omega) = 1, \\[4pt]
\left[\alpha_i^{t_0}(\tau,\omega)(1 - \alpha_j^{t_0}(\tau,\omega))L(Y_\tau(\omega)) + \alpha_j^{t_0}(\tau,\omega)(1 - \alpha_i^{t_0}(\tau,\omega))F(Y_\tau(\omega)) \right. \\[4pt]
\left. + \alpha_i^{t_0}(\tau,\omega)\alpha_j^{t_0}(\tau,\omega)M(Y_\tau(\omega))\right] \Big/ \left(\alpha_i^{t_0}(\tau,\omega)\right. \\[4pt]
\left. + \alpha_j^{t_0}(\tau,\omega) - \alpha_i^{t_0}(\tau,\omega)\alpha_j^{t_0}(\tau,\omega)\right) \quad \text{if } 2 > \alpha_i^{t_0}(\tau,\omega) + \alpha_j^{t_0}(\tau,\omega) > 0, \\[4pt]
\dfrac{(\alpha_i^{t_0})'(\tau,\omega)L(Y_\tau(\omega)) + (\alpha_j^{t_0})'(\tau,\omega)F(Y_\tau(\omega))}{(\alpha_i^{t_0})'(\tau,\omega) + (\alpha_j^{t_0})'(\tau,\omega)} \quad \text{if } \alpha_i^{t_0}(\tau,\omega) = \alpha_j^{t_0}(\tau,\omega) = 0,
\end{cases}
\tag{4.4}
$$

if $\tau_i(t_0,\omega) = \tau_j(t_0,\omega)$.

In the last case, thus where $\tau_i(t_0,\omega) = \tau_j(t_0,\omega)$, the function $W_i(\cdot)$ has been obtained by using limiting arguments similar to the one used in eq. (4.2). For $\alpha_i(\cdot) = \alpha_j(\cdot) = 0$, $W_i(\cdot)$ has been derived by applying L'Hopital's rule. Here one uses the assumptions on existence and positivity of the right-derivative of the intensity function $\alpha(\cdot)$.

The definition of simple strategies does not *a priori* exclude the possibility that both firms choose an intensity function α that turns out to be inconsistent with the cumulative distribution function G. In equilibrium it should naturally be the case that inconsistencies of this kind do not occur. Therefore, we introduce the notion of α-*consistency*.

DEFINITION 4.2 *A tuple of simple strategies* $((G_i^{t_0}, \alpha_i^{t_0}))_{i=1,2}$ *for the subgame starting at* $t_0 \geq 0$ *is* α-consistent *if for* $i = 1, 2$ *it holds that for all* $\omega \in \Omega$ *and* $t \geq t_0$,

$$
\alpha_i^{t_0}(t,\omega) - \alpha_i^{t_0}(t-,\omega) \neq 0 \Rightarrow G_i^{t_0}(t,\omega) - G_i^{t_0}(t-,\omega) =
$$

$$
= \left(1 - G_i^{t_0}(t-,\omega)\right)\frac{\alpha_i^{t_0}(t,\omega)}{\alpha_i^{t_0}(t,\omega) + \alpha_j^{t_0}(t,\omega) - \alpha_i^{t_0}(t,\omega)\alpha_j^{t_0}(t,\omega)}.
$$

Definition 4.2 requires that at time $\tau(t_0,\omega)$ the jump in the cumulative distribution function for both firms should be equal to the probability that the firm invests by playing the game as depicted in Figure 4.1. Note that if $\alpha_i^{t_0}(t,\omega) - \alpha_i^{t_0}(t-,\omega) \neq 0$ and $\alpha_i^{t_0}(t,\omega) = 1$, then α-consistency implies that $G_i^{t_0}(t,\omega) = 1$.

An α-equilibrium for the subgame starting at t_0 is then defined as follows.

DEFINITION 4.3 *A tuple of simple strategies* $s^* = \left(s^*(\omega)\right)_{\omega \in \Omega}$, $s^*(\omega) \in S^s(t_0,\omega)$, *all* $\omega \in \Omega$, *is an* α-equilibrium *for the subgame starting at* t_0 *if for all* $\omega \in \Omega$, $s^*(\omega)$ *is* α-consistent *and*

$$
\forall_{i \in \{1,2\}} \forall_{s_i \in S_i^s(t_0,\omega)} : V_i(t_0, s^*(\omega)) \geq V_i(t_0, s_i, s_{-i}^*(\omega)).
$$

The concept of α-equilibrium relies on open-loop strategies. As in deterministic timing games we want to rule out incredible threats and therefore we require a more robust equilibrium concept, comparable to subgame perfect equilibrium for games in discrete time, using closed-loop strategies.

DEFINITION 4.4 *A closed-loop strategy for player $i \in \{1,2\}$ is for all $\omega \in \Omega$ a collection of simple strategies*

$$\left((G_i^t(\cdot,\omega), \alpha_i^t(\cdot,\omega))\right)_{0 \le t < \infty},$$

with $(G_i^t(\cdot,\omega), \alpha_i^t(\cdot,\omega)) \in S_i^s(t,\omega)$ for all $t \ge 0$ that satisfies the following intertemporal consistency conditions for all $\omega \in \Omega$:

1 $\forall_{0 \le t \le u \le v < \infty} : v = \inf\{\tau > t | Y_\tau = Y_v\} \Rightarrow G_i^t(v,\omega) = G_i^u(v,\omega);$

2 $\forall_{0 \le t \le u \le v < \infty} : v = \inf\{\tau > t | Y_\tau = Y_v\} \Rightarrow \alpha_i^t(v,\omega) = \alpha_i^u(v,\omega).$

For all $\omega \in \Omega$, the set of closed-loop strategies for player $i \in \{1,2\}$ is denoted by $S_i^{cl}(\omega)$. As before, we define the strategy space to be $S^{cl}(\omega) = \prod_{i \in \{1,2\}} S_i^{cl}(\omega)$, $\omega \in \Omega$.

The intertemporal consistency conditions differ from their deterministic counterparts in Fudenberg and Tirole (1985). Taking their conditions without adaptation implies that one requires that for each firm the probability of having invested before time v starting at time t equals the probability of not having invested before time u starting from t times the probability of having invested before time v starting at time u. This is not a sensible requirement in the stochastic case. Consider for example a situation with one firm such that investment yields higher revenues for higher values of Y. So, the probability of investment is monotonic in Y. Let $0 \le t \le \tau \le u \le v$ and suppose that for certain $\omega \in \Omega$, Y is strictly increasing on $[t, \tau]$, strictly decreasing on $(\tau, u]$ and strictly increasing on $(u, v]$ and that $Y_t = Y_v$. Consider a simple strategy with $G^t(t,\omega) = 1/4$ and $G^t(\tau,\omega) = G^t(u,\omega) = G^t(v,\omega) = 1/2$. Intertemporal consistency in the Fudenberg and Tirole (1985) sense would then imply that $G^u(v,\omega) = 0$, whereas one would expect $G^u(v,\omega) = G^t(t,\omega) = 1/4$. That is, due to randomness, first passage times are important, not time as such.

A consistent α-equilibrium is now defined in the standard way.

DEFINITION 4.5 *A tuple of closed-loop strategies $\bar{s} = \left(\bar{s}(\omega)\right)_{\omega \in \Omega}$, $\bar{s}(\omega) \in S^{cl}(\omega)$, all $\omega \in \Omega$, is a consistent α-equilibrium if for all $t \in [0, \infty)$, the corresponding tuple of simple strategies $\left((G_1^t, \alpha_1^t), (G_2^t, \alpha_2^t)\right)$ is an α-equilibrium for the subgame starting at t.*

Since we have defined strategies and equilibria path-wise we will, for notational convenience, in the remainder drop ω as an argument.

2.2   Preemption Games

The coordination problem that we want to consider arises in cases where there exists an incentive to be the first mover. These games are called *preemption games*, because there is an incentive to preempt the competitor. Apart from the assumptions already made we introduce five additional assumptions:

1 there exists a unique Y_F such that $L(Y) = F(Y) = M(Y)$ for all $Y \geq Y_F$ and $F(Y) > M(Y)$ for all $Y < Y_F$;

2 $L(0) < F(0)$;

3 $F(\cdot)$ is strictly increasing for $Y < Y_F$;

4 $L(\cdot) - F(\cdot)$ is strictly quasi-concave on $[0, Y_F)$.

Note that in Fudenberg and Tirole (1985), $L(\cdot)$, $F(\cdot)$ and $M(\cdot)$ are functions of time, whereas in this model they are functions of the value of the stochastic process Y.

Because of these assumptions there exists a unique $Y_P \leq Y_F$ such that $L(Y) < F(Y)$ for all $0 \leq Y < Y_P$, $L(Y_P) = F(Y_P)$, and $L(Y) > F(Y)$ for all $Y_P < Y < Y_F$. Furthermore, define Y_L to be the location of the maximum of the discounted leader value.[9] It is assumed that $Y_L > Y_P$, i.e. no war of attrition arises. For the remainder define the following stopping times $T_P^t = \inf\{u \geq t | Y_u \geq Y_P\}$ and $T_F^t = \inf\{u \geq t | Y_u \geq Y_F\}$.[10]

In case firms are identical, coordination on a non-symmetric equilibrium is hard to establish in a noncooperative setting. Therefore, we concentrate on equilibria that are supported by symmetric strategies.[11] In Appendix A the following theorem is proved.

---

[9]In case of exogenous firm roles, i.e. where the firms know beforehand which one of them is the first investor, it is optimal for the leader to invest at the moment t that $Y_t = Y_L$, when $Y_0 \leq Y_L$.

[10]The existence of Y_L and Y_F need not be assumed but can be obtained from solving optimal stopping problems. For the general semimartingale case existence is not readily guaranteed. If the solution to eq. (4.1) satisfies the Markov property and some other technical conditions, existence and uniqueness of Y_L and Y_F can be obtained (see e.g. Shiryaev (1978)).

[11]The focus on symmetric strategies is, however, not *a priori* clear. There is a growing literature on equilibrium selection started by Harsanyi and Selten (1988) that shows that in games with symmetric players, asymmetric equilibria can survive (cf. Kandori et al. (1993) and Young (1998)).

THEOREM 4.1 *There is a consistent α-equilibrium with symmetric strategies, which is given by the tuple of closed-loop strategies*

$$(\bar{s}^t)_{t \geq 0} = \left((G_1^t, \alpha_1^t), (G_2^t, \alpha_2^t) \right)_{t \geq 0},$$

where for $i = 1, 2$, $t \geq 0$ and $u \geq t$

$$G_i^t(u) = \begin{cases} 0 & \text{if } u < T_P^t, \\ \dfrac{L(Y_{T_P^t}) - M(Y_{T_P^t})}{L(Y_{T_P^t}) - 2M(Y_{T_P^t}) + F(Y_{T_P^t})} & \text{if } T_P^t \leq u < T_F^t, \\ 1 & \text{if } u \geq T_F^t, \end{cases} \qquad (4.5)$$

$$\alpha_i^t(u) = \begin{cases} 0 & \text{if } u < T_P^t, \\ \dfrac{L(Y_{T_P^t}) - F(Y_{T_P^t})}{L(Y_{T_P^t}) - M(Y_{T_P^t})} & \text{if } T_P^t \leq u < T_F^t, \\ 1 & \text{if } u \geq T_F^t. \end{cases} \qquad (4.6)$$

Moreover, if Y has continuous sample paths a.s. the strategies in (4.5) and (4.6) constitute the unique consistent α-equilibrium.

Starting at $t_0 \geq 0$, this equilibrium says that no investment takes place until $T_P^{t_0}$. At $T_P^{t_0}$ at least one firm invests. Note that it may well be possible that $T_P^{t_0} = t_0$, i.e. that $Y_0 \geq Y_P$. This is a case that cannot be analysed in the framework of e.g. Weeds (2002). The probability with which firm i invests is determined by the intensity function and corresponds with the jump in the function $G_i^{t_0}(\cdot)$ which implies that the strategies satisfy the α-consistency condition of Definition 4.2. The probability of investment at time $T_P^{t_0}$ is determined by balancing the three possible scenarios: firm 1 invests and firm 2 does not, firm 2 invests and firm 1 does not, and both firm 1 and firm 2 invest. It turns out that $\alpha_i^{t_0}(T_P^{t_0})$ is such that firm i's expected value equals $F(Y_{T_P^{t_0}})$ which is the value that it can guarantee anyway. This property is called the principle of *rent equalisation*. Note that if $Y_{T_P^{t_0}} = Y_P$, then $\alpha_i^{t_0}(T_P^{t_0}) = 0$ since $L(Y_P) = F(Y_P)$. The intensity function is increasing in $L(\cdot) - F(\cdot)$ and decreasing in $L(\cdot) - M(\cdot)$. This can be explained by the fact that if the first mover advantage, $L(\cdot) - F(\cdot)$, increases it becomes more attractive to become the leader, i.e. firms will increase the intensity of their sequence of atoms. Conversely, if the difference between the leader payoff and the payoff of mutual investment increases, firms are less willing to risk mutual investment and therefore they decrease the intensity of the sequence of atoms. If $t \geq T_F^{t_0}$ both firms have invested with probability one.

3.   The Standard Model

In this section we apply the equilibrium concept introduced in the previous section to the model analysed in Dixit and Pindyck (1996, Section 9.3).[12] This model considers an investment project with sunk costs $I > 0$. After the investment is made, the firm can produce one unit of product at any point in time. Since the number of firms is two, market supply is $Q \in \{0, 1, 2\}$. The price, P, is given by inverse market demand $D(Q)$ multiplied by a shock Y which follows a geometric Brownian motion process. So, $P = YD(Q)$. In Figure 4.2 the three value functions are plotted. If the leader invests at $Y < Y_F$ the follower's value is maximised when the follower invests at Y_F.

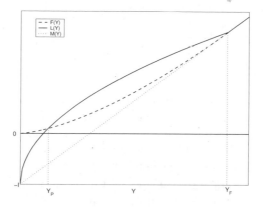

Figure 4.2. Value functions in the Dixit and Pindyck model.

In the remainder of this chapter we will only consider the subgame starting at $t_0 = 0$. Therefore, we will, for notational convenience, drop the time superscripts for strategies and stopping times. The equilibrium outcome depends on the value Y_0, which is the initial value of $(Y_t)_{0 \le t < \infty}$. To determine the outcomes, three regions have to be distinguished. The first region is defined by $Y_0 \le Y_P$. If we restrict ourselves to symmetric equilibrium strategies, it follows from Theorem 4.1 that there are three possible equilibrium outcomes. In the first outcome firm 1 is the leader and invests at Y_P and firm 2 is the follower and invests at Y_F. Note that in this case the symmetric equilibrium strategies lead to an asymmetric equilibrium outcome. In this particular outcome firm 1 is the first one to invest in the repeated game depicted in Figure 4.1. The second outcome

---

[12]This model is a simplified version of the model of Smets (1991) and is also extensively analysed in Nielsen (2002), Huisman and Kort (1999), and Huisman (2001).

is the symmetric counterpart: firm 2 is the leader and invests at Y_P and firm 1 is the follower and invests at Y_F. The third possibility is that both firms invest simultaneously at Y_P, i.e. both firms invest in the same round of the repeated game depicted in figure 4.1. However, this equilibrium arises with probability zero. To see this, note that since a geometric Brownian motion has continuous sample-paths and at Y_P it holds that $L(Y_P) = F(Y_P)$, it can be concluded from eq. (4.6) that $\alpha(\tau) = \alpha(T_P) = 0$. Now it directly follows from eq. (4.3) that the probability of joint investment is zero. Using the same kind of limiting argument as in eq. (4.2), we obtain that the probability that player i is the only one who invests at $t = \tau$, $\mathbb{P}(i|\tau)$, is given by

$$\mathbb{P}(i|\tau) = \frac{\alpha_i(\tau)(1 - \alpha_j(\tau))}{\alpha_i(\tau) + \alpha_j(\tau) - \alpha_i(\tau)\alpha_j(\tau)}. \qquad (4.7)$$

By applying L'Hopital's rule, while imposing symmetry, one then obtains that in equilibrium

$$\mathbb{P}(1|\tau) = \mathbb{P}(2|\tau) = \frac{\alpha_i'(T_P)}{\alpha_i'(T_P) + \alpha_j'(T_P)} = \frac{1}{2}. \qquad (4.8)$$

So, with equal probability either firm becomes the leader. Due to the definition of Y_P, i.e. $L(Y_P) = F(Y_P)$, it follows that the expected value of each player equals

$$V_i(\tau, \bar{s}^\tau) = W_i(\tau, \bar{s}^\tau) = \tfrac{1}{2}(L(Y_P) + F(Y_P)) = F(Y_P).$$

In the second region it holds that $Y_P < Y_0 < Y_F$. There are three possible outcomes. Firstly, since $L(Y)$ exceeds $F(Y)$ in case $Y \in (Y_P, Y_F)$, it can be obtained from eq. (4.6) that $\alpha_1(0) > 0$. Due to $\tau = 0$ and eq. (4.7) we know that with probability

$$\frac{\alpha_1(0)(1 - \alpha_2(0))}{\alpha_1(0) + \alpha_2(0) - \alpha_1(0)\alpha_2(0)},$$

firm 1 invests at $t = 0$ and firm 2 invests at T_F. A second scenario is given by the symmetric counterpart of the first scenario. Finally, equation (4.2) implies that the firms invest simultaneously at $t = 0$ with probability

$$\frac{\alpha_1(0)\alpha_2(0)}{\alpha_1(0) + \alpha_2(0) - \alpha_1(0)\alpha_2(0)} > 0,$$

leaving them with a low value of $M(Y_0) < F(Y_0)$. The expected payoff of each firm then equals

$$W_i(\tau, \bar{s}^\tau) =$$
$$\frac{\alpha_i(0)(1 - \alpha_j(0))L(Y_0) + \alpha_j(0)(1 - \alpha_i(0))F(Y_0) + \alpha_i(0)\alpha_j(0)M(Y_0)}{\alpha_i(0) + \alpha_j(0) - \alpha_i(0)\alpha_j(0)}$$
$$= F(Y_0),$$

where the latter equation follows from eq. (4.6). Since there are first mover advantages in this region, each firm is willing to invest with positive probability. However, this implies via eq. (4.2) that the probability of simultaneous investment, leading to a low payoff $M(Y_0)$, is also positive. Since the firms are both assumed to be risk neutral, they will fix the probability of investment such that their expected value equals $F(Y_0)$, which is also their payoff if they let the other firm invest first.

When Y_0 is in the third region $[Y_F, \infty)$, according to eqs. (4.2) and (4.6) the outcome exhibits joint investment at Y_0. The value of each firm is again $F(Y_0)$.

4.   The Interaction of Competition and Uncertainty

In this section we describe some consequences of the simultaneous modelling of strategic interaction and investment uncertainty. To do so, we consider the basic game theoretic real option model as described in Smets (1991) and Huisman (2001, Chapter 7). First, we briefly describe that model and its results. For further details the reader is referred to Huisman (2001, Chapter 7). Then we address the issue of equilibrium selection in the presence of multiple equilibria. We also compare the resulting equilibria of the model with uncertainty and its deterministic counterpart. From the previous section it might be clear that the presence of strategic interaction erodes the option value of waiting with investment. By performing a simulation we test whether in a preemption equilibrium the option value significantly differs from zero and from the option value in the monopoly case. We conclude this section by comparing welfare results for the model with uncertainty and the deterministic model.

In the standard game theoretic real option model there are two firms who have the opportunity to invest in the same project at sunk costs $I > 0$. Both firms are assumed to be risk-neutral and have the same discount rate $0 < r < 1$. At time $t \geq 0$ the profit flow of firm $i \in \{1, 2\}$ equals

$$Y_t D_{N_i N_j},$$

where for $k \in \{1, 2\}$,

$$N_k = \begin{cases} 0 & \text{if firm } k \text{ has not invested,} \\ 1 & \text{if firm } k \text{ has invested.} \end{cases}$$

Uncertainty is captured by the stochastic process $(Y_t)_{t\geq 0}$ which is assumed to follow a geometric Brownian motion, i.e.

$$dY_t = \mu Y_t dt + \sigma Y_t dW_t,$$
$$Y_0 = y,$$

where $y > 0$, $0 < \mu < r$ is the trend, $\sigma > 0$ is the volatility, and $(W_t)_{t\geq 0}$ is a Wiener process, i.e. $dW_t \stackrel{iid}{\sim} N(0, dt)$. The following restrictions are made on the deterministic part of the profit flow:

$$D_{10} > D_{11} > D_{00} > D_{01}. \tag{4.9}$$

Furthermore, it is assumed that there is a first mover advantage, i.e.

$$D_{10} - D_{00} > D_{11} - D_{01}. \tag{4.10}$$

Given $Y > 0$, it can be shown that the value for the follower equals

$$F(Y) = \begin{cases} \frac{Y_F^{1-\beta_1}}{\beta_1} \frac{D_{11}-D_{01}}{r-\mu} Y^{\beta_1} + \frac{Y D_{01}}{r-\mu} & \text{if } Y < Y_F, \\ \frac{Y D_{11}}{r-\mu} - I & \text{if } Y \geq Y_F, \end{cases}$$

where β_1 is the positive root of the quadratic equation $\frac{1}{2}\sigma^2\beta^2 + (\mu - \frac{1}{2}\sigma^2)\beta - r = 0$. It can be shown that $\beta_1 > 1$. The optimal (unique) threshold for investment of the follower, Y_F, is given by

$$Y_F = \frac{\beta_1}{\beta_1 - 1} \frac{(r-\mu)I}{D_{11} - D_{01}}.$$

The value for the leader at $Y < Y_F$ then equals

$$L(Y) = \frac{Y D_{10}}{r-\mu} + \left(\frac{Y}{Y_F}\right)^{\beta_1} \frac{Y_F(D_{11} - D_{10})}{r-\mu}.$$

The preemption threshold Y_P is a value such that $L(Y_P) = F(Y_P)$. It can be shown that it is unique and that it satisfies $0 < Y_P < Y_F$.

Suppose that one of the firms is assigned the leader role, i.e. the other firm cannot invest earlier than this firm. In this case, the competitive pressure is taken away and the leader can determine the optimal investment threshold Y_L. It can be shown to be unique and is given by

$$Y_L = \frac{\beta_1}{\beta_1 - 1} \frac{(r-\mu)I}{D_{10} - D_{00}},$$

where it holds that $L(Y_L) > L(Y_P)$.

Suppose that both firms decide to invest simultaneously at time T_θ, where

$$T_\theta = \inf\{t \geq 0 | Y_t \geq \theta\},$$

for some $\theta > 0$. The value for each firm of joint investment at $Y > 0$ equals

$$J(Y,\theta) = \begin{cases} \frac{Y D_{00}}{r-\mu} + \left(\frac{Y}{\theta}\right)^{\beta_1} \left(\frac{\theta(D_{11}-D_{00})}{r-\mu} - I\right) & \text{if } Y < \theta, \\ \frac{Y D_{11}}{r-\mu} - I & \text{if } Y \geq \theta. \end{cases}$$

The optimal joint investment threshold, Y_J, is given by

$$Y_J = \frac{\beta_1}{\beta_1 - 1} \frac{(r-\mu)I}{D_{11} - D_{00}}.$$

This threshold is unique as well and it satisfies $Y_J > Y_P$. For further reference, define the stopping times $T_P = \inf\{t \geq 0 | Y_t \geq Y_P\}$, $T_F = \inf\{t \geq 0 | Y_t \geq Y_F\}$, $T_L = \inf\{t \geq 0 | Y_t \geq Y_L\}$, and $T_J = \inf\{t \geq 0 | Y_t \geq Y_J\}$.

To describe the equilibria of the investment game, we distinguish two scenarios. In the first scenario, there exists $Y \in (0, Y_F)$ such that $L(Y) \geq J(Y, Y_J)$. In this scenario we have a situation similar to the model described in Section 3, i.e. the unique symmetric equilibrium is supported by the strategies described in Theorem 4.1. In the other scenario it holds that $L(Y) < J(Y, Y_J)$, for all $Y \in (0, Y_F)$. In this case a preemption equilibrium still exists, but there is also a continuum of joint investment equilibria. Here both firms tacitly collude by refraining from investment until demand has reached a level that is so high that it is optimal for both of them to invest simultaneously. Therefore, Boyer et al. (2001) call these *tacit collusion equilibria*. The closed-loop strategies that support the latter consistent α-equilibria for $i \in \{1,2\}$ are for all $t \geq 0$ and $s \geq t$ given by

$$G_i^t(s) = \alpha_i^t(s) = \begin{cases} 0 & \text{if } s < T^*, \\ 1 & \text{if } s \geq T^*, \end{cases}$$

for any $T^* \in [T_S^t, T_J^t]$, where $T_S^t = \inf\{s \geq t | Y_t \geq Y_S\}$ and

$$Y_S = \min\{\theta | \forall_{Y \geq 0} : J(Y,\theta) \geq L(Y)\}.$$

It can be shown that the latter scenario prevails if and only if $f > g$, where

$$f = \beta_1 \frac{D_{10} - D_{11}}{D_{11} - D_{01}} + \left(\frac{D_{11} - D_{00}}{D_{11} - D_{01}}\right)^{\beta_1},$$ (4.11)

$$g = \left(\frac{D_{10} - D_{00}}{D_{11} - D_{01}}\right)^{\beta_1}.$$ (4.12)

In order to avoid the problem of simultaneous investment that can arise in the preemption equilibrium we assume for the remainder of this section that $\omega \in \tilde{\Omega} = \{\omega \in \Omega | Y_0 < Y_P\}$.

4.1 Equilibrium Selection

Consider the scenario where both the preemption and the joint investment equilibria exist, which occurs when $f > g$. It can be shown that the equilibrium where both firms invest at T_J is Pareto dominant. In many contributions[13] it is assumed that this is the equilibrium that firms coordinate on, because of the Pareto dominance. However, it is argued in the equilibrium selection literature (cf. Harsanyi and Selten (1988)) that Pareto dominance is not the correct criterion to select equilibria. The Pareto dominant equilibrium is the equilibrium whose outcome is most beneficial for all players *together*. That is, if firms could make binding agreements on the timing of investment they would choose the Pareto dominant equilibrium. However, antitrust law forbids binding agreements of this type. Therefore, another equilibrium selection mechanism should be applied in the presence of multiple equilibria. In this subsection we use the concept of *risk dominance* that has been introduced in Harsanyi and Selten (1988).

Consider the symmetric bimatrix game depicted in Figure 4.3, where the payoffs are such that $a > d$ and $b \geq c$. With this payoff structure

	J	P
J	(a, a)	(c, d)
P	(d, c)	(b, b)

Figure 4.3. A symmetric 2x2 game.

there are two pure strategy Nash equilibria with payoffs (a, a) and (b, b).

---

[13]Cf. Fudenberg and Tirole (1985), Huisman (2001), and Pawlina and Kort (2001).

Suppose that $a > b$, i.e. the equilibrium with payoffs (a, a) is Pareto dominant.

Suppose that each player is uncertain about the action of the other player and that they both have a non-informative prior, that is, they attach equal probabilities to the other player playing each strategy. The expected payoff of playing action J is then equal to $\frac{a+c}{2}$ while the expected payoff of playing action P equals $\frac{d+b}{2}$. Suppose that $b-c > a-d$. Then an expected utility maximiser will never choose action J, i.e. action P is risk-dominant. In general, an equilibrium is risk-dominant if and only if it maximises the product of the gains from unilateral deviation. Furthermore, from the evolutionary game theory literature it is known that in 2x2 games it holds that under the replicator dynamics (cf. Samuelson (1997, Chapter 2)) or under adaptive learning (cf. Young (1998, Chapter 4)), the risk-dominant equilibrium has the larger basin of attraction. That is, it is more likely to survive evolutionary pressure in the long-run.

The concept of risk dominance is an equilibrium selection device that is based on individual preferences and not, as is the case with Pareto dominance, on group preferences. Therefore, risk dominance seems to be a more appropriate selection tool. However, we will show that in the basic game theoretic real option model the Pareto dominant and risk-dominant equilibria coincide.

If, somehow, the firms can coordinate on any joint investment equilibrium they will coordinate on investing at time T_J. Therefore, we consider a strategy game where both firms can choose between playing either the optimal joint investment strategy, i.e. investment at time T_J or the preemption strategy as described in Theorem 4.1. We denote the first strategy by J and the latter by P. Let $V_i(s_i, s_j)$, $s_i, s_j \in \{J, P\}$, denote the expected value for firm i when firm i plays s_i and firm j plays s_j. This gives the following values for a, b, c and d in Figure 4.3. If both players play J, then both firms invest simultaneously at time T_J. This gives

$$a = V_i(J, J)$$
$$= \mathbb{E}\left(\int_0^{T_J} e^{-rt} Y_t D_{00} dt \right) + \mathbb{E}\left(e^{-rT_J} \right) J(Y_J, Y_J).$$

If both firms play strategy P, then, since $\omega \in \tilde{\Omega}$, one firm becomes the leader with probability $1/2$ at time T_P while the other firm becomes the follower. Therefore, the expected payoff equals

$$b = V_i(P,P)$$
$$= \mathbb{E}\left(\int_0^{T_P} e^{-rt}Y_t D_{00}dt\right) + \mathbb{E}\left(e^{-rT_P}\right)\tfrac{1}{2}(L(Y_P)+F(Y_P)).$$

If firm i plays strategy J while firm j plays strategy P, then firm j will invest at time T_P. The best response for firm i is to be the follower and invest at time T_F. Therefore, we get

$$c = V_i(J,P)$$
$$= \mathbb{E}\left(\int_0^{T_P} e^{-rt}Y_t D_{00}dt\right) + \mathbb{E}\left(e^{-rT_P}\right)F(Y_P).$$

The symmetric counterpart results in

$$d = V_i(P,J)$$
$$= \mathbb{E}\left(\int_0^{T_P} e^{-rt}Y_t D_{00}dt\right) + \mathbb{E}\left(e^{-rT_P}\right)L(Y_P).$$

Since $L(Y_P) = F(Y_P)$ we have that $b = c = d$. Combining this with the following lemma leads to the conclusion that the strategy game has two pure Nash equilibria, namely (J,J) and (P,P).

LEMMA 4.1 *In the strategy game the following holds for all $i \in \{1,2\}$:*

$$V_i(J,J) > V_i(P,J).$$

Proof. Let the starting point of the geometric Brownian motion be given by y. First note that since $Y_P < Y_J$ and $1 - \beta_1 < 0$, it holds that

$$\mathbb{E}\left(e^{-rT_J}\right)J(Y_J,Y_J) - \mathbb{E}\left(e^{-rT_P}\right)J(Y_P,Y_J)$$
$$= \left(\frac{y}{Y_J}\right)^{\beta_1}\frac{Y_J D_{00}}{r-\mu} - \left(\frac{y}{Y_P}\right)^{\beta_1}\frac{Y_P D_{00}}{r-\mu}$$
$$= \frac{y^{\beta_1}D_{00}}{r-\mu}\left(Y_J^{1-\beta_1} - Y_P^{1-\beta_1}\right) < 0,$$

where the integrals are calculated in Appendix B. Using this result we obtain that

$$
\begin{aligned}
V_i(J,J) - V_i(P,J) =& \mathbb{E}\left(\int_{T_P}^{T_J} e^{-rt} Y_t D_{00} dt\right) + \mathbb{E}\left(e^{-rT_J}\right) J(Y_J, Y_J) \\
& - \mathbb{E}\left(e^{-rT_P}\right) L(Y_P) \\
>& \frac{y^{\beta_1} D_{00}}{r - \mu}\left(Y_J^{1-\beta_1} - Y_P^{1-\beta_1}\right) + \mathbb{E}\left(e^{-rT_J}\right) J(Y_J, Y_J) \\
& - \mathbb{E}\left(e^{-rT_P}\right) J(Y_P, Y_J) \\
=& 0,
\end{aligned}
$$

which proves the lemma.   □

Since $b = c = d$ it now follows immediately that $a - d > b - c$, which implies that the equilibrium (J, J) is risk-dominant. In the remainder we will therefore identify a scenario with $f > g$ with the joint investment equilibrium (J, J) as opposed to a scenario with $f < g$ which we identify with the equilibrium (P, P).

4.2   The Impact of Uncertainty on Equilibria

In this subsection we analyse the impact of uncertainty on the equilibrium outcome of the investment timing game. To do so, we consider two situations: a deterministic one which is characterised by setting $\sigma = 0$, and a stochastic case which is characterised by $\sigma = 0.2$. Note that with $\sigma = 0$, applying L'Hopital's rule gives $\beta_1 = \frac{r}{\mu}$. As has been mentioned before, there are two possible equilibria, joint investment or preemption, depending on f and g.

To gain insight on the impact of uncertainty we simulate both models ($\sigma = 0$ and $\sigma = 0.2$) 10000 times. For each simulation run we check for both models whether a preemption equilibrium or a joint investment equilibrium results (by comparing f and g). Then we calculate the percentage of cases in which a different equilibrium type is obtained.

The simulation procedure is as follows. In each simulation run we (pseudo)-randomly sample a value for D_{10}, D_{11}, D_{00} and D_{01} from the interval $[10, 200]$ such that conditions (4.9) and (4.10) are satisfied. The sunk investment cost, I, is randomly sampled from the interval $[100, 500]$. As parameter values we take $r = 0.1$ and $\mu = 0.06$. After 10000 runs we obtain that in 33.82% of the simulations the presence of uncertainty gives a different equilibrium prediction. This gives some evidence that the addition of uncertainty to the standard deterministic investment timing game can lead to more accurate equilibrium predictions.

4.3   The Effect of Competition on the Value of Waiting

As has been observed before, the presence of competition can lead to an erosion of the option value of waiting with investment. In a joint adoption equilibrium, the option value is fully taken into account. In a preemption equilibrium, however, competitive pressure makes the option of waiting less valuable. This is obvious since one can show that the preemption point is reached earlier a.s. than the optimal time of investment when the competitive pressure is taken away by exogenously determined leader and follower roles (see Huisman (2001, Chapter 7) for a detailed exposition of this point). In Huisman (2001, Chapter 7) it is also shown that firms can make an investment with a negative present value, implying a negative option value. The present value of investment at Y_P equals $L(Y_P) - \frac{Y_P D_{00}}{r-\mu}$.

We test whether in the preemption equilibrium the option value is significantly (at 95%) different from the case without competition, i.e. the case where one firm is exogenously assigned the leader role. In order to perform this test we simulate 1000 scenarios in a similar way as described above, with the restriction that we only sample scenarios where $f < g$, i.e. scenarios where the preemption equilibrium is the unique symmetric equilibrium. In each simulation run we calculate the values of $L(Y_P) - \frac{Y_P D_{00}}{r-\mu}$, which are stored in a vector x, and $L(Y_L) - \frac{Y_L D_{00}}{r-\mu}$, which are stored in a vector y. It is assumed that the entries in x are iid draws from a distribution with unknown mean $\mu_x = \mathbb{E}(L(Y_P) - \frac{Y_P D_{00}}{r-\mu})$ and unknown variance σ_x^2. Similarly, we assume that y consists of iid draws from a distribution with unknown mean $\mu_y = \mathbb{E}(L(Y_L))$ and unknown variance σ_y^2. We test the null hypothesis

$$H_0 : \mu_x = \mu_y.$$

The central limit theorem gives that

$$\sqrt{n}(\bar{x} - \mu_x) \xrightarrow{d} \mathcal{N}(0, \sigma_x^2),$$
$$\sqrt{n}(\bar{y} - \mu_y) \xrightarrow{d} \mathcal{N}(0, \sigma_y^2),$$

where n is the number of observations, $\bar{x}$ is the sample mean of x and $\bar{y}$ is the sample mean of y. Since it is assumed that both series are sampled from independent distributions, taking the convolution of both distributions gives that under the null hypothesis it holds that,

$$\sqrt{n}(\bar{x} - \bar{y}) \xrightarrow{d} \mathcal{N}(0, \sigma_x^2 + \sigma_y^2).$$

Define the test statistic

$$T = \frac{n(\bar{x} - \bar{y})^2}{\hat{\sigma}_x^2 + \hat{\sigma}_y^2},$$

where $\hat{\sigma}_x^2 = \frac{1}{n}\sum_{i=1}^{n}(x_i - \bar{x})^2$ is the sample variance of x and $\hat{\sigma}_y^2$ is the sample variance of y. Under the null hypothesis it holds that

$$T \xrightarrow{d} \chi_1^2.$$

The critical value at 0.95 is given by 3.84. In our simulation we find $T = 4159.21$, which implies that the null hypothesis is rejected at 95%.

Testing the null hypothesis

$$H_0 : \mathbb{E}(L(Y_P) - \tfrac{Y_P D_{00}}{r-\mu}) = 0,$$

gives a value $T = 220.03$ (where $\bar{y}$ and $\hat{\sigma}_y^2$ are set to zero). So, at 95% we find evidence that the option value in case of competition is significantly different from zero and significantly different from the monopoly option value.

4.4   The Effect of Uncertainty on Welfare Predictions

To assess the welfare effects of uncertainty in the investment timing game, we consider, for simplicity, the case of a new market model, i.e. we assume that $D_{01} = D_{00} = 0$. Since consumer surplus is contained in total welfare, we have to specify a demand function. To do so, assume that the market is characterised by an inverse demand function $P : \mathbb{R}_+ \to \mathbb{R}_+$ and a cost function $C : \mathbb{R}_+ \to \mathbb{R}_+$ such that

$$P(q) = b - aq, \qquad b > 0, a > 0, q \leq \tfrac{b}{a},$$
$$C(q) = cq, \qquad 0 < c < b.$$

If only one firm is active on the market it operates as a monopolist, so that

$$D_{10} = \max_{q}\{P(q)q - cq\}.$$

Solving this optimisation problem yields the monopoly quantity $q^m = \frac{b-c}{2a}$, the monopoly price $p^m = \frac{b+c}{2}$ and $D_{10} = \frac{(b-c)^2}{4a}$.

If both firms are active it is assumed that they engage in quantity competition leading to a Cournot equilibrium, i.e. for $i \in \{1, 2\}$ it holds that

$$D_{11} = \max_{q_i}\{P(q_i + q_j)q_i - C(q_i)\}.$$

Solving this problem gives the duopoly quantity $q^d = \frac{b-c}{3a}$, the duopoly price $p^d = \frac{b+2c}{3}$ and $D_{11} = \frac{(b-c)^2}{9a}$. Note that $D_{10} > D_{11}$ which implies that there is a first mover advantage.

The following lemma shows that in a new market model the joint investment scenario does not arise.

LEMMA 4.2 *In a new market model* $(D_{01} = D_{00} = 0)$ *it holds that* $f < g$.

Proof. Denote $x = \frac{D_{10}}{D_{11}}$ and define (cf. (4.11) and (4.12))

$$h(x) = f - g = \beta_1(x-1) + 1 - x^{\beta_1}, \qquad x \geq 1.$$

Note that $h(1) = 0$. Furthermore, we have for all $x > 1$,

$$h'(x) = \beta_1(1 - x^{\beta_1 - 1}) < 0,$$

since $\beta_1 - 1 < 0$. Hence, $h(x) < 0$ for all $x > 1$. $\qquad\square$

Note that the demand function equals $D(p) = \frac{b}{a} - \frac{1}{a}p$. The consumer surplus if one firm is active or if both firms are active are denoted by CS^m and CS^d, respectively, and given by

$$CS^m = \int_{p^m}^{b} D(p)dp = \frac{1}{4}\left(b(b+c) - \frac{b^2 - c^2}{2a}\right),$$

$$CS^d = \int_{p^d}^{b} D(p)dp = \frac{1}{2}\left(b - \frac{b-c}{3a}\right)\frac{b+2c}{3}.$$

Let $\omega \in \tilde{\Omega}$. In the preemption equilibrium the expected discounted consumer surplus equals

$$\mathbb{E}(CS(y)) = \mathbb{E}\left(\int_{T_P}^{T_F} e^{-rt}Y_t CS^m dt\right) + \mathbb{E}\left(\int_{T_F}^{\infty} e^{-rt}Y_t CS^d dt\right)$$

$$= \frac{y^{\beta_1}CS^m}{r - \mu}\left(Y_P^{1-\beta_1} - Y_F^{1-\beta_1}\right) + \left(\frac{y}{Y_F}\right)^{\beta_1}\frac{Y_F CS^d}{r - \mu},$$

where y is the starting point of the geometric Brownian motion. The integrals are calculated in Appendix B. The expected producer surplus is given by

$$
\mathbb{E}(PS(y)) = \mathbb{E}\left(\int_{T_P}^{T_F} e^{-rdt} Y_t D_{10} dt\right) + 2\mathbb{E}\left(\int_{T_F}^{\infty} e^{-rdt} Y_t D_{11} dt\right)
$$
$$
- \left(\mathbb{E}\left(e^{-rT_P}\right) + \mathbb{E}\left(e^{-rT_F}\right)\right) I
$$
$$
= \frac{y^{\beta_1} D_{10}}{r - \mu}\left(Y_P^{1-\beta_1} - Y_F^{1-\beta_1}\right) + 2\left(\frac{y}{Y_F}\right)^{\beta_1} \frac{Y_F D_{11}}{r - \mu}
$$
$$
- \left(\left(\frac{y}{Y_P}\right)^{\beta_1} + \left(\frac{y}{Y_F}\right)^{\beta_1}\right) I.
$$

Expected welfare is now defined by

$$
\mathbb{E}(W(y)) = \mathbb{E}(CS(y)) + \mathbb{E}(PS(y)).
$$

In order to test whether the addition of uncertainty leads to significantly different welfare predictions, we simulate a vector of 1000 welfare results under certainty ($\sigma = 0$), denoted by W^c, and a vector of 1000 welfare results under uncertainty ($\sigma = 0.2$), denoted by W^u. For each series it is assumed that the observations are iid samples from independent distributions with unknown means μ_c and μ_u and unknown variances, σ_c^2 and σ_u^2, respectively.

We test the null hypothesis that $\mathbb{E}(W^c) = \mathbb{E}(W^u)$, i.e.

$$
H_0 : \mu_c = \mu_u.
$$

Define the test statistic

$$
T = \frac{n(\bar{W}^c - \bar{W}^u)^2}{\hat{\sigma}_c^2 + \hat{\sigma}_u^2},
$$

where n is the number of observations, $\bar{W}^c$ and $\bar{W}^u$ are the sample means of W^c and W^u, respectively, and $\hat{\sigma}_c^2$ and $\hat{\sigma}_u^2$ are the sample variances of W^c and W^u, respectively. As in the previous subsection one can show that under the null hypothesis

$$
T \xrightarrow{d} \chi_1^2.
$$

In each simulation run we randomly sample values $b \in [20, 60]$, $c \in [20, 60]$, $a \in [0.5, 5]$ and $I \in [100, 500]$ in such a way that both D_{10} and D_{11} are in the interval $[10, 200]$. The geometric Brownian motion is sampled from $\tilde{\Omega}$, i.e. $y < Y_P$. The parameter values are chosen at $r = 0.1$ and $\mu = 0.06$. This results in $T = 60.66$, which implies that the null hypothesis is rejected at 95%. So, the welfare predictions from the stochastic model are significantly different from the predictions of the deterministic model.

Testing the null hypothesis

$$H_0 : \mu_u \geq \mu_c,$$

using the standard test yields a value of $7.79 > 1.96$. This implies that welfare under uncertainty is significantly lower than under certainty. There are two opposing effects. On the one hand, firms are less willing to invest under uncertainty which lowers consumer surplus. On the other hand, uncertainty takes away some of the competitive pressure which is beneficial for the producer surplus. Our simulation shows that the former effect significantly outweighs the latter effect.

5. Conclusion

At present, only a few contributions deal with the effects of strategic interactions on the option value of waiting associated with investments under uncertainty.[14] However, due to the importance of studying the topic of investment under uncertainty in an oligopolistic setting, it can be expected that more papers will appear in the immediate future. This chapter shows that taking both uncertainty and competition into account leads to significantly different results for e.g. equilibrium and welfare predictions, than treating both aspects separately. Furthermore, we propose a method to solve a coordination problem frequently occurring in such oligopoly models. This is especially important, since in those papers that already exist this coordination problem is not treated in a satisfactory way. For instance, Weeds (2002) explicitly makes the assumption that the stochastic process always starts at a value lower than the preemption value, i.e. $Y_0 < Y_P$. Furthermore, her result does not hold for stochastic processes with non-continuous sample-paths. In Nielsen (2002), Grenadier (1996) and Dutta et al. (1995) it is assumed that at the preemption point only one firm can succeed in investing. There are two reasons for this assumption to be unsatisfactory. Firstly, in all these contributions the firms are assumed to be identical so there is no *a priori* ground for this assumption. Secondly, the firms can invest simultaneously if it is optimal for both, so it seems unsatisfactory to exclude this possibility simply because of the fact that it is not optimal for both firms to invest.

The reason for our outcomes to be more realistic is the following. When there is an incentive to be the first to invest, i.e. if Y is such

---

[14]For a survey see Grenadier (2000).

that $L(Y) > F(Y) > M(Y)$ both firms are willing to take a risk. Since they are both assumed to be risk neutral they will risk so much that their expected value equals F, which equals their payoff if they allow the other firm to invest first. Employing the results of Section 2 learns that in this case there is a positive probability that both firms invest exactly at the same time, leaving them with the low payoff M. In our framework, this risk is explicitly taken into account by the firms, as opposed to most contributions in this field. In order to obtain realistic conclusions in game theoretic real option models it is inevitable that all aspects concerning the option effect and the strategic aspect should be taken into account.

Appendix
A.   Proof of Theorem 4.1

First notice that since Y is a semimartingale and hence right-continuous, continuity of $L(\cdot)$, $F(\cdot)$ and $M(\cdot)$ implies that every G-function and every α-function is right-continuous. Also, the strategy $(\bar{s}^t)_{0 \le t < \infty}$ satisfies the intertemporal consistency conditions of Definition 4.4. Hence, the closed-loop strategies are well-defined. Furthermore, for all $t \ge 0$, $\bar{s}^t$ satisfies α-consistency.

Let $t \ge 0$. The expected value of $\bar{s}^t$ for player i can be obtained by considering three cases.

1 $Y_\tau \ge Y_F$

This implies that $\alpha_i^t(\tau) = \alpha_j^t(\tau) = 1$. The expected value is then given by $V_i(t, \bar{s}^t) = M(Y_\tau) = F(Y_{T_P^t})$.

2 $Y_P < Y_\tau < Y_F$

This implies that $\alpha_i^t(\tau) = \alpha_j^t(\tau) = \alpha \in (0, 1]$. The expected value then equals

$$V_i(t, \bar{s}^t) = W_i(\tau, \bar{s}^t)$$
$$= \frac{1}{2 - \alpha} \Big[(1 - \alpha)L(Y_\tau) + (1 - \alpha)F(Y_\tau) + \alpha M(Y_\tau) \Big]$$
$$= F(Y_{T_P^t}).$$

3 $Y_\tau = Y_P$

This implies that $\alpha_i^t(\tau) = \alpha_j^t(\tau) = \alpha(\tau^t) = 0$. The expected value is given by

$$V_i(t, \bar{s}^t) = W_i(\tau, \bar{s}^t)$$
$$= \frac{\alpha'}{2\alpha'}[L(Y_\tau) + F(Y_\tau)]$$
$$= F(Y_{T_P^t}),$$

since Y_P is defined such that $L(Y_P) = F(Y_P)$.

So, $V_i(t, \bar{s}^t) = F(Y_{T_P^t})$.

Take any strategy for player i, (G_i^t, α_i^t) and denote $\tilde{s}^t = ((G_i^t, \alpha_i^t), \bar{s}_j^t)$. Then it holds that

$$V_i(t, \tilde{s}^t) = \int_t^{\tau-} L(Y_s) dG_i^t(s) + \left(1 - G_i^t(\tau-)\right) W_i(\tau, \tilde{s}^t).$$

Consider the following cases:

1 $\tau_i < \tau_j$
   In this case $W_i(\tau, \tilde{s}^t) = L(Y_\tau) = L(Y_{\tau_i})$. Hence, $V^i(t, \tilde{s}^t) \leq F(Y_{T_P^t})$, since for all $u < T_P^t(= \tau_j)$ it holds that $F(Y_u) > L(Y_u)$.

2 $\tau_i > \tau_j$
   For this case it holds that

$$\left(1 - G_i^t(\tau-)\right) W_i(\tau, \tilde{s}^t) = \left(1 - G_i^t(\tau-)\right) W_i(\tau_j, \tilde{s}^t)$$
$$= \left(1 - G_i^t(\tau-)\right) \frac{G_i^t(\tau) - G_i^t(\tau-)}{1 - G_i^t(\tau-)} \left[(1 - \alpha_j^t(\tau)) L(Y_\tau)\right.$$
$$\left. + \alpha_j^t(\tau) M(\tau)\right] + \left(1 - G_i^t(\tau-)\right) \frac{1 - G_i^t(\tau)}{1 - G_i^t(\tau-)} F(Y_\tau)$$
$$= \left(G_i^t(\tau) - G_i^t(\tau-)\right) F(Y_\tau) + \left(1 - G_i^t(\tau)\right) F(Y_\tau)$$
$$= \left(1 - G_i^t(\tau-)\right) F(Y_\tau).$$

So,

$$V_i(t, \tilde{s}^t) = \int_t^{T_P^t-} L(Y_s) dG_i^t(s) + \left(1 - G_i^t(T_P^t-)\right) F(Y_{T_P^t})$$
$$\leq F(Y_{T_P^t}).$$

3 $\tau_i = \tau_j$, $a_i \equiv \alpha_i^t(\tau) \neq \alpha_j^t(\tau) \equiv a_j$
   In this case we obtain that, given that firm j plays its equilibrium

strategy a_j,

$$W_i(t, \tilde{s}^t) = \frac{a_i(1-a_j)L(Y_\tau) + a_j(1-a_i)F(Y_\tau) + a_i a_j M(Y_\tau)}{a_i + a_j - a_i a_j}$$

$$= \frac{1}{a_i(L(Y_\tau) - M(Y_\tau)) + (1-a_i)(L(Y_\tau) - F(Y_\tau))}$$
$$\times \Big[a_i(F(Y_\tau) - M(Y_\tau))L(Y_\tau) + (1-a_i)(L(Y_\tau)$$
$$- F(Y_\tau))F(Y_\tau) + a_i(L(Y_\tau) - F(Y_\tau))M(Y_\tau) \Big]$$

$$= F(Y_\tau).$$

So,

$$V_i(t, \tilde{s}^t) = \int_t^{\tau^-} L(Y_s)dG_i^t(s) + \big(1 - G_i^t(\tau-)\big)F(Y_\tau)$$
$$\leq F(Y_{T_P^t}).$$

Therefore, we conclude that $V_i(t, \tilde{s}^t) \leq V_i(t, \bar{s}^t)$. Hence, $\bar{s}^t$ is an α-equilibrium for the subgame starting at time t.

The uniqueness result is proved in the following way. Let $t_0 \geq 0$ be the starting point of a subgame. We only consider symmetric strategies. First, we show that if $t \geq T_F^{t_0}$, then it should hold that $G^{t_0}(t) = \alpha^{t_0}(t) = 1$. Then we show that for $t < T_P^{t_0}$ it should hold that $G^{t_0}(t) = \alpha^{t_0}(t) = 0$. Thirdly, we show that $\tau = T_P^{t_0}$. Finally, we calculate the equilibrium value of $\alpha^{t_0}(\tau)$.

Let $t \geq T_F^{t_0}$ and suppose that in a symmetric equilibrium $\alpha^{t_0}(T_F^{t_0}) < 1$. Then there is a positive probability that no firm invests at time $T_F^{t_0}$. If a firm deviates and invests, it obtains $L(Y_{T_F^{t_0}})$, which is strictly larger than the value of waiting, since the optimal investment threshold, Y_L, is such that $Y_L < Y_F$ due to strict quasi-concavity of $L(\cdot) - F(\cdot)$. Hence, postponing investment reduces the value for a firm due to discounting and thus $\alpha^{t_0}(t) = 1$. Taking into account α-consistency this implies that for all $t \geq T_F^{t_0}$ we should have $\alpha^{t_0}(t) = G^{t_0}(t) = 1$.

If $t < T_P^{t_0}$ it is strictly dominant to set $G^{t_0}(t) = \alpha^{t_0}(t) = 0$. Suppose this strategy is not chosen. Then if a firm deviates it gets the leader role with positive probability, leading to a lower expected payoff since $F(Y_t) > L(Y_t)$.

Suppose $\tau > T_P^{t_0}$. The expected payoff at time τ for each firm is given by

$$\frac{1-\alpha}{2-\alpha}(L(Y_\tau) + F(Y_\tau)) + \frac{\alpha}{2-\alpha}M(Y_\tau).$$

Because of intertemporal consistency it should hold that τ is the stopping time for some value Y_S that satisfies $Y_S > Y_P$. Therefore, Y approaches Y_S from below on the interval $[t_0, \tau)$. Since Y has continuous sample paths and $L(Y_t) > F(Y_t)$ and $L(Y_t) > M(Y_t)$ for $t \in (T_P^{t_0}, T_F^{t_0})$, this implies that there exists an $\varepsilon > 0$ such that

$$\frac{(1-\alpha)(L(Y_\tau) + F(Y_\tau)) + \alpha M(Y_\tau)}{2-\alpha}$$
$$< \frac{2(1-\alpha)L(Y_{\tau-\varepsilon}) + \alpha L(Y_{\tau-\varepsilon})}{2-\alpha}$$
$$= L(Y_{\tau-\varepsilon}).$$

Hence, investing at $\tau - \varepsilon$, by which the payoff $L(Y_{\tau-\varepsilon})$ is obtained, gives a higher expected value. Therefore, $\alpha^{t_0}(T_P^{t_0}) > 0$. The corresponding jump in $G^{t_0}(T_P^{t_0})$ follows from α-consistency. At time $T_P^{t_0}$ at least one firm invests. By definition it is optimal for the follower to invest at $T_F^{t_0}$. Hence, for all $t \in (T_P^{t_0}, T_F^{t_0})$ it should hold that $G^{t_0}(t) = G^{t_0}(T_P^{t_0})$.

Finally, the atom at $T_P^{t_0}$ should be such as to simultaneously maximise for $i \in \{1, 2\}$ the expected value, which equals (cf. (4.4))

$$\frac{\alpha_i(1-\alpha_j)L(Y_{T_P^{t_0}}) + (1-\alpha_i)\alpha_j F(Y_{T_P^{t_0}}) + \alpha_i\alpha_j M(Y_{T_P^{t_0}})}{\alpha_i + \alpha_j - \alpha_i\alpha_j}, \qquad (4.13)$$

with respect to α_i. The first order conditions then read for $i \in \{1, 2\}$:

$$(\alpha_i + \alpha_j - \alpha_i\alpha_j)\Big((1-\alpha_j)L(Y_{T_P^{t_0}}) - \alpha_j F(Y_{T_P^{t_0}}) + \alpha_j M(Y_{T_P^{t_0}})\Big)$$
$$-(1-\alpha_j)\Big(\alpha_i(1-\alpha_j)L(Y_{T_P^{t_0}}) + (1-\alpha_i)\alpha_j F(Y_{T_P^{t_0}}) + \alpha_i\alpha_j M(Y_{T_P^{t_0}})\Big) = 0.$$

Imposing symmetry $\alpha_i = \alpha_j = \alpha$ yields

$$(1-\alpha)L(Y_{T_P^{t_0}}) - F(Y_{T_P^{t_0}}) + \alpha M(Y_{T_P^{t_0}}) = 0$$
$$\Longleftrightarrow \quad \alpha = \frac{L(Y_{T_P^{t_0}}) - F(Y_{T_P^{t_0}})}{L(Y_{T_P^{t_0}}) - M(Y_{T_P^{t_0}})}. \qquad (4.14)$$

The second order derivative of (4.13) with respect to α_i is given by

$$-\frac{2\alpha_j(1-\alpha_j)\big(\alpha_j M(Y_{T_P^{t_0}}) + (1-\alpha_j)(L(Y_{T_P^{t_0}}) + F(Y_{T_P^{t_0}}))\big)}{(\alpha_i + \alpha_j - \alpha_i\alpha_j)^3} < 0,$$

for all $\alpha_i, \alpha_j > 0$. Hence, the solution in (4.14) gives indeed a maximum.

$\square$

B.   Some Integrals

In this appendix we calculate some of the integrals that are used in the text. Let in the following $(Y_t)_{t\geq 0}$ be a geometric Brownian motion with starting point $Y_0 = y$. Let β_1 be the positive root of the quadratic equation $\frac{1}{2}\sigma^2\beta^2 + (\mu - \frac{1}{2}\sigma^2)\beta - r = 0$ and let D denote the instant payoff flow. Furthermore, let T_P and T_F be the stopping times of Y_P and Y_F, respectively, such that $T_P < T_F$ a.s. It can be obtained from Dixit and Pindyck (1996, Chapter 9) that

$$\mathbb{E}\left(e^{-rT_P}\right) = \left(\frac{y}{Y_P}\right)^{\beta_1},$$

and

$$\mathbb{E}\left(\int_0^{T_P} e^{-rt}Y_t D dt\right) = \frac{y}{r-\mu} - \left(\frac{y}{Y_P}\right)^{\beta_1}\frac{Y_P D}{r-\mu}.$$

Define $S(Y)$ for all $Y \leq Y_F$ by

$$S(Y) = \mathbb{E}\left(\int_{T_F}^{\infty} e^{-rt}Y_t D dt\right).$$

Suppose that $Y_t < Y_F$. Then, in a small time interval $[t, t+dt]$, Y_F will not be reached a.s. Therefore, because of the strong Markov property[15] of the geometric Brownian motion, $S(Y)$ should satisfy

$$S(Y) = e^{-rdt}\mathbb{E}\big(S(Y+dY)\big).$$

Rewriting gives

$$e^{-rdt}\mathbb{E}(dS) = 0. \tag{4.15}$$

Applying Ito's lemma[16] on the expectation results in

$$\mathbb{E}(dS) = \mathbb{E}\Big(\big[\mu Y S'(Y) + \tfrac{1}{2}\sigma^2 Y^2 S''(Y)\big]dt + \sigma Y S'(Y)dw\Big)$$
$$= [\mu Y S'(Y) + \tfrac{1}{2}\sigma^2 Y^2 S''(Y)]dt.$$

Using this result and a Taylor series expansion on e^{-rdt} at $-rdt = 0$, eq. (4.15) becomes

$$S(Y) = (1 - rdt + o(dt))\Big(S(Y) + \mu Y S'(Y) + \tfrac{1}{2}\sigma^2 Y^2 S''(Y)\Big)dt$$
$$\Longleftrightarrow \mu Y S'(Y)dt + \tfrac{1}{2}\sigma^2 Y^2 S''(Y)dt - rS(Y)dt + o(dt) = 0.$$

---

[15]See Section 7.1 of Chapter 2.
[16]idem.

Dividing by dt and letting $dt \downarrow 0$ results in the following second order differential equation

$$\mu Y S'(Y) + \tfrac{1}{2}\sigma^2 Y^2 S''(Y) - r S(Y) = 0.$$

The general solution of this equation is given by

$$S(Y) = A_1 Y^{\beta_1} + A_2 Y^{\beta_2},$$

where $\beta_1 > 1$ and $\beta_2 < 0$ are the roots of the characteristic equation

$$\tfrac{1}{2}\sigma^2 \beta^2 + (\mu - \tfrac{1}{2}\sigma^2)\beta - r = 0.$$

Note that if $Y \to 0$, then $dY \to 0$. This leads to the boundary condition $S(0) = 0$. Since $\beta_2 < 0$, this implies that $A_2 = 0$. Furthermore, if $Y \to Y_F$, then $T_F \downarrow 0$. Hence,

$$\lim_{Y \to Y_F} S(Y) = \mathbb{E}\left(\int_0^\infty e^{-rt} Y_t D dt \right)$$

$$= \frac{Y_F D}{r - \mu}.$$

Using this boundary condition, one obtains that $A_1 = Y_F^{-\beta_1}\frac{Y_F D}{r-\mu}$ and hence

$$\mathbb{E}\left(\int_{T_F}^\infty e^{-rt} Y_t D dt \right) = \left(\frac{y}{Y_F} \right)^{\beta_1} \frac{Y_F D}{r - \mu}.$$

Using this result we get

$$\mathbb{E}\left(\int_{T_P}^{T_F} e^{-rt} Y_t D dt \right) = \mathbb{E}\left(\int_{T_P}^\infty e^{-rt} Y_t D dt \right) - \mathbb{E}\left(\int_{T_F}^\infty e^{-rt} Y_t D dt \right)$$

$$= \frac{y^{\beta_1} D}{r - \mu}\left(Y_P^{1-\beta_1} - Y_F^{1-\beta_1} \right).$$

Chapter 5

THE EFFECTS OF INFORMATION ON STRATEGIC INVESTMENT

1. Introduction

Two main forces that influence a firm's investment decision are uncertainty about the profitability of the investment project and the behaviour of potential competitors, having an option to invest in the same project. In Chapter 3 the uncertainty aspect has been studied in the case of a single firm. In this chapter the influence of both uncertainty and competition on the strategic considerations of a firm's investment decision and the resulting welfare effects are investigated.

The framework that is used here assumes imperfect information that arrives stochastically over time. The informational structure in this chapter is identical to the one introduced in Chapter 3. So, as to the project only two states are possible: either the project is profitable or it yields a loss. Firms have an identical belief in the project being profitable. This belief is updated over time due to information that becomes available via signals that arrive according to a Poisson process. The signal can either be good or bad: in the first case it indicates that the project is profitable, whereas in the latter case investment yields a loss. However, the signals may not provide perfect information. With an exogenously given fixed probability the signal gives the correct information. For simplicity, it is assumed that the signals can be observed without costs. They can be thought of for example as arising from media or publicly available marketing research. As an example of the duopoly model with signals, consider two soccer scouts who are considering to contract a player. In order to obtain information on the player's quality both scouts go to matches in which the wanted player plays. If he performs well, this can be seen as a signal indicating high revenues, but if he performs poorly, this is a signal that the investment is not profitable. This induces an option value of waiting for more signals to arrive and hence getting a better approximation of the actual profitability of the project.

On the side of the economic fundamentals underlying the model it is assumed that there are both a first mover and a second mover advantage. The first mover effect results from a Stackelberg advantage obtained by the first investor. The second mover advantage arises, because after one of the firms has invested, the true state of the project becomes known to both firms. The firm that has not invested yet benefits form this in that it can take its investment decision under complete information. In this chapter it is shown that, depending on the prior beliefs on the profitability of the project and the magnitudes of the first and second mover advantages, either a preemption game or a war of attrition arises. The latter occurs if the information spillover exceeds the first mover Stackelberg effect. In the reverse case a preemption game arises. Even both types of games may occur in the same scenario: in a war of attrition there exists a positive probability that no firm undertakes the investment. Then it may happen – if enough good signals arrive – that at a certain point in time the first mover outweighs the information spillover, implying that a preemption game arises. It is shown that at the preemption point two things can happen in equilibrium. Firstly, one firm can invest while the other firm first waits to get the information spillover before it decides whether to invest or not. In this case the resulting market structure is a Stackelberg one. Secondly, both firms can invest simultaneously, thus resulting in e.g. a Cournot market. in that case both firms prefer a symmetrical situation in the output market above accepting the information spillover together with the Stackelberg disadvantage that is obtained upon investment by the competitor.

In this chapter it is shown that the presence of information streams and uncertainty concerning the profitability of a new market leads to hybrid welfare results. We investigate the impact of information on expected *ex ante* welfare. For the monopoly case it is found that welfare may in fact be decreasing in the quantity and quality of the signals. This is mainly due to the fact that when signals appear more frequently over time, or provide more reliable information, the option value of waiting for more information increases, which leads to investment at a later date, lowering consumer surplus. This result may extend to the duopoly case. One would expect that competitive pressure together with better information leads to earlier investment and thus to higher expected consumer surplus. There is, however, an opposite effect closely linked to the market structure. In equilibrium there is a certain probability that the actual outcome is a Stackelberg equilibrium. If this is the case and the market turns out to be bad there is only one firm that looses the sunk investment costs (namely the leader), while the follower will not invest at all. There is also a probability that the market ends up in a Cournot equilibrium with simultaneous investment at the preemption point. If the market turns out to be bad in this case there are two firms that loose the sunk investment costs. When more information is available, the information spillover is less valuable. This implies that a Cournot market will arise with a higher probability when the quality of information rises. In that case the resulting downward pressure on expected producer surplus (losing twice the sunk investment costs instead of once) might outweigh the increase in expected consumer surplus.

Secondly, simulations indicate that for low levels of quantity and quality of the signals a duopoly yields significantly higher levels of expected welfare. The intuition behind this result is straightforward. When the information stream is poor in both quantity and quality, the option value of waiting for a monopolist is low. Since for competing firms this value is already low due to competition, the standard dead-weight loss argument applies here. We also find, however, that with high levels of quantity and quality of the signals, monopoly leads to significantly higher welfare levels than a duopoly. This is because of two reasons. Firstly, duopoly stimulates preemption which is bad for welfare because a significant value of waiting exists in case the expected information gain per unit of time is large. Secondly, the possibility of simultaneous investment in a preemptive duopoly has a negative effect on expected producer surplus, because there exists a possibility that the project turns out to be bad. These effects are larger than the increase in expected consumer surplus.

Most of the literature on optimal investment deals with the effects of either uncertainty or competition. The real option theory concerns itself with investment decisions under uncertainty (cf. Dixit and Pindyck (1996)). In this literature nature chooses a state of the world at each point in time, influencing the profitability of the investment project. The problem is then to find an optimal threshold level of an underlying variable (e.g. price or output value of the firm), above which the investment should be undertaken. A recent contribution in this area dealing with technology adoption is Alvarez and Stenbacka (2001) who include the opportunity to update the technology with future superior versions.

In the strategic interaction literature a number of models have been developed, dealing with different situations such as patent races and technology adoption. In general, a distinction can be made between two types of models. Firstly, there are preemption games in which two firms try to preempt each other in investing (cf. Fudenberg and Tirole (1991)).

The equilibrium concept used in such games is developed in Fudenberg and Tirole (1985). Another class is the war of attrition, which is first introduced by Maynard Smith (1974) in the biological literature and later adopted for economic situations (cf. Tirole (1988)). Originally, the war of attrition describes two animals fighting over a prey. In an economic context one can think of two firms considering adopting a new technology. Both know that for one firm it would be optimal to invest, but neither wants to be the first to invest, since waiting for an even newer technology would be better. The equilibrium concept used in this type of game is introduced in Hendricks et al. (1988).

The literature combining both aspects is small indeed, see Grenadier (2000) for a survey. A first attempt to combine real option theory with timing games was made in Smets (1991). Huisman (2001) provides some extensions to this approach and applies this framework to technology adoption problems. Recent contributions include, e.g., Boyer et al. (2001) and Weeds (2002).

This chapter extends the strategic real options literature in the direction of imperfect information. Jensen (1982) was the first to introduce uncertainty and imperfect information in a one-firm-model dealing with technology adoption. In Mamer and McCardle (1987) the impact on the timing of innovation of costs, speed and quality of information arriving over time is studied for a one-firm model as well as a duopoly. However, due to an elaborate information structure, Mamer and McCardle (1987) did not obtain explicit results. Hoppe (2000) considers a duopoly framework in which it is *a priori* uncertain whether an investment project is profitable or not. The probability with which the project is profitable is exogenously given, fixed and common knowledge. As soon as one firm invests, the true profitability of the project becomes known. This creates informational spillovers that yield a second mover advantage.

The observation that a game of technology adoption under uncertainty is either a preemption game or a war of attrition dates back to Jensen (1992a). However, where Jensen (1992a) examines a two-stage adoption game, the present chapter provides an extension of these results to the case of an infinite horizon continuous time framework. Moreover, as has been mentioned before, in our framework both types of games can occur within the same scenario. The equilibrium concept that we use is discussed in detail in Chapter 4.

The present chapter is related to Décamps and Mariotti (2000) who also consider a duopoly model where signals arrive over time. Differences are that in Décamps and Mariotti (2000) only bad signals exist and that signals are perfectly informative. This means that after receiving one signal the game is over since the firms are sure that the project is not profitable, while in our framework it could still be possible that the project is good. In Décamps and Mariotti it holds that, as long as no signal arrives, the probability that the project is good continuously increases over time and the firms are assumed to be asymmetric, which also induces uncertainty regarding the players' types, whereas we consider identical firms. Furthermore, Décamps and Mariotti apply the Bayesian equilibrium concept, whereas in our model this is not the case. Another implication is that a coordination problem between the two firms that occurs in our framework is not present in Décamps and Mariotti (2000). This coordination problem concerns the issue of which firm will be the first to invest in the preemption equilibrium. Another duopoly paper where information arrives over time is Lambrecht and Perraudin (2003). There, the information relates to the behaviour of the competitor: each firm has a certain belief about when the other firm will invest and this belief is updated by observing the other firm's behaviour.

The chapter is organised as follows. In Section 2 the model is described. Then, in Section 3 we analyse the model for the scenario that the firm roles, i.e. leader and follower, are exogenously determined. In Section 4 the exogenous firm roles are dropped and the model is analysed for the case where the firms are completely symmetric. In Section 5 a welfare measure is introduced and welfare effects are discussed. Finally, in Section 6 some conclusions will be drawn.

2. The Model

The model presented in this section describes a new market situation where two identical firms have the opportunity to invest in a project with uncertain revenues. Time is continuous and indexed by $t \in [0, \infty)$. The project can be good (denoted by H) or bad (denoted by L). The firm that is the first to invest becomes the leader if the other firm does not invest at the same point in time. The other firm then automatically becomes the follower. A second possibility is that both firms invest at exactly the same point in time. After investment has taken place by at least one firm the state of the project becomes immediately known to both firms. Hence, this creates a second mover advantage. If the firms do not invest simultaneously, the follower decides on investment immediately after the true state of the project is revealed. It is assumed that this does not take any time. So, if one firm invests at time $t \geq 0$, the follower will either invest at time t as well or not invest at all. We distinguish this case from the case of mutual investment where both firms also invest at the same time $t \geq 0$, but without one of the firms having the second mover advantage.[1] That is, in case of mutual investment both firms are at the time of investment uncertain as to the true state of the project.

In case the project is good the leader's revenues equal $U_L^H > 0$. If the project is bad the leader's revenues equal $U_L^L = 0$. The sunk costs of investment are given by $I > 0$. If the project is good, the follower will immediately invest as well and get revenues $U_F^H > 0$. The follower will also incur the sunk costs I. It is assumed that $U_L^H > U_F^H > I$. Hence, there is a first mover advantage if the project turns out to yield high revenues and investment is profitable for both firms. If the project is bad the payoff for the follower equals $U_F^L = U_L^L = 0$. So, if the project is bad the follower observes this due to the second mover advantage and thus refrains from investment. This implies that in case of a bad project only the leader incurs a loss that is equal to the sunk costs of investment. To see who is in the best position, the leader or the follower, the second mover advantage has to be compared with the first mover advantage of being the leader.

If both firms invest simultaneously and the project turns out to be good, both receive $U_M^H > 0$, where $U_F^H < U_M^H < U_L^H$. The revenues can be seen as an infinite stream of payoffs π_j^i discounted at rate $r \in (0,1)$, i.e. $U_j^i = \int_0^\infty e^{-rt}\pi_j^i dt = \frac{1}{r}\pi_j^i$, $i = H,L$, $j = L,M,F$. Example 5.1 illustrates this framework.

EXAMPLE 5.1 *Consider a new market for a homogeneous good. Two firms have the opportunity to enter the market, that can be either good or bad. Let market demand be given by $P(Q) = Y - Q$ for some $Y > 0$ if the market is good (H) and by $P(Q) = 0$ if the market is bad (L). The cost function is given by $C(q) = cq$, for some $0 \le c \le Y$. It is assumed that if the firms invest they engage in quantity competition. If the market turns out to be bad, then the action to take is not to produce, i.e. $U_L^L = U_F^L = U_M^L = 0$. Suppose that there is one firm that invests in the market first. This firm then is the Stackelberg leader.[2] In case the market is good the follower solves the following profit maximisation*

---

[1] The assumption that the follower reacts immediately might seem unrealistic, but is not very restrictive. If for example there is a time lag between investment of the leader and the follower this only has an influence on the payoffs via extra discounting by the follower. The important point is that the game ends as soon as one firm has invested, because then the decision of the other firm is made as well. The fact that actual investment may take place at a later date is irrelevant.

[2] It is assumed that firms can only set capacity once, thereby fixing the production level forever. This resolves the commitment problem mentioned in Dixit (1980).

problem

$$\max_{q_F \geq 0} \frac{1}{r} q_F [P(q_L + q_F) - c],$$

where r is the discount rate. This yields $q_F = \frac{Y - c - q_L}{2}$. Using this reaction, the leader maximises its stream of profits. Solving the corresponding maximisation problem yields $q_L = \frac{Y-c}{2}$, which results in $q_F = \frac{Y-c}{4}$, and the payoffs $U_L^H = \frac{(Y-c)^2}{8r}$ and $U_F^H = \frac{(Y-c)^2}{16r}$, respectively. In case both firms invest simultaneously, the Cournot-Nash outcome prevails. Straightforward computations yield $U_M^H = \frac{(Y-c)^2}{9r}$. Note that $U_L^H > U_M^H > U_F^H$.[3]

It is assumed that both firms have an identical belief $p \in [0,1]$ in the project being good that is common knowledge. If the leader invests at a point in time where the belief in a good project equals p, the leader's *ex ante* expected payoff equals

$$L(p) = p(U_L^H - I) + (1-p)(-I) = pU_L^H - I.$$

The follower only invests in case of a good project. Therefore, if the leader invests when the belief in a good project equals p, the *ex ante* expected payoff for the follower equals

$$F(p) = p(U_F^H - I).$$

In case of mutual investment at belief p, each firm has an *ex ante* expected payoff that equals

$$M(p) = pU_M^H - I.$$

Define by p_M the belief such that the *ex ante* expected profit for the follower equals the *ex ante* expected profit of mutual investment, i.e. p_M is such that $F(p_M) = M(p_M)$. Note that, when $p \geq p_M$, both firms will always invest simultaneously, i.e. before the true state of the project is known, yielding payoffs

$$l(p) = \begin{cases} L(p) & \text{if } p < p_M, \\ M(p) & \text{if } p \geq p_M, \end{cases}$$

---

[3]For our framework it is not essential that the first mover has an infinite Stackelberg advantage. The main point is that it should be the case that the first mover has a higher discounted present value if the market is good. If for example after a certain point in time the market has a standard Cournot structure, then the discounted present value for the leader is still higher.

for the leader and

$$f(p) = \begin{cases} F(p) & \text{if } p < p_M, \\ M(p) & \text{if } p \geq p_M, \end{cases}$$

for the follower. A graphical representation of these payoffs is given in Figure 5.1.

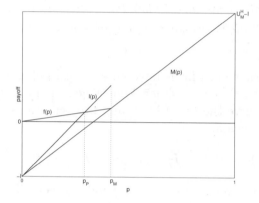

Figure 5.1. Payoff functions.

At the moment that the investment opportunity becomes available, both firms have an identical prior belief about the project yielding high revenues, say p_0, which is common knowledge. Occasionally, the firms obtain information in the form of signals about the profitability of the project. These signals are observed by both firms simultaneously and are assumed to arrive according to a Poisson process with parameter $\mu > 0$. Information arriving over time will in general be heterogeneous regarding the indication of the profitability level of the project. We distinguish two types of signals as in Chapter 3: a signal can either indicate high revenues (an h-signal) or low revenues (an l-signal). A signal revealing the true state of the project occurs with the common knowledge probability $\lambda > \frac{1}{2}$, see Table 5.1.[4]

Let n denote the number of signals and let g and b be the number of h-signals and l-signals, respectively, so that $n = g + b$. Given that at a certain point in time n signals have arrived, g of which were h-signals,

---

[4]Without loss of generality it can be assumed that $\lambda > \frac{1}{2}$, since if the converse holds we can redefine the h-signals to be l-signals and vice versa. Then a signal again reveals the true state of the project with probability $1 - \lambda > \frac{1}{2}$. If $\lambda = \frac{1}{2}$ the signal is uninformative and the problem becomes a deterministic one since the information arriving over time has no influence on the firms' decision processes.

	h	l
H	λ	$1 - \lambda$
L	$1 - \lambda$	λ

Table 5.1. Conditional probabilities of h- and l-signals.

the firms then calculate their belief in a good project in a Bayesian way. Define $k = 2g - n = g - b$, so that $k > 0$ ($k < 0$) indicates that more (less) h-signals than l-signals have arrived. After defining the prior odds of a bad project as $\zeta = \frac{1-p_0}{p_0}$, it is obtained from (3.1) that the belief in a good project is a function of k and is given by

$$p(k) = \frac{\lambda^k}{\lambda^k + \zeta(1 - \lambda)^k}.$$ (5.1)

Note that the inverse of this function gives the number of h-signals in excess of l-signals that is needed to obtain a belief equal to p. The inverse function equals

$$k(p) = \frac{\log(\frac{p}{1-p}) + \log(\zeta)}{\log(\frac{\lambda}{1-\lambda})}.$$ (5.2)

3.   Exogenous Firm Roles

Before we turn to the more interesting case where it is endogenously determined which firm invests first, we now look at the simpler case of exogenous firm roles. There are two cases. The former being that only firm 1 is allowed to be the first investor and the latter being the symmetric counterpart. Suppose that only firm 1 is allowed to be the first investor. Then, firm 1 does not need to take into account the possibility that firm 2 preempts. Firm 2 can choose between the follower role, i.e. waiting to incur the second mover advantage, and investing at the same time as firm 1, i.e. without waiting for the true state of the project to become known. These two cases can lead to different forms of competition. For example, in the first case firm 1 is the Stackelberg leader and in the second case quantity competition can lead to a Cournot-Nash equilibrium. Firm 1 should invest at the moment that its belief in a good project exceeds a certain threshold. From Chapter 3 it follows that this threshold belief, denoted by p_L, is given by (cf. (3.14))

$$p_L = \frac{1}{\Psi(U_L^H / I - 1) + 1},$$ (5.3)

where (cf. (3.15))

$$\Psi = \frac{\beta(r+\mu)(r+\mu(1-\lambda)) - \mu\lambda(1-\lambda)(r+\mu(1+\beta-\lambda))}{\beta(r+\mu)(r+\mu\lambda) - \mu\lambda(1-\lambda)(r+\mu(\beta+\lambda))},$$

and (cf. 3.9)

$$\beta = \frac{r+\mu}{2\mu} + \tfrac{1}{2}\sqrt{(\tfrac{r}{\mu}+1)^2 - 4\lambda(1-\lambda)}.$$

Hence, as soon as p exceeds p_L, the leader invests. Then, the follower immediately decides whether or not to invest, based on the true state of the project that is immediately revealed after the investment by the leader. Note that p_L will not be reached exactly, since the belief $p(k)$ jumps along with the discrete variable k. Hence, the leader invests when $p = p(\lceil k_L \rceil)$, where $k_L = k(p_L)$.

The above story only holds if $p(\lceil k_L \rceil) < p_M$. If the converse holds, firm 1 knows that firm 2 will not choose the follower role, but will invest immediately as well yielding U_M^H instead of U_L^H if the project turns out to be good. Therefore, the threshold in this case is equal to

$$\tilde{p}_L = \frac{1}{\Psi(U_M^H/I - 1) + 1}.$$

Note that since $U_L^H > U_M^H$ it holds that $\tilde{p}_L > p_L$.

When p_0 is contained in the region $(p_M, 1]$, both firms will immediately invest, yielding for both a discounted payoff stream $U_M^H - I$ if the project is good, and $-I$ if the project is bad. Here the belief is such that the follower prefers to receive the mutual investment payoff rather than being a follower, implying that it takes the risk of making a loss that equals the sunk costs of investment when the project value is low.

4.   Endogenous Firm Roles

Let the firm roles now be endogenous. This implies that both firms are allowed to be the first investor. Define the preemption belief, denoted by p_P, to be the belief at which $L(p_P) = F(p_P)$ (cf. Figure 5.1). This gives

$$p_P = \frac{I}{U_L^H - U_F^H + I}.$$

Note that $p_P < p_M$. As soon as p reaches p_P (if ever), both firms want to be the leader and try to preempt each other, which erodes the option value. It does not vanish completely, however, since $L(p_P) > 0$. Furthermore, define $k_P = k(p_P)$. For the analysis an important part is played by the positioning of k_L, which can be smaller or larger than k_P. Since the mapping $p \mapsto \dfrac{\log(\frac{p}{1-p})+\log(\zeta)}{\log(\frac{\lambda}{1-\lambda})}$ is monotonic it holds that

$$k_L > k_P \iff \Psi < \frac{U_L^H - U_F^H}{U_L^H - I}. \tag{5.4}$$

Note that if $k_L > k_P$ then $\lceil k_L \rceil \geq \lceil k_P \rceil$. The right-hand side of the second inequality in (5.4) can be seen as the relative price that the follower pays for waiting to obtain the information spillover if the market is good. Since Ψ decreases with λ and usually with μ (cf. Proposition 3.2), Ψ increases with the value of the information spillover. For if Ψ is low, then this implies that the quality and the quantity of the signals are relatively high. Therefore, if a firm becomes the leader it provides relatively less information to its competitor for low values of Ψ compared to when Ψ is high. So, expression (5.4) implies a comparison between the first mover advantage and the second mover advantage. In what follows we consider the two cases: $\lceil k_L \rceil \geq \lceil k_P \rceil$ and $\lceil k_L \rceil < \lceil k_P \rceil$.

4.1 Dominant First Mover Advantage

Suppose that $\lceil k_L \rceil \geq \lceil k_P \rceil$. This implies that firms try to preempt each other in investing in the project. We apply the equilibrium concept introduced in Fudenberg and Tirole (1985), which is extended for the present setting involving uncertainty in Chapter 4, to solve the game. The application of this equilibrium concept requires the use of several stopping times. Define for all starting points $t_0 \geq 0$, $T_P^{t_0} = \inf\{t \geq t_0 | p_t \geq p_P\}$ and $T_M^{t_0} = \inf\{t \geq t_0 | p_t \geq p_M\}$, where $p_t \equiv p(k_t)$ and k_t is the number of h-signals in excess of l-signals at time t. Note that $T_M^{t_0} \geq T_P^{t_0}$ a.s. for all $t_0 \geq 0$. In what follows we consider three different starting points, namely $p_{t_0} \geq p_M$, $p_P \leq p_{t_0} < p_M$ and $p_{t_0} < p_P$.

If $p_{t_0} \geq p_M$ the value of mutual investment is greater than or equal to the value of being the second investor. If $p_{t_0} > p_M$ this implies that no firm wants to be the follower and hence that both firms will invest immediately. If $p_{t_0} = p_M$ firms are indifferent between being the follower and simultaneous investment. Note that whether or not $p_M > p_L$ is irrelevant, since if it were not the case, then no firm would be willing to wait until p_L is reached, because of the sheer fear of being preempted by the other firm.

Next, let $p_P \leq p_{t_0} < p_M$ be the starting point of the game. Both firms try to preempt in this scenario, since the value for the leader is higher than the value for the follower. This implies that in a symmetric equilibrium[5] each firm invests with a positive probability. Here both firms want to be the first investor, since the expected Stackelberg leader payoff is sufficiently large, or the belief in a good project is sufficiently high, so that it is optimal to take the risk that the project has a low payoff. On the other hand, if the firms invest with positive probability, the probability that both firms simultaneously invest is also positive. This would lead to the mutual investment payoff. However, this payoff is not large enough for simultaneous investment as such to be optimal since $t_0 < T_M^{t_0}$. We conclude that there is a trade-off here between the probability of being the leader on the one hand and the probability of (a suboptimal) simultaneous investment on the other hand. As is proved in Proposition 5.1 below, the intensity with which the firms invest equals $\frac{L(p)-F(p)}{L(p)-M(p)}$. Hence, this intensity increases with the first mover advantage and decreases with the difference between the leader and the mutual investment payoff. The latter makes sense because if this difference is large the firms will try to avoid simultaneous investment by lowering their investment intensity.

From Chapter 4 we know that it is optimal if one of the two firms invests as soon as the preemption region is reached. This means that if this happens the game depicted in Figure 4.1 is played. Hence, since immediately after investment by the leader the follower decides on investment, the game ends exactly at the point in time where the preemption region is reached. Again, the position of p_L is of no importance, since the leader curve lies above the follower curve, implying that both firms will try to become the leader.

The last region is the region where $p_{t_0} < p_P$. As long as $t_0 \leq t < T_P^{t_0}$, the leader curve lies under the follower curve, and since in this case $k_L \geq k_P$, p_L has not been reached yet. Hence, no firm wants to be the leader and both firms abstain from investment until enough h-signals have arrived to make investment more attractive than waiting.

Formally, the above discussion can be summarised in a consistent α-equilibrium. This equilibrium concept for game theoretic real option models is described in detail in Section 2. The strategies used in these timing games consist of a function $G^{t_0}(\cdot)$, where $G_i^{t_0}(t)$ gives the probability that firm i has invested before and including time $t \geq t_0$, and an intensity function $\alpha^{t_0}(\cdot)$. The intensity function serves as an endogenous

---

[5]Since the firms are identical, a symmetric equilibrium seems to be the most plausible candidate. See Footnote 11 in Chapter 4 for a more elaborate discussion of this point.

coordination device in cases where it is optimal for one firm to invest but not for both. In coordinating firms make a trade-off between succeeding in investing first and the risk of both investing at the same time.

PROPOSITION 5.1 *If* $\Psi \leq \frac{U_L^H - U_F^H}{U_L^H - I}$, *then a symmetric consistent α-equilibrium is given by the tuple of closed-loop strategies* $\left((G_1^t, \alpha_1^t), (G_2^t, \alpha_2^t)\right)_{t \in [0,\infty)}$, *where for* $i = 1, 2$

$$
G_i^t(s) = \begin{cases} 0 & \text{if } s < T_P^t, \\ \dfrac{L(p_{T_P^t}) - M(p_{T_P^t})}{L(p_{T_P^t}) - 2M(p_{T_P^t}) + F(p_{T_P^t})} & \text{if } T_P^t \leq s < T_M^t, \\ 1 & \text{if } s \geq T_M^t, \end{cases} \tag{5.5}
$$

$$
\alpha_i^t(s) = \begin{cases} 0 & \text{if } s < T_P^t, \\ \dfrac{L(p_{T_P^t}) - F(p_{T_P^t})}{L(p_{T_P^t}) - M(p_{T_P^t})} & \text{if } T_P^t \leq s < T_M^t, \\ 1 & \text{if } s \geq T_M^t. \end{cases} \tag{5.6}
$$

For a proof of this proposition, see Appendix A.

4.2   Dominant Second Mover Advantage

Suppose that $p_L < p_P$. Now the problem becomes somewhat different. Let $t_0 \geq 0$. For $t > T_P^{t_0}$ the game is exactly the same as in the former case. The difference arises if $t \geq t_0$ is such that $p_t \in [p_L, p_P)$. In this region it would have been optimal to invest for the leader in case the leader role had been determined exogenously. However, since the leader role is endogenous and the leader curve lies below the follower curve, both firms prefer to be the follower. In other words, a war of attrition (cf. Hendricks et al. (1988)) arises. Two asymmetric equilibria of the war of attrition arise trivially: firm 1 invests always with probability one and firm 2 always with probability zero, and vice versa. However, since the firms are assumed to be identical there is no *a priori* reason to expect that they coordinate on one of these asymmetric equilibria.

We know that the game ends as soon as $T_P^{t_0}$ is reached. Note however that before this happens p_L can be reached several times, depending on the arrival of h- and l-signals. Note that p only changes if a new signal arrives. There is a war of attrition for $k \in K = \{\lceil k_L \rceil, \ldots, \lceil k_P \rceil - 1\}$. To keep track of the points in time where a war of attrition occurs, define the following increasing sequence of stopping times: $T_1^{t_0} = \inf\{t \geq t_0 | p_t = \lceil p_L \rceil\}$, $T_{n+1}^{t_0} = \inf\{t > T_n^{t_0} | \exists_{k \in K, k \neq k_{T_n^{t_0}}} : p_t = p(k)\}$, $n = 1, 2, 3, \ldots$, with the corresponding levels of h-signals in excess of l-signals $k_n = k(p_{T_n^{t_0}})$. Note that n is the number of signals that have arrived up until and including time $T_n^{t_0}$ since the first time the war of attrition region has been reached.

To find a symmetric equilibrium we argue in line with Fudenberg and Tirole (1991) that for a symmetric equilibrium it should hold that for each point in time, the expected revenue of investing directly equals the value of waiting a small period of time dt and investing when a new signal arrives.[6] The expected value of investing at each point in time depends on the value of k at that point in time. Let $k_t \in K$ for some $t \geq t_0$. Denoting the probability that the other firm invests at belief $p(k_t)$ by $\gamma(k_t)$, the expected value of investing at time t equals

$$V_1(p_t) = \gamma(k_t)M(p_t) + (1 - \gamma(k_t))L(p_t). \qquad (5.7)$$

The value of waiting for an infinitesimal small amount of time equals the weighted value of becoming the follower and of both firms waiting, i.e.

$$V_2(p_t) = \gamma(k_t)F(p_t) + (1 - \gamma(k_t))\tilde{V}(p_t), \qquad (5.8)$$

where $\tilde{V}(p)$ is the value of waiting when both firms do so. Let $\gamma(\cdot)$ be such that $V_1(\cdot) = V_2(\cdot)$.

To actually calculate $\gamma(k)$ for all $k \in K$, we use the fact that only for certain values of p the probability of investment needs to be calculated. These probabilities are the beliefs that result from the signals, i.e. for the beliefs p such that $p = p(k)$, $k \in K$. For notational convenience we take k as dependent variable instead of p. For example, we write $V(k)$ instead of $V(p(k))$. To calculate the isolated atoms – the probabilities of investment – in the war of attrition, $\gamma(\cdot)$, the value of waiting $\tilde{V}(\cdot)$ needs to be determined. It is governed by the following equation:

$$\tilde{V}(k) = e^{-rdt}\{(1 - \mu dt)\tilde{V}(k) + \mu dt[p(k)(\lambda V_1(k+1) + (1-\lambda)V_1(k-1)) +$$
$$+ (1 - p(k))(\lambda V_1(k-1) + (1-\lambda)V_1(k+1))]\}.$$
$$(5.9)$$

Eq. (5.9) arises from equalising the value of $\tilde{V}(k)$ to the value an infinitesimally small amount of time later. In this small time interval, nothing happens with probability $1 - \mu dt$. With probability μdt a signal arrives. The belief a firm has in a good project is given by $p(k)$. If the project is indeed good, an h-signal arrives with probability λ, and an l-signal arrives with probability $1 - \lambda$. Vice versa if the project is bad. If a signal arrives then investing yields either $V_1(k+1)$ or $V_1(k-1)$. After

---

[6]It might seem strange that a firm then also invests when a bad signal arrives. Note however that it is always optimal for one firm to invest in the war of attrition region.

letting $dt \downarrow 0$ and substituting eqs. (5.1) and (5.7) into eq. (5.9) it is obtained that

$$\tilde{V}(k) = \frac{\mu}{r+\mu} \Big[\frac{\lambda^{k+1} + \zeta(1-\lambda)^{k+1}}{\lambda^k + \zeta(1-\lambda)^k} \big(\gamma(k+1)M(k+1) + (1-\gamma(k+1)) \big.$$

$$L(k+1)\big) + \lambda(1-\lambda) \frac{\lambda^{k-1} + \zeta(1-\lambda)^{k-1}}{\lambda^k + \zeta(1-\lambda)^k} \big(\gamma(k-1)M(k-1) \big.$$

$$+ (1-\gamma(k-1))L(k-1)\big) \Big].$$

$$(5.10)$$

Substituting eq. (5.10) into eq. (5.8) yields, after equating eqs. (5.8) and (5.7) and rearranging:

$$a_k \gamma(k) + b_k = (1 - \gamma(k))(c_k \gamma(k+1) + d_k \gamma(k-1) + e_k), \qquad (5.11)$$

where

$$a_k = M(k) - L(k) - F(k),$$

$$b_k = L(k),$$

$$c_k = \frac{\mu}{r+\mu} \frac{\lambda^{k+1} + \zeta(1-\lambda)^{k+1}}{\lambda^k + \zeta(1-\lambda)^k} \big(M(k+1) - L(k+1) \big),$$

$$d_k = \frac{\mu}{r+\mu} \lambda(1-\lambda) \frac{\lambda^{k-1} + \zeta(1-\lambda)^{k-1}}{\lambda^k + \zeta(1-\lambda)^k} \big(M(k-1) - L(k-1) \big),$$

$$e_k = \frac{\mu}{r+\mu} \Big(\frac{\lambda^{k+1} + \zeta(1-\lambda)^{k+1}}{\lambda^k + \zeta(1-\lambda)^k} L(k+1)$$

$$+ \lambda(1-\lambda) \frac{\lambda^{k-1} + \zeta(1-\lambda)^{k-1}}{\lambda^k + \zeta(1-\lambda)^k} L(k-1) \Big).$$

To solve for $\gamma(\cdot)$ note that if $k < \lceil k_L \rceil$, no firm will invest, since the option value of waiting is higher than the expected revenues of investing. Therefore $\gamma(\lceil k_L \rceil) = 0$. On the other hand, if $k \geq \lceil k_P \rceil$ the firms know that they enter a preemption game, i.e. $\gamma(\lceil k_P \rceil) = G_i^t(T_P^t)$, where $G_i^t(T_P^t)$ can be obtained from Proposition 5.1. Note that it is possible that $\lceil k_P \rceil = \lceil k_M \rceil$. Then the game proceeds from the war of attrition directly into the region where mutual investment is optimal. This happens if $T_M^t = T_P^t$. In this case the expected payoff is governed by $M(\cdot)$. For other values of k, we have to solve a system of equations, where the k-th entry is given by eq. (5.11). The complete system is given by

$$\text{diag}(\gamma)\mathbf{A}\gamma + \mathbf{B}\gamma = \mathbf{b}, \qquad (5.12)$$

where diag$(\cdot)$ is the diagonal operator, $\gamma = (\gamma(\lceil k_L \rceil - 1), \ldots, \gamma(\lceil k_P \rceil))$, $\mathbf{b} = (0, e_{\lceil k_L \rceil} - b_{\lceil k_L \rceil}, \ldots, e_k - b_k, \ldots, e_{\lceil k_P \rceil - 1} - b_{\lceil k_P \rceil - 1}, 1)$,

$$
\mathbf{A} = \begin{bmatrix}
0 & \cdots\cdots\cdots\cdots\cdots\cdots\cdots\cdots\cdots\cdots\cdots\cdots & 0 \\
d_{\lceil k_L \rceil} & 0 & c_{\lceil k_L \rceil} & 0 & \cdots\cdots\cdots\cdots & 0 \\
\vdots & \ddots & \ddots & \ddots & & \vdots \\
0 & \cdots & d_k & 0 & c_k & \cdots & 0 \\
\vdots & & \ddots & \ddots & \ddots & & \vdots \\
0 & \cdots\cdots\cdots\cdots & 0 & d_{\lceil k_P \rceil - 1} & 0 & c_{\lceil k_P \rceil - 1} \\
0 & \cdots\cdots\cdots\cdots\cdots\cdots\cdots\cdots\cdots\cdots\cdots & 0
\end{bmatrix},
$$

and $\mathbf{B} =$

$$
\begin{bmatrix}
1 & 0 & \cdots\cdots\cdots\cdots\cdots\cdots\cdots\cdots\cdots\cdots\cdots\cdots & 0 \\
-d_{\lceil k_L \rceil} & a_{\lceil k_L \rceil} + e_{\lceil k_L \rceil} & -c_{\lceil k_L \rceil} & \cdots\cdots\cdots\cdots\cdots\cdots\cdots\cdots & 0 \\
\vdots & & \ddots & & & \vdots \\
0 & \cdots & -d_k & a_k + e_k & -c_k & \cdots & 0 \\
\vdots & & & \ddots & & & \vdots \\
0 & \cdots\cdots\cdots\cdots\cdots & -d_{\lceil k_P \rceil - 1} & a_{\lceil k_P \rceil - 1} + e_{\lceil k_P \rceil - 1} & -c_{\lceil k_P \rceil - 1} \\
0 & \cdots\cdots\cdots\cdots\cdots\cdots & 0 & 1
\end{bmatrix}.
$$

The system of equations (5.12) cannot be solved analytically. However, for any specific set of parameter values, a numerical solution can be determined. The following lemma shows that a solution always exists. The proof can be found in Appendix B.

LEMMA 5.1 *The system of equations (5.12) has a solution. Furthermore, $\gamma(k) \in [0,1]$ for all $k \in K$.*

Define $n_t = \sup\{n | T_n^{t_0} \le t\}$ to be the number of signals that has arrived up until time $t \ge t_0$. In the following proposition a symmetric consistent α-equilibrium is stated.

PROPOSITION 5.2 *If $\Psi > \frac{U_L^H - U_F^H}{U_L^H - I}$, then a consistent α-equilibrium is given by the tuple of closed-loop strategies $\left((G_1^t, \alpha_1^t), (G_2^t, \alpha_2^t)\right)_{t \in [0,\infty)}$,* *where for* $i = 1, 2$

$$
G_i^t(s) = \begin{cases} 0 & \text{if } s < T_1^t \\ \sum_{n=n_t}^{n_s} \frac{\gamma(k_n)}{1-\gamma(k_n)} \prod_{n'=n_t}^n \left(1 - \gamma(k_{n'})\right) & \text{if } T_1^t \le s < T_P^t, \\ \left(1 - G_i^t(T_P^t-)\right) \frac{L(p_{T_P^t})-M(p_{T_P^t})}{L(p_{T_P^t})-2M(p_{T_P^t})+F(p_{T_P^t})} & \text{if } T_P^t \le s < T_M^t, \\ 1 & \text{if } s \ge T_M^t, \\ & \text{or } s > T_P^t \text{ and } H, \end{cases}
$$

(5.13)

$$
\alpha_i^t(s) = \begin{cases} 0 & \text{if } s < T_P^t, \\ \frac{L(p_{T_P^t})-F(p_{T_P^t})}{L(p_{T_P^t})-M(p_{T_P^t})} & \text{if } T_P^t \le s < T_M^t, \\ 1 & \text{if } s \ge T_M^t. \end{cases}
$$

(5.14)

The proof of Proposition 5.2 can be found in Appendix C.

An illustration of the case where the second mover advantage outweighs the first mover advantage can be found in the following example.

EXAMPLE 5.2 *As an example consider a situation whose characteristics are given in Table 5.2. For this example the preemption belief is given by*

$U_L^H = 13.3$	$r = 0.1$
$U_F^H = 13$	$\mu = 2$
$U_M^H = 13.2$	$\lambda = 0.7$
$I = 2$	$p_0 = 0.5$

Table 5.2. Parameter values.

$p_P = 0.87$. *The minimal belief that an exogenous leader needs to invest optimally is given by* $p_L = 0.51$. *Using eq. (5.2) this implies that a war of attrition arises for* $k \in \{1, 2\}$. *Solving the system of equations given in (5.12) yields the vector of probabilities with which each firm invests in the project. It yields* $\gamma(1) = 0.4547$ *and* $\gamma(2) = 0.7613$.

From this example one can see that the probability of investment increases rapidly and is substantial. Both firms know that, given that the project is good, it is better to become the leader. So, as the belief in a good project increases, both firms invest with higher probability.

5. Welfare Analysis

Welfare effects resulting from investment under uncertainty have been reported by e.g. Jensen (1992b) and Stenbacka and Tombak (1994). In both papers the timing of investment does not depend on the arrival of signals. In these papers the uncertainty comprises the time needed to successfully implement the investment, i.e. the time between investment and the successful implementation of the investment is stochastic. The models in Jensen (1992b) and Stenbacka and Tombak (1994) allow for the critical levels to be explicit points in time. In our model, the critical level is not measured in units of time but measured as a probability, i.e. a belief. To perform a welfare analysis, however, it is necessary to incorporate the time element in the model.

Suppose for the sake of convenience that $p_0 < p_P < p_L$, i.e. a symmetric consistent α-equilibrium of this game is given in Proposition 5.1. This equilibrium implies that as soon as $\lceil k_P \rceil$ is reached, at least one firm invests and the game ends. Given the belief in a good project $p \in [p_P, p_M)$, the probability of mutual investment, denoted by $b(p)$, is given by (cf. (4.2)).

$$b(p) = \frac{L(p) - F(p)}{L(p) - 2M(p) + F(p)}.$$

Let CS_M^l denote the discounted value of consumer surplus if the project is $l \in \{L, H\}$ and simultaneous investment takes place. Furthermore, let CS_S^H and CS^L denote the infinite discounted stream of consumer surplus in the Stackelberg equilibrium if the project is good, and the infinite discounted stream of consumer surplus if the project is bad and one firm invests, respectively.

If the critical number of h-signals in excess of l-signals is given by $k \geq 0$ with first passage time t, the expected discounted total surplus if the project gives high revenues is given by

$$ES^H(k,t) = e^{-rt}\Big[(b \circ p)(k)(2U_M^H + CS_M^H)$$
$$+ \big(1 - (b \circ p)(k)\big)(U_L^H + U_F^H + CS_S^H) - 2I\Big],$$

whereas if the project gives a low revenue the expected total surplus equals

$$ES^L(k,t) = e^{-rt}\Big[(b \circ p)(k)(CS_M^L - 2I) + \big(1 - (b \circ p)(k)\big)(CS^L - I)\Big].$$

The expected total surplus with critical level k and first passage time t is then given by

$$W(k,t) = p(k)ES^H(k,t) + (1 - p(k))ES^L(k,t).$$

So far, there is no difference with the ideas in Jensen (1992b) and Stenbacka and Tombak (1994). To incorporate the uncertainty regarding the first passage time through k, we define the *ex ante* expected total surplus $W(k)$ to be the expectation of $W(k,t)$ over the first passage time through k. That is,

$$W(k) = \mathbb{E}_k\big(W(k,t)\big)$$
$$= \int_0^\infty W(k,t)f_k(t)dt, \qquad (5.15)$$

where $f_k(\cdot)$ is the pdf of the first passage time through k.

Denote the modified Bessel function with parameter ρ by $I_\rho(\cdot)$, i.e.

$$I_\rho(x) = \sum_{l=0}^\infty \frac{1}{l!\Gamma(l+\rho+1)} \left(\frac{x}{2}\right)^{2l+\rho},$$

where $\Gamma(\cdot)$ denotes the gamma function. The pdf of the first passage time through $k \geq 0$ can now be established as is done in the following proposition, the proof of which can be found in Appendix D.

PROPOSITION 5.3 *Let $k_0 = 0$ a.s. The probability density function $f_k(\cdot)$ of the first passage time through $k \geq 0$ is given by*

$$f_k(t) = \frac{\lambda^k+\zeta(1-\lambda)^k}{1+\zeta}\big(\lambda(1-\lambda)\big)^{-k/2}\frac{k}{t}I_k(2\mu\sqrt{\lambda(1-\lambda)}t)e^{-\mu t},$$

for all $t \geq 0$.

From the standard theory of industrial organization it is well-known that monopoly gives lower social welfare than competition. However, in the following example it is shown that in the presence of uncertainty this need not hold. In the remainder let CS_{mon} and W_{mon} denote the present value of the infinite flow of consumer surplus and the *ex ante* expected total surplus, respectively, in the case of a monopolist. The critical level of investment for the monopoly case is obtained from Chapter 3 (cf. (3.14) and (3.15)). We use the economic situation described in Example 5.1, i.e. a new market model with affine inverse demand and linear costs. Consider the parametrisation as given in Table 5.3. From Example 5.1 we can conclude that the monopoly price

$Y = 5$	$r = 0.1$
$c = 2$	$p_0 = 0.4$
$I = 5$	

Table 5.3. Parameter values.

is given by $P_{mon} = \frac{Y+c}{2}$, the price in case of mutual investment is

given by $P_M = \frac{Y+2c}{3}$, and the price in the Stackelberg case is given by
$P_S = \frac{Y+3c}{4}$. Given that the market is good, the flow of consumer surplus
is then given by $\int_{P_P}^{Y} P^{-1}(p)dp = \frac{1}{2}(Y-P_P)^2$, where P_P is the equilibrium
price. Hence, $CS_{mon}^H = \int_0^\infty e^{-rt}\frac{1}{2}(Y - P_{mon})^2 dt = \frac{(Y-P_{mon})^2}{8r}$. Similarly,
$CS_M^H = \frac{(Y-P_M)^2}{6r}$, $CS_S^H = \frac{(Y-P_S)^2}{32r}$, and $CS_{mon}^L = CS_M^L = CS^L = 0$.

We want to analyse the effect of the quantity and quality of information on welfare in both the monopolistic and the duopoly case. First, consider the case where $\lambda = 0.6$ and μ varies from 2 up to 5. Calculations lead to Figure 5.2. As can be seen from the figure, one cannot derive a

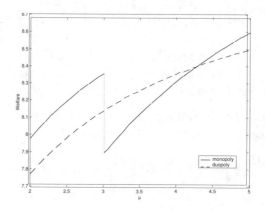

Figure 5.2.   Welfare as a function of μ.

clear-cut result saying that competition is better than monopoly ore vice versa. The main effect at work here is due to the discreteness of the investment threshold. In the duopoly case a Stackelberg equilibrium arises for all values of μ. The investment threshold equals $\lceil k_d \rceil = 1$. Welfare increases, because more information is (in this case) better. The jump in the curve for welfare under monopoly occurs because at $\mu \approx 3$ the investment threshold $\lceil k_m \rceil$ jumps from 1 to 2. This happens since k_m is increasing in μ, but $\lceil k_m \rceil$ is not for a certain range of values. As soon as there is a jump, the monopolist waits longer, which reduces expected consumer surplus.

Secondly, we analyse the effect of the quality of information on welfare by taking $\mu = 4$ and by letting λ vary from 0.55 to 0.8. This yields Figure 5.3. This case is even less clear-cut than the former. The jumps occur due to discreteness of the investment threshold just as before. We will describe monopoly and duopoly separately to get some feeling for the different effects at work. First, we consider the monopoly case, since it is the easier case. At $\lambda \approx 0.575$ $\lceil k_m \rceil$ jumps form 1 to 2, which accounts

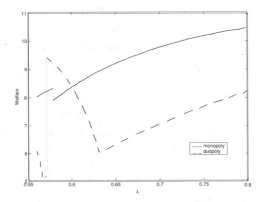

Figure 5.3. Welfare as a function of λ.

for the drop in welfare. For the rest, an increase in λ reduces the risk of investment while the market is good, which results in increasing welfare levels.

In the duopoly case there are more effects. The jump at $\lambda \approx 0.57$ occurs since $\lceil k_d \rceil$ jumps from 2 to 1, due to competitive pressure. This is good for consumer surplus, thence the increase. For λ between 0.57 and 0.635, a Stackelberg equilibrium arises. Welfare decreases over this range since for increasing λ the probability of simultaneous investment at the preemption point increases monotonically. Therefore, the expected loss (due to sunk investment costs) in case the market turns out to be bad is increasing in λ which has a negative effect on welfare. From $\lambda \approx 0.635$ onwards, a Nash equilibrium arises where both firms always invest simultaneous. For higher λ this means that the probability of a bad market is smaller, which increases expected welfare, although the welfare level is lower than under monopoly.

A final remark concerns the range where λ is in between 0.55 and 0.65. Here $\lceil k_m \rceil = 1$ and $\lceil k_d \rceil = 2$, i.e. in a monopolistic market investment takes place at an earlier date than in a duopoly, given an identical sample path of the information process. This is due to the fact that the discounted value of the project is higher for a monopolist than for a firm that faces competition. This higher discounted value has a dampening effect on the waiting time.

In the above analysis only the preemption case is considered. From a mathematical point of view the advantage of considering the preemption case is that one knows that the game stops as soon as the preemption level is reached. This allows for the use of the distribution of the first passage time in the definition of *ex ante* expected total surplus. In case the information spillover outweighs the Stackelberg effect a war of attrition arises. To make a comparable welfare analysis for this case one has to consider all possible paths for the arrival of signals. So, not only the distribution for the first passage time, but also the distribution of all passage times have to be considered, conditional on the fact that the preemption value is not reached. Such an analysis is not analytically tractable. However, one could estimate the *ex ante* expected total surplus by use of simulations. Also in this case ambiguous results regarding the welfare effects of monopoly and duopoly can be expected, depending on the position of the critical investment level for a monopolist relative to p_L. An additional effect concerning the welfare comparison of monopoly and duopoly in case of a war of attrition is the free rider effect. In a duopoly both firms like the other to invest first so that it does not need to take the risk that the project has low value. Consequently firms invest too late, leading to a lower consumer surplus.

6.   Conclusions

Non-exclusivity is a main feature that distinguishes real options from their financial counterparts (Zingales (2000)). A firm having a real investment opportunity often shares this possibility with one or more competitors and this has a negative effect on profits. The implication is that, to come to a meaningful analysis of the value of a real option, competition must be taken into account.

This chapter considers a duopoly where both firms have the same possibility to invest in a new market with uncertain payoffs. As time passes uncertainty is gradually resolved by the arrival of new information regarding the quality of the investment project in the form of signals. Generally speaking, each firm has the choice of being the first or second investor. A firm moving first reaches a higher market share by having a Stackelberg advantage. However, being the second investor implies that the investment can be undertaken knowing the payoff with certainty, since by observing the performance in the market of the first investor it is possible to obtain full information regarding the quality of the investment project.

The outcome mainly depends on the speed at which information arrives over time. If the quality and quantity of the signals is sufficiently high, the information advantage of the second investor is low so that the Stackelberg advantage of the first investor dominates, which always results in a preemption game. In the other scenario, initially a war of attrition prevails where it is preferred to wait for the competitor to undertake the risky investment. During the time where this war of attrition goes on it happens with positive probability that both firms refrain from investment. It can then be the case that so many bad signals arrive that the belief in a good project again becomes so low that the war of attrition is ended and that no firm invests for the time being. On the other hand, it can happen that so many positive signals in excess of bad signals arrive that at some point in time the Stackelberg advantage starts to exceed the value of the information spillover. This then implies that the war of attrition turns into a preemption game.

From the industrial organisation literature it is known that a monopoly is bad for social welfare. In our model the welfare issue is more complicated, mainly because we look at expected *ex ante* social welfare. We find evidence that a duopolistic market structure is more desirable in cases where there is few and qualitatively poor information. On the other hand, a monopolistic market structure is better if quantity and quality of information are high. The main reasons for this conclusion are, firstly, the low expected producer surplus in the duopoly case due to a high probability of simultaneous investment, resulting in a higher probability that both firms loose the sunk investment costs. Secondly, if a lot of information arrives over time (in expectation) the value of postponing investment increases. However, in a duopoly framework the presence of competition still makes that investment takes place soon. Furthermore, we show that more or better information does not necessarily lead to higher expected welfare. In the monopoly case this is mainly due to the fact that, again, more signals arriving over time raises the value of waiting. Therefore, the monopolist delays investment, which is bad for consumer surplus. In the duopoly case the resulting equilibrium market structure (Stackelberg or Cournot) plays an important role.

Finally, departing from the modelling framework of this chapter two interesting topics for future research can be distinguished. Firstly, one could include the possibility for firms to invest in the quantity and quality of the signals. This would then give rise to an optimal R&D model, that also includes the problem of optimal sampling. Secondly, it is interesting to allow for entry and exit in this model. This would then lead to an analysis of the optimal number of firms from a social welfare perspective, thereby making it possible to compare with existing literature like e.g. Mankiw and Whinston (1986).

Appendix

A.   Proof of Proposition 5.1

Let $(\Omega, \mathcal{F}, (\mathcal{F}_t)_{t \geq 0}, P)$ be the filtered probability space underlying the stochastic process governing the arrival of signals. First notice that for each $\omega \in \Omega$ and $i = 1, 2$, the strategy $(G_i^t, \alpha_i^t)_{t \in [0, \infty)}$ satisfies the intertemporal consistency and α-consistency conditions of Definitions 4.4 and 4.2, respectively. Hence, the closed-loop strategies are well-defined. Let $t \in [0, \infty)$. It will be shown that $(G_i^t, \alpha_i^t)_{i=1,2}$ is an α-equilibrium for the game starting at t. Due to discounting, it is a dominant strategy to invest with positive probability only at points in time when new information arrives. Since p_t has non-continuous sample paths, due to the Poisson arrivals of signals, the function $G^t(\cdot)$ has to be a step function. We consider three cases.

1 $t = T_M^t$ (i.e. $p_t \geq p_M$)
   Given that firm j plays its closed-loop strategy, firm i has three possible strategies. First, firm i can play $G_i^t(t) = 0$, i.e. it does not invest. Then firm i's expected payoff equals $F(p_t)$. If firm i invests with an isolated atom equal to $\nu > 0$, then the expected payoff equals $F(p_t) + \nu(M(p_t) - F(p_t)) \geq F(p_t)$. Finally, suppose that $\alpha_i^t(t) = a > 0$. Using the theory from Chapter 4 and the probabilities in (4.2) and (4.7) one can see that, since $\alpha_j^t(t) = 1$, the expected payoff for firm i is given by

$$\tfrac{1}{a + \alpha_j^t(t) - a\alpha_j^t(t)}\Big(a(1 - \alpha_j^t(t))L(p_t) + (1 - a)\alpha_j^t(t)F(p_t) + a\alpha_j^t(t)M(p_t)\Big)$$
$$= F(p_t) + a(M(p_t) - F(p_t)) \geq F(p_t).$$

   So, maximising the expected payoff gives $a = 1$.

2 $t < T_P^t$ (i.e. $p_t < p_P$)
   Given the strategy of firm j, if firm i does not invest, its value is $W(p_t)$. Since $T_L \geq T_P$, we know it is not optimal to invest yet. Hence, $W(p_t) > L(p_t)$. If firm i invests with an isolated atom equal to $\nu > 0$, then its expected payoff equals $W(p_t) + \nu(L(p_t) - W(p_t)) \leq W(p_t)$. Investing with an interval of atoms, i.e. $\alpha_i^t(t) = a > 0$, gives an expected payoff equal to $L(p_t)$. Hence it is optimal to set $G_i^t(t) = 0$.

3 $t = T_P^t < T_M^t$ (i.e. $p_P \leq p_t < p_M$)
   Investing with probability zero, i.e. $G_i^t(t) = 0$ yields an expected payoff equal to $F(p_t)$, given that firm j plays its strategy, i.e. $G_i^t(t) = 1$. If firm i invests with an isolated jump equal to $\nu > 0$, then

$$\mathbb{P}(\text{both firms invest simultaneously}) = \nu\alpha_j^t(t),$$
$$\mathbb{P}(\text{firm } i \text{ invests first}) = \nu(1 - \alpha_j^t(t)),$$
$$\mathbb{P}(\text{firm } j \text{ invests first}) = 1 - \nu.$$

   Given $\alpha_j^t(t) = \tfrac{L(t) - F(t)}{L(t) - M(t)}$ the expected payoff for firm i is given by

$$\nu\alpha_j^t(t)M(p_t) + \nu(1 - \alpha_j^t(t))L(p_t) + (1 - \nu)F(p_t) = F(p_t).$$

Finally, if firm i plays $\alpha_i^t(t) = a > 0$, then the expected payoff is given by

$$\frac{1}{a + \alpha_j^t(t) - a\alpha_j^t(t)}\Big(a\alpha_j^t(t)M(p_t) + a(1 - \alpha_j^t(t))L(p_t) + (1 - a)\alpha_j^t(t)F(p_t)\Big)$$
$$= F(p_t).$$

Hence, in each case a unilateral deviation does not yield a higher expected payoff. □

B.   Proof of Lemma 5.1

It is easy to see that the war of attrition region K is finite with cardinality, say, n. Hence, the system in (5.12) gives rise to a function $f : \mathbb{R}^n \to \mathbb{R}^n$ where the k-th entry is given by

$$f_k(x) = a_k x_k + b_k - (1 - x_k)(c_k x_{k+1} + d_k x_{k-1} - e_k), \qquad k = 1, \ldots, n.$$

A solution for the system (5.12) is equivalent to $x \in \mathbb{R}^n$ such that $f(x) = 0$.

Let $k \in K$ and let $x \in \mathbb{R}^n$ such that $x_k = 1$ be fixed. We have

$$f_k(x) = a_k + b_k = M(k) - L(k) - F(k) + L(k) < 0, \qquad (5.16)$$

since we are in the attrition region. Furthermore, note that

$$b_k - e_k = \frac{\lambda^k}{\lambda^k + \zeta(1 - \lambda)^k}\left(U_L^H \frac{\mu}{r + \mu}(\lambda U_L^H + (1 - \lambda)U_L^H)\right) - \Big(1 - $$
$$\frac{\mu}{r + \mu}\frac{\lambda^{k+1} + \zeta(1 - \lambda)^{k+1} + \lambda(1 - \lambda)(\lambda^{k-1} + \zeta(1 - \lambda)^{k-1})}{\lambda^k + \zeta(1 - \lambda)^k}\Big)I$$
$$= \frac{\mu}{r}\big(p(k)U_L^H - I\big) = \frac{\mu}{r}L(k) > 0.$$

Using this observation we obtain that if $x \in \mathbb{R}^n$ is such that $x_k = 0$,

$$f_k(x) = b_k - e_k - c_k x_{k+1} - d_k x_{k-1}$$
$$= \frac{\mu}{r}L(k) - \frac{\mu}{r + \mu}\frac{\lambda^{k+1} + \zeta(1 - \lambda)^{k+1}}{\lambda^k + \zeta(1 - \lambda)^k}x_{k+1}\Big(M(k + 1) - L(k + 1)\Big)$$
$$- \frac{\mu}{r + \mu}\frac{\lambda^{k-1} + \zeta(1 - \lambda)^{k-1}}{\lambda^k + \zeta(1 - \lambda)^k}x_{k-1}\Big(M(k - 1) - L(k - 1)\Big)$$
$$> 0,$$

$$(5.17)$$

since $M(k) \le L(k)$ for all $k \le \lceil k_P \rceil$. Hence, for all $k \in K$ and all $x \in \mathbb{R}^n$ we have $x_k = 0 \Rightarrow f_k(x) > 0$ and $x_k = 1 \Rightarrow f_k(x) < 0$. Since

$[0,1]^n$ is a convex and compact set and $f(\cdot)$ is continuous on $[0,1]^n$, there exists a stationary point $x^* \in [0,1]^n$, i.e. for all $x \in [0,1]^n$ it holds that $xf(x^*) \le x^* f(x^*)$.

Let $k \in \{1,\ldots,n\}$. Suppose that $x_k^* > 0$. Then there exists an $\varepsilon > 0$ such that $x = x^* - \varepsilon \mathbb{1}_k \in [0,1]^n$, where $\mathbb{1}_k$ denotes the k-th unity vector. This gives $f_k(x^*) \ge 0$, since

$$xf(x^*) - x^* f(x^*)$$
$$= -\varepsilon f_k(x^*) \le 0.$$

Similarly, if $x_k^* < 1$ there exists an $\varepsilon > 0$ such that $x = x^* + \varepsilon \mathbb{1}_k \in [0,1]^n$. Since x^* is a stationary point this yields $f_k(x^*) \le 0$. Hence, if $0 < x_k^* < 1$ this implies that $f_k(x^*) = 0$. Now suppose that $x_k^* = 0$. Then $f_k(x^*) \le 0$, which contradicts (5.17). Finally, suppose that $x_k^* = 1$. Then $f_k(x^*) \ge 0$, which contradicts (5.16). $\qquad\square$

C.   Proof of Proposition 5.2

By Lemma 5.1 there exists an $x \in [0,1]^n$ such that $f(x) = 0$. For all $k \in K$, let $\gamma(k) = x_k$. Furthermore, it is easy to see that $(G_i^t, \alpha_i^t)_{i=1,2}$ satisfies the intertemporal and α-consistency conditions for each $t \in [0,\infty)$.

We prove that for each subgame starting at t, the simple strategy (G_i^t, α_i^t) is an α-equilibrium. The case where t is such that $p_t < p_L$ is exactly the same as the case where $t < T_P^t < T_M^t$ in the proof of Proposition 5.1. The same holds true for the case where $t = T_M^t$. Consider the region for the war of attrition, i.e. t is such that $p_t \in [p_L, p_P)$. Then $k_t \in K$. Suppose that firm i invests with an interval of atoms and suppose $\alpha_i^t(t) = a$. Then given that firm j invests with an isolated jump equal to $\gamma(k_t)$, we get in analogy of (4.2) and (4.7) that

$$\mathbb{P}(\text{firm } i \text{ invests first}) = 1 - \gamma(k_t),$$
$$\mathbb{P}(\text{firm } j \text{ invests first}) = \gamma(k_t)(1 - a),$$
$$\mathbb{P}(\text{firms invest simultaneously}) = a\gamma(k_t).$$

Hence, the expected payoff for firm i is given by

$$a\gamma_j(k_t)M(p_t) + (1 - \gamma_j(k_t))L(p_t) + \gamma_j(k_t)(1 - a)F(p_t).$$

This expected payoff is maximised for $a = 0$. Hence, firm i will not play an interval of atoms. Suppose firm i plays an isolated atom equal to $\nu \in [0,1]$. Then its expected payoff equals

$$\nu V_1(p_t) + (1 - \nu)V_2(p_t),$$

and is hence independent of ν since, by definition, $\gamma_j(k_t)$ is such that $V_1(p_t) = V_2(p_t)$. Therefore, any $\nu \in [0,1]$, and in particular $\nu = \gamma(k_t)$, maximises the expected payoff. $\qquad\square$

D. Proof of Proposition 5.3

The proof follows Feller (1971, Section 14.6) and is probabilistic in nature. Note that the process starts at $t_0 = 0$ with $k_0 = 0$ a.s. Arriving at $k \neq 0$ at time $t > 0$ can only be possible if a jump has occurred before t. Assume that the first jump occurred at time $t - x$. The conditional probability of the position $k \neq 0$ at time t is denoted by $P_k(t)$. It is the convolution of the probability that the process was at $k+1$ at time x or at $k-1$ at time x and the probability of an arrival of an l-signal or an h-signal, respectively. Since the arrival of signals follows a Poisson process with parameter μ and hence the inter-arrival times are exponentially distributed with parameter μ, $P_k(t)$ is given by

$$P_k(t) = \int_0^t \mu e^{-\mu(t-x)} \Big[q_1(k-1)P_{k-1}(x) + q_2(k+1)P_{k+1}(x) \Big] dx, \quad (5.18)$$

where

$$q_1(k-1) = \frac{\lambda^k + \zeta(1-\lambda)^k}{\lambda^{k-1} + \zeta(1-\lambda)^{k-1}}, \quad (5.19)$$

is the probability of reaching state k from state $k-1$ and

$$q_2(k+1) = \lambda(1-\lambda)\frac{\lambda^k + \zeta(1-\lambda)^k}{\lambda^{k+1} + \zeta(1-\lambda)^{k+1}}, \quad (5.20)$$

is the probability of reaching state k from state $k+1$. That is, $P_k(t)$ is the convolution of the distribution of reaching $k+1$ or $k-1$ at time $t - x$ and the distribution of the arrival of one signal in the interval $(t - x, t]$. For $k = 0$, the probability of no jump up to t, which equals $1 - \int_0^t \mu e^{-\mu t} dt = e^{-\mu t}$, must be added, i.e.

$$P_0(t) = e^{-\mu t} + \int_0^t \mu e^{-\mu(t-x)} \Big[q_1(-1)P_{-1}(x) + q_2(1)P_1(x) \Big] dx, \quad (5.21)$$

Denoting the Laplace transform of $P_k(\cdot)$ by $\pi_k(\cdot)$ we get from eqs. (5.18) and (5.21)

$$\pi_k(\gamma) = \frac{\mu}{\mu + \gamma}[q_1(k-1)\pi_{k-1}(\gamma) + q_2(k+1)\pi_{k+1}(\gamma)] \quad \text{for } k \neq 0,$$
$$(5.22)$$

$$\pi_0(\gamma) = \frac{1}{\mu + \gamma} + \frac{\mu}{\mu + \gamma}[q_1(-1)\pi_{-1}(\gamma) + q_2(1)\pi_1(\gamma)]. \quad (5.23)$$

By substituting eqs. (5.19) and (5.20) into eq. (5.22) one obtains the following second order linear difference equation

$$\mu\lambda(1-\lambda)F_{k+1}(\gamma) - (\mu+\gamma)F_k(\gamma) + \mu F_{k-1}(\gamma) = 0, \qquad (5.24)$$

where

$$F_k(\gamma) = \frac{\pi_k(\gamma)}{\lambda^k + \zeta(1-\lambda)^k}.$$

The roots of the characteristic equation of eq. (5.24) are

$$\beta_\gamma = \frac{\mu+\gamma - \sqrt{(\mu+\gamma)^2 - 4\mu^2\lambda(1-\lambda)}}{2\mu\lambda(1-\lambda)},$$

and

$$\sigma_\gamma = \frac{\mu+\gamma + \sqrt{(\mu+\gamma)^2 - 4\mu^2\lambda(1-\lambda)}}{2\mu\lambda(1-\lambda)}$$

$$= \frac{4\mu^2\lambda(1-\lambda)}{2\mu\lambda(1-\lambda)\left(\mu+\gamma - \sqrt{(\mu+\gamma)^2 - 4\mu^2\lambda(1-\lambda)}\right)}$$

$$= \frac{1}{\lambda(1-\lambda)}\beta_\gamma^{-1}.$$

The general solution for $k \neq 0$ is therefore given by

$$F_k(\gamma) = A_\gamma\beta_\gamma^k + \frac{1}{\lambda(1-\lambda)}B_\gamma\beta_\gamma^{-k}.$$

Note that for $k \geq 0$ it holds that $\beta_\gamma^k \to 0$ as $\gamma \to \infty$, but that $\sigma_\gamma^k \to \infty$ as $\gamma \to \infty$. Since $\pi_k(\gamma)$ and hence $F_k(\gamma)$ are bounded as $\gamma \to \infty$, we get for $k \geq 0$ that $B_\gamma = 0$. Similarly, we get for $k \leq 0$ that $A_\gamma = 0$. So, a solution to eq. (5.24) is given by

$$F_k(\gamma) = \begin{cases} F_0(\gamma)\beta_\gamma^k & k \geq 0 \\ \frac{1}{\lambda(1-\lambda)}F_0(\gamma)\beta_\gamma^{-k} & k < 0, \end{cases}$$

and hence,

$$\pi_k(\gamma) = \begin{cases} \frac{\lambda^k + \zeta(1-\lambda)^k}{1+\zeta}\beta_\gamma^k\pi_0(\gamma) & k \geq 0 \\ \frac{\lambda^k + \zeta(1-\lambda)^k}{1+\zeta}\frac{1}{\lambda(1-\lambda)}\beta_\gamma^{-k}\pi_0(\gamma) & k < 0, \end{cases} \qquad (5.25)$$

Solving for $\pi_0(\gamma)$ using eq. (5.23) gives

$$\pi_0(\gamma) = \frac{1}{\beta_\gamma}\frac{\lambda(1-\lambda)}{(\mu+\gamma)\lambda(1-\lambda) - \mu(1+\lambda^2(1-\lambda)^2)}.$$

Hence, eq. (5.25) is well-defined.

If at time t the process is at $k \geq 0$, the first passage through k must have occurred at time $\tau \leq t$. In this case, the conditional probability of being at k again at time t equals the probability of being at state 0 at time $t - \tau$ times the probability of a first passage through k at time τ, i.e.

$$P_k(t) = \int_0^t F_k(\tau) P_0(t - \tau) d\tau, \qquad (5.26)$$

where $F_k(\cdot)$ is the distribution of the first passage time through k. The Laplace transform of eq. (5.26) is given by

$$\pi_k(\gamma) = f_k(\gamma) \pi_0(\gamma).$$

From eq. (5.25) we therefore conclude that the Laplace transform of $F_k(\cdot)$ equals $f_k(\gamma) = \frac{\lambda^k + \zeta(1-\lambda)^k}{1+\zeta} \beta_\gamma^k$. Feller (1971) shows that for $\gamma > 1$, $(\gamma - \sqrt{\gamma^2 - 1})^k$ is the Laplace transform of the density $\frac{k}{t} I_k(t)$. Applying the mapping $\gamma \mapsto \frac{\gamma}{2\mu\sqrt{\lambda(1-\lambda)}}$ is a change of scale and applying the mapping $\gamma \mapsto \gamma + \mu$ reflects multiplication of the density by $e^{-\mu t}$. Applying both mappings gives

$$(\gamma - \sqrt{\gamma^2 - 1})^k \mapsto \left(\frac{\gamma + \mu - \sqrt{(\gamma + \mu)^2 - 4\mu^2 \lambda(1 - \lambda)}}{2\mu\sqrt{\lambda(1 - \lambda)}} \right)^k$$

$$= \frac{\lambda^k + \zeta(1-\lambda)^k}{1+\zeta} \beta_\gamma^k \left(\frac{1+\zeta}{\lambda^k + \zeta(1-\lambda)^k} (\lambda(1-\lambda))^{k/2} \right).$$

Hence, the pdf of the first passage time through k is given by

$$f_k(t) = \frac{\lambda^k + \zeta(1-\lambda)^k}{1+\zeta} \left(\lambda(1-\lambda) \right)^{-k/2} \frac{k}{t} I_k(2\mu\sqrt{\lambda(1-\lambda)}t) e^{-\mu t},$$

which proves the proposition. $\square$

II

COOPERATION, SPILLOVERS, AND INVESTMENT

Chapter 6

SPILLOVERS AND STRATEGIC COOPERATIVE BEHAVIOUR

1. Introduction

In standard noncooperative game theory it is assumed that players cannot make binding agreements. That is, each cooperative outcome must be sustained by Nash equilibrium strategies. At the other end of the spectrum, in cooperative game theory, players have no choice but to cooperate. The standard transferable utility (TU) model assumes that all players involved want to come to an agreement and the main task is to propose socially acceptable solutions. Non-cooperative theory tries to predict the outcome of strategic situations using equilibrium concepts that at least require the predicted strategy combinations to be robust against unilateral deviations.

Both approaches seem to be diametrically opposed. Many real life situations, however, exhibit both cooperative and strategic features. Neither approach suffices in these cases. Examples of these situations can be found in parliaments where governments are based on multiple-party coalitions. Here non-cooperative theory obviously does not work, since agreements have to be made. Also TU theory is not sufficiently rich, since typically not all parties represented in parliament are part of the government. Furthermore, TU theory does not take into account the spillover effects from coalitions on the parties outside. These spillovers measure the impact of government policy on the opposition parties and thus reflect in some way the parties' relative positions in the political spectrum.

This kind of spillovers is present in many situations. For example, one can think of a situation where a group of people needs to be connected to a source, like in a telecommunication network. In the literature, many solution concepts have been introduced (cf. Bird (1976)), but these do not take into account the strategic considerations of players not to join in the public enterprise. However, spillovers occur if one assumes that publicly accessible networks can be built by smaller groups, hence creating a special type of free-rider effect. In order to find a fair solution, these possible spillovers should be taken into account.

As another example, one can think of a group of firms that compete in an oligopolistic industry. In assessing the benefits of a merger, a crucial part is played by comparing the profit when joining another firm (merging) and when staying out. The spillover model allows for the analysis of all intermediate cases in between a completely non-cooperative (e.g. Cournot-Nash) situation and a fully cooperative (monopoly) situation.

From the aforementioned examples one can conclude that in many cooperative situations, a socially acceptable solution concept should incorporate the strategic options that result from spillovers. Essentially, spillovers induce a non-cooperative aspect in cooperative situations. They provide incentives for players to join or to stay out of a coalition. In TU games, these spillovers are not taken into account, but one implicitly assumes that players do not have a better alternative than to stay in the group. As mentioned before, in the government example, this is typically not the case. In short, cooperative game theory lacks the strategic outside options players have, whereas non-cooperative theory, on the other hand, does not allow for explicit cooperation.

To capture spillovers in a cooperative model, a new class of games is introduced, namely *spillover games*. This class of games builds on ideas introduced in Van der Rijt (2000) for government situations. In a spillover game, each coalition is assigned a value, as in a TU game. In addition, all the players outside the coalition are separately assigned a value as well, capturing the spillovers from the coalition to the outside players. We restrict ourselves to a coalitional structure where there is one coalition (e.g. a government, a group building a public network, a cartel) and a group of singletons outside. This allows us to redefine some basic concepts of TU theory, while not assuming *ex ante* that all players are fully cooperating.

The model of spillover games is explicitly aimed at analysing the influence of a coalition S on the payoffs of the players outside S. In this sense, spillover games differ fundamentally from games in partition function form (cf. Bloch (1996) and Yi (1997)), where for each coalition S the influence of the possible coalition structures on the player set outside S on the payoff to coalition S is analysed. Hence, the causality of spillovers in spillover games is reversed compared to partition function form games.

The structure of the chapter is as follows. In Section 2 the class of spillover games is introduced. Our three main applications are presented: government situations, public-private connection problems, and mergers in oligopolistic markets. In Section 3 we introduce the core concept for the class of spillover games and present a balancedness result reminiscent of TU theory. In Section 4 we take a closer look at public-private connection problems and and apply the core concept to these problems. Section 5 analyses government situations in more detail. A power index is introduced that is constructed in a similar way as the Shapley value for TU games. Finally, Section 6 deals with the Cournot model for oligopolistic markets and shows how this type of non-cooperative games can be transformed into a spillover game in a natural way. Furthermore, a compromise value (in the same spirit as for TU games) is introduced.

2.   The Model

A *spillover game* is a tuple $\mathcal{G} = (N, \mathcal{W}, v, z)$, where $N = \{1, \ldots, n\}$ is the set of players, $\mathcal{W} \subset 2^N$ is a set of coalitions that can cooperate and v and z are payoff functions, to be specified below.

One main feature of our model is the assumption that exactly one coalition of players will cooperate. Contrary to TU games, however, we do not impose that the resulting coalition is the grand coalition. In the example of government formation, the grand coalition would be a very extreme outcome.

The set $\mathcal{W} \subset 2^N$ contains those coalitions which can actually cooperate. An element of $\mathcal{W}$ is called a *winning coalition*. In a government situation, a natural choice for $\mathcal{W}$ is the collection of coalitions which have a majority in parliament.

We assume that $\mathcal{W}$ satisfies the following properties:

- $N \in \mathcal{W}$.

- $S \subset T, S \in \mathcal{W} \Rightarrow T \in \mathcal{W}$ (monotonicity).

The first property ensures that the game is not trivial, in the sense that there is at least one winning coalition. The second property states that if a small group of players S can cooperate (e.g. have a majority), then a larger coalition $T \supset S$ is also winning.

The (nonnegative) payoff function $v : 2^N \rightarrow \mathbb{R}_+$ assigns to every coalition $S \subset N$ a value $v(S)$. If $S \in \mathcal{W}$, then $v(S)$ represents the total payoff to the members of S in case they cooperate. For $S \notin \mathcal{W}$ we simply impose $v(S) = 0$.

Suppose that the players in S cooperate. Then the members of S do not only generate a payoff to themselves. Their cooperation also affects the players outside S. The payoffs to the other players, which are called *spillovers* (wrt S), are given by the vector $z^S \in \mathbb{R}_+^{N \setminus S}$. Again, we simply put $z^S = 0$ for $S \notin W$. Note that whereas the members of S still have the freedom to divide the amount $v(S)$ among themselves, the payoffs to the players outside S are individually fixed.

Spillovers (wrt S) are called *positive*, if the total payoff to every coalition $U \subset N \setminus S$ is higher than what U can earn on its own, so if

$$\sum_{i \in U} z_i^S \geq v(U), \tag{6.1}$$

for every $U \subset N \setminus S$. Likewise, spillovers are *negative* if for every $U \subset N \setminus S$ the reverse inequality holds in (6.1). Note that if for different coalitions U not the same inequality holds, spillovers are neither positive nor negative.

A set of winning coalitions $W \subset 2^N$ is called *N-proper* if $S \in W$ implies $N \setminus S \notin W$. In the context of coalition formation in politics, this property relates to the fact that a coalition and its complement can not have a majority at the same time.

In the remainder of this section, we provide three examples to illustrate the spillover model.

EXAMPLE 6.1 (PUBLIC-PRIVATE CONNECTION PROBLEM) *Consider a group of players that can be connected to a source. If a player is connected to the source, he receives some fixed benefit. On the other hand, by creating connections costs are incurred. Each player can construct a direct link between the source and himself, or he can connect himself via other players.*

There are two types of connections: public and private. If a player constructs a public link, other players can use this link to get to the source. A private connection can only be used by the player who constructs it.

When constructing a network, players can cooperate in order to reduce costs. We assume that if a group of players cooperate, the players within that coalition construct an optimal public network, which by definition is open for use by other players. Once this optimal public network for the coalition is constructed, the players outside can decide whether or not to connect to the source, using the public network in place, possibly complemented with private connections. The corresponding payoffs to these individual players are the spillovers that result from the formation *of this coalition. We call the resulting model a public-private connection (ppc) problem. Note that in principle every coalition can build the public network and hence, $\mathcal{W} = 2^N$.*

In Section 4 we introduce ppc problems more formally and analyse their corresponding games.

EXAMPLE 6.2 (GOVERNMENT SITUATION) *Consider a parliament with four parties[1]: the communists (COM), socialists (SOC), Christian democrats (CD) and liberals (LIB). The seats are divided as follows:*

party	COM	SOC	CD	LIB
share of seats	0.1	0.3	0.25	0.35

This gives rise to a spillover game with $N = \{COM, SOC, CD, LIB\}$ and an N-proper set $\mathcal{W}$ of coalitions having a majority:

$$\mathcal{W} = \{\{SOC, CD\}, \{SOC, LIB\}, \{CD, LIB\}, \{COM, SOC, CD\},$$
$$\{COM, SOC, LIB\}, \{COM, CD, LIB\}, \{SOC, CD, LIB\}, N\}.$$

For the winning coalitions the payoffs could look as follows (the first entry in the two-dimensional z-vectors corresponds to COM):[2]

S	$v(S)$	z^S
$\{SOC, CD\}$	12	$(4, 3)$
$\{SOC, LIB\}$	10	$(2, 7)$
$\{CD, LIB\}$	15	$(0, 4)$
$\{COM, SOC, CD\}$	19	0
$\{COM, SOC, LIB\}$	13	6
$\{COM, CD, LIB\}$	14	4
$\{SOC, CD, LIB\}$	18	1
N	16	

Obviously, COM and LIB do not have much in common, which is reflected by a relatively low payoff to coalitions in which both are involved. The central position of CD is reflected by the relatively high spillover it experiences when a coalition forms in which it is not involved. If all four parties get together, the result will not be stable, which is reflected by the low value for N.

---

[1] This example is inspired by the model presented in Van der Rijt (2000).

[2] It is not within the scope of this book to provide an underlying model from which these coalition values can be derived. We simply give some *ad hoc* numbers to illustrate the concept of spillover game.

EXAMPLE 6.3 (MERGERS IN AN OLIGOPOLISTIC MARKET) *Consider a group of firms in an oligopolistic market. We assume that these firms play a Cournot game (Cournot (1838)) and that the outcome will be the Cournot-Nash equilibrium of this game.*

If the firms merge (and, hence, form a cartel) their total profit increases in general. Indeed, in the extreme case of full cooperation, a de facto monopoly will ensue with corresponding monopoly profits. We can also consider the situation in which only a coalition of firms $S \subset N$ decides to merge. Clearly, this will increase the total profit of the firms in S. But not only will the members of S be affected by the merger. By cooperating, the merged firms influence the market price, and hence, the profits of the other firms. In section 6, we show how these merger profits and corresponding externalities can be captured in a spillover game.

The previous three examples demonstrate the versatility of the spillover model. Basically, the model can be used to serve the following three purposes:

- In many OR problems like in Example 6.1 spillovers play a role. What one usually does in such problems, is to create a corresponding TU game and analyse its properties and solutions. Important information is lost in this way.

- Also, if one wants to analyse a (political) coalition problem like in Example 6.2, it does not suffice to consider only the payoffs to the resulting coalition. Obviously, the spillovers to the remaining players should also be taken into account and a spillover game provides a concise way of doing this.

- Finally, also in non-cooperative situations like in Example 6.3, the analysis usually focuses on the cooperating players rather than at all parties involved. A spillover game is a nice vehicle that can carry the results of oligopoly, cartel (monopoly) and any form of cooperation (merger) in between.

3.   The Core

In this section we extend the definition of core for TU games to the class of spillover games. Furthermore, we characterise nonemptiness of the core by means of a balancedness property.

A payoff vector $x \in \mathbb{R}^N$ belongs to the *S-core* if for every coalition, the total payoff to the members of that coalition exceeds its value. So, for $S \in \mathcal{W}$ we define the S-core by

$$C_S(\mathcal{G}) = \{x \in \mathbb{R}^N \mid \sum_{i \in S} x_i = v(S), x_{N \setminus S} = z^S, \forall_{T \subset N} : \sum_{i \in T} x_i \geq v(T)\},$$

or, equivalently,

$$C_S(\mathcal{G}) = \{x \in \mathbb{R}_+^N \mid \sum_{i \in S} x_i = v(S), x_{N\setminus S} = z^S, \forall_{T \in \mathcal{W}} : \sum_{i \in T} x_i \geq v(T)\}.$$

An allocation in the S-core is stable in the sense that there is no other winning coalition T that objects to the proposed allocation on the basis of it being able to obtain more if it cooperates. The *core* of $\mathcal{G}$ consists of all undominated payoff vectors in the union of all S-cores, so

$$C(\mathcal{G}) = undom(\bigcup_{S \in \mathcal{W}} C_S(\mathcal{G})),$$

where $undom(A) = \{x \in A \mid \neg \exists_{y \in A} : y \gneqq x\}$.

For TU games, Bondareva (1993) and Shapley (1967) characterised nonemptiness of the core by means of the concept of *balancedness*. We establish a similar result for the class of $\mathcal{W}$-stable spillover games. A game $\mathcal{G} = (N, \mathcal{W}, v, z)$ is called $\mathcal{W}$-*stable* if

$$S, T \in \mathcal{W}, S \cap T = \emptyset \Rightarrow \left\{ \begin{array}{l} \sum_{i \in T} z_i^S \geq v(T), \\ \sum_{i \in S} z_i^T \geq v(S). \end{array} \right.$$

The idea behind $\mathcal{W}$-stability is that there can exist no two disjoint winning coalitions with negative spillovers. For, if two such coalitions were present, the game would have no stable outcome in the sense that both these coalitions would want to form. Note that positive spillover games and spillover games with N-proper $\mathcal{W}$ belong to the class of $\mathcal{W}$-stable games.

For $S \subset N$, we define e^S to be the vector in $\mathbb{R}^N$ with $e_i^S = 1$ if $i \in N$ and $e_i^S = 0$ if $i \notin N$. A map $\lambda : \mathcal{W} \to \mathbb{R}_+$ is called S-*subbalanced* if

$$\sum_{T \in \mathcal{W}} \lambda(T) e_S^T \leq e_S^S.$$

We denote the set of all such S-subbalanced mappings by $\mathcal{B}^S$.

A game $\mathcal{G} = (N, \mathcal{W}, v, z)$ is S-*subbalanced* if for all S-subbalanced $\lambda : \mathcal{W} \to \mathbb{R}_+$ it holds that

$$\sum_{T \in \mathcal{W}} \lambda(T) \left[v(T) - \sum_{i \in (N\setminus S) \cap T} z_i^S \right] \leq v(S).$$

Suppose winning coalition S forms, giving its members a total payoff of $v(S)$. Next, consider a winning coalition T and consider the situation where T forms. The payoff to T would then be $v(T)$, but some of its members would have to forego the spillovers resulting from the formation of S. So, after subtracting these opportunity costs, the net payoff to T equals the expression inside the brackets. A game is S-subbalanced if dividing the net payoffs of all winning coalitions T in an S-subbalanced way yields a lower payoff than $v(S)$.

THEOREM 6.1 *Let $\mathcal{G} = (N, \mathcal{W}, v, z)$ be a $\mathcal{W}$-stable spillover game. Then $C(\mathcal{G}) \neq \emptyset$ if and only if there exists an $S \in \mathcal{W}$ such that $\mathcal{G}$ is S-subbalanced.*

Proof. See Appendix A.   □

4.   Public-Private Connection Problems

In many allocation decisions resulting from Operations Research (OR) problems, spillovers occur naturally. In this section, we analyse public-private connection (ppc) problems as described in Example 6.1. We address two main questions: which coalition will cooperate and how should the value of this coalition be divided among its members?

Before formally introducing ppc problems, we start with an example.

EXAMPLE 6.4 *Consider the ppc problem depicted in Figure 6.1, where * is the source, the bold numbers indicate the players, the numbers between parentheses represent the benefits if the players are connected to the source and the numbers on the edges are the corresponding construction costs.*

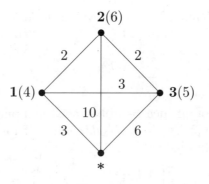

Figure 6.1.   A ppc problem

First, consider the grand coalition. The best this coalition can do is to build a public network connecting all players to the source, creating links $\{*, 1\}$, $\{1, 2\}$ and $\{2, 3\}$. The net payoff equals $4 + 6 + 5 - (3 + 2 + 2) = 8$.

Next, consider coalition $\{2\}$[3]. It is optimal for this coalition to create $\{*,1\}$ and $\{1,2\}$, giving player 2 a payoff of $6 - (2+3) = 1$. The construction of these public links results in spillovers for players 1 and 3. Player 1 can use the public network and does not have to create an extra private link, so his spillover equals his benefit of 4. Player 3 can also use the public network, complemented with the private connection $\{2,3\}$, giving him a spillover of $5 - 2 = 3$.

Next, consider $\{3\}$. Since every path to the source is more expensive that his benefit, player 3 will not construct a network at all, giving him a payoff of 0. Player 1 then has to construct a private link $\{*,1\}$ with spillover 1 and player 2, who cannot use 1's private link, will have to construct $\{*,1\}$ and $\{1,2\}$ privately, giving him a spillover of 1 as well.

Doing this for every possible coalition, we obtain a spillover game $\mathcal{G} = (N, \mathcal{W}, v, z)$ with $N = \{1,2,3\}$, $\mathcal{W} = 2^N$ and the following payoffs:

S	$\emptyset$	$\{1\}$	$\{2\}$	$\{3\}$	$\{1,2\}$	$\{1,3\}$	$\{2,3\}$	N
$v(S)$	0	1	1	0	5	3	4	8
z^S	$(1,1,0)$	$(4,2)$	$(4,3)$	$(1,1)$	3	4	4	

A *public-private connection* or *ppc problem* is a tuple $(N, *, b, c)$, where $N = \{1, \ldots, n\}$ is a set of agents, $*$ is a source, $b : N \to \mathbb{R}_+$ is a nonnegative benefit function and $c : E_{N^*} \to \mathbb{R}_+$ is a nonnegative cost function, where $N^* = N \cup \{*\}$. E_S is defined as the set of all edges between pairs of elements of $S \subset N^*$, so that (S, E_S) is the complete graph on S:

$$E_S = \{\{i,j\} \mid i, j \in S, i \neq j\}.$$

$b(i)$ represents the benefits if player $i \in N$ is connected to $*$ and $c(\{i,j\})$ represents the costs if a link between $i \in N^*$ and $j \in N^*$ is formed.

Links can be created either publicly or privately, as described in Example 6.1. To avoid unnecessary diversions, we simply assume that the optimal public network for each coalition is unique.

A network of edges is a set $K \subset E_{N^*}$. By $N(K) \subset N$ we denote the set of players that are connected to the source in network K.

A ppc problem $(N, *, b, c)$ gives rise to a *public-private connection* or *ppc game* $(N, \mathcal{W}, v, z)$ with $\mathcal{W} = 2^N$,

$$v(S) = \max_{K \subset E_{N^*}} \left\{ \sum_{i \in S \cap N(K)} b(i) - \sum_{k \in K} c(k) \right\}, \qquad (6.2)$$

---

[3]It may seem strange that a single player or even the empty coalition can build a public network. For the sake of expositional clarity, we do not *a priori* exclude this possibility.

for all $S \subset N$ and

$$z_i^S = \max_{L \subset E_{N^*} \backslash K_S} \{b(i)I_{N(K_S \cup L)}(i) - \sum_{\ell \in L} c(\ell)\},$$

for all $S \subset N, i \in N \backslash S$, where K_S denotes the unique network K that maximises (6.2), and $I_A(i)$ equals 1 if $i \in A$ and 0 if $i \notin A$.

Although players outside S can use the public network created by S, the spillovers need not be positive. This is caused by the assumption that only the players within the coalition that eventually builds the public network can cooperate, whereas the players outside can only build private links. As a result, the costs of a particular connection may have to be paid more than once by the players outside the coalition and consequently, they are worse off than when they cooperate.

Let us return to the ppc problem in Example 6.4. To find a suitable solution for this problem, we first consider the core of the corresponding ppc game $\mathcal{G}$. The S-cores are given in the following table.

S	$C_S(\mathcal{G})$
$\emptyset$	$\emptyset$
$\{1\}$	$\{(1,4,2)\}$
$\{2\}$	$\{(4,1,3)\}$
$\{3\}$	$\emptyset$
$\{1,2\}$	$Conv(\{(4,1,3),(1,4,3)\})$
$\{1,3\}$	$Conv(\{(3,4,0),(1,4,2)\})$
$\{2,3\}$	$Conv(\{(4,4,0),(4,1,3)\})$
N	$Conv(\{(4,1,3),(4,4,0),(3,5,0),(1,5,2),(1,4,3)\})$

Since the N-core (weakly) dominates all the other cores, we have $C(\mathcal{G}) = C_N(\mathcal{G})$. Note that there are some core elements that are supported by other coalitions as well, all of which contain player 2. The core element $(4,1,3)$ is even supported by every coalition containing player 2.

In Figure 6.2 we depict the four S-cores that yield core elements and (therefore) lie in the hyperplane with total payoff 8. The payoff to player 1 is in normal typeface, the payoff to player 2 is italic and the payoff to player 3 is bold. The N-core $C_N(\mathcal{G})$ is the shaded pentagon, $C_{\{1,2\}}$ is the line segment with the triangles, $C_{\{2,3\}}$ is the line segment with the stars and $C_{\{2\}}$ is the point $(4,1,3)$.

To solve the ppc problem, suppose for the moment that all players cooperate. We have already seen that it is optimal for the grand coalition to connect all its members to the source. Since the benefits of a coalition do not depend on the shape of the network that is formed as long as everyone is connected, the optimal network in this ppc problem,

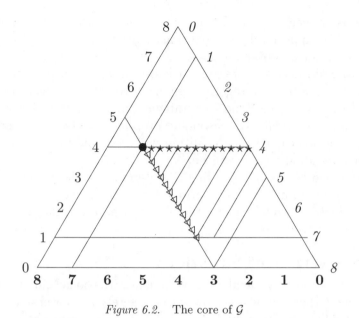

Figure 6.2. The core of $\mathcal{G}$

$\{\{*,1\},\{1,2\},\{2,3\}\}$, is actually a *minimum cost spanning tree* (Claus and Kleitman (1973)). In this context, Bird (1976) proposed that each player pays the costs of the (unique) link that is adjacent to him and lies on the path between him and the source. So, one way to solve a ppc problem is to assume that construction costs are divided using Bird's rule and everyone gets his own benefit. According to this Bird-like procedure, player 1 receives $4 - 3 = 1$, player 2 gets $6 - 2 = 4$ and player 3 gets $5 - 2 = 3$. This yields the core element $(1,4,3)$ as solution.

This procedure, however, has some elementary flaws. The nice properties of the Bird rule for mcst problems follow from the assumption that all players *have to* cooperate and connect to the source. Moreover, this rule does not take the spillovers into account. The strategic option of players not to participate in a coalition undermines the Bird approach. Player 1 will never agree to the proposed payoff vector $(1,4,3)$, since he will be better off leaving the grand coalition, which will lead to a payoff (spillover) of 4. Knowing this, player 3 can argue that he should at least receive 3, his spillover when player 2 forms a coalition on his own. Taking this into account, the payoff vector $(4,1,3)$ seems a more reasonable outcome. Because player 2 on his own will build a network that also connects player 1 to the source, the latter player occupies a position of power in this ppc problem, which should somehow be reflected in his payoff.

The payoff vector $(4, 1, 3)$ is a core element of the corresponding ppc game and is supported by all coalitions containing player 2. This payoff, however, is not acceptable to player 2. He can argue that if he were to refuse to build his optimal public network, it would then be optimal for players 1 and 3 to work together, giving player 2 a spillover of 4.

By considering this kind of strategic threats of the players not to cooperate, any seemingly reasonable proposal can be dismissed. As a result, it is not clear which coalition will eventually emerge and what the corresponding payoffs will be.

This phenomenon of free-riding is well-known in the context of public goods. Although it is socially optimal for all the players to cooperate in order to provide a public good, the players separately have the strategic incentive not to do so.

5.   Government Situations

In this section, we analyse government situations and introduce a power index that can be used to indicate the relative power of the parties involved. On the basis of Example 6.2 we introduce the concept of marginal vector for spillover games, which we use to define a power index that is reminiscent of the Shapley value for TU games. Contrary to its TU counterpart, strategic considerations play an important role in our definition of marginal vector.

EXAMPLE 6.5 *Recall the government situation in Example 6.2. To construct a marginal vector, assume that first the largest party, LIB, enters. Since this party on itself is not winning, its marginal contribution is zero. To keep things simple, we assume that parties always join if the coalition in place is not yet winning. Hence, the second largest party, SOC, joins, creating a winning coalition. Its payoff equals the marginal contribution to the existing coalition, which equals 10-0=10. Next, the third largest, CD has the choice whether to join or not. If it joins, its marginal contribution is 18-10=8. If it does not join, the worst that can happen is that coalition {COM, SOC, LIB} eventually cooperates, giving CD a payoff (spillover) of 6. Hence, CD joins the existing coalition. Finally, COM decides not to join, giving it a spillover of 1 rather than the marginal contribution of -2. So, the resulting coalition will be {SOC, CD, LIB} with payoff 1 to COM, 10 to SOC, 8 to CD and 0 to LIB.*

The procedure described in the previous example to solve the coalition formation problem resembles the well-known concept of marginal vector for TU games. The crucial difference, however, is that contrary to the

TU case, in our context players do not have to join the existing coalition. As long as there is a winning coalition in place and the worst that can happen if a player does not join is better than joining, that player has the option to stay outside.

5.1 The Power Index

In order to define the concept of marginal vector, we need to introduce some more notation. An *ordering* on the player set N is a bijection $\sigma : \{1, \ldots, n\} \rightarrow N$, where $\sigma(k) = i$ means that player $i \in N$ is at position k. The set of all $n!$ orderings on N is denoted by $\Pi(N)$. The set of predecessors of player $i \in N$ according to ordering $\sigma \in \Pi(N)$ is denoted by $P_i^\sigma = \{j \in N \,|\, \sigma^{-1}(j) < \sigma^{-1}(i)\}$.

Let $(N, \mathcal{W}, v, z)$ be a spillover game. The *marginal vector corresponding to σ*, $\sigma \in \Pi(N)$, denoted by $M^\sigma(N, \mathcal{W}, v, z)$, is defined recursively. By S_k^σ we denote the current coalition after the first k players have entered and we initialise $S_0^\sigma = \emptyset$. Let $k \in \{1, \ldots, n\}$. Player $i = \sigma(k)$ has to decide whether to join the current coalition S_{k-1}^σ or not. The minimum payoff if he does not join equals

$$m_i^\sigma = \min_{T \subset N \setminus \{i\} : T \cap P_i^\sigma = S_{k-1}^\sigma} z_i^T .$$

If he does join, his marginal contribution equals

$$c_i^\sigma = v(S_{k-1}^\sigma \cup \{i\}) - v(S_{k-1}^\sigma).$$

We assume that i does not join S_{k-1}^σ if this latter coalition is already winning and the worst that can happen to i if it stays outside, m_i^σ, is better than his marginal contribution c_i^σ. So,

$$S_k^\sigma = \begin{cases} S_{k-1}^\sigma & \text{if } S_{k-1}^\sigma \in \mathcal{W} \text{ and } m_i^\sigma > c_i^\sigma, \\ S_{k-1}^\sigma \cup \{i\} & \text{otherwise} \end{cases}$$

and

$$M_i^\sigma(N, \mathcal{W}, v, z) = \begin{cases} z_i^{S_n^\sigma} & \text{if } S_{k-1}^\sigma \in \mathcal{W} \text{ and } m_i^\sigma > c_i^\sigma, \\ c_i^\sigma & \text{otherwise.} \end{cases}$$

According to this procedure, the coalition $S^\sigma = S_n^\sigma$ eventually forms and in the resulting marginal vector, $v(S^\sigma)$ is divided among the members of S^σ and the players in $N \setminus S^\sigma$ get their corresponding spillovers.

The solution that is computed in Example 6.5 is the marginal vector that corresponds to the ordering based on the shares of the seats. Of course, this procedure can be performed with all orderings on the parties, each leading to a marginal vector. The *Shapley value* (cf. Shapley

(1953)) is defined as the average of these marginal vectors:

$$\Phi(N, \mathcal{W}, v, z) = \frac{1}{n!} \sum_{\sigma \in \Pi(N)} M^\sigma(N, \mathcal{W}, v, z).$$

The Shapley value can be interpreted as an *expected* payoff vector if coalition formation is performed by the marginal vector procedure and the orderings on the players are equally likely. Note that the total payoff to the players according to different marginal vectors need not be the same. Contrary to each marginal vector separately, the Shapley value is not "supported" by a single coalition, but it induces a probability measure $\mathbb{P}$ on all (winning) coalitions in a natural way:

$$\mathbb{P}(S) = \frac{|\{\sigma \in \Pi(N) \mid S^\sigma = S\}|}{n!}.$$

EXAMPLE 6.6 *In Example 6.5, the Shapley value can be obtained by cal-culating all marginal vectors following a similar procedure for all permu-tations as has been illustrated for the permutation* (LIB, SOC, CD, COM). *This yields*

$$\Phi(N, \mathcal{W}, v, z) = \frac{1}{24}(24, 140, 172, 116).$$

The induced probabilities are presented in the following table (winning coalitions not mentioned have probability 0).

S	$\mathbb{P}(S)$
$\{CD, LIB\}$	$\frac{1}{6}$
$\{COM, SOC, CD\}$	$\frac{1}{4}$
$\{COM, SOC, LIB\}$	$\frac{1}{4}$
$\{COM, CD, LIB\}$	$\frac{1}{6}$
$\{SOC, CD, LIB\}$	$\frac{1}{6}$

According to these probabilities on the coalitions, COM and LIB will be part of the coalition with probability $\frac{2}{3}$ and SOC and CD with prob-ability $\frac{3}{4}$, which reflects the latter two parties' centrality in the political spectrum.

The strategic element in our definition of marginal vector is that a player can choose not to join when it is in his interest to stay separate. We assume that players are cautionary in that they only decide not to join when the worst that can happen when doing so is better than the payoff if they join.[4] This strategic element can be extended in several ways.

---

[4]This is quite standard practise in cooperative game theory. Usually, a non-cooperative game is turned into a TU game by assigning values to coalitions based on the maximin principle, i.e. by maximising the worst case scenario.

For example, one can assume that the players play a sequential move extensive form game and the resulting marginal vector is the payoff vector corresponding to a subgame perfect equilibrium. One would then have to make some additional assumptions about what happens when indifferences occur and there are multiple equilibria. In our approach, we assume that player i decides to join whenever $m_i^\sigma = c_i^\sigma$.

6. Mergers in Oligopolistic Markets

In this section we show how to construct a spillover game out of an oligopolistic market that is characterised by Cournot competition. The general case of constructing a spillover game from a non-cooperative game is presented in Appendix B. Furthermore, a way to divide the surplus of a merger in a spillover game that is based on the compromise (or τ-value) for TU games[5] is presented.

Consider a market with n firms. The inverse demand function is given by $P : \mathbb{R}_+^n \to \mathbb{R}_+$. The production technology of each firm i, $i = 1, \ldots, n$, is represented by the cost function $C_i : \mathbb{R}_+ \to \mathbb{R}_+$. The profit function for firm i is the function $\pi_i : \mathbb{R}_+^n \to \mathbb{R}$, which is defined by

$$\pi_i(q_i, q_{-i}) = P(q_1, \ldots, q_n)q_i - C_i(q_i),$$

where $(q_i, q_{-i}) = (q_1, \ldots, q_{i-1}, q_i, q_{i+1}, \ldots, q_n)$. Simultaneously solving the profit maximisation problem for all firms yields the Cournot-Nash equilibrium profits, $\bar{\pi} = (\bar{\pi}^1, \ldots, \bar{\pi}^n)$.

The oligopolistic market can be turned into a spillover game $\mathcal{G} = (N, \mathcal{W}, v, z)$ in the following way. Let $N = \{1, \ldots, n\}$ and $\mathcal{W} = 2^N$. The Cournot-Nash equilibrium corresponds to a situation where $S = \emptyset$ with $v(\emptyset) = 0$ and $z^\emptyset = \bar{\pi}$. Subsequently, let $S = \{i\}$ for some $i \in N$. This still corresponds to a Cournot situation, i.e. $v(\{i\}) = \bar{\pi}_i$ and $z^{\{i\}} = \bar{\pi}_{-i}$.

For any coalition S consisting of more than one firm, we assume that there are economies of scale so that the coalition (or cartel or merged firm) can produce the product at the lowest possible costs. So, if $2 \leq |S| \leq n-1$, we basically have a Cournot situation with $n - |S| + 1$ firms:

$$\begin{cases} \max_{q^S \in \mathbb{R}_+^S} \{ P(q^S, q_{N \setminus S}) \sum_{i \in S} q_i^S - \sum_{i \in S} C_i(q_i) \}, \\ \max_{q_j \in \mathbb{R}_+} \{ P(q^S, q_{N \setminus S}) q_j - C_j(q_j) \} \qquad \text{for all } j \in N \setminus S. \end{cases}$$

This gives the vector of equilibrium profits $(\bar{\pi}^S, \bar{\pi}^{N \setminus S})$, where $\bar{\pi}^{N \setminus S} = (\bar{\pi}_j)_{j \in N \setminus S}$, leading to the values $v(S) = \bar{\pi}^S$ and $z^S = \bar{\pi}^{N \setminus S}$.

---

[5]See Section 4.2 of Chapter 2

For the grand coalition N, we simply solve the monopoly problem and obtain

$$v(N) = \max_{q^N \in \mathbf{R}_+^N} \left\{ P(q^N) \sum_{i \in N} q_i^N - \sum_{i \in N} C_i(q_i) \right\}.$$

The Shapley value can be used as an indication of the market power that firms have when they decide to merge. The advantage of using the framework of spillover games for oligopolistic markets is that it incorporates in one model such extreme cases as fully non-cooperative competition and fully cooperative collusion. Furthermore, all intermediate cases are included as well. The Shapley value averages out the profits in all these cases, thereby indicating the relative power of firms in the market.

Note, however, that the Shapley value only considers one coalition for each permutation. In other words, it is implicitly assumed that there can only be one merger at a time. There is no *a priori* reason why there could not be two or more mergers in one market at the same time.

As an example, consider a market with three firms. The linear inverse demand function is specified by $P(q_1, q_2, q_3) = b - a(q_1 + q_2 + q_3)$, $a > 0$, $b > 0$. It is assumed that the cost functions have constant marginal costs, i.e. for firm i it holds that $C_i(q) = c_i q$, $0 < c_1 \leq c_2 \leq c_3$. Additionally, it is assumed that $b \geq 3c_1 - c_2 - c_3$, $b \geq 2c_1 - c_3$, and $b \geq c_1$.[6] For this spillover game the appropriate values for v and z are given in Table 6.1.

S	$v(S)$	z^S
$\emptyset$		$\left(\frac{(b+c_2+c_3-3c_1)^2}{16a}, \frac{(b+c_1+c_3-3c_2)^2}{16a}, \frac{(b+c_1+c_2-3c_3)^2}{16a} \right)$
$\{1\}$	$\frac{(b+c_2+c_3-3c_1)^2}{16a}$	$\left(\frac{(b+c_1+c_3-3c_2)^2}{16a}, \frac{(b+c_1+c_2-3c_3)^2}{16a} \right)$
$\{2\}$	$\frac{(b+c_1+c_3-3c_2)^2}{16a}$	$\left(\frac{(b+c_2+c_3-3c_1)^2}{16a}, \frac{(b+c_1+c_2-3c_3)^2}{16a} \right)$
$\{3\}$	$\frac{(b+c_1+c_2-3c_3)^2}{16a}$	$\left(\frac{(b+c_2+c_3-3c_1)^2}{16a}, \frac{(b+c_1+c_3-3c_2)^2}{16a} \right)$
$\{1,2\}$	$\frac{(b+c_3-2c_1)^2}{9a}$	$\frac{(b+c_1-2c_3)^2}{9a}$
$\{1,3\}$	$\frac{(b+c_2-2c_1)^2}{9a}$	$\frac{(b+c_1-2c_2)^2}{9a}$
$\{2,3\}$	$\frac{(b+c_1-2c_2)^2}{9a}$	$\frac{(b+c_2-2c_1)^2}{9a}$
N	$\frac{(b-c_1)^2}{4a}$	

Table 6.1. Values for v and z.

It is not clear *a priori* what will happen in a market like this. For $b = 50$, $a = 1$, $c_1 = 5$, $c_2 = 10$, $c_3 = 15$ the Shapley value is given by $\Phi(\mathcal{G}) \approx (280, 147, 80)$. The prediction for the possible mergers gives a

---

[6]These assumptions ensure that all equilibrium profits are non-negative.

clear cut answer, namely $\mathbb{P}(N) = 1$. So, all firms will merge into one firm.

With the same values for b and a, and cost parameters $c_1 = 5$, $c_2 = 6$ and $c_3 = 10$ the Shapley value equals $\Phi(\mathcal{G}) \approx (211, 184, 67)$ and the probability measure on coalitions gives $\mathbb{P}(\{1,3\}) = \mathbb{P}(\{2,3\}) = \frac{1}{6}$, and $\mathbb{P}(N) = \frac{2}{3}$.

Finally, with constant marginal costs $c_1 = c_2 = c_3 = 10$ one obtains $\Phi(\mathcal{G}) = (100, 100, 100)$ and $\mathbb{P}(\{1\}) = \mathbb{P}(\{2\}) = \mathbb{P}(\{3\}) = \frac{1}{3}$. Hence, in this case no merger will take place. From the above examples one can deduce that apparently the magnitude of the synergy effects of collusion are important. Consider for example the case where firms are symmetric. Take any permutation of N. From Table 6.1 one can see that the first firm is indifferent between joining or not. It was assumed, in defining the Shapley value, that in case of indifference a player joins. The firm that arrives second has to compare its marginal contribution with the worst-case outside option. Joining the coalition means that the third firm gets an equal profit to the two firms in the cartel (since firms are symmetric). If marginal costs equal c the marginal contribution of the second firm equals $\frac{7(b-c)^2}{144a} < \frac{(b-c)^2}{16a}$. Hence, the second firm will never join. Then the same holds for the third firm.

The Shapley value gives an *ex ante* indication for the power of each firm in an oligopolistic market that may enter into negotiations that lead to a merger with one or more firms. Suppose that a group of firms $S \subset N$ – that forms a winning coalition ($S \in \mathcal{W}$) – has negotiated and intents to merge. The question now is how to divide the surplus $v(S)$ among the participating firms. One can think of a solution concept that is similar to the compromise value for TU games.

6.1 The Compromise Value

We want to define a compromise value for a general spillover game $\mathcal{G} = (N, \mathcal{W}, v, z)$. In order to do so, we need to redefine the *utopia vector* $M(v)$ and the *minimum right vector* $m(v)$ for TU games. For players outside the coalition S, $i \in N \backslash S$, it is reasonable to assume that both their utopia payoff and their minimum right is equal to z_i^S.

The utopia payoff of a player in the coalition S is equal to its marginal contribution to the merged firm, just like in a TU game. In other words, the other players in S can not be expected to honour a claim by player $i \in S$ that entails more than the marginal contribution. So, for each $S \in \mathcal{W}$ we have a utopia vector $M^S(\mathcal{G}) \in \mathbb{R}^N$ where for each $i \in S$ we have,

$$M_i^S(\mathcal{G}) = \begin{cases} v(S) - v(S \setminus \{i\}) & \text{if } i \in S \\ z_i^S & \text{if } i \notin S. \end{cases}$$

The difference with the compromise value for TU games becomes clear in the minimum right vector. In standard TU theory a player i has no choice but to participate in the grand coalition N. In a spillover game, however, each player has in principle the choice to join a coalition or not. Therefore, the minimum right of a player $i \in S$ has to take into account the outside options player i has. As in a TU game the minimum right of a player *within* the coalition is given by $\max_{\{T \in 2^N | T \subset S, i \in T\}} \{v(T) - \sum_{j \in T \setminus \{i\}} M_j^S(\mathcal{G})\}$. That is, player $i \in S$ can make a claim on the remainder of $v(T)$ when all other players got their utopia payoff, for any subcoalition T that entails player i. Furthermore, player i can always leave the coalition S and see what payoff she gets *outside* the coalition. Whatever happens with coalition $S \setminus \{i\}$ after player i left, she can never get less than the minimum spillover value she gets for any (winning) subcoalition of $S \setminus \{i\}$. That is, any player i can credibly threaten to leave the coalition S if she gets no more than $\min_{\{T \in \mathcal{W} | i \notin T, S \setminus \{i\} \subset T\}} z_i^T$. The minimum claim of player $i \in S$ is therefore the maximum of the minimum claim within coalition S and what can happen outside coalition S. In other words, the minimum right vector for coalition S, $m^S(\mathcal{G})$, gives for player i,

$$m_i^S(\mathcal{G}) = \begin{cases} \max\left(\max_{\{T \in 2^N | T \subset S, i \in T\}} \left\{v(T) - \sum_{j \in T \setminus \{i\}} M_j^S(\mathcal{G})\right\}, \right. & \\ \left. \min_{\{T \in \mathcal{W} | i \notin T, S \setminus \{i\} \subset T\}} z_i^T\right) & \text{if } i \in S \\ z_i^S & \text{if } i \notin S. \end{cases}$$

The *S-compromise value*, $\tau^S(\mathcal{G}) \in \mathbb{R}_+^N$, for coalition S is then defined to be the intersection of the line $\{x \in \mathbb{R}^N | \exists_{\lambda \in [0,1]} : x = \lambda m^S(\mathcal{G}) + (1 - \lambda)M^S(\mathcal{G})\}$ with the hyperplane $\{y \in \mathbb{R}^N | \forall_{i \notin S} : x_i = z_i^S, \sum_{i \in S} x_i = v(S)\}$. That is, $\tau^S(\mathcal{G})$ is the efficient convex combination of $m^S(\mathcal{G})$ and $M^S(\mathcal{G})$. One can show that

$$\tau^S(\mathcal{G}) = m^S(\mathcal{G}) + \lambda(M^S(\mathcal{G}) - m^S(\mathcal{G})),$$

where $\lambda \in [0,1]$ is such that $\sum_{i \in S} \tau_i^S(\mathcal{G}) = v(S)$. Note that for all players $i \notin S$ it holds that $\tau_i^S(\mathcal{G}) = m_i^S(\mathcal{G}) = M_i^S(\mathcal{G}) = z_i^S$.

The S-compromise value exists only if for coalition S it holds that

- $M^S \geq m^S$;

- $\sum_{i \in S} m_i^S \leq v(S)$.

A coalition S that satisfies both conditions is called *S-compromise admissible*. If the first condition is not satisfied the minimum right of at least one player is larger than its marginal contribution to the coalition S. Therefore, the other players in S do not want to honour this player's minimum claim. Conversely, in case the second condition is violated, the surplus that coalition S generates is not large enough to satisfy all minimum claims. So, the outside options of at least a part of the players in S are such that there is no incentive even to consider the formation of coalition S. The two conditions can be seen as minimum requirements for the stability of a coalition. Any coalition that does not satisfy both conditions can be seen as unstable, since the strategic aspects of the game are stronger than the benefits of cooperation.

Let us consider the oligopolistic example with affine inverse demand and linear costs, where $b = 50$, $a = 1$, $c_1 = 5$, $c_2 = 10$, $c_3 = 15$. Consider the the possible merger between the firms in coalition $S = \{1, 2\}$. The utopia payoffs are given by $M^S(\mathcal{G}) = (236, 111, 69)$. All subcoalitions of S that include firm 1 are $T = \{1\}$ and $T = \{1, 2\}$. For these coalitions we have

$$\max_{\{T \in 2^N | T \subset S, i \in T\}} \left\{ v(T) - \sum_{j \in T \setminus \{i\}} M_j^S(\mathcal{G}) \right\} = \max\{225, 225\} = 225.$$

(6.3)

Furthermore, the winning coalitions T that include the players in $S \setminus \{i\}$, but exclude player i are $T = \{2\}$ and $T = \{2, 3\}$. Therefore we get

$$\min_{\{T \in \mathcal{W} | i \notin T, S \setminus \{i\} \subset T\}} z_i^T = \min\{225, 278\} = 225.$$

(6.4)

The minimum right of firm 1 equals the maximum of (6.3) and (6.4), i.e. $m_1^S(\mathcal{G}) = 225$. A similar exercise for firm 2 leads to $m^S = (225, 100, 69)$. Solving $\sum_{i \in S} m_i^S + \lambda(M_i^S - m_i^S) = v(S)$ for λ gives $\lambda = \frac{1}{2}$. The S-compromise value is therefore equal to $\tau^S = (230.5, 105.5, 69)$.

Calculating the utopia payoff and minimum right for every possible merger we get the S-compromise values as given in Table 6.2.

At the end of this chapter we return to the government example from Section 5 to illustrate the interpretation of S-compromise admissibility as a stability requirement on coalitions. Consider the coalition $S = \{COM, CD, LIB\}$. The utopia payoff of COM is equal to $M_{COM}^S = -1$. Since by definition $m^S \geq 0$, this coalition does not satisfy the first requirement of S-compromise admissibility. So, CD and LIB do not want to have COM in their coalition.

S	M^S	m^S	τ^S
$\{1\}$	$(225, 100, 25)$	$(225, 100, 25)$	$(225, 100, 25)$
$\{2\}$	$(225, 100, 25)$	$(225, 100, 25)$	$(225, 100, 25)$
$\{3\}$	$(225, 100, 25)$	$(225, 100, 25)$	$(225, 100, 25)$
$\{1, 2\}$	$(236, 111, 69)$	$(225, 100, 69)$	$(230.5, 105.5, 69)$
$\{1, 3\}$	$(253, 136, 53)$	$(225, 136, 25)$	$(239, 136, 39)$
$\{2, 3\}$	$(278, 111, 36)$	$(278, 100, 25)$	$(278, 105.5, 30.5)$
$\{1, 2, 3\}$	$(370, 228, 170)$	$(225, 100, 25)$	$(278.65, 146.25, 78.65)$

Table 6.2. S-compromise values for a merger situation.

Secondly, consider coalition $S = \{SOC, CD, LIB\}$. We have that $M^S = (1, 3, 8, 6)$. Furthermore, we get

$$m_{SOC}^S = \max\left\{ \max\{4, 0, 0\}, \min\{4, 4\} \right\} = 4$$

$$m_{CD}^S = \max\left\{ \max\{9, 0, 0\}, \min\{7, 6\} \right\} = 9$$

$$m_{LIB}^S = \max\left\{ \max\{7, 0, 0\}, \min\{3, 0\} \right\} = 7.$$

So, the minimum right of SOC is based on either the remainder of $v(\{SOC, CD, LIB\})$ when the other parties get their utopia payoff, the spillover of coalition $\{CD, LIB\}$, or the spillover of coalition $\{COM, CD, LIB\}$. The minimum rights of CD and LIB are based on the remainder of $v(\{SOC, CD, LIB\})$ when the other parties get their utopia payoff. Since $\sum_{i \in S} m_i^S > v(S)$, this coalition is not S-compromise admissible. The total of the minimum rights can not be supported by the surplus these three parties generate. For completeness, all utopia payoffs, minimum rights and S-compromise values are denoted in Table 6.3.

S	M^S	m^S	τ^S
$\{SOC, CD\}$	$(4, 12, 12, 3)$	$(4, 4, 6, 3)$	$(4, 36/7, 48/7, 3)$
$\{SOC, LIB\}$	$(2, 10, 7, 10)$	$(2, 4, 7, 0)$	$(2, 25/4, 7, 15/4)$
$\{CD, LIB\}$	$(0, 4, 15, 15)$	$(0, 4, 6, 0)$	$(0, 4, 75/8, 45/8)$
$\{COM, SOC, CD\}$	$(7, 19, 19, 0)$	$(4, 4, 6, 0)$	$(139/31, 199/31, 251/31, 0)$
$\{COM, SOC, LIB\}$	$(3, 13, 6, 13)$	$(1, 4, 6, 0)$	$(5/3, 7, 6, 13/3)$
$\{COM, CD, LIB\}$	$(-1, 4, 14, 14)$	not defined	not S-compromise admissible
$\{SOC, CD, LIB\}$	$(1, 3, 8, 6)$	$(1, 4, 9, 7)$	not S-compromise admissible
N	$(-2, 2, 3, -3)$	not defined	not S-compromise admissible

Table 6.3. S-compromise values for a government situation.

Appendix

A. Proof of Theorem 6.1

Let $S \in \mathcal{W}$. Then

$$C_S(\mathcal{G}) \neq \emptyset$$

$$\Longleftrightarrow \{x \in \mathbb{R}_+^N \mid \sum_{i \in S} x_i = v(S), x_{N \setminus S} = z^S, \forall_{T \in \mathcal{W}} : \sum_{i \in T} x_i \geq v(T)\} \neq \emptyset$$

$$\Longleftrightarrow v(S) = \min_{x \in \mathbb{R}^N} \{\sum_{i \in S} x_i \mid \forall_{T \in \mathcal{W}} : \sum_{i \in T} x_i \geq v(T), \forall_{i \in S} : x_i \geq 0, x_{N \setminus S} = z^S\}$$

$$\Longleftrightarrow v(S) = \max_{\lambda, \mu, \psi} \{\sum_{T \in \mathcal{W}} \lambda(T) v(T) + \sum_{i \in N \setminus S} \mu_i z_i^S - \sum_{i \in N \setminus S} \psi_i z_i^S \mid$$

$$\sum_{i \in S} \mu_i e^{\{i\}} + \sum_{i \in N \setminus S} \mu_i e^{\{i\}} - \sum_{i \in N \setminus S} \psi_i e^{\{i\}} + \sum_{T \in \mathcal{W}} \lambda(T) e^T = e^S, \lambda, \mu, \psi \geq 0\}.$$

The last step follows directly from applying the duality theorem of linear programming. Note that nonemptiness of the primal feasible set follows from $\mathcal{W}$-stability and that the dual feasible set is always nonempty. Defining $\zeta_i = \mu_i - \psi_i$ for all $i \in N \setminus S$, we obtain

$$v(S) = \max_{\lambda, \mu, \zeta} \{\sum_{T \in \mathcal{W}} \lambda(T) v(T) + \sum_{i \in N \setminus S} \zeta_i z_i^S \mid$$

$$\sum_{i \in S} \mu_i e^{\{i\}} + \sum_{i \in N \setminus S} \zeta_i e^{\{i\}} + \sum_{T \in \mathcal{W}} \lambda(T) e^T = e^S, \lambda, \mu \geq 0\}$$

$$\Longleftrightarrow \forall_{S-\text{balanced}} \lambda : \sum_{T \in \mathcal{W}} \lambda(T) v(T) + \sum_{i \in N \setminus S} \zeta_i z_i^S \leq v(S),$$

$$\text{where } \forall_{i \in N \setminus S} : \zeta_i = \sum_{T \in \mathcal{W} : i \in T} \lambda(T)$$

$$\Longleftrightarrow \forall_{S-\text{balanced}} \lambda : \sum_{T \in \mathcal{W}} \lambda(T) v(T) + \sum_{i \in N \setminus S} \sum_{T \in \mathcal{W} : i \in T} \lambda(T) z_i^S \leq v(S)$$

$$\Longleftrightarrow \forall_{S-\text{balanced}} \lambda : \sum_{T \in \mathcal{W}} \lambda(T) \left[v(T) - \sum_{i \in (N \setminus S) \cap T} z_i^S \right] \leq v(S).$$

Since $C(\mathcal{G}) \neq \emptyset$ if and only if there exists an $S \in \mathcal{W}$ such that $C_S(\mathcal{G}) \neq \emptyset$, the assertion follows. $\square$

B.   Constructing a Spillover Game from a Non-Cooperative Game

Let $G = (N, \{A_i\}_{i \in N}, \{u_i\}_{i \in N})$ be a game in strategic form, where N is the set of players, A_i is the set of strategies for player $i \in N$ and $u_i : \prod_{j \in N} A_j \to \mathbb{R}_+$ is the (nonnegative) payoff function for player $i \in N$. This game might, for example, arise from an economy with externalities as is for example the case in Chander and Tulkens (1997). For each coalition $S \in 2^N$, define $A_S = \prod_{i \in S} A_i$ and $u_S = \sum_{i \in S} u_i$. Note that it is implicitly assumed that utilities are transferable, e.g. that they are in monetary terms. Furthermore, we define for each coalition $S \in 2^N$ the associated *S-induced game*, which is given by the tuple $G_S = (\{S\} \cup N \backslash S, \{A_S\} \cup \{A_i\}_{i \in N \backslash S}, \{u_S\} \cup \{u_i\}_{i \in N \backslash S})$. The S-induced game is a noncooperative game where coalition S acts as one player against the singletons in $N \backslash S$. Note that for all $i \in N$, $G_{\{i\}} = G_\emptyset = G$.

For the sake of argument, assume that for each $S \in 2^N$ the S-induced game has a unique Nash equilibrium payoff. Let $x^S \in A_S \times \prod_{i \in N \backslash S} A_i$ be a strategy profile that supports the unique Nash equilibrium payoff in G_S. Using these Nash equilibrium payoffs we can generate a cooperative game where for each coalition S the value is given by $v(S) = u_S(x^S)$. Note that $v(N)$ equals the maximum total payoff to the grand coalition and, hence, corresponds to a Pareto optimal strategy profile. Attached to the value for S is a vector of payoffs for the agents not in S, z^S, where for all $i \in N \backslash S$, $z_i^S = u_i(x^S)$. The vector z^S captures the spillovers that arise when coalition S forms.

Chapter 7

THE TIMING OF VERTICAL MERGERS UNDER UNCERTAINTY

1. Introduction

In Part I of this book, a variety of investment problems under uncertainty has been discussed. A very prominent example of an investment decision taken under uncertainty is the decision of two firms to merge. Usually, mergers take place in waves during economic booms. Empirical evidence on the procyclicality of merger waves has been reported by Maksimovic and Philips (2001). In general, one distinguishes between *horizontal* and *vertical* mergers. A horizontal merger occurs when two (or more) firms that are operating on the same product market merge. A vertical merger takes place when two (or more) firms that operate in different product markets merge.

The possibility of a merger should be seen as a real option to two firms operating in an uncertain market. From an uncertainty point of view there is a key difference between horizontal and vertical mergers. In horizontal mergers the firms are facing the same market uncertainty, which influences their profit stream. In a vertical merger the firms face different, although possibly correlated, market uncertainty.

The standard example of a vertical merger is where a firm producing intermediate goods (the *upstream* firm) merges with a firm that uses the intermediate good to produce a final product (the *downstream* firm). The uncertainty that both firms face is different, but it seems reasonable to assume that, since the demand of the downstream firm for intermediate goods influences the profit stream of the upstream firm, they are correlated. Another example of a vertical merger is one between cross-border firms. The recent merger between Air France and KLM Royal Dutch Airlines can serve as an example. Although both firms produce

165

the same service, flights, this is not a horizontal merger. Namely, the uncertainty both airlines face is different. This has for a large part to do with landing rights. Since Air France is the main airline serving French airports it is extremely vulnerable to shifts in the demand for flights from France. Similarly, KLM is vulnerable to shifts in the demand for flights from The Netherlands. Since the number of cross-border mergers has been increasing over the past decade (cf. Di Giovanni (2004)) the issue of the timing of cross-border mergers becomes more important.

The problem of optimal timing of a horizontal merger is addressed in Lambrecht (2004). He develops a model with two firms who can merge to obtain a synergy effect. The synergy effect is the real option in this case. Obtaining this synergy effect can be achieved by incurring some sunk costs (e.g. legal costs, costs of restructuring the organisation, etc.). Since he assumes that both firms face the same product market uncertainty the optimal threshold can be found by applying the standard techniques of real options theory (cf. Dixit and Pindyck (1996)). Furthermore, the (Pareto) optimal terms of the mergers (i.e. the profit share each firm gets) is determined. Lambrecht (2004) shows that mergers are procyclical: it is optimal to merge only in a bull market. He also finds that hostile takeovers take place at a later date than (friendly) mergers.

In Chapter 6 the importance of coalitional spillovers has been emphasised in finding a "fair" allocation of revenues that are earned cooperatively. In mergers this also holds true. The value of the outside option for each firm (i.e. staying separate) should be taken into account in determining the terms of the merger. In horizontal mergers the market uncertainty is not crucial in determining the terms of the merger, since both firms face exactly the same uncertainty.

In vertical mergers, however, uncertainty plays a crucial role in determining the terms of the merger and thereby also in the timing of the merger. This is seen by the following argument. At the point where two firms merge, a new firm is created that faces market uncertainty. This uncertainty consists of a combination of the uncertainty that both firms faced separately before the merger. The exact combination depends on the relative importance of the two markets for the merged firm. Suppose that we can find an optimal threshold for the merged firm to actually make the sunk costs and obtain the synergy effect that the merger creates. This threshold is then based on the *combined* uncertainty for both firms. Consider now a spillover game for the merger situation at the threshold. The minimum right of each firm can be calculated and it might very well turn out that the coalition of firms considering the merger is not compromise admissible. Since the minimum right of each firm takes into account the outside (stand-alone) option, this implies that the synergy effect that is obtained by the merger is high enough to cover the sunk costs, but is smaller than the sum of the stand-alone profits. That is, it is impossible to find a profit share for both firms that makes it in both firms' interest to actually merge. Hence, strategic considerations may lead to a delay of a merger that is in itself optimal from an economic point of view.

In this chapter a model is developed that addresses some of the issues that arise when combining multiple sources of uncertainty and strategic considerations in the timing of (vertical) mergers. The model considers two firms whose profits consist of a deterministic profit flow and a multiplicative stochastic shock modelled via a geometric Brownian motion. The firms can decide to merge by incurring a sunk cost and in return the newly formed firm gets a deterministic profit flow that is higher than the sum of its parts (the synergy effect). Based on the relative importance of both markets in the merged firm it is shown that the uncertainty for the merged firm follows a geometric Brownian motion as well. A threshold is obtained at which it is optimal for the firms to merge, i.e. to incur the sunk cost and obtain the synergy effect. This is the optimal time for a merger to take place. A spillover game is then constructed to assess whether the merger is compromise admissible (and, hence, strategically viable) at the threshold. By means of simulations the effects of certain parameters on the expected optimal merging time and the expected compromise admissible merging time are measured. It is shown that in most cases the merger takes place at a substantially later point in time than the optimal merging time.

2. The Model

Consider two firms, indexed by $i \in \{1, 2\}$, that operate in separate, but related markets. The profit flow of firm i at time $t \in [0, \infty)$, π_t^i, consists of a deterministic part, denoted by $D_i > 0$, and a stochastic component, denoted by X_t^i. The deterministic component can be thought of as resulting from Cournot competition in the product market as is illustrated in Chapters 4 and 5. The stochastic shock is assumed to be multiplicative, that is,

$$\pi_t^i = X_t^i D_i.$$

The stochastic shock follows a geometric Brownian motion with trend μ_i and volatility σ_i, i.e.

$$dX_t^i = \mu_i X_t^i dt + \sigma_i X_t^i dW_t^i,$$

where W^i is a Wiener process, so $dW_t^i \sim \mathcal{N}(0, dt)$. The instantaneous correlation between W^1 and W^2 equals $\rho \in [-1, 1]$. This implies that $dW_t^1 dW_t^2 = \rho dt$. It is assumed that the discount rate for both firms is identical and equal to $r \in (0, 1)$. Furthermore, in order for the problem to have a finite solution it is assumed that $\mu_i < r$, for $i \in \{1, 2\}$.

Let $D = D_1 + D_2$ denote the total deterministic profit flow of the separate firms. There is an option for both firms to merge, leading to a joint deterministic profit flow $D_m = \alpha D$. Due to synergy effects it is assumed that $\alpha > 1$. In order for the firms to merge, some sunk costs have to be incurred. These costs can be thought of to comprise for example the legal costs of the merger (including the costs incurred for getting formal approval by competition authorities), the costs of restructuring the two organisations to facilitate the merger, etc. These costs are denoted by $M > 0$. After the merger it is assumed that the importance of market 1 in the new firm is given by a share $\gamma \in (0, 1)$. So, the stochastic shock that the merged firm faces at time t, denoted by Y_t, equals[1]

$$Y_t = (X^1)^\gamma (X^2)^{1-\gamma}.$$

The following proposition shows that Y follows a geometric Brownian motion. Its proof can be found in Appendix A.

PROPOSITION 7.1 *There exists a Wiener process* $(W_t)_{t \geq 0}$, *such that the stochastic process* $(Y_t)_{t \geq 0}$ *follows a geometric Brownian motion, equal to*

$$dY_t = \mu Y_t dt + \sigma Y_t dW_t, \tag{7.1}$$

where

$$\mu = \gamma \mu_1 + (1 - \gamma) \mu_2 - \frac{1}{2} \gamma (1 - \gamma) \left((\sigma_1^2 - \sigma_2^2) - 2\sigma_1 \sigma_2 (1 - \rho) \right), \tag{7.2}$$

and

$$\sigma = \sqrt{\gamma^2 \sigma_1^2 + (1 - \gamma)^2 \sigma_2^2 - 2\gamma(1 - \gamma)\sigma_1 \sigma_2 \rho}. \tag{7.3}$$

Note that $\mu < r$. Furthermore, it holds that $\mu < \gamma \mu_1 + (1-\gamma)\mu_2$. Hence, the trend of the uncertainty faced by the merged firm is less than the weighted average of the uncertainty the separated firms face. If $\rho > 0$, this is offset by a smaller volatility, $\sigma^2 < \gamma^2 \sigma_1^2 + (1 - \gamma)^2 \sigma_2^2$. If $\rho < 0$,

---

[1]This functional form is best understood by considering the deterministic case, i.e. $\sigma_1 = \sigma_2 = 0$. Then it holds that $X_t^i = e^{\mu_i t}$ for $i = 1, 2$. Hence, the growth rate of the profit of firm i equals μ_i. The growth rate of the merged firm should then equal $\gamma \mu_1 + (1 - \gamma)\mu_2$. In other words, $Y = e^{\gamma \mu_1 + (1-\gamma)\mu_2} = (X^1)^\gamma (X^2)^{1-\gamma}$.

however, the converse holds and the merged firm faces more uncertainty. Hence, if the uncertainty for both firms is positively correlated, a merger can be seen as an act of diversification, thereby lowering the volatility. If the uncertainty is negatively correlated, the merged firm faces more risk. This leads us to predict that mergers will be seen sooner between firms operating in positively correlated markets.

The optimal time for a merger to take place can now be found in a similar way as has been done in Chapter 4. We have to find a threshold of the stochastic process Y, Y^*, at which it becomes optimal for a firm having a current deterministic profit flow D, and facing a multiplicative stochastic shock Y, to invest an amount M, in order to obtain the new deterministic profit stream D_m. This threshold can be shown to equal (cf. Huisman (2001) for an analogy)

$$Y^* = \frac{\beta_1}{\beta_1 - 1} \frac{(r - \mu)M}{D_m - D} = \frac{\beta_1}{\beta_1 - 1} \frac{(r - \mu)M}{(\alpha - 1)D},$$

where β_1 is the positive root of the characteristic equation,

$$\frac{1}{2}\sigma^2 \beta(\beta - 1) + \mu\beta - r = 0.$$

Since this threshold is reached from below, we conclude that it is optimal to merge only in bull markets. This is a similar finding as reported in Lambrecht (2004).

Associated to this merger problem we can create a spillover game $\mathcal{G}$, with $N = \{1,2\}$ and $\mathcal{W} = 2^N$ at each point in time $t \geq 0$. Given that the stochastic processes are at X_t^1, X_t^2, and $Y_t = (X_t^1)^\gamma (X_t^2)^{1-\gamma}$, respectively, the expected payoffs of staying separate and merging at time t are,[2]

$$v_t(\{1\}) = z_{1,t}^{\{2\}} = \mathbb{E}\left(\int_t^\infty e^{-rdt} X_t^1 D_1\right) = X_t^1 \frac{D_1}{r - \mu_1},$$

$$v_t(\{2\}) = z_{2,t}^{\{1\}} = \mathbb{E}\left(\int_t^\infty e^{-rdt} X_t^2 D_2\right) = X_t^2 \frac{D_2}{r - \mu_2},$$

and

$$v_t(N) = \mathbb{E}\left(\int_t^\infty e^{-rdt} Y_t D_m\right) - M = Y_t \frac{D_m}{r - \mu} - M,$$

respectively. The strategic viability of a merger at time t can be assessed by looking at the minimum rights of the firms for coalition $S = \{1,2\}$, $m_1^S(t)$ and $m_2^S(t)$. As in the merger example of Chapter 6 it is easy to

---

[2]The expectations are calculated in a similar way as in Chapter 4.

show that

$$m_1^S(t) = X_t^1 \frac{D_1}{r - \mu_1},$$

and

$$m_2^S(t) = X_t^2 \frac{D_2}{r - \mu_2},$$

respectively.

Define the stopping time T_m, by

$$T_m = \inf\{t \geq 0 | Y_t \geq Y^*\}.$$

So, it is optimal to conduct the merger at time T_m. However, if at time T_m it holds that

$$m_1^S(T_m) + m_2^S(T_m) > v_{T_m}(\{N\}) = (X_{T_m}^1)^\gamma (X_{T_m}^2)^{1-\gamma} \frac{D_m}{r - \mu} - M,$$

then the merger is not compromise admissible. That is, no division of the merger surplus can be found that makes both firms better off than the stand-alone option. So, the merger should take place at the first time $T \geq 0$, where both $Y_t \geq Y^*$, and the merger is compromise admissible, i.e. when

$$T = \inf \left\{ t \geq 0 | Y_t \geq Y^*, X_t^1 \frac{D_1}{r - \mu_1} + X_t^2 \frac{D_2}{r - \mu_2} \right.$$
$$\left. \leq (X_t^1)^\gamma (X_t^2)^{1-\gamma} \frac{D_m}{r - \mu} - M \right\}.$$

Note that $T \geq T_m$ (a.s.). Hence, the outside options firms have in a vertical merger delay the merger. The magnitude of this effect is assessed by means of simulations in the next section.

3.   The Effect of the Stand-Alone Option on the Timing of Mergers

In this section, the effect of combining an optimal stopping problem with a spillover game is analysed by means of a numerical example of the model as described in Section 2. For the benchmark case of the model we choose the parameter values as given in Table 7.1. So, we start from a situation where the two firms are symmetric and face a stochastic shock with trend 0.04 and volatility 0.1. The correlation between the Wiener processes W^1 and W^2 is taken to be zero. The synergy effect of a merger

$D_1 = 50$	$\mu_1 = 0.04$	$\sigma_1 = 0.1$
$D_2 = 50$	$\mu_2 = 0.04$	$\sigma_2 = 0.1$
$M = 100$	$\alpha = 1.5$	$\gamma = 0.5$
$r = 0.1$	$\rho = 0$	

Table 7.1. Parameter values.

allows for an increase in the deterministic profit flow of 50% and both markets are assumed to of equal weight for the merged firm. Finally, the discount rate is set at 10%.

Deviating from this benchmark case we study the (*ceteris paribus*) effects of changing the parameters μ_1, σ_1, α, γ, and ρ, respectively. In each case we calculate the expected time for the optimal and compromise admissible thresholds to be hit, i.e. $\mathbb{E}(T_m)$ and $\mathbb{E}(T)$, respectively. These expectations are approximated by calculating the sample mean over 500 simulations for each scenario.

First we vary the trend in the geometric Brownian motion of firm 1. We take values for μ_1 in the interval [0.01,0.08]. This leads to Figure 7.1. The figure shows that $\mathbb{E}(T_m)$ decreases if μ_1 increases. Since the trend

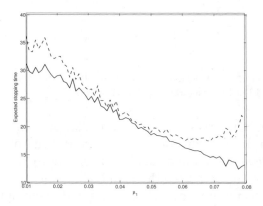

Figure 7.1. Expected first passage times of the optimal (solid line) and compromise admissible (dashed line) thresholds as a function of μ_1.

in the growth of the profit stream of firm 1 increases, the trend in the growth of the profit stream of the merged firm, μ, increases as well. Therefore, the threshold Y^* will be reached sooner. The effect on $\mathbb{E}(T)$ is more ambiguous. Here two effects are at work. Firstly, for increasing μ_1, the threshold Y^* is reached sooner. This has a downward effect on $\mathbb{E}(T)$. On the other hand, the stand-alone option of firm 1 becomes larger as well. Therefore, the probability that a merger is economically viable, but not strategically viable (i.e. not compromise admissible) increases. This results in an upward pressure for $\mathbb{E}(T)$. In this simulation, for values of μ_1 in the interval $[0.01, 0.06]$, the former effect dominates, whereas for values $\mu_1 > 0.07$, the latter effect dominates. Furthermore, the difference between $\mathbb{E}(T_m)$ and $\mathbb{E}(T)$ seems to be smaller the more symmetric both firms are. This indicates that for symmetric firms the probability that a merger is economically but not strategically viable, is lower than for less symmetric firms.

The results of the simulation where the parameter σ_1 is varied over the interval $[0, 0.2]$ are reported in Figure 7.1 Here we see that if uncer-

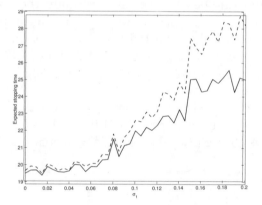

Figure 7.2.   Expected first passage times of the optimal (solid line) and compromise admissible (dashed line) thresholds as a function of σ_1.

tainty for one of the firms grows, both $\mathbb{E}(T_m)$ and $\mathbb{E}(T)$ increase as is perfectly in synch with intuition. Furthermore, one observes that the difference between $\mathbb{E}(T_m)$ and $\mathbb{E}(T)$ increases as σ_1 increases. This effect results form the fact that the stand-alone option for firm 2 is not affected by an increase in σ_1. Both the stand-alone option for firm 1 and the expected joint profit flow of the merged firm decrease. However, since the deterministic profit flow of the merged firm is higher, the value of the merged firm decreases faster with σ_1 than the stand-alone value of firm 1. Hence, the probability that a merger is economically but not strategically viable increases with σ_1.

The effect of the synergy parameter, α, on the expected first passage times of the optimal and compromise admissible thresholds is depicted in Figure 7.2. The effects are straightforward. If α increases, the threshold Y^* decreases and, hence, its first passage time. Since the expected value of the merged firm increases with α and the stand-alone values of both

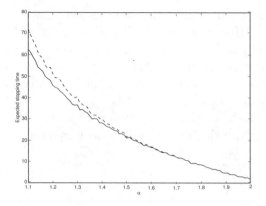

Figure 7.3. Expected first passage times of the optimal (solid line) and compromise admissible (dashed line) thresholds as a function of α.

firms are unaffected, the probability that a merger is economically but not strategically viable decreases. Hence, both $\mathbb{E}(T_m)$ and $\mathbb{E}(T)$ are decreasing with α, and the difference between the two expected first passage time decreases as well.

Varying the weight of the market on which firm 1 operates leads to Figure 7.3. Here, the effects are less clear-cut. Still one can observe some

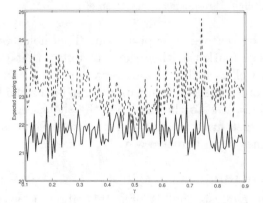

Figure 7.4. Expected first passage times of the optimal (solid line) and compromise admissible (dashed line) thresholds as a function of γ.

trends. The expected first passage time of Y^* seems hardly affected by changes in γ. This comes as no surprise since it is assumed that both firms are symmetric in the economic fundamentals as well as in the uncertainty that they face. Also $\mathbb{E}(T)$ does not seem to vary much with

γ. This is due to the fact that the stand-alone values of both firms are independent of γ. However, the more equal the weight of both markets in the merged firms the closer $\mathbb{E}(T_m)$ and $\mathbb{E}(T)$ get.[3] Symmetry enhances the expected value of the merged firm since uncertainty in both markets is diversified more. This holds because in the benchmark case we assume that the correlation between W^1 and W^2 is zero.

Finally, the effects of the correlation coefficient, ρ, can be found in Figure 7.4. The more the uncertainty in both markets is correlated, the

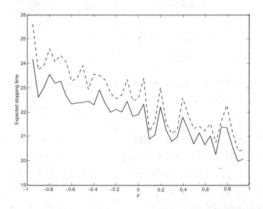

Figure 7.5. Expected first passage times of the optimal (solid line) and compromise admissible (dashed line) thresholds as a function of ρ.

sooner Y^* will be reached in expectation. This holds because if there is a boom in, say, market 1, then the probability that there is a boom in market 2 as well is higher for higher values of ρ. Furthermore, the expected value of the merged firm will increase faster in a boom than the stand-alone values, due to the fact that the shocks enter the expected value for the merged firm in a multiplicative way, whereas they enter the stand-alone values in an additive way.

4.   Implications

Although the analysis that is presented above is very rudimentary and needs to be thoroughly extended, some implications for vertical, or cross-border mergers can be drawn. Based on the simulation results in Section 3 one expects that the most profitable mergers are the ones between equally sized firms ($\gamma \approx \frac{1}{2}$) that operate in correlated markets (high ρ) with a similar trend ($\mu_1 \approx \mu_2$). In these cases a merger is, in

---

[3]We see a similar "symmetry effect" with varying μ_1.

expectation, sooner both economically and strategically viable. Furthermore, the difference between $\mathbb{E}(T_m)$ and $\mathbb{E}(T)$ is typically smaller. This implies that one can use economic "momentum" better than in other cases. Namely, as soon as Y^* is reached it is optimal to start exploiting the synergy effects of a merger. Hence, the sooner it is strategically viable to merge, the higher the probability of a successful merger.

This might explain why many (cross-border or vertical) mergers take place relatively late in an economic boom. Consider two firms, one relatively small firm and one relatively large firm, that operate on markets with different trends and a very low correlation between uncertainty. Even though the synergy effects may be high, a merger might not be successful. This is the case because, even though a merger is economically viable, the firms will find it hard to agree on the terms of the merger since the stand-alone values are relatively high. This leads to postponement of the merger and, hence, to the destruction of (shareholder) value.

The analysis in this chapter can be extended to include more firms. Suppose that there are two firms in market 1 and there is one firm in market 2. Both firms in market 1 could consider a merger with the firm in market 2. This might lead to preemptive effects, much in the spirit of Chapters 4 and 5. This could lead to mergers taking place too soon from an economic point of view and therefore to a high probability of the merger failing. This is a topic for further research.

Appendix
A. Proof of Proposition 7.1

With Ito's lemma (see Section 7 of Chapter 2) we find that

$$dY =\gamma(X^1)^{\gamma-1}(X^2)^{1-\gamma}dX^1 + (1-\gamma)(X^1)^{\gamma}(X^2)^{-\gamma}dX^2$$
$$- \frac{1}{2}\gamma(1-\gamma)\Big((X^1)^{\gamma-2}(X^2)^{1-\gamma}(dX^1)^2 + (X^1)^{\gamma}(X^2)^{-\gamma-1}(dX^2)^2\Big)$$
$$+ \gamma(1-\gamma)(X^1)^{\gamma-1}(X^2)^{-\gamma}dX^1 dX^2$$
$$=\gamma\mu_1 Y\, dt + \gamma\sigma_1 Y\, dW^1 + (1-\gamma)\mu_2 Y\, dt + (1-\gamma)\sigma_2 Y\, dW^2$$
$$- \frac{1}{2}\gamma(1-\gamma)(\sigma_1^2 + \sigma_2^2)Y\, dt + \gamma(1-\gamma)\sigma_1\sigma_2\rho Y\, dt$$
$$\equiv \mu dt + \gamma\sigma_1 Y\, dW^1 + (1-\gamma)\sigma_2 Y\, dW^2,$$

where μ is defined as in (7.2).

Consider

$$d\tilde{W}^1 \equiv \gamma\sigma_1 dW^1 \sim \mathcal{N}(0,\gamma^2\sigma_1^2 dt)$$

and

$$d\tilde{W}^2 \equiv (1 - \gamma)\sigma_2 dW^2 \sim \mathcal{N}(0, (1 - \gamma)^2 \sigma_2^2 dt).$$

Note that

$$Cov(dW^1, dW^2) = \mathbb{E}(dW^1 dW^2) = \rho dt.$$

Hence, it holds that

$$Cov(d\tilde{W}^1, d\tilde{W}^2) = \gamma(1 - \gamma)\sigma_1 \sigma_2 \rho dt.$$

Define

$$d\tilde{W} = d\tilde{W}^1 + d\tilde{W}^2.$$

Then it holds that

$$d\tilde{W} \sim \mathcal{N}(0, [\gamma^2 \sigma_1^2 + (1 - \gamma)^2 \sigma_2^2 - 2\gamma(1 - \gamma)\sigma_1 \sigma_2 \rho]dt).$$

Note that

$$\gamma \sigma_1 Y dW^1 + (1 - \gamma)\sigma_2 Y dW^2 = Y d\tilde{W}$$
$$= Y \sigma dW,$$

where W is a Wiener process and σ is as defined in (7.3).   □

III

BOUNDED RATIONALITY AND MARKET EVOLUTION

Chapter 8

MULTI-LEVEL EVOLUTION IN COURNOT

OLIGOPOLY

1.   Introduction

The economic decisions that an individual has to make are often very complicated. Each individual has to take into account not only her own objectives, actions and possible strategies, but also the social environment in which he operates. In the literature it has been argued that assuming rational behaviour by individuals, as is standard in the neoclassical paradigm, is too strong an assumption. To quote Young (1998): "This [rationality] is a rather extravagant and implausible model of human behavior, especially in the complex, dynamic environments that economic agents typically face". Furthermore, it is felt that the role of *equilibrium* in economic models needs to be reconsidered. One may look at the equilibria arising in neoclassical models as being the outcome of a dynamic process of interaction during which evolution to an equilibrium is established. Evolution then works as a way to select an equilibrium. The importance of equilibrium selection has also been recognised by Harsanyi and Selten (1988). They stick however to the neoclassical paradigm with rational individuals in an essentially static environment. Equilibrium selection then takes place by a rational procedure that can be described by a homotopy. Lately, it has been argued that the equilibrium selection process should be seen as an evolutionary process and hence be modelled explicitly. The way this has been done is to apply ideas from evolution theory in game theory (see e.g. Maynard Smith (1982)). Evolution results from the actions of essentially non-rational or boundedly rational agents. The main question is whether in the long-run evolution leads to a rational equilibrium, that is, do the equilibria arising in models based on the neoclassical paradigm give a good description of the long-run in an evolutionary setting. The field of evolutionary economics has grown rapidly during the last decade. This development has been accompanied by an increasing interest in experimental economics to study the evolution of economic behaviour.

There are several ways to include evolutionary ideas into economic theory. One way, that stays close to standard non-cooperative game theory, is by looking at evolutionary stable strategies (ESS). An ESS is a strategy that is robust against small perturbations. As such it is a refinement of the Nash equilibrium concept (see e.g. Van Damme (1994) or Weibull (1995)). The ESS concept, however, is a static one. In the biological literature a dynamic process has been introduced called the replicator dynamics (cf. Taylor and Jonker (1978) or Van Damme (1991)). The replicator dynamics is a differential equation that is the result of an underlying game theoretic model. It describes the dynamics of the fractions of two different populations that influence each other's existence by interaction. One can think for example of a predator-prey model. It can be shown that an ESS of the underlying game is asymptotically stable for the replicator dynamics. The behavior of the populations in the replicator dynamics is completely pre-programmed and deterministic.

If the behaviour of players is stochastically perturbed one can use the concept of stochastic stability that has been introduced by Foster and Young (1990), Kandori et al. (1993) and Young (1993). Intuitively, stochastically stable states are those states that remain to be played after evolution has done its work by letting the perturbations converge to zero. Taking this limit can be defended by the argument that, as time goes along, players learn to understand their environment better which decreases the probability of them making mistakes which results in less perturbations. The stochastically stable states are the remaining states in the long-run that can be said to have survived the process of evolution.

In oligopoly theory this idea has been applied by Vega–Redondo (1997). He showed that when firms imitate the firm that makes the highest profits, combined with experimentation or trial and error in a Cournot setting, the market converges to the Walrasian equilibrium. The importance of imitation and trial and error in evolutionary economic processes has already been stressed by Alchian (1950). He claimed that profit maximisation is not a meaningful criterion for selecting an action in an essentially uncertain situation. Recently, an experimental study by Offerman et al. (2002) shows that in a Cournot market where agents know the demand function, the cost function, as well as all quantities produced and profits earned by the others, the market either settles in the Walrasian equilibrium or in the collusion equilibrium. The latter results when firms set quantities in such a way that industry profit is maximised. Hence, Vega–Redondo (1997) explains only part of this experimental result.

This chapter presents a framework in which we allow for two levels of evolution. At the first level firms can change their behaviour. The evolution of behaviour leads to different evolutionary paths at the second – quantity setting – level. We show that the stochastically stable state of this two-stage evolutionary process is either the collusive equilibrium resulting from cooperative behaviour or the Walrasian equilibrium resulting from competitive behaviour. Therewith, this chapter gives a theoretical explanation for the experimental results of Offerman et al. (2002). Which way evolution goes – competition or cooperation – depends on the inclination to cooperative behaviour within the group of firms in the market. This inclination to cooperation can be seen as an agreement on patience between firms and is therefore a representation of the social environment in which firms operate. It is assumed that the inclination to cooperate is exogenously given. The importance of the interrelationships of the environment and the prevailing types of economic behaviour which appear through a process of economic selection, has been stressed by Alchian (1950). In the ultra-long run, the inclination to cooperative behaviour might also be subject to evolution. For simplicity we don't investigate this venue. By allowing for the simultaneous existence of more than one behavioural rule and by introducing a meta-level where firms evaluate their behaviour, this chapter extends the model of Vega–Redondo (1997) in two ways that, to our knowledge, have not been pursued so far in the existing literature.

In modelling the interaction on two levels, a Markov chain on the quantity-setting level as well as a Markov chain on the behavioural level are defined, where the transition probabilities of the latter depend on the state of the quantity-setting chain. It is difficult to analyse the limit distribution of the large Markov chain that is obtained by combining the two levels, for it would require an analysis of all possible interrelationships between behavioural and quantity adaptation. Fortunately, one can simplify the analysis and obtain an approximation of the stochastically stable states of the entire process by using the theory of nearly-complete decomposable systems developed by Simon and Ando (1961), Ando and Fisher (1963), and Courtois (1977).

At both levels, the decision-making process of firms is boundedly rational. At the quantity-setting level, firms are assumed to imitate in a prescribed way. This corresponds to firms using rules of thumb in conducting their day to day business. At the behavioural level, firms evaluate their strategy and change their behaviour if the profitability of their current behaviour is not satisfactory.

Although the use of multiple behavioural rules in stochastic evolutionary models has not been explored in great depth, the idea has been applied in a (static and deterministic) ESS setting, notably in the literature on indirect evolution (cf. Güth and Yaari (1992)). In this literature evolution works on preferences rather than on strategies. For example, Bester and Güth (1998) develop a model in which agents can be either altruistic or spiteful. Given the player's preferences she plays a best response. Altruism then leads to the cooperative outcome and spitefulness leads to the competitive outcome. Possajennikov (2000) extends the Bester and Güth (1998) model and gives conditions under which either altruism or spitefulness is evolutionary stable. This chapter gives a first application of the theory of nearly-complete decomposable systems in evolutionary economics. In Chapter 9 a more elaborate behavioural model is analysed.

The chapter is organised as follows. In Section 2 the model is explained in detail. First the quantity setting level is modelled. Afterwards, the behavioural level is modelled and both levels are united in one stochastic dynamic system. In Section 3 it is proved that under suitable conditions either cooperative or competitive behaviour is stochastically stable. This leads to the conclusion that (approximately) either the collusion equilibrium or the Walrasian equilibrium arises. Finally, Section 4 concludes.

2.   The Model

Let be given a market for a homogeneous good with n firms, indexed by $I_n = \{1, 2, \ldots, n\}$. Competition takes place by quantity setting. The profit of firm i, $i \in I_n$, when it produces γ_i and the other firms produce together $\gamma_{-i} := \sum_{j \neq i} \gamma_j$ is given by

$$\pi(\gamma_i, \gamma_{-i}) = P(\gamma_i + \gamma_{-i})\gamma_i - C(\gamma_i),$$

where $P : \mathbb{R}_+ \to \mathbb{R}_+$ is the inverse demand function, which is assumed to be strictly decreasing and $C : \mathbb{R}_+ \to \mathbb{R}_+$ is the cost function. It is assumed that each firm can choose from a finite discrete set of possible production levels, $\Gamma(\delta) := \{0, \delta, 2\delta, \ldots, v\delta\}$, for some $v \in \mathbb{N}$ and $\delta > 0$.

The behaviour of firm $i \in I_n$ is denoted by $\theta_i \in \Theta = \{0, 1\}$, where $\theta_i = 1$ denotes cooperative behaviour and $\theta_i = 0$ denotes competitive behaviour. The state-space is given by $\Omega = \Gamma(\delta)^n \times \Theta^n$. A typical element $\omega \in \Omega$ is denoted $\omega = (\gamma, \theta)$, where $\gamma = (\gamma_1, \ldots, \gamma_n) \in \Gamma(\delta)^n$ and $\theta = (\theta_1, \ldots, \theta_n) \in \Theta^n$. The cardinality of Θ^n will be denoted by N and the cardinality of $\Gamma(\delta)^n$ by m. Let $\Sigma(S)$ denote the ordered set of all permutations on a finite set S. Then we define $\gamma(k) = \Sigma(\Gamma(\delta)^n)_k$, $k = 1, \ldots, m$, and $\theta(I) = \Sigma(\Theta^n)_I$, $I = 1, \ldots, N$.

2.1 The Quantity Setting Level

Firms that behave cooperatively are assumed to imitate the exemplary firm, i.e. the firm that produces the output that generates the highest industry profits if all firms were to produce the same quantity. Therefore, these firms are called *exemplary imitators*. Given a vector of output levels $\gamma \in \Gamma(\delta)^n$ their best-response correspondence is given by

$$BE(\gamma) = \{q \in \Gamma(\delta) | \exists_{j \in I_n} : q = \gamma_j, \forall_{k \in I_n} : \pi(q, (n-1)q) \geq \pi(\gamma_k, (n-1)\gamma_k)\}.$$

If a firm acts competitively, it imitates the firm that makes the highest profit. Firms behaving competitively are called *profit imitators*. Given a vector of output levels $\gamma \in \Gamma(\delta)^n$ their best-response correspondence is given by

$$BP(\gamma) = \{q \in \Gamma(\delta) | \exists_{j \in I_n} : q = \gamma_j, \forall_{k \in I_n} : \pi(q, \gamma_{-j}) \geq \pi(\gamma_k, \gamma_{-k})\}.$$

Let $\theta(I)$ be a given permutation on Θ^n. Firm i chooses an output level from $BE(\gamma)$ if $\theta(I)_i = 1$. If $\theta(I)_i = 0$, firm i chooses an element from $BP(\gamma)$. To do so, firm i uses a probability distribution with full support, $\eta_{E,i}^\gamma(\cdot)$ on $BE(\gamma)$ if $\theta(I)_i = 1$ and $\eta_{P,i}^\gamma(\cdot)$ on $BP(\gamma)$ if $\theta(I)_i = 0$.

The market now works as follows. At any time t, $t \in \mathbb{N}$, every firm gets the opportunity to adapt its output with probability p, $0 < p < 1$. This probability can be interpreted as the fraction of periods in which a firm updates its quantity. Given the vector of output levels $\gamma^{t-1} \in \Gamma(\delta)^n$, $\gamma_i^t \in BP(\gamma^{t-1})$ if firm i is a profit imitator and $\gamma_i^t \in BE(\gamma^{t-1})$ if firm i is an exemplary imitator. These dynamics define a Markov chain on $\Gamma(\delta)^n \times \Gamma(\delta)^n$, with transition matrix M_0^I. The dynamic process evolving according to this Markov chain is called the *pure imitation dynamics*dynamics,quantity.

The actual quantity choice can be influenced by several aspects. For example, a firm can experiment and choose another quantity. Another possibility is that firms make mistakes in their imitative behaviour. Finally, a firm may be replaced by a new firm that has the same behaviour, but sets a different quantity.[1] Since these effects are outside the model, we treat them as stochastic perturbations and hence we assume that

---

[1] In the original, biological, literature this is called a mutation.

with probability $\varepsilon > 0$ firm i chooses any output level using a probability distribution $\nu_i(\cdot)$ with full support. Imitation and experimentation define a Markov chain on $\Gamma(\delta)^n \times \Gamma(\delta)^n$ with transition matrix M_ε^I. A typical element is given by

$$M_\varepsilon^I(k,l) = \prod_{i \in I_n} \Big\{ (1-\varepsilon) \big[p \mathbb{1}_{(\theta(I)_i=0)} \eta_{P,i}^{\gamma(k)}(\gamma(l)_i) + p \mathbb{1}_{(\theta(I)_i=1)} \eta_{E,i}^{\gamma(k)}(\gamma(l)_i)$$

$$+ (1-p) \mathbb{1}_{(\gamma(k)_i=\gamma(l)_i)} \big] + \varepsilon \nu_i(\gamma(l)_i) \Big\},$$

where $\mathbb{1}_{(\cdot)}$ is the indicator function. It is reasonable to assume that as time passes firms learn to use the rule of thumb given by exemplary or profit imitation ever better. For this reason we focus on the situation where the probability of mistakes ε converges to zero. That is, we analyse the Markov chain with transition matrix

$$M^I := \lim_{\varepsilon \downarrow 0} M_\varepsilon^I.$$

Since M^I is an irreducible matrix, this Markov chain is ergodic and thus has a unique invariant probability measure $\mu^I(\cdot)$. For further reference the k-th element of the invariant measure will be denoted by μ_k^I, i.e. $\mu_k^I = \mu^I(\gamma(k))$.

2.2   The Behavioural Level

It is reasonable to assume that each firm knows *ex ante* that cooperation yields higher profits than competition. Since anti-trust laws forbid explicit coordination the question is whether there can be non-cooperative coordination on the cooperative outcome. The idea is to model behavioural adaptation by using a reciprocal-like argument. If a firm acts cooperatively and sees that it leads to profits that are close enough to the collusion profit it will not change its behaviour. If however, cooperative behaviour does not give enough profit *relative* to competitive behaviour, the firm will change its behaviour to competition. Since it is impossible for firms to observe the behaviour of the other firms, the behavioural decision needs to be based on observable data, i.e. quantities and profits. If all firms behave perfectly cooperatively and set the optimal collusion quantity, the total profit realised in the market equals the collusion profit, denoted by π^m. So the best a firm can hope for is to earn the n-th fraction of π^m, which is the firm's utopia profit. The behavioural decision of the firm will be based on the difference between this utopia profit and the actual profit in the industry.

Since full cooperation yields more profits than anything else, it is assumed that within the group of firms there is a certain inclination to cooperative behaviour. This inclination can be seen as a measure of patience of firms to reach the cooperative outcome. In this chapter we are not concerned about the evolution or origins of this inclination but simply assume that it is reflected by an exogenous and constant parameter $\tilde{\lambda} > 0$. A firm will then behave cooperatively as long as the difference between the utopia profit and the actual realised industry profit is not larger than $\tilde{\lambda}$. Another way to look at $\tilde{\lambda}$ is to see it as a measure of the intensity of competition in a market. The higher $\tilde{\lambda}$ the less fierce competition is. For a discussion on measures of competition the reader is referred to Boone (2000).

Given a behavioural permutation $\theta(I) \in \Theta^n$ and a quantity permutation $\gamma(k) \in \Gamma(\delta)^n$, the behaviour that firm i will choose if it can adapt its behaviour is given by

$$\theta^k(I)_i = \begin{cases} 1 & \text{if } \pi^m - \sum_{j \in I_n} \pi(\gamma(k)_j, \gamma(k)_{-j}) \leq \tilde{\lambda} \\ 0 & \text{otherwise.} \end{cases} \tag{8.1}$$

For each $I = 1, \ldots, N$, let $b(I)$ be the number of firms behaving cooperatively, i.e. $b(I) = |\{i \in I_n | \theta(I)_i = 1\}|$.

It is assumed that each period a firm adapts its behaviour with probability $0 < \tilde{p} < 1$. Together with eq. (8.1) this yields a dynamic process that defines a Markov chain of pure behavioural adaptation dynamics.[2] With probability $\tilde{\varepsilon} > 0$ each firm makes a mistake or experiments and chooses any behaviour using a probability measure $\tilde{\nu}_i(\cdot)$ with full support. Given a vector of quantities $\gamma(k) \in \Gamma(\delta)^n$, the probability of changing from $\theta(I)$ to $\theta(J)$ is then given by

$$\lambda_{\tilde{\varepsilon}}^k(I, J) = \prod_{i \in I_n} \left\{ (1 - \tilde{\varepsilon}) \left[\tilde{p} \mathbb{1}_{(\theta(J)_i = \theta^k(I)_i)} + (1 - \tilde{p}) \mathbb{1}_{(\theta(J)_i = \theta(I)_i)} \right] \right.$$
$$\left. + \tilde{\varepsilon} \tilde{\nu}_i(\theta(J)_i) \right\}.$$

As before, it is assumed that as time passes, firms get a better grip on the market situation and therefore the analysis is restricted to the dynamics where the experimentation probability converges to zero. To

---

[2]The postulated types of behaviour might give the impression that exemplary imitating implies solving a profit maximisation problem, whereas profit imitation does not. Therefore it may seem that switching from cooperative to competitive behaviour implies loosing rationality since exemplary imitators are more sophisticated. However, profit imitation can in fact also be seen as a form of profit maximisation. The only difference is that it requires less computational burden. Therefore, switching from cooperative to competitive behaviour merely implies that the firm is not willing any more to endure a heavier computational burden for behaviour that it considers not to give the desired result.

that end define for each $k = 1, \ldots, m$ and $I, J = 1, \ldots, N$,

$$\lambda_{IJ}^k := \lim_{\bar{\varepsilon} \downarrow 0} \lambda_{\bar{\varepsilon}}^k(I, J). \tag{8.2}$$

So, we consider the situation where evolution has forced the probability of mistakes on both the quantity setting level and the behavioural level to be infinitely small, but strictly positive.

To complete the model, we construct a Markov chain on Ω whose transition matrix is denoted by Q. At the beginning of each period firms simultaneously adapt their behaviour and output level based on the present state of the world. A typical element of Q is then given by

$$Q_{k_I l_J} = \lambda_{IJ}^k M^I(k, l).$$

Note that Q is a stochastic and irreducible matrix. The matrix Q is constructed by making blocks of all permutations on Θ^n. Within these blocks all permutations on $\Gamma(\delta)^n$ are stored. Hence, the coordinate k_I implies the quantity vector $\gamma(k)$ in block I, i.e. with behaviour vector $\theta(I)$. Since Q is irreducible the Markov chain has a unique invariant distribution which is denoted by $\mu(\cdot)$.

To facilitate the analysis in the next section define the stochastic and irreducible matrix Q^* with typical element

$$Q_{k_I l_J}^* = \begin{cases} M^I(k, l) & \text{if } I = J \\ 0 & \text{if } I \neq J. \end{cases}$$

Note that Q^* is a block diagonal matrix with blocks $Q_I^* = M^I$, $I = 1, \ldots, N$. Furthermore, a scalar ζ and a matrix C are defined such that

$$\zeta C_{k_I l_J} = \begin{cases} \lambda_{IJ}^k M^I(k, l) & \text{if } I \neq J \\ -\sum_{K \neq I} \lambda_{IK}^k M^I(k, l) & \text{if } I = J, \end{cases}$$

and

$$\zeta = \max_{k_I} \left\{ \sum_{K \neq I} \sum_{l=1}^m Q_{k_I l_K} \right\}$$
$$= \max_{k_I} \left\{ \sum_{K \neq I} \lambda_{IK}^k \right\}.$$

Note that $Q = Q^* + \zeta C$. For the results to be obtained in Section 3 to hold, the interaction between the blocks Q_I^* should be relatively small. It is most natural to achieve this by making assumptions on the probability of behavioural revision $\tilde{p}$ relative to the probability of quantity revision p, i.e. it is assumed that $\tilde{p}$ is small enough, which will be made precise in Proposition 8.2.

3. Analysis

In this section we prove that in the long-run the system settles down either in the Walrasian equilibrium or in the collusion equilibrium. To do so we need some additional notation.

Define the collusion equilibrium q^m to be the quantity that maximises industry profits. That is, q^m satisfies

$$P(nq^m)q^m - C(q^m) \geq P(nq)q - C(q), \qquad \forall q \in \mathbb{R}_+.$$

Let q_r^*, $r = 0, 1, \ldots, n$, be defined by

$$
\begin{aligned}
P((n-r)q_r^* + rq^m)q_r^* - C(q_r^*) \\
\geq P((n-r)q_r^* + rq^m)q - C(q), \qquad \forall q \in \mathbb{R}_+.
\end{aligned}
\tag{8.3}
$$

Furthermore, let I_0 and I_1 be such that $\theta(I_0) = (0, \ldots, 0)$ and $\theta(I_1) = (1, \ldots, 1)$. Note that q_0^* is the Walrasian output level q^*. It is assumed that the finite grid is such that $q^m, q_r^* \in \Gamma(\delta)^n$ for all $r = 0, 1, \ldots, n$.

On the quantity setting level, denote the *monomorphic* state $(q, \ldots, q) \in \Gamma(\delta)^n$ by $\overline{\gamma}(q)$. For $\theta(I) \in \Theta^n$, the *bimorphic* state $\overline{\gamma}_I(q, q') \in \Gamma(\delta)^n$ is defined by

$$
\overline{\gamma}_I(q, q')_i = \begin{cases} q & \text{if } \theta(I)_i = 0 \\ q' & \text{if } \theta(I)_i = 1, \end{cases}
$$

for all $i \in I_n$. Furthermore, k_I^* is defined to be the permutation on $\Gamma(\delta)^n$ such that $\gamma(k_I^*) = \overline{\gamma}_I(q_{b(I)}^*, q^m)$.

The first proposition that is proved determines the limit distribution on the quantity setting level for a Markov chain with transition matrix M^I, $I = 1, \ldots, N$, i.e. the limit distribution of block Q_I^* is determined. To prove the proposition two lemmas are needed, the proofs of which can be found in the appendix. To simplify notation, denote for each $I = 1, \ldots, N$,

$$
\begin{aligned}
\mathcal{A}_I = &\{\{\overline{\gamma}(q)\} | q \in \Gamma(\delta)\} \cup \Big\{ \{\overline{\gamma}(q, q')\} | q, q' \in \Gamma(\delta), \\
&\pi(q, (n - b(I) - 1)q + b(I)q') > \pi(q', (n - b(I))q + (b(I) - 1)q'), \\
&\pi(q', (n-1)q') > \pi(q, (n-1)q') \Big\}.
\end{aligned}
$$

This set contains all monomorphic states and those bimorphic states where both the exemplary imitators as well as the profit imitators can not be better off. The first lemma determines the set of recurrent classes for the imitation dynamics.

LEMMA 8.1 *Let $\theta(I) \in \Theta^n$ be a behaviour vector. The set of recurrent classes for the pure imitation dynamics with transition matrix M_0^I is given by $\mathcal{A}_I$.*

The next lemma is an extension of the claim in Vega–Redondo (1997, p. 381). It claims that any deviation from $q_{b(I)}^*$ yields less profit for a profit imitator.

LEMMA 8.2 *Let $\theta(I) \in \Theta^n$ be a behaviour vector.*
$\forall_{k \in \{1,2,\ldots,n-b(I)-1\}} \forall_{q \neq q_{b(I)}^*}$:

$$P(kq_{b(I)}^* + (n - b(I) - k)q + b(I)q^m)q_{b(I)}^* - C(q_{b(I)}^*)$$
$$> P(kq_{b(I)}^* + (n - b(I) - k)q + b(I)q^m)q - C(q).$$

The first proposition can now be stated as follows.

PROPOSITION 8.1 *Let $\theta(I) \in \Theta^n$ be a behaviour vector. The limit distribution $\mu^I(\cdot)$ of the Markov chain with transition matrix M^I is a well-defined element of $\Delta(\Gamma(\delta)^n)$. Moreover, $\mu_{k_I^*}^I = 1$.*

Proof. The theory used to prove the proposition is described in detail in Section 6.1 of Chapter 2. For $I \in \{1, \ldots, N\}$ such that $I = I_0$ the result follows from Vega–Redondo (1997). For $I = I_1$ the result trivially follows (see also Offerman et al. (2002)). Hence, let $I \notin \{I_0, I_1\}$.

In the following we use the idea of costs between two states $\gamma(k)$ and $\gamma(l)$. Let $d(\gamma(k), \gamma(l)) = \sum_{i \in I_n} 1_{(\gamma(k)_i \neq \gamma(l)_i)}$. The costs between $\gamma(k)$ and $\gamma(l)$ are then defined by

$$c(\gamma(k), \gamma(l)) = \min_{j=1,\ldots,m} \{d(\gamma(k), \gamma(j)) | M_0^I(j, l) > 0\},$$

i.e. $c(\gamma(k), \gamma(l))$ gives the minimum number of mutations from $\gamma(k)$ that is needed for the imitation dynamics to have positive probability of reaching $\gamma(l)$. In the remainder the argument of $\gamma(\cdot)$ is suppressed.

First, we build a $\overline{\gamma}_I(q_{b(I)}^*, q^m)$-tree H^*, with minimal costs. Then it is shown that for any state $\gamma \neq \overline{\gamma}_I(q_{b(I)}^*, q^m)$ and any γ-tree H_γ the costs will be higher. Young (1993) has shown that the minimum cost tree is among the γ-trees where γ is an element of a recursive class of the pure imitation dynamics. Thus, following Lemma 8.1 only the elements of $\mathcal{A}_I$ need to be considered. So, take $\{\gamma\} \in \mathcal{A}_I$. There are four possibilities.

1. $\gamma = \overline{\gamma}(q)$, $q \neq q_{b(I)}^*$, $q \neq q^m$. This case can be subdivided in two parts.

   (a) $\pi(q, (n - b(I) - 1)q + b(I)q^m) \geq \pi(q^m, (n - b(I) - 1)q + b(I)q^m)$.
   Consider the following sequence of events.

i One exemplary imitator mutates to q^m, while the other firms cannot revise their output. Denote the resulting by state by γ'. This gives cost $c(\gamma, \gamma') = 1$.

ii Next, all exemplary imitators get the opportunity to revise their output. With positive probability they all choose q^m.

iii Finally, all profit imitators may adapt their output level. With positive probability they all stay at q.

So, there is a path with positive probability that leads to state $\overline{\gamma}(q, q^m) \in \mathcal{A}_I$ at cost 1.

(b) $\pi(q, (n - b(I) - 1)q + b(I)q^m) < \pi(q^m, (n - b(I))q + (b(I) - 1)q^m)$. Consider the sequence of events where first one exemplary imitator mutates to q^m. Second, all exemplary imitators get the opportunity to update their quantity. With positive probability they all choose q^m. Finally, all profit imitators get the opportunity to update their quantity and with positive probability they will also choose q^m. Hence, it takes one mutation of an exemplary imitator to q^m to reach with positive probability the state $\overline{\gamma}(q^m) \in \mathcal{A}_I$. Therefore, $c(\gamma, \overline{\gamma}(q^m)) = 1$.

2 $\gamma = \overline{\gamma}(q, q')$, $q, q' \neq q^*_{b(I)}$, $q, q' \neq q^m$. This case too can be subdivided in two parts.

(a) $\pi(q, (n - b(I) - 1)q + b(I)q^m) > \pi(q^m, (n - b(I))q + (b(I) - 1)q^m)$. As before it takes one mutation of an exemplary imitator to q^m to reach $\overline{\gamma}(q, q^m)$ with positive probability.

(b) $\pi(q, (n - b(I) - 1)q + b(I)q^m) < \pi(q^m, (n - b(I))q + (b(I) - 1)q^m)$. State $\overline{\gamma}(q^m)$ can be reached with positive probability using one mutation of an exemplary imitator.

3 $\gamma = \overline{\gamma}(q^*_{b(I)}, q)$, $q \neq q^m$. It takes one mutation of an exemplary imitator to reach $\overline{\gamma}_I(q^*_{b(I)}, q^m)$ with positive probability.

4 $\gamma = \overline{\gamma}(q, q^m)$, $q \neq q^*_{b(I)}$.[3] It takes one mutation of a profit imitator to $q^*_{b(I)}$ to reach $\overline{\gamma}_I(q^*_{b(I)}, q^m)$ with positive probability. When one profit imitator mutates to $q^*_{b(I)}$ and when, after that, all profit imitators revise their output, then, by applying Lemma 8.2 with $k = 1$, one can see that all profit imitators will choose $q^*_{b(I)}$ with positive probability, thus reaching $\overline{\gamma}_I(q^*_{b(I)}, q^m)$.

---

[3] Note that $q = q^m$ also belongs to this case.

By tying all states of the form of case 1 and 2 to states of the form of case 4 and tying all states of the form of cases 3 and 4 to $\overline{\gamma}_I(q_{b(I)}^*, q^m)$, we have constructed a $\overline{\gamma}_I(q_{b(I)}^*, q^m)$-tree H^* with $c(H^*) = |\mathcal{A}_I| - 1$.

As shown above, to leave any state $\gamma \in \mathcal{A}_I \setminus \{\overline{\gamma}_I(q_{b(I)}^*, q^m)\}$ it takes at least one mutation. Consider now $\overline{\gamma}_I(q_{b(I)}^*, q^m)$. Suppose that for two periods to come, no exemplary imitator can revise its output. If one profit imitator mutates to, say, q and all profit imitators afterwards get the opportunity to revise their output, then by applying Lemma 8.2 with $k = n - b(I) - 1$, one can see that all profit imitators will choose $q_{b(I)}^*$. So, it takes at least two mutations to leave $\overline{\gamma}_I(q_{b(I)}^*, q^m)$. Hence for every $\gamma \in \mathcal{A}_I \setminus \{\overline{\gamma}_I(q_{b(I)}^*, q^m)\}$ and any γ-tree H_γ we have

$$c(H_\gamma) > |\mathcal{A}_I| - 1 = c(H^*).$$

Thus, $\mu^I(\overline{\gamma}_I(q_{b(I)}^*, q^m)) = \mu_{k_I^*}^I = 1$. $\qquad \square$

Since Q is an irreducible matrix, there is a unique invariant probability measure, whose support gives the stochastically stable states. It is however very hard to calculate the invariant probability measure explicitly or to derive any general result. We therefore aggregate the dynamic process over the quantity-setting level, by using the result of Proposition 8.1. For this aggregated Markov chain it is easy to derive the unique invariant probability measure by applying the same techniques as before. Then we use the theory of nearly-complete decomposability developed by e.g. Courtois (1977) and explained in Section 6.2 of Chapter 2 to conclude that the invariant probability measure of the aggregated Markov chain is an approximation of order $O(\zeta)$ of the invariant probability measure of the original Markov chain with transition matrix Q. The states in the support of the approximate invariant measure are called the *stochastically stable* states. These are the states that are observed approximately most of the times in the long-run of the Markov chain governed by the transition matrix Q.

Consider the Markov chain on $\Theta^n \times \Theta^n$ with transition matrix $\tilde{M}$, a typical element of which is given by

$$\begin{aligned}
p_{IJ} &= \sum_{k=1}^{m} \mu_k^I \sum_{l=1}^{m} Q_{k_I l_J} \\
&= \sum_{k=1}^{m} \mu_k^I \lambda_{IJ}^k \sum_{l=1}^{m} M^I(k, l) \\
&= \sum_{k=1}^{m} \mu_k^I \lambda_{IJ}^k = \lambda_{IJ}^{k_I^*}.
\end{aligned}$$

Note that the matrix $\tilde{M}$ is indeed an aggregate version of Q where aggregation has taken place over the quantity setting level using the invariant probability measures. Furthermore, remark that $\lambda_{IJ}^{k_I^*}$ is the limit of a pure behavioural adaptation process and a mutation process where the probability of a mutation converges to zero. Let us first consider the pure behavioural adaptation process.

LEMMA 8.3 *For the set of recurrent states for the pure behavioural adaptation dynamics, denoted by $\tilde{A}$, it holds that $\tilde{A} \subset \{\theta(I_0), \theta(I_1)\}$.*

Proof. The proof of this lemma is trivial. Note that $\tilde{M}(I, J) = \lambda_{IJ}^{k_I^*}$. Hence, we only need to consider the quantity vectors that are stochastically stable in the quantity setting level. Let $\theta \in \Theta^n \backslash \tilde{A}$. Suppose that all firms may change behaviour, which happens with positive probability. Then all firms choose the same behaviour. So, the system reaches either $\theta(I_0)$ or $\theta(I_1)$. $\qquad\square$

Note that it can happen that $\tilde{\lambda}$ is so large that only $\theta(I_1)$ is a recurrent state. Conversely, $\tilde{\lambda}$ can be so small that $\theta(I_0)$ is the only recurrent state.

Let r_{01} be the smallest number such that

$$\pi^m - \Big[P(r_{01}q^m + (n - r_{01})q_{n-r_{01}}^*)(r_{01}q^m + (n - r_{01})q_{n-r_{01}}^*)$$
$$- r_{01}C(q^m) - (n - r_{01})C(q_{n-r_{01}}^*)\Big] \leq \tilde{\lambda}.$$

So, if the system is in the monomorphic state where all firms are competitive and set the Walrasian quantity, r_{01} is the minimum number of firms needed to switch to cooperative behaviour and setting the collusion quantity to make cooperation more profitable than competition. Conversely, let r_{10} be the minimum number of firms needed to switch from cooperation to competition to make competition more profitable, given the system is in the cooperative monomorphic state. That is, r_{10} is such that

$$\pi^m - \Big[P((n - r_{10})q^m + r_{10}q_{r_{10}}^*)((n - r_{10})q^m + r_{10}q_{r_{10}}^*)$$
$$- (n - r_{10})C(q^m) - r_{10}C(q_{r_{10}}^*)\Big] > \tilde{\lambda}.$$

Furthermore, let $\lambda_2(Q_I^*)$ denote the second largest eigenvalue of Q_I^* in absolute value. The following proposition can now be proved.

PROPOSITION 8.2 *If all elementary divisors of Q are linear and ζ is such that*

$$\zeta < \tfrac{1}{2}\Big[1 - \max_{I=1,\ldots,N} |\lambda_2(Q_I^*)|\Big],$$

then the unique invariant probability measure $\mu(\cdot)$ of Q can be approxi-mated by a well defined element $\tilde{\mu}(\cdot) \in \Delta(\Omega)$ of order $O(\zeta)$. For $\tilde{\mu}(\cdot)$ it holds that

1 If $r_{01} < r_{10}$, then $\tilde{\mu}_{k^*_{I_1}} = 1$;

2 If $r_{01} > r_{10}$, then $\tilde{\mu}_{k^*_{I_0}} = 1$;

3 If $r_{01} = r_{10}$, then $0 < \tilde{\mu}_{k^*_{I_0}} = 1 - \tilde{\mu}_{k^*_{I_1}} < 1$.

Proof. Section 6.2 of Chapter 2 shows that the conditions on ζ and the elementary divisors of Q are sufficient for Q to be nearly-complete decomposable. This implies that one can apply the theorems proved by Simon and Ando (1961) to approximate the unique invariant probability measure $\mu(\cdot)$ of Q by the invariant probability measure of $\tilde{M}$, $\tilde{\mu}(\cdot)$.

Since $\tilde{M}$ is an irreducible matrix the invariant probability measure $\tilde{\mu}(\cdot)$ is unique. The procedure to prove the proposition is the same as in the proof of Proposition 8.1, i.e. we build θ-trees and the ones with minimal costs get positive measure. Since only the elements of $\tilde{A}$ are to be considered we only need to compare $c(\theta(I_0), \theta(I_1))$ and $c(\theta(I_1), \theta(I_0))$. The proof follows then trivially. Suppose that $r_{01} < r_{10}$. Then $c(\theta(I_0), \theta(I_1)) = r_{01} < r_{10} = c(\theta(I_1), \theta(I_0))$. Since we only need to consider the stochastically stable states from the quantity setting level, we conclude that $\tilde{\mu}_{k^*_{I_1}} = 1$. The other cases are proved in a similar way.

□

Note that if $\tilde{\lambda} > \pi^m$, the system will always settle in the cooperative outcome. The condition on ζ can always be satisfied by taking $\tilde{p}$ small enough. Linearity of the elementary divisors of Q can be obtained by an appropriate choice of the $\tilde{\nu}_i$, $i = 1, \ldots, n$.

Proposition 8.2 establishes that if $r_{01} < r_{10}$, then the basin of attraction of collusion is larger than the basin of attraction of competition. This implies that in the long-run, only the collusion outcome will be observed a significant fraction of time. This does not imply that the market will never be in the Walrasian equilibrium. On the contrary, it is very well possible that the market settles in the Walrasian equilibrium for prolonged periods of time. If $r_{01} > r_{10}$, the reverse story holds. In the degenerate case where $r_{01} = r_{10}$, both the collusion outcome and the Walrasian equilibrium will be observed a significant fraction of time in the long-run. The values of r_{01} and r_{10} critically depend on the value of $\tilde{\lambda}$. In general, these values cannot be calculated analytically. Numerical methods can be used in such cases. Note that in the case of a linear cost function, the values of r_{01} and r_{10} cannot be determined since all firms make zero profits. This is due to the fact that the profit imitators choose their quantity such that the price equals the marginal costs. Therefore, a collusion will arise if $\pi^m \leq \tilde{\lambda}$ and a Walrasian equilibrium will arise otherwise.

4. Conclusion

In this chapter we extended the model of Vega–Redondo (1997) in two ways. Multiple behavioural rules are allowed and behavioural adaptation is introduced. This set-up leads to the conclusion that either competition or cooperation is stochastically stable (unless $r_{01} = r_{10}$, in which case both are stochastically stable), depending on the structure of the market and the inclination to cooperative behaviour. Competition leads to the Walrasian equilibrium and cooperation leads to the collusion equilibrium. This chapter can therefore be seen as providing a theoretical underpinning for some of the experimental results found by Offerman et al. (2002).

In their experiment Offerman et al. (2002) randomly match individuals into groups of three persons. Each person is given the inverse demand function and the cost function. Individuals do not know to whom they are matched. In each round, each individual chooses an output level given the information that she gets. Offerman et al. (2002) use three informational treatments. The one that corresponds to our model is the treatment in which after each round every individual is informed about the revenues, costs, profits, and quantities of all firms in her group. Furthermore, the aggregate quantity as well as the market price of each person's group is given. Following Vega–Redondo (1997) one would expect that every group eventually settles at the Walrasian equilibrium. However, this is not the case. The collusion equilibrium is also reached quite often in this experiment. According to the theory presented in this chapter, the co-existence of both equilibria is the result of different levels of inclination to cooperative behaviour within the groups.

It is a natural further step to drop the assumption of a common inclination to cooperative behaviour and replace it with individual levels. This could then facilitate an analysis into the impact of these levels on the resulting market outcome. Furthermore, the model might be extended with more behavioural rules. Offerman et al. (2002) for instance pose several other plausible behavioural rules. In this perspective, it would be interesting to distinguish between behavioural rules by attaching costs of using the rules, for instance based on the level of information that is available. If lots of information is available, profit imitation is a feasible behavioural rule that does not require much intellectual or computational skills. Therefore, it can be seen as a cheap behavioural rule. If only aggregate quantities are known, profit imitation is not feasible any more. Fictitious play for instance, still is. However, fictitious play requires more skills and can therefore be regarded as more expensive. It is conjectured by Offerman et al. (2002) that these costs are influencing the resulting equilibria in different information treatments. Finally, an extension of this model could accommodate for entry and exit in the market. In fact, Alós-Ferrer et al. (1999) already extended the Vega–Redondo (1997) model in this direction, that is, without the possibility of behavioural adaptation.

Appendix
A.   Proof of Lemma 8.1

Note that every element of $\mathcal{A}_I$ is a recurrent class. We prove the converse claim. Let $\gamma \in \Gamma(\delta)^n$ be such that there is no $A \in \mathcal{A}_I$ satisfying $\gamma \in A$. We will show that there is a path from γ to a state in $\mathcal{A}_I$ which has positive probability.

Take $q \in \{\gamma_j | \pi(\gamma_j, \gamma_{-j}) = \max_{i \in I_n} \pi(\gamma_i, \gamma_{-i})\}$ and denote any exemplary choice in γ by q'. With positive probability all profit imitators choose q and all exemplary imitators choose q' next period. So, next period's state will be $\overline{\gamma}(q, q')$. There are two possibilities.

1   $q = q'$; then $\{\overline{\gamma}(q, q')\} = \{\overline{\gamma}(q)\} \in \mathcal{A}_I$.

2   $q \neq q'$. There are two cases[4].

    (a) $\pi(q, (n - b(I) - 1)q + b(I)q') \geq \pi(q', (n - b(I))q + (b(I) - 1)q')$
       and $\pi(q', (n - 1)q') \geq \pi(q, (n - 1)q)$.
       Then it holds that

$$q \in BP(\overline{\gamma}(q, q'))$$

    and

$$q' \in BE(\overline{\gamma}(q, q')).$$

    So, with positive probability state $\overline{\gamma}(q, q')$ is reached and $\{\overline{\gamma}(q, q')\} \in \mathcal{A}_I$.

    (b) $\pi(q, (n - b(I) - 1)q + b(I)q') < \pi(q', (n - b(I))q + (b(I) - 1)q')$
       and $\pi(q', (n - 1)q') \geq \pi(q, (n - 1)q)$.
       With positive probability, all firms choose q' leading to the monomorphic state $\overline{\gamma}(q') \in \mathcal{A}_I$.

This proves the lemma.   □

---

[4]Since q' is an exemplary choice, $\pi(q', (n - 1)q') \geq \pi(q, (n - 1)q)$.

B.   Proof of Lemma 8.2

Note that since $P(\cdot)$ is strictly decreasing it holds for all $k \in \{1, \ldots, n - b(I) - 1\}$ that

$$q > q^*_{b(I)} \Rightarrow P((n - b(I))q^*_{b(I)} + b(I)q^m)$$
$$> P(kq^*_{b(I)} + (n - b(I) - k)q + b(I)q^m),$$
$$q < q^*_{b(I)} \Rightarrow P((n - b(I))q^*_{b(I)} + b(I)q^m)$$
$$< P(kq^*_{b(I)} + (n - b(I) - k)q + b(I)q^m).$$

Therefore, we have for all $q \neq q^*_{b(I)}$

$$[P((n-b(I))q^*_{b(I)} + b(I)q^m) - P(kq^*_{b(I)} + (n - b(I) - k)q + b(I)q^m)]q^*_{b(I)}$$
$$< [P((n - b(I))q^*_{b(I)} + b(I)q^m) - P(kq^*_{b(I)} + (n - b(I) - k)q + b(I)q^m)]q.$$

Substracting $C(q) - C(q^*_{b(I)})$ from both sides and rearranging terms gives

$$[P((n - b(I))q^*_{b(I)} + b(I)q^m)q^*_{b(I)} - C(q^*_{b(I)})] + [P(kq^*_{b(I)} + (n - b(I) - k)q +$$
$$+ b(I)q^m)q - C(q)] < [P((n - b(I))q^*_{b(I)} + b(I)q^m)q - C(q)]$$
$$+ [P(kq^*_{b(I)} + (n - b(I) - k)q + b(I)q^m)q^*_{b(I)} - C(q^*_{b(I)})].$$

From eq. (8.3) it can be seen that the first term on the left hand side is as least as large as the first term on the right hand side. $\square$

Chapter 9

EVOLUTION OF CONJECTURES IN COURNOT OLIGOPOLY

1. Introduction

The technique of nearly-complete decomposable systems has been used in Chapter 8 to construct a dynamic evolutionary model that can explain why different oligopolistic markets can end up in different types of equilibria. We modelled a situation where firms can behave either competitively or cooperatively. Depending on the (exogenously given) intensity of competition we showed that the market ends up in either the Walrasian or the collusion equilibrium.

In this chapter we take a different approach to answer the same question. Again, we will develop a nearly-complete decomposable system with dynamics at two levels. At the quantity level firms do not imitate as in Chapter 8 and most of the evolutionary literature, but myopically maximise their profit based on a conjecture about the behaviour of the other firms. At the behavioural level, firms imitate the conjecture of the firm that makes the highest profit.

The question under which conditions collusion (or cartel formation) in oligopolistic markets is possible is an important issue in the theory of industrial organisation. It is particularly interesting for anti-trust policies. There are several ways in which the issue has been addressed in the literature. The static Cournot or Bertrand models don't allow for a cooperative outcome. Experimental evidence, e.g. by Friedman (1967), Axelrod (1984), and Offerman et al. (2002), suggests that cooperation or cartel formation (tacit collusion) does arise in oligopolistic markets.

In the literature many contributions try to explain sustainability of tacit collusion. For most of these models it holds that extensions to the basic static model are needed in order to get cooperation as a possi-

197

ble equilibrium outcome, e.g. by assuming incomplete information or asymmetries in the firms' technologies. There is, however, a very simple way of obtaining a collusive outcome in the static model, namely by introducing conjectural variations, a concept that dates back to Bowley (1924). This approach assumes that firms take into account the reaction of the market to their own quantity choice. For example, the standard best-reply dynamics is compatible with conjectural variations stating that the market does not respond to one's own actions. The problem is that conjectural variations are essentially a dynamic concept, but are mostly used in a static environment. Kalai and Stanford (1985) show that there are repeated game formulations of Cournot markets that can result in beliefs in the spirit of conjectural variations without abandoning full rationality. In a recent paper Friedman and Mezzetti (2002) show how conjectural variations can be used in an oligopoly model. They consider a differentiated product market with boundedly-rational, price-setting firms that at each point in time maximise their profit over an infinite time horizon based on a conjectural variation. These authors also study an adaptation process of the conjectural variation where adaptation takes place if the observed price change is substantially larger than the price change predicted by the conjectural variation. They show that under certain conditions the Nash equilibrium always constitutes a stable steady-state. Furthermore, as substitutability among firms increases, a more cooperative outcome can be sustained as a stable steady-state. In the limit (perfect substitutability) this leads to full cooperation.

An important step in the evolution of economic thinking has been the interest of economists for the theory of evolution applied to economic phenomena. Several contributions to the literature have set off the development of this field. First there is the concept of bounded rationality introduced by Herbert Simon (cf. Simon (1957)). The bounded rationality approach replaces the assumption of full rationality of economic agents. Secondly, in neoclassical economics the objective of agents is to maximise some absolute quantity (e.g. utility or profit), whereas Alchian (1950) already pointed out that *relative* payoffs are often of more interest.

In this chapter, the concept of stochastic stability introduced by Foster and Young (1990) is used to analyse an oligopoly model with boundedly rational firms which are ultimately interested in relative profits. The first paper in industrial organisation which applies the concept of stochastic stability is Vega–Redondo (1997). He considers a Cournot oligopolistic market where firms choose their quantity level by imitating the most successful firm, i.e. the firm that makes the highest profit. He shows that the unique stochastically stable state is given by the Walrasian equilibrium. This model has been extended by Alós-Ferrer et al. (1999) by allowing for entry and exit. They find that if there are decreasing returns to scale, then the market will eventually settle in a Walrasian equilibrium. In case of increasing returns to scale, a monopoly will arise eventually.

As mentioned before, an experimental study by Offerman et al. (2002) shows that not only the Walrasian equilibrium may survive in a Vega-Redondo framework, but also the collusion equilibrium. This experimental evidence seems to suggest that the behavioural assumptions in Vega–Redondo (1997) are too restrictive. There are attempts in the literature to construct models with more behavioural rules. For example, Schipper (2003) models myopic optimisers (best-repliers) and profit imitators à la Vega–Redondo (1997). He finds that the market eventually converges to a situation where the myopic optimisers play a best-reply to the imitators and the imitators play a semi-Walrasian quantity taking into account the existence of the best-repliers. In this model, neither the Walrasian equilibrium nor the collusion equilibrium is obtained. Kaarbøe and Tieman (1999) use a similar model to show that in supermodular games a Nash equilibrium is always selected in the limit.

In all the papers mentioned above agents either cannot change their behaviour, or changing behaviour is modelled as an exogenous random process. The model presented in this chapter gives more flexibility to the behavioural assumptions underlying the results of these papers by endogenising the behavioural choice. It is assumed that firms base their quantity choice in a boundedly rational way on observations from the past and on their conjectures about competitors' reactions to their behaviour. The latter aspect is modelled by using a variable that measures the – supposed – immediate reaction of others to one's own actions. The quantity dynamics is then modelled in such a way that a firm chooses the quantity that maximises next period's profit given the quantity choices of the previous period and its own conjecture. Hence, at the quantity level, firms are assumed to be myopic optimisers. This quantity dynamics is extended with random noise to capture aspects of the quantity choice that are not explained by the model. One can think for example of experimentation by firms which leads to a different quantity choice than would be expected from myopic optimisation. The noise part can also be interpreted as firms making mistakes in their myopic optimisation process. It might also capture the fact that a firm is replaced by a new firm that has the same conjecture, but starts with another quantity choice. The last aspect reflects what biologists call mutation.

It may happen that after some time a firm realises that it is making less profit than its competitors. In such a case, its conjecture is apparently not correct. In such cases, firms adapt their conjecture. They make this decision in a boundedly rational way, namely by imitating the conjecture of the firm that has the highest profit. This dynamics is called the conjecture dynamics. Here too a random noise term is added to capture experiments, mistakes or mutations. By allowing evolution at the behavioural level this chapter is related to the literature on indirect evolution (cf. Güth and Yaari (1992)). The main difference is that in this chapter it is not assumed that given a behavioural pattern agents act rationally. Boundedly rational behaviour enters here at both the behavioural and the quantity-setting level.

The quantity dynamics and the conjecture dynamics, together with the noise terms, lead to an ergodic Markov chain having a unique invariant probability measure. A simulation study is conducted to study the behaviour of this Markov chain. It is found that the collusion, Cournot-Nash, and Walrasian equilibria are played more frequently than other quantities. Furthermore, in the long-run the Walrasian equilibrium gets played more often.

To see if the Walrasian equilibrium can theoretically be supported as the most likely long-run outcome of the model, we look at the stochastically stable states of the Markov chain. The stochastically stable states are the states in the support of the unique invariant probability measure of the limit Markov chain when the error probabilities for both the quantity dynamics and the conjecture dynamics converge to zero. Due to the complexity of the dynamics it is not possible to get analytical results on the stochastically stable states. However, by construction of the model the Markov chain can be decomposed in a chain that governs the quantity dynamics and a chain that describes the conjecture dynamics. It is shown that – given the conjectures – the quantity dynamics has a unique invariant probability measure. The Markov chain is then aggregated over the quantity level using this measure and a Markov chain is obtained that is solely based on the conjecture dynamics. It is shown that this aggregated Markov chain has a unique invariant probability measure. The theory of nearly-complete decomposability as developed by Simon and Ando (1961), Ando and Fisher (1963) and Courtois (1977) provides conditions under which the invariant measure of the aggregated chain is an approximation of the invariant measure of the original chain.

Following this path of analysis it is obtained that the market will eventually settle in the Walrasian equilibrium, just like in Vega–Redondo (1997). So, even with the more elaborate behavioural structure of this model, the Walrasian equilibrium is still, by approximation, the only stochastically stable state. This results from the fact that imitative behaviour drives cooperative behaviour out, just as in Vega–Redondo

(1997) profit imitation drives out cooperative quantity setting. As such this chapter provides even more evidence of the appeal of the Walrasian equilibrium as a prediction of the outcome of an evolutionary process. This result only holds, however, if the frequency of the conjecture dynamics is sufficiently low. Then, the quantity dynamics has time to settle in its equilibrium. Otherwise, anything can happen, although the simulations suggest that the dynamics mainly evolves around the collusion, Cournot-Nash and Walrasian equilibria.

The chapter is organised as follows. In Section 2 the model is formally introduced. Section 3 presents a simulation study, whereas in Section 4 the model is analysed analytically. Section 5 concludes.

2. The Model

Let be given a dynamic market for a homogeneous good with n firms, indexed by $I_n = \{1, 2, \ldots, n\}$. At each point in time, $t \in \mathbb{N}$, competition takes place in a Cournot fashion, i.e. by means of quantity setting. Inverse demand is given by a smooth function $P : \mathbb{R}_+ \to \mathbb{R}_+$ satisfying $P'(\cdot) < 0$. The production technology is assumed to be the same for each firm and is reflected by a smooth cost function $C : \mathbb{R}_+ \to \mathbb{R}_+$, satisfying $C'(\cdot) > 0$. If at time $t \in \mathbb{N}$ the vector of quantities is given by $q \in \mathbb{R}_+^n$, the profit for firm $i \in I_n$ at time t is given by

$$\pi(q_i, q_{-i}) = P(q_i + Q_{-i})q_i - C(q_i),$$

where $q_{-i} = (q_j)_{j \neq i}$ and $Q_{-i} = \sum_{j \neq i} q_j$.

Each firm $i \in I_n$ chooses quantities from a finite grid Γ_i. Define $\Gamma = \prod_{i \in I_n} \Gamma_i$. For further reference let $q(k)$, $k = 1, \ldots, m$, be the k-th permutation of Γ. It is assumed that in setting their quantities firms conjecture that their change in quantity results in an immediate change in the total quantity provided by their competitors. This can also be seen to reflect the firm's conjecture of the competitiveness of the market. Formally, firm $i \in I_n$ conjectures a value for the partial derivative of Q_{-i} with respect to q_i. Using this conjecture, the firm wants to maximise next period's profit. Hence, the firm is a myopic optimiser, which reflects its bounded rationality. The first-order condition for profit maximisation of firm i reads

$$P'(q_i + Q_{-i})\left(1 + \frac{\partial Q_{-i}}{\partial q_i}\right)q_i + P(q_i + Q_{-i}) - C'(q_i) = 0. \qquad (9.1)$$

As can be seen from eq. (9.1) we assume that there is only a first order conjecture effect. Furthermore, we assume that it is linear. These assumptions add to the firm's bounded rationality.[1]

To facilitate further analysis, the conjectures are parameterised by a vector $\alpha \in \mathbb{R}^n$ such that for all $i \in I_n$

$$(1 + \alpha_i)\frac{n}{2} = 1 + \frac{\partial Q_{-i}}{\partial q_i}.$$

Given a vector of conjectures an equilibrium for the market is given by $q \in \mathbb{R}_+^n$ such that for all $i \in I_n$ the first-order condition (9.1) is satisfied. Note that if all firms $i \in I_n$ have a conjecture $\alpha_i = -1$, the equilibrium coincides with the Walrasian equilibrium. Furthermore, if all firms have $\alpha_i = \frac{2-n}{n}$ or $\alpha_i = 1$, the equilibrium coincides with the Cournot-Nash equilibrium or the collusion equilibrium, respectively. Therefore, the conjectures $\alpha_i = -1$, $\alpha_i = \frac{2-n}{n}$, and $\alpha_i = 1$ will be called the Walrasian, Cournot-Nash, and collusion conjectures, respectively.

Each firm chooses its conjecture from a finite grid Λ on $[-1, 1]$, where it is assumed that $\Lambda \supset \{-1, \frac{2-n}{n}, 1\}$. The bounds of this finite grid represent the extreme cases of full competition ($\alpha = -1$) and collusion ($\alpha = 1$). For further reference, let $\alpha(I)$, $I = 1, \ldots, N$, be the I-th permutation of $\Lambda^n = \prod_{i \in I_n} \Lambda$.

The dynamics of the market takes place in discrete time and consists of both a quantity dynamics and a conjecture dynamics. The quantity dynamics works as follows. At the beginning of period $t \in \mathbb{N}$, each firm gets the opportunity to revise its output with probability $0 < p < 1$. The output is chosen so that it maximises this period's profit based on last period's quantities and the firm's conjecture. That is, firm $i \in I_n$ seeks to find $q_i^t \in \Gamma_i$ so as to approximate as closely as possible the first-order condition from eq. (9.1), i.e. $q_i^t \in B(q_{-i}^{t-1}, \alpha_i^{t-1})$, where for $q_{-i} \in \prod_{j \neq i} \Gamma_j$ and $\alpha_i \in \Lambda_i$,

$$B(q_{-i}, \alpha_i) = \arg\min_{q \in \Gamma_i} \left\{ \left| P'(q + Q_{-i})(1 + \alpha_i)\frac{n}{2}q + P(q + Q_{-i}) - C'(q) \right| \right\}.$$

If there are ties, firm i chooses any quantity from $B(q_{-i}^{t-1}, \alpha_i^{t-1})$ using a probability measure $\eta_i(\cdot)$ with full support. The dynamics described above constitutes the *pure quantity dynamics*. The actual quantity choice can be influenced by several other aspects. For example, a

---

[1] The first-order and linearity assumptions are also made throughout the static literature on conjectural variations. This seems incompatible with the assumption of fully rational firms in these models.

firm can experiment and choose another quantity. Another possibility is that firms make mistakes in their optimisation process. Finally, a firm may be replaced by a new firm that has the same conjecture, but sets a different quantity to start with. This is what biologists refer to as mutation. To capture these effects we assume that each firm experiments or makes a mistake with probability $\varepsilon > 0$ and chooses any quantity from Γ_i using a probability measure $\nu_i(\cdot)$ with full support. Given a conjecture vector $\alpha(I)$ for some $I \in \{1, \ldots, N\}$ and an error probability ε, the quantity dynamics gives rise to a Markov chain on Γ with transition matrix M_I^ε, a typical element of which is given by

$$
M_I^\varepsilon(k, l) = \prod_{i \in I_n} \Bigg\{ (1 - \varepsilon) \Big[p \mathbb{1}_{\left(q_i(l) \in B(q_{-i}(k), \alpha_i(I))\right)} \eta_i(q_i(l))
$$
$$
+ (1 - p) \mathbb{1}_{\left(q_i(k) = q_i(l)\right)} \Big] + \varepsilon \nu_i\left(q_i(l)\right) \Bigg\},
$$

(9.2)

where $\mathbb{1}_{(\cdot)}$ denotes the indicator function and the part between square brackets gives the transition probabilities for the pure quantity dynamics.

The conjecture dynamics takes place at the end of period t, when each firm i gets the opportunity to revise its conjecture with probability $0 < \tilde{p} < 1$. The idea behind this revision is that once in a while a firm analyses its past performance and it assesses the correctness of its conjecture by looking at the performance of the other firms. It is assumed that each firm can observe the individual quantity choices of its competitors and therefore it can also deduce the conjectures that its competitors use. It can then imitate the firm that made the highest profit in period t. Since deriving the conjectures requires effort we assume that firms change their conjecture less often than their quantity choice which is reflected in assuming that $\tilde{p} < p$.[2] Formally, firm i's choice α_i^t is such that $\alpha_i^t \in \tilde{B}(\alpha^{t-1}, q^t)$, where for given $\alpha \in \Lambda^n$ and $q \in \Gamma$,

$$
\tilde{B}(\alpha, q) = \arg\max_{\gamma \in \Lambda} \Big\{ \exists_{j \in I_n} : \alpha_j = \gamma, \forall_{k \in I_n} : \pi(q_j, q_{-j}) \geq \pi(q_k, q_{-k}) \Big\}.
$$

If there are ties, firm i chooses any element from $\tilde{B}(\alpha^{t-1}, q^t)$ using a probability measure $\tilde{\eta}_i(\cdot)$ with full support. This dynamic process is called

---

[2]One could argue that since the firm can derive its competitors' conjectures it can always optimally react. However, it would have to gather more information than just quantity choices. This requires effort and, hence, costs. Therefore, we assume that conjecture updating takes place less often than the application of the rule of thumb of quantity adjustment with fixed conjectures.

the *pure conjecture dynamics*. As in the quantity dynamics we allow for mistakes or experimentation. So, each firm chooses with probability $\tilde{\varepsilon} > 0$ any conjecture using a probability measure $\tilde{\nu}_i(\cdot)$ with full support. For each $k \in \{1, \ldots, m\}$ and corresponding quantity vector $q(k)$, and error probability $\tilde{\varepsilon}$, the conjecture dynamics gives rise to a Markov chain on Λ^n with transition matrix $\lambda_k^{\tilde{\varepsilon}}$. The transition probability from $\alpha(I)$ to $\alpha(J)$ is given by

$$
\lambda_k^{\tilde{\varepsilon}}(I, J) = \prod_{i \in I_n} \left\{ (1 - \tilde{\varepsilon}) \left[\tilde{p} \mathbb{1}_{\left(\alpha_i(J) \in \tilde{B}(\alpha(I), q(k)) \right)} \tilde{\eta}_i(\alpha_i(J)) \right.\right.
$$
$$
\left.\left. + (1 - \tilde{p}) \mathbb{1}_{\left(\alpha_i(J) = \alpha_i(I) \right)} \right] + \tilde{\varepsilon} \tilde{\nu}_i \left(\alpha_i(J) \right) \right\},
$$
(9.3)

where the part between square brackets gives the transition probabilities for the pure conjecture dynamics.

The combined quantity and conjecture dynamics yield a Markov chain on $\Gamma \times \Lambda^n$ with transition matrix $Q^{\varepsilon, \tilde{\varepsilon}}$. Entries in this transition matrix are grouped according to the conjecture index. So, the k-th row in $Q^{\varepsilon, \tilde{\varepsilon}}$ consists of the transition probabilities from the state with conjectures $\alpha(1)$ and quantities $q(k)$. The $m*(I-1)+k$-th row contains the transition probabilities from the state with conjectures $\alpha(I)$ and quantities $q(k)$. A typical element of $Q^{\varepsilon, \tilde{\varepsilon}}$ is given by

$$
Q^{\varepsilon, \tilde{\varepsilon}}(k_I, l_J) = M_I^\varepsilon(k, l) \lambda_k^{\tilde{\varepsilon}}(I, J),
$$
(9.4)

which should be read as the transition probability form the state with conjectures $\alpha(I)$ and quantities $q(k)$ to the state with conjectures $\alpha(J)$ and quantities $q(l)$.

3.   A Simulation Study

Since for all $i \in I_n$, the probability distributions $\nu_i(\cdot)$ and $\tilde{\nu}_i(\cdot)$ have full support, the Markov chain $Q^{\varepsilon, \tilde{\varepsilon}}$ is ergodic and, hence, has a unique invariant probability measure. To gain some insight in the long-run behaviour of the Markov chain a simulation study has been conducted. The demand side of the market is described by an inverse demand function given by

$$
P(Q) = 45 - \sqrt{3Q}.
$$

It is assumed that all firms have access to the same technology which is represented by the cost function

$$
C(q) = q\sqrt{q}.
$$

This description is the same as the one used in the experiment conducted by Offerman et al. (2002). The focus in that paper is on the frequencies of the Walrasian (full competition), Cournot-Nash, and collusion quantities, respectively. The Walrasian quantity, denoted by q^w, solves the inequality

$$P(nq^w)q^w - C(q^w) \geq P(nq^w)q - C(q) \qquad \forall q \in \mathbb{R}_+.$$

The Cournot-Nash (q^n) and collusion (q^c) quantities solve

$$P(nq^n)q^n - C(q^n) \geq P((n-1)q^n + q)q - C(q) \qquad \forall q \in \mathbb{R}_+,$$

and

$$P(nq^c)q^c - C(q^c) \geq P(nq)q - C(q) \qquad \forall q \in \mathbb{R}_+,$$

respectively. Following Offerman et al. (2002) and taking $n = 3$ firms, these quantities are given by $q^w = 100$, $q^n = 81$, and $q^c = 56.25$, respectively. The Walrasian, Cournot-Nash, and collusion conjectures equal $-1, -1/3$, and 1, respectively.

For the simulation, the quantity grid for all firms is taken to be $\Gamma = \{49, 50, \ldots, 108\}$ and the quantity grid is set to $\Lambda = \{-1, -\frac{1}{3}, 1\}$. This implies that the state space is 5,832,000 dimensional. The probabilities of quantity and conjecture adaptation are set to $p = 0.9$ and $\tilde{p} = 0.4$, respectively. We simulate 200 runs of 150 time periods. For each simulation the error probabilities ε and $\tilde{\varepsilon}$ are iid uniformly drawn from the interval $[0.001, 0.2]$.

The frequencies of the conjectures and the running frequencies of the aggregate quantities are shown in Figure 9.1. The running frequency for quantity Q has window size four, i.e. it is the frequency of all observations in the set $\{Q - 4, Q - 3, \ldots, Q + 4\}$. As can be seen from this figure, the Walrasian quantity has the highest frequency, with two other peaks at the Cournot-Nash quantity and the collusion quantity. The frequencies of the conjectures chosen paint a similar picture.

If the sample is split into short-run (first 50 periods of each run) and long-run (last 50 periods of each run) data, the frequencies are as depicted in Figures 9.2 and 9.3. These findings show that all three equilibria are being played in the long-run. If we look at prices, one of the simulation runs led to a price-run depicted in Figure 9.4. This price-run stays very close to Offerman et al. (2002) who report that both the collusion and Walrasian equilibria occur approximately half of the time. In Figure 9.4 one can see that the collusion price prevails in the first half of the run, whereas the Walrasian price prevails in the second half.

Figures 9.1, 9.2, and 9.3 show an interesting feature, namely that the Walrasian equilibrium is played more frequently in the long-run than in the short-run. In the next section we provide theoretical evidence

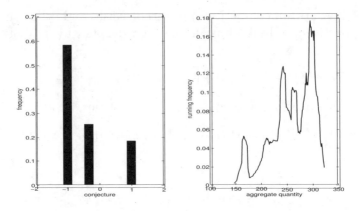

Figure 9.1.   Frequencies of conjectures (left panel) and running frequencies of aggregate quantities (right panel).

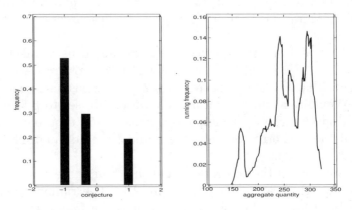

Figure 9.2.   Short-run frequencies of conjectures (left panel) and running frequencies of aggregate quantities (right panel).

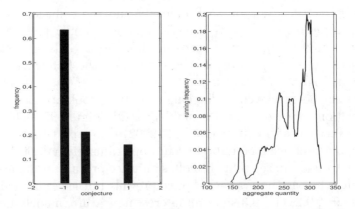

Figure 9.3.   Long-run frequencies of conjectures (left panel) and running frequencies of aggregate quantities (right panel).

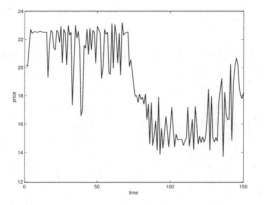

Figure 9.4. Simulated prices.

that the Walrasian equilibrium has, approximately, the largest basin of attraction when the error probabilities converge to zero. In fact, the Walrasian is the only state that has a basin of attraction in this limiting case.

4. A Theoretical Analysis

For each ε and $\tilde{\varepsilon}$ the chain $Q^{\varepsilon,\tilde{\varepsilon}}$ is ergodic, hence there is a unique invariant probability measure. In line with other papers on stochastic stability (cf. Kandori et al. (1993), Young (1993), and Vega–Redondo (1997)) we are interested in the long-run behaviour of the dynamics when evolution has forced the probabilities of mistakes to zero. The standard argument for considering this limiting case is that firms learn to play the game better as time evolves. That is, we are interested in the (unique) invariant probability measure $\mu(\cdot)$ of the Markov chain with transition matrix Q, where[3]

$$Q = \lim_{\tilde{\varepsilon}\downarrow 0}\lim_{\varepsilon\downarrow 0} Q^{\varepsilon,\tilde{\varepsilon}}. \tag{9.5}$$

The support of $\mu(\cdot)$ constitutes the set of stochastically stable states. Note that, contrary to the standard literature we have two levels of evolution in this model. Due to the complexity of the combined dynamics, one cannot determine $\mu(\cdot)$ exactly. It turns out, however, that we can find an approximation, $\tilde{\mu}(\cdot)$, of this measure which can be analysed.

---

[3]The order of limits is crucial in the results to be proved. First evolution drives the error probability of the quantity dynamics to zero and after that the error probability for the conjecture dynamics. Since it is assumed that quantity adaptation takes places more frequent than conjecture adaptation ($\tilde{p} < p$), this is a straightforward assumption.

As a point of departure the first level of evolution, the quantity dynamics, is studied. For each $I = 1, \ldots, N$, let $M_I = \lim_{\varepsilon \downarrow 0} M_I^\varepsilon$ be the limit Markov chain when the error in the quantity dynamics converges to zero. Note that M_I has a unique invariant probability measure, say $\mu^I(\cdot)$. To facilitate further analysis it is assumed that for any vector of conjectures there is a unique equilibrium, i.e. a unique vector of quantities that solves eq. (9.1) for all firms. Furthermore, we assume that this equilibrium is an element of the quantity grid Γ.

ASSUMPTION 9.1 *For all $\alpha \in \Lambda^n$ there exists a unique $q^\alpha \in \Gamma$ such that for all $i \in I_n$,*

$$P'(q_i^\alpha + Q_{-i}^\alpha)(1 + \alpha_i)\frac{n}{2}q_i^\alpha + P(q_i^\alpha + Q_{-i}^\alpha) - C'(q_i^\alpha) = 0.$$

Let the permutation on Γ that corresponds to q^α be denoted by $k(I)$, i.e. $q(k(I)) = q^\alpha$. The following proposition states that for each vector of conjectures $\alpha(I)$ the unique stochastically stable state of the quantity dynamics is given by $q^{\alpha(I)}$.

THEOREM 9.1 *Let $I \in \{1, \ldots, N\}$ be given. Under Assumption 9.1, the unique invariant probability measure $\mu^I(\cdot)$ of the Markov chain with transition matrix M_I is such that*

$$\mu^I(q^{\alpha(I)}) = 1.$$

Proof. The proposition is proved using the theory developed by Milgrom and Roberts (1991). First note that for all $i \in I_n$, Γ_i is a compact subset of $\mathbb{R}_+$. Define for all $i \in I_n$ the (continuous) function $\tilde{\pi}_i : \mathbb{R}_+ \times \mathbb{R}_+^{n-1} \to \mathbb{R}_+$, given by

$$\tilde{\pi}_i(q_i, q_{-i}) = - \left| P'(q_i + Q_{-i})(1 + \alpha_i(I))\frac{n}{2}q_i + P(q_i + Q_{-i}) - C'(q_i) \right|.$$

Consider the strategic form game $\langle I_n, (\Gamma_i)_{i \in I_n}, (\tilde{\pi}_i)_{i \in I_n} \rangle$. Let $S \subset \Gamma$, denote by S_i the projection of S on Γ_i and define $S_{-i} = \prod_{j \neq i} S_j$. For all $i \in I_n$ the set of undominated strategies with respect to S is given by the set

$$U_i(S) = \left\{ q_i \in \Gamma_i \middle| \forall_{y \in S_i} \exists_{q_{-i} \in S_{-i}} : \tilde{\pi}_i(q_i, q_{-i}) \geq \tilde{\pi}_i(y, q_{-i}) \right\}.$$

Let $U(S) = \prod_{i \in I_n} U_i(S)$, the k-th iterate of which is given by $U^k(S) = U\left(U^{k-1}(S)\right)$, $k \geq 2$, where $U^1(S) = U(S)$. Note that since $q^{\alpha(I)}$ is unique we have

$$U^\infty(\Gamma) = \{q^{\alpha(I)}\}.$$

Following Milgrom and Roberts (1991) we say that $\{q^t\}_{t\in\mathbb{N}}$ is *consistent with adaptive learning* if

$$\forall_{\hat{t}\in\mathbb{N}}\exists_{\bar{t}>\hat{t}}\forall_{\tilde{t}\geq\bar{t}}: q^{\tilde{t}} \in U\big(\{q^s|\hat{t} \leq s < \tilde{t}\}\big).$$

Let $\hat{t} \in \mathbb{N}$, take $\bar{t} = \hat{t} + 1$ and let $\tilde{t} = \bar{t} + k$ for some $k \in \{0, 1, 2, \dots\}$. Then

$$\{q^s|\hat{t} \leq s < \tilde{t}\} = \{q^s|s = \hat{t}, \dots, \bar{t} + k - 1\}.$$

Let $\{q^t\}_{t\in\mathbb{N}}$ be generated by the pure quantity dynamics, i.e. the quantity dynamics without the experimentation (or mutation) part. Then we have by definition

$$\forall_{y\in\Gamma_i} : \tilde{\pi}_i(q_i^{\tilde{t}}, q_{-i}^{\tilde{t}-1}) \geq \tilde{\pi}_i(y, q_{-i}^{\tilde{t}-1}).$$

Furthermore, it holds that $q^{\tilde{t}-1} \in \{q^s|\bar{t} \leq s < \tilde{t}\}$. Hence, we can conclude that $\{q^t\}_{t\in\mathbb{N}}$ is consistent with adaptive learning. From Milgrom and Roberts (1991, Theorem 7) one obtains that $\|q^t - q^{\alpha(I)}\| \to 0$ as $t \to \infty$. Since Γ is finite we have

$$\exists_{\bar{t}\in\mathbb{N}}\forall_{t\geq\bar{t}} : q^t = q^{\alpha(I)}.$$

So, $\{q^{\alpha(I)}\}$ is the only recurrent state of the (mutation-free) pure quantity dynamics. From Young (1993) we know that the stochastically stable states are among the recurrent states of the mutation-free dynamics. Hence, $\mu^I(q^{\alpha(I)}) = 1$. □

Before we turn to Theorem 9.2, the following lemma is introduced, which plays a pivotal role its proof. It compares the equilibrium profits for different conjectures. Suppose that the market is in a monomorphic state, i.e. all firms have the same conjecture. The question is what happens to equilibrium profits if k firms deviate to another conjecture. If $n - k$ firms have a conjecture equal to α and k firms have a conjecture equal to α', let the (unique) equilibrium quantities be denoted by q_k^α and $q_k^{\alpha'}$, respectively.

LEMMA 9.1 *For all* $k \in \{1, 2, \dots, n-1\}$ *and* $\alpha > \alpha'$ *it holds that*

$$P\big((n-k)q_k^\alpha + kq_k^{\alpha'}\big)q_k^{\alpha'} - C(q_k^{\alpha'}) > P\big((n-k)q_k^\alpha + kq_k^{\alpha'}\big)q_k^\alpha - C(q_k^\alpha).$$

The proof of this lemma can be found in Appendix A. Lemma 9.1 plays a similar role as the claim in Vega–Redondo (1997, p. 381). The main result in that paper is driven by the fact that if at least one firm plays the Walrasian quantity against the other firms playing another quantity, the firm with the Walrasian quantity has a strictly higher profit. In our model the dynamics is more elaborate. Suppose that all firms have the Walrasian conjecture and that the quantity dynamics is in equilibrium, i.e. the Walrasian equilibrium. If at least one player has another conjecture not only its own equilibrium quantity changes, but also the equilibrium *quantities* of the firms that still have the Walrasian *conjecture*. Lemma 9.1 states that the firms with the lower conjecture still have the highest equilibrium profit. This is intuitively clear form the first-order condition (9.1). The firms with the lower conjecture increase their production until the difference between the price and the marginal costs reaches a lower, but positive, level than the firms with the higher conjecture. Therefore, the total profit of having a lower conjecture is higher. This happens because the firms do not realise that in the future their behaviour will be imitated by other firms which puts downward pressure on industry profits.

Some additional notation and assumptions are needed in the following. For a matrix A let $\lambda_j(A)$ denote the j-th largest eigenvalue in absolute value of A. Furthermore, define $\lambda_k(I,J) = \lim_{\bar{\varepsilon}\downarrow 0}\lambda_k^{\bar{\varepsilon}}(I,J)$ and let $\zeta = \max_{k_I}\left\{\sum_{K\neq I}\sum_{l=1}^{m}Q_{k_I l_K}\right\}$. The following assumptions are made.

ASSUMPTION 9.2 *All elementary divisors of Q are linear.*

ASSUMPTION 9.3 $\zeta < \frac{1}{2}\left[1 - \max_{I\in\{1,\dots,N\}}\lambda_2(M_I)\right].$

Since the probability measures $\nu_i(\cdot)$ and $\tilde{\nu}_i(\cdot)$ have full support for all $i \in I_n$, all eigenvalues of Q will generically be distinct and, hence, Assumption 9.2 will generically be satisfied. Let $\alpha(1)$ be the monomorphic state where all firms have the Walrasian conjecture, i.e. $\alpha(1) = (-1,\dots,-1)$ We can now state the following theorem.

THEOREM 9.2 *Suppose that Assumptions 9.1–9.3 hold. Then there exists an ergodic Markov chain on Λ^n with transition matrix $\tilde{Q}$ and unique invariant probability measure $\tilde{\mu}(\cdot)$. For $\tilde{\mu}(\cdot)$ it holds that $\tilde{\mu}(q^{\alpha(1)}) = 1$. Furthermore, $\tilde{\mu}(\cdot)$ is an approximation of $\mu(\cdot)$ of order $O(\zeta)$.*

Proof. The approximation result follows from the theory of nearly-complete decomposability (cf. Section 6.2 of Chapter 2). First, define

$$Q^* = \begin{bmatrix} M_1 & 0 & \cdots & 0 \\ 0 & \ddots & \ddots & \vdots \\ \vdots & \ddots & \ddots & 0 \\ 0 & \cdots & 0 & M_N \end{bmatrix},$$

and take the matrix C such that

$$\zeta C_{k_I l_J} = \begin{cases} \lambda_k(I, J) M_I(k, l) & \text{if } I \neq J \\ -\sum_{K \neq I} \lambda_k(I, K) M_I(k, l) & \text{if } I = J. \end{cases}$$

Note that $Q = Q^* + \zeta C$. So, the transition matrix Q has been decomposed into a block diagonal matrix Q^*, where each diagonal block is the transition matrix for the quantity dynamics of a given vector of conjectures, and a matrix that reflects the conjecture dynamics. The constant ζ can be interpreted as the maximum degree of coupling between subsystems M_I.

Given the result of Theorem 9.1 one can aggregate Q using $\mu^I(\cdot)$ in the following way. Define a Markov chain on Λ^n with transition matrix $\tilde{Q}$ which has typical element

$$\begin{aligned} \tilde{Q}(I, J) &= \sum_{k=1}^{m} \mu^I\big(q(k)\big) \sum_{l=1}^{m} Q_{k_I l_J} \\ &= \sum_{k=1}^{m} \mu^I\big(q(k)\big) \lambda_k(I, J) \sum_{l=1}^{m} M_I(k, l) \\ &= \sum_{k=1}^{m} \mu^I\big(q(k)\big) \lambda_k(I, J) = \lambda_{k(I)}(I, J). \end{aligned}$$

Note that the transition matrix $\tilde{Q}$ is the limit of a sequence of ergodic Markov chains with transition matrices $\tilde{Q}^{\tilde{\varepsilon}}$ with $\tilde{Q}^{\tilde{\varepsilon}}(I, J) = \lambda_{k(I)}^{\tilde{\varepsilon}}(I, J)$.

So, $\tilde{Q}$ has a unique invariant probability measure $\tilde{\mu}(\cdot)$. Under Assumptions 9.2 and 9.3 the matrix Q is nearly-completely decomposable. From Courtois (1977, Section 3.2) this directly implies that $\tilde{\mu}(\cdot)$ is an $O(\zeta)$ approximation of $\mu(\cdot)$.

The result on $\tilde{\mu}(\cdot)$ is obtained by using the techniques developed by Freidlin and Wentzell (1984). First we establish the set of recurrent states for the mutation-free dynamics of $\tilde{Q}^{\tilde{\varepsilon}}$. This is the dynamics without the experimentation part and is thus equal for all $\tilde{\varepsilon} > 0$. From (9.3) one can see that the transition probabilities for this dynamics are equal to the transition probabilities of going from one vector of conjectures $\alpha(I)$ to another vector $\alpha(J)$ given that the current quantity vector is the equilibrium $q^{\alpha(I)}$. So, the dynamics of $\tilde{Q}^{\tilde{\varepsilon}}$ is the pure conjecture dynamics if the quantity dynamics gets sufficient time to settle in equilibrium. Let the transition matrix for this aggregated pure conjecture dynamics be denoted by $\tilde{Q}_0$.

LEMMA 9.2 *The set $\mathcal{A}$ of recurrent states for the aggregated mutation-free conjecture dynamics with transition matrix $\tilde{Q}_0$ is given by the set of monomorphic states, i.e.*

$$\mathcal{A} = \{\{(\alpha, \ldots, \alpha)\}|\alpha \in \Lambda\}.$$

The proof of this lemma can be found in Appendix B.

To find the stochastically stable state, first an $\alpha(1)$-tree H^* with minimal costs is built (cf. Section 6.1 of Chapter 2). Then it is shown that for any state $\alpha \in \mathcal{A}\backslash\{\alpha(1)\}$ and any α-tree H_α the costs will be higher. From Freidlin and Wentzell (1984, Lemma 6.3.1) one can then conclude that $\alpha(1)$ is the unique element in the support of $\tilde{\mu}(\cdot)$. Young (1993) has shown that the minimum cost tree is among the α-trees where α is an element of a recurrent class of the mutation-free dynamics. Thus, from Lemma 9.2 we know that we only need to consider the monomorphic states in $\mathcal{A}$. This implies that for all α-trees H_α, $\alpha \in \mathcal{A}$, we have $c(H_\alpha) \geq |\mathcal{A}| - 1$, since one always needs at least one experiment to leave a monomorphic state.

Consider $\alpha(1)$ and the $\alpha(1)$-tree H^* that is constructed in the following way. Let $\alpha \in \mathcal{A}\backslash\{\alpha(1)\}$. For all $i \in I_n$ we have $\alpha_i > \alpha_i(1)$. Suppose that one firm i experiments to $\alpha_i(1) = -1$, while the other firms cannot revise their output. According to Lemma 9.1 with $k = 1$ this firm has a higher profit in quantity equilibrium than the other firms. If one period later all other firms $j \neq i$ get the opportunity to revise their conjectural variation (which happens with positive probability) they will all choose $\alpha_j(1) = -1$. Hence, one mutation suffices to reach $\alpha(1)$ and therefore $c(H^*) = |\mathcal{A}| - 1$.

Conversely, let H_α be an α-tree for some $\alpha \in \mathcal{A}\backslash\{\alpha(1)\}$. Then somewhere in this tree there is a path between $\alpha(1)$ and a monomorphic state α' with $\alpha'_i > -1$ for all $i \in I_n$. Suppose that starting from $\alpha(1)$ one firm i experiments to α'_i. From Lemma 9.1 with $k = n - 1$ it is obtained that firm i has a strictly lower profit than the other firms in quantity equilibrium. So, to drive the system away from $\alpha(1)$ to α' at least two mutations are needed. Hence, $c(H_\alpha) > c(H^*)$. $\square$

Theorem 9.2 gives a result on the convergence of market interaction to the Walrasian equilibrium that is similar to the result of Vega–Redondo (1997). Apparently, profit imitation is such a strong force that it also drives this more elaborate behavioural model to the Walrasian equilibrium. Note, however, that the result in Theorem 9.2 is an approximation. It might well be that the support of $\mu(\cdot)$ consists of more states than just the Walrasian equilibrium. This is actually suggested by the simulations in Section 3.

A crucial assumption is the one on the maximum degree of coupling between subsystems M^I, ζ, as stated in Assumption 9.3. This parameter should not be too large. Intuitively, this condition requires that the interaction between subsystems M^I is sufficiently low, i.e. that the conjecture dynamics does not happen too frequent. In Proposition 9.1 a sufficient condition on $\tilde{p}$ is given for Assumption 9.3 to hold.

PROPOSITION 9.1 *If* $\tilde{p} < 1 - \left(\frac{3}{4}\right)^{1/n}$, *then Assumption 9.3 is satisfied.*

Proof. Let $I \in \{1, 2, \ldots, N\}$. From Bauer et al. (1969) we obtain an upper bound for the second largest eigenvalue of M^I:

$$\lambda_2(M^I) \leq \min \left\{ \max_{1 \leq \theta, \rho \leq m} \frac{1}{2} \sum_{i=1}^m v_i^1(M^I) \left| \frac{M^I(i, \theta)}{v_\theta^1(M^I)} - \frac{M^I(i, \rho)}{v_\rho^1(M^I)} \right|, \right.$$
$$\left. \max_{1 \leq \theta, \rho \leq m} \frac{1}{2} \sum_{i=1}^m |M^I(\theta, i) - M^I(\rho, i)| \right\}, \tag{9.6}$$

where $v^1(M^I)$ is the eigenvector corresponding to the largest eigenvalue of M^I. Since M^I is a stochastic matrix we have that

$$v_i^1(M^I) = \mu_i^I = \mathbb{1}_{(q=q^{\alpha(I)})}.$$

Consider the first term on the right hand side of (9.6). For $\theta = k(I)$ and $\rho \neq k(I)$, we get

$$\frac{1}{2} \sum_{i=1}^m v_i^1(M^I) \left| \frac{M^I(i, k(I))}{v_{k(I)}^1(M^I)} - \frac{M^I(i, \rho)}{v_\rho^1(M^I)} \right|$$
$$= \frac{1}{2} \left| \frac{M^I(k(I), k(I))}{\mu_{k(I)}^I} - \frac{M^I(k(I), \rho)}{\mu_\rho^I} \right|$$
$$= \infty,$$

since $\mu^I(q(\rho)) = 0$ and $\frac{M^I(k(I), k(I))}{\mu_{k(I)}^I} = M^I(k(I), k(I)) = 1$.

The maximum of the second term on the right hand side of (9.6) is attained for $\theta = k(I)$ and some $\rho \neq k(I)$, such that $q(k(I))$ is not a best response to $q(\rho)$. One obtains that

$$\frac{1}{2} \sum_{i=1}^m |M^I(k(I), i) - M^I(\rho, i)| \leq \frac{1}{2} |M^I(k(I), k(I))| = \frac{1}{2},$$

since $q(k(I))$ is a best response to $q(k(I))$. Hence, we find that $\lambda_2(M^I) \leq \frac{1}{2}$ for all $I = 1, \ldots, N$. So, we have that

$$\frac{1}{2} [1 - \max_{I=1,\ldots,N} \lambda_2(M^I)] \geq \frac{1}{4}.$$

Note that it holds that

$$\zeta = \max_{k_I}\left\{ \sum_{K\neq I}\sum_{l=1}^{m} Q_{k_I l_K} \right\}$$

$$= \max_{k_I}\left\{ \sum_{K\neq I} \lambda_k(I,K) \right\}$$

$$= \max_{k_I}\left\{ 1 - \lim_{\tilde{\varepsilon}\downarrow 0} \lambda_k^{\tilde{\varepsilon}}(I,I) \right\}.$$

Furthermore, by definition we have that

$$\lambda_k^{\tilde{\varepsilon}}(I,I) \geq \prod_{i\in I_n}\left\{ (1-\tilde{\varepsilon})(1-\tilde{p}) + \tilde{\varepsilon}\tilde{\nu}_i(\alpha_i(I)) \right\}.$$

Therefore, we conclude that

$$\zeta \leq 1 - \lim_{\tilde{\varepsilon}\downarrow 0} \prod_{i\in I_n}\left\{ (1-\tilde{\varepsilon})(1-\tilde{p}) + \tilde{\varepsilon}\tilde{\nu}_i(\alpha_i(I)) \right\}$$

$$= 1 - (1-\tilde{p})^n < \frac{1}{4}$$

$$\Longleftrightarrow \tilde{p} < 1 - \left(\frac{3}{4}\right)^{1/n},$$

which proves the proposition.   □

5.   Discussion

The model presented in this chapter extends existing evolutionary models of e.g. Vega–Redondo (1997), Schenk-Hoppé (2000) and Schipper (2003) by allowing for dynamics at two levels. We model quantity dynamics based on myopic optimisation by firms that includes the conjectured market response to the firm's own quantity-setting behaviour which is modelled by means of a conjecture parameter. At a second level, we allow firms to change or adapt their behaviour in the sense that they can change their conjecture. This decision is also modelled to be boundedly rational. Firms look at their competitors and imitate the behaviour of the most successful firm.

The main conclusion of Theorem 9.2 is that if behavioural adjustment takes place at a sufficiently lower rate than quantity adjustment, the market ends up in the Walrasian equilibrium in the long-run. To be more precise, the Walrasian equilibrium is the only outcome that will be observed a significant amount of time in the long-run. A sufficient condition for this result to hold is that the conjecture dynamics occurs at a sufficiently low frequency. A simulation study shows that in the long-run also the collusion and Cournot-Nash equilibria can arise at a significant frequency. The main point of Theorem 9.2 is, however, that even with more elaborate behavioural dynamics than e.g. Vega–Redondo (1997), evolution still selects the Walrasian equilibrium. The appeal of this equilibrium lies in the fact that if behaviour is guided by profit imitation, i.e. relative payoffs, this leads to spitefulness in a firm's actions. This in turn leads to selection of the Walrasian equilibrium.

An important feature of our model that triggers the result of Theorem 9.2 is the fact that we model an explicit dynamic process where firms learn from the past. This induces them to adapt their behaviour if their profit falls behind their competitors' profits. This contrasts, for example, standard repeated games where time plays an implicit role. To quote Vives (1999): in a "pure repeated game framework [...] history matters only because firms threaten it to matter". Therefore, a collusion outcome can be sustained as an equilibrium in such models. The combination of time having an explicit role and boundedly rational firms has important consequences for the long-run outcome of market interaction since it avoids folk theorem-like results and instead pins down a unique equilibrium outcome.

Appendix
A.   Proof of Lemma 9.1

Since all firms are identical and solutions to the first-order conditions are unique, firms with the same conjecture have the same equilibrium quantity. Therefore, the equilibrium quantities q_k^α and $q_k^{\alpha'}$ satisfy

$$P'\big((n-k)q_k^\alpha + kq_k^{\alpha'}\big)(1+\alpha)\frac{n}{2}q_k^\alpha + P\big((n-k)q_k^\alpha + kq_k^{\alpha'}\big) - C'(q_k^\alpha) = 0$$

$$P'\big((n-k)q_k^\alpha + kq_k^{\alpha'}\big)(1+\alpha')\frac{n}{2}q_k^{\alpha'} + P\big((n-k)q_k^\alpha + kq_k^{\alpha'}\big) - C'(q_k^{\alpha'}) = 0.$$

These first-order conditions imply that

$$P'\big((n-k)q_k^\alpha + kq_k^{\alpha'}\big)(1+\alpha)\frac{n}{2}q_k^\alpha - C'(q_k^\alpha)$$
$$= P'\big((n-k)q_k^\alpha + kq_k^{\alpha'}\big)(1+\alpha')\frac{n}{2}q_k^{\alpha'} - C'(q_k^{\alpha'}).$$

(9.7)

Suppose that $q_k^\alpha \geq q^{\alpha'}$. There are two possible cases:

1 if $C'(q_k^\alpha) \geq C'(q_k^{\alpha'})$, then (9.7) immediately gives a contradiction;

2 if $C'(q_k^\alpha) < C'(q_k^{\alpha'})$, then according to (9.7) it should hold that

$$-P'\big((n-k)q_k^\alpha + kq_k^{\alpha'}\big)(1+\alpha)\frac{n}{2}q_k^\alpha \leq P'\big((n-k)q_k^\alpha + kq_k^{\alpha'}\big)(1+\alpha')\frac{n}{2}q_k^{\alpha'}.$$

This implies that $\frac{q_k^\alpha}{q_k^{\alpha'}} \leq \frac{1+\alpha'}{1+\alpha}$. However, since $\frac{q_k^\alpha}{q_k^{\alpha'}} \geq 1$ and $\frac{1+\alpha'}{1+\alpha} < 1$ this gives a contradiction.

According to the mean-value theorem there exists a $q \in (q_k^\alpha, q_k^{\alpha'})$ such that

$$C'(q) = \frac{C(q_k^{\alpha'}) - C(q_k^\alpha)}{q_k^{\alpha'} - q_k^\alpha},$$

since the cost function is continuous. Furthermore, it holds that

$$C'(q) < \max\{C'(q_k^\alpha), C'(q_k^{\alpha'})\}$$
$$\leq P\big((n-k)q_k^\alpha + kq_k^{\alpha'}\big)$$
$$\Longleftrightarrow P\big((n-k)q_k^\alpha + kq_k^{\alpha'}\big)q_k^{\alpha'} - C(q_k^{\alpha'}) > P\big((n-k)q_k^\alpha + kq_k^{\alpha'}\big)q_k^\alpha - C(q_k^\alpha),$$

which proves the lemma. □

B.   Proof of Lemma 9.2

Given a monomorphic state, the pure conjecture dynamics remains in the same monomorphic state with probability one. So $\mathcal{A} \supset \{\{(\alpha,\ldots,\alpha)\}|\alpha \in \Lambda\}$. Conversely, let $\alpha \in \Lambda^n\backslash\mathcal{A}$. With positive probability all firms may adjust their conjecture and with positive probability all choose the same conjecture, leading to a monomorphic state. Hence,

$$\mathcal{A} \subset \{\{(\alpha,\ldots,\alpha)\}|\alpha \in \Lambda\},$$

which proves the lemma. □

Chapter 10

BOUNDED RATIONALITY IN A FINANCE ECONOMY WITH INCOMPLETE MARKETS

1. Introduction

In Chapters 8 and 9 we analysed the effects of bounded rationality in a partial equilibrium model. In this chapter we turn to a general equilibrium model with incomplete financial markets. The main focus of this chapter is to describe a boundedly rational price-adjustment process that converges to an equilibrium price vector. It turns out that the simplicial algorithm for calculating stationary points of a continuous function on a polytope as developed by Talman and Yamamoto (1989) has a nice interpretation that can be used to give a boundedly rational explanation for price formation on financial markets.

The theory of general equilibrium with incomplete markets originates from the classical general equilibrium theory and the theory of finance. The general equilibrium approach dates back to Walras (1874), who gave the first systematic account of general equilibrium. Existence of a general equilibrium was not proved, however, until the nineteen fifties by Arrow and Debreu (1954). Textbook expositions can be found in e.g. Hildenbrand and Kirman (1988) and Mas–Colell et al. (1995). There has been extensive criticism towards the static and deterministic nature of general equilibrium theory, started notably by Hicks (1939).

The first general equilibrium model with time and uncertainty was developed in Arrow (1953). This model, known as the Arrow-Debreu model, describes two periods of time, today and the future. There is a finite number of possible states of the future, but which one will occur is unknown at present. It is assumed that agents can trade in both present as well as future commodities. An equilibrium price vector is such that all markets clear. In that sense, the Arrow-Debreu model is a

217

straightforward generalisation of the standard general equilibrium model as explained in Debreu (1959). A more elaborate model involving spot markets for today's commodities and future markets for future goods has been explored by Radner (1972).

The theory of financial economics has its roots in Fisher (1930). He presented a model of a sequence economy in which there is a short-term bond that can be used to redistribute income. The formalisation of incomplete markets dates back to Diamond (1967). Markets are incomplete if not all possible future allocations can be attained by trading on markets. Hence, the basic Arrow-Debreu and Radner models assume complete markets. In this chapter the simplest general equilibrium model with incomplete markets as is explained in e.g. Magill and Quinzii (1996) is considered. There are two periods of time (present and future), a finite number of possible future states, one consumption good and a number of financial securities that can be used to transfer income from the present to the future. For the consumption good there are spot markets, so at present one cannot trade the consumption good for the future. The financial market is incomplete if not all possible income streams for present and future can be attained by trading on financial markets.

Existence of equilibrium in a two-period general equilibrium model with multiple consumption goods and (possibly) incomplete markets is proved in Geanakoplos and Polemarchakis (1986). They prove existence on the set of no-arbitrage prices. These are prices such that it is impossible to create a portfolio of assets which generates a non-negative income stream in the future and has non-positive costs at present. The proof uses a fixed point argument for functions on compact sets. Therefore, since the set of no-arbitrage prices can be unbounded, the proof of Geanakoplos and Polemarchakis (1986) uses a compact truncation of this set. In this chapter we present an existence proof for the one consumption good model that uses a stationary point argument without truncating the set of no-arbitrage prices. Other existence proofs use some transformation of the underlying model. Hens (1991) for example, introduces an artificial asset to translate the present to the future. The approach taken by Hirsch et al. (1990) shows existence of equilibrium in a model with state prices. Then it is argued that each equilibrium in the original model corresponds one-to-one to an equilibrium in state prices.

Given that an equilibrium exists the question arises how to compute one. There is a homotopy method introduced in Herings and Kubler (2002) that requires differentiability assumptions on the utility functions. In this chapter we show that one can use the simplicial approach developed by Talman and Yamamoto (1989), which does not require additional assumptions to the ones needed to prove existence. Note that the Talman and Yamamoto (1989) algorithm is defined for functions on polytopes. The set of no-arbitrage prices for the model can however be an unbounded polyhedron. Since it is shown that in equilibrium asset prices cannot be unbounded, the algorithm uses an increasing sequence of polytopes and converges to an equilibrium in a finite number of steps. There are simplicial algorithms for functions on polyhedra, notably by Dai et al. (1991) and Dai and Talman (1993). These algorithms cannot be applied, however, since they assume pointedness of the polyhedron or linear functions, respectively.

Since a general equilibrium model can (and generally will) have multiple equilibria, the method used to calculate an equilibrium should ideally also be an equilibrium selection device. The homotopy method of Herings and Kubler (2002) qualifies as a selection method, only in that there homotopy method can be seen as a weighted average of Walrasian tatonnement and Smale's global Newton method (cf. Kamyia (1990)). The Talman and Yamamoto (1989) approach, however, can be used as a selection device based on underlying behavioural assumptions of the market maker. Namely, it assumes a boundedly rational market maker that maximises the market's turn-over. It does so by, given a starting vector of asset prices, collecting all demand and supply orders and by relatively increasing the price of the asset that has the greatest excess demand. This continues until another asset has the greatest excess demand. Then the price of this asset will be relatively increased. This procedure eventually converges to an equilibrium. The demand and supply orders of the agents represent the agents' valuations of their portfolios in the different states of the future.

The two period model can be given a more dynamic interpretation where the present represents a point in time just after a fundamental change has taken place in the economy that influences for example utility functions, endowments or future payoffs to assets. The starting vector of asset prices for the market maker is then the equilibrium price vector from just before the shock. Such an interpretation implicitly assumes bounded rationality since the agents are one-period forward looking.

The chapter is organised as follows. In Section 2 the economic model is described. In Section 3 we prove the existence of equilibrium and in Section 4 we interpret the simplicial algorithm of Talman and Yamamoto (1989) as describing a boundedly rational path of asset prices. In Section 5 the algorithm is presented in some detail and illustrated by means of a numerical example.

2.   The Finance Economy

The General Equilibrium model with Incomplete markets (GEI) explicitly includes incomplete financial markets in a general equilibrium framework. In this chapter the simplest version is used. It consists of two time periods, $t = 0, 1$, where $t = 0$ denotes the present and $t = 1$ denotes the future. At $t = 0$ the state of nature is known to be $s = 0$. The state of nature at $t = 1$ is unknown and denoted by $s \in \{1, 2, \ldots, S\}$. In the economy there are $I \in \mathbb{N}$ consumers, indexed by $i = 1, \ldots, I$. There is one consumption good that can be interpreted as income. A consumption plan for consumer $i \in \{1, \ldots, I\}$ is a vector $x^i \in \mathbb{R}_+^{S+1}$, where x_s^i gives the consumption level in state $s \in \{0, 1, \ldots, S\}$.[1]

Each consumer $i = 1, \ldots, I$, is characterised by a vector of initial endowments, $\omega^i \in \mathbb{R}_+^{S+1}$, and a utility function $u^i : \mathbb{R}_+^{S+1} \to \mathbb{R}$. Denote aggregate initial endowments by $\omega = \sum_{i=1}^{I} \omega^i$. Regarding the initial endowments and utility functions we make the following assumptions.

ASSUMPTION 10.1 *The vector of aggregate initial endowments is strictly positive, i.e.*

$$\omega \in \mathbb{R}_{++}^{S+1}.$$

ASSUMPTION 10.2 *For each agent $i = 1, \ldots, I$, the utility function u^i satisfies:*

1 continuity on $\mathbb{R}_+^{S+1}$;

2 strict monotonicity on $\mathbb{R}_+^{S+1}$;

3 strict quasi-concavity on $\mathbb{R}_+^{S+1}$.

Assumption 10.1 ensures that in each period and in each state of nature there is at least one agent who has a positive amount of the consumption good. Assumption 10.2 ensures that the consumer's demand is a continuous function.

It is assumed that the market for the consumption good is a spot market. The consumers can smoothen consumption by trading on the asset market. At the asset market, $J \in \mathbb{N}$ financial contracts are traded, indexed by $j = 1, \ldots, J$. The future payoffs of the assets are put together in a matrix

$$V = (V^1, \ldots, V^J) \in \mathbb{R}^{S \times J},$$

where V_s^j is the payoff of one unit of asset j in state s. The following assumption is made with respect to V.

---

[1] In general we denote for a vector $x \in \mathbb{R}^{S+1}$, $x = (x_0, x_1) \in \mathbb{R} \times \mathbb{R}^S$ to separate x_0 in period $t = 0$ and $x_1 = (x_1, \ldots, x_S)$ in period $t = 1$.

ASSUMPTION 10.3 *There are no redundant assets, i.e. $rank(V) = J$.*

Actually, Assumption 10.3 can be made without loss of generality; if there are redundant assets then a no-arbitrage argument guarantees that its price is uniquely determined by the other assets. Let the marketed subspace be denoted by $\langle V \rangle = Span(V)$. That is, the marketed subspace consists of those income streams that can be generated by trading on the asset market. If $S = J$, the marketed subspace consists of all possible income streams, i.e. markets are complete. If $J < S$ there is idiosyncratic risk and markets are incomplete.

A *finance economy* is defined as a tuple $\mathcal{E} = \left((u^i, \omega^i)_{i=1,...,I}, V \right)$. Given a finance economy $\mathcal{E}$, agent i can trade assets by buying a portfolio $z^i \in \mathbb{R}^J$ given the (row)vector of prices $q = (q_0, q_1) \in \mathbb{R}^{J+1}$, where q_0 is the price for consumption in period $t = 0$ and $q_1 = (q_1, \dots, q_J)$ is the vector of security prices with q_j the price of security j, $j = 1, \dots, J$. Given a vector of prices $q = (q_0, q_1) \in \mathbb{R}^{J+1}$, the budget set for agent $i = 1, \dots, I$ is given by

$$B^i(q) = \left\{ x \in \mathbb{R}_+^{S+1} \Big| \exists_{z \in \mathbb{R}^J} : q_0(x_0 - \omega_0^i) \leq -q_1 z, x_1 - \omega_1^i = Vz \right\}. \quad (10.1)$$

Given the asset payoff matrix V we will restrict attention to asset prices that generate no arbitrage opportunities, i.e. asset prices q such that there is no portfolio generating a semi-positive income stream. In other words, we only consider asset prices that exclude the possibility of "free lunches". The importance of restricting ourselves to no-arbitrage prices becomes clear from the following well-known theorem (cf. Magill and Quinzii (1996)).

THEOREM 10.1 *Let $\mathcal{E}$ be a finance economy satisfying Assumption 10.2. Then the following conditions are equivalent:*

1 $q \in \mathbb{R}^{J+1}$ permits no arbitrage opportunities;

2 $\forall_{i=1,...,I} : \arg\max\{u^i(x^i) | x^i \in B^i(q)\} \neq \emptyset$;

3 $\exists_{\pi \in \mathbb{R}_{++}^S} : q_1 = \pi V$;

4 $B^i(q)$ is compact for all $i = 1, \dots, I$.

The vector $\pi \in \mathbb{R}_{++}^S$ can be interpreted as a vector of state prices. Condition 3 therefore states that a no-arbitrage price for security j equals the present value of security j given the vector of state prices π. As a consequence of this theorem, in the remainder we restrict ourselves to the set of no-arbitrage prices

$$Q = \{q \in \mathbb{R}^{J+1} | q_0 > 0, \exists_{\pi \in \mathbb{R}_{++}^S} : q_1 = \pi V\}. \quad (10.2)$$

Under Assumption 10.2, Theorem 10.1 shows that the demand function $x^i(q)$, maximising agent i's utility function $u^i(x)$ on $B^i(q)$, is well-defined for all $i = 1, \ldots, I$, and all $q \in Q$. Since the budget correspondence $B^i : Q \to \mathbb{R}_+^{S+1}$ is upper- and lower-semicontinuous, Berge's maximum theorem gives that $x^i(q)$ is continuous on Q. Because the mapping $z^i \mapsto Vz^i + \omega^i$ is continuous, one-to-one and onto, the security demand function $z^i(q)$, determined by $Vz^i(q) = x_1^i(q) - \omega_1^i$, is a continuous function on Q.

Define the *excess demand* function $f : Q \to \mathbb{R}^{J+1}$ by

$$f(q) = \big(f_0(q), f_1(q)\big) = \Big(\sum_{i=1}^{I} (x_0^i(q) - \omega_0^i), \sum_{i=1}^{I} z^i(q) \Big).$$

Note that since there are no initial endowments of asset j, $j = 1, \ldots, J$, excess demand is given by $\sum_{i=1}^{I} z_j^i(q)$. With respect to the excess demand function we can derive the following result.

PROPOSITION 10.1 *Under Assumptions 10.1–10.3 the excess demand function $f : Q \to \mathbb{R}^J$ satisfies the following properties:*

1 continuity on Q;

2 homogeneity of degree 0;

3 $(f_0(q), Vf_1(q)) \geq -\omega$ for all $q \in Q$;

4 for all $q \in Q$, $qf(q) = 0$ (Walras' law).

The proof of this proposition is elementary and is, therefore, omitted.

A *financial market equilibrium* (FME) for a finance economy $\mathcal{E}$ is a tuple $\big((\bar{x}^i, \bar{z}^i)_{i=1,\ldots,I}, \bar{q}\big)$ with $\bar{q} \in Q$ such that:

1 $\bar{x}^i \in \arg\max\{u^i(x^i)|x^i \in B^i(\bar{q})\}$ for all $i = 1, \ldots, I$;

2 $V\bar{z}^i = \bar{x}_1^i - \omega_1^i$ for all $i = 1, \ldots, I$;

3 $\sum_{i=1}^{I} \bar{z}^i = 0$.

Note that the market-clearing conditions for the financial markets imply that the goods market also clears, since there is only one consumption good.

3.   Existence of Equilibrium

Existence of equilibrium is proved on the space of asset prices $\bar{Q}$, where

$$\bar{Q} = \{q \in \mathbb{R}^{J+1}|q_0 \geq 0, \exists_{\pi \in \mathbb{R}_+^S} : q_1 = \pi V\}.$$

Before proving a general existence theorem we present the following lemmata.

LEMMA 10.1 *Under Assumption 10.3 it holds that* $\bar{Q} = cl(Q)$.

Proof. Since $\bar{Q}$ is a finitely generated cone it is a closed set (cf. Rockafellar (1970, Theorem 19.1)) and hence $cl(Q) \subset \bar{Q}$.

Let $\bar{q} \in \bar{Q}$. Then $\bar{q}_0 \geq 0$ and there exists a $\bar{\pi} \in \mathbb{R}_+^S$ satisfying $\bar{q}_1 = \bar{\pi}V$. Take any $(\pi^\nu)_{\nu \in \mathbb{N}}$ in $\mathbb{R}_{++}^S$ converging to $\bar{\pi}$. Such a sequence exists, since $\bar{\pi} \in \mathbb{R}_+^S$. Moreover, take $q_0^\nu = \max\{\bar{q}_0, \frac{1}{\nu}\}$ for all $\nu \in \mathbb{N}$. Define $q^\nu = (q_0^\nu, q_1^\nu)$, where $q_1^\nu = \pi^\nu V$. Clearly, $q^\nu \in Q$ for all $\nu \in \mathbb{N}$ and $q^\nu \to \bar{q}$ since $q_0^\nu \to \bar{q}_0$ and $q_1^\nu = \pi^\nu V \to \bar{\pi}V = \bar{q}_1$. Consequently, $(q^\nu)_{\nu \in \mathbb{N}}$ is a sequence in Q converging to $\bar{q}$. Hence, $\bar{Q} \subset cl(Q)$.   □

An important result needed to prove existence of an FME is the existence of a convergent sequence of state prices to the boundary.

LEMMA 10.2 *Let* $(q^\nu)_{\nu \in \mathbb{N}}$ *be a sequence in* Q *converging to* $\bar{q} \in \partial\bar{Q}\backslash\{0\}$. *Then under Assumption 10.3 there exists a sequence of state prices* $(\pi^\nu)_{\nu \in \mathbb{N}}$ *in* $\mathbb{R}_{++}^S$ *converging to some* $\bar{\pi} \in \mathbb{R}_+^S$ *satisfying* $\bar{q}_1 = \bar{\pi}V$. *Moreover, if* $\bar{q}_0 > 0$, *it holds that* $\bar{\pi} \in \partial\mathbb{R}_+^S$.

Proof. Define

$$\bar{Q}_1 = \{q_1 \in \mathbb{R}^J | \exists_{\pi_1 \in \mathbb{R}_+^S} : q_1 = \pi_1 V\}.$$

Since $\bar{Q}_1$ is a finitely generated cone it consists of all nonnegative linear combinations of finitely many directions $\{q^1, \ldots, q^m\} \subset \bar{Q}_1$. Hence, there exist corresponding vectors $\pi^1, \ldots, \pi^m \in \mathbb{R}_+^S$ such that for all $k = 1, \ldots, m$, $q^k = \pi^k V$.

From Carathéodory's theorem (cf. Rockafellar (1970, Theorem 17.1)) we know that for every $\nu \in \mathbb{N}$, the vector q_1^ν can be written as

$$q_1^\nu = \sum_{k \in K_\nu} \lambda_k^\nu q^k,$$

where $\lambda_k^\nu \geq 0$ for all $k \in K_\nu$ and K_ν is such that $\{q^k | k \in K_\nu\}$ is a set of linearly independent vectors. Take

$$\pi^\nu = \sum_{k \in K_\nu} \lambda_k^\nu \pi^k,$$

then $\pi^\nu \in \mathbb{R}_+^S$ and $\pi^\nu V = q_1^\nu$, for all $\nu \in \mathbb{N}$.

Since $\bar{Q}_1$ is finitely generated, there exists a subsequence of $(q_1^\nu)_{\nu \in \mathbb{N}}$ generated from the same subset K of linearly independent elements of $\{q^1, \ldots, q^m\}$. Without loss of generality we take it to be the sequence itself. Since $(q_1^\nu)_{\nu \in \mathbb{N}}$ is convergent and hence bounded, and $\{q^k | k \in K\}$ is a set of linearly independent vectors, we have that λ_k^ν, $k \in K$, $\nu \in \mathbb{N}$, is unique and thus bounded. Therefore, the sequence $(\pi^\nu)_{\nu \in \mathbb{N}}$ is bounded.

Since $q^\nu \in Q$ for all $\nu \in \mathbb{N}$, there exists a $\tilde{\pi}^\nu \in \mathbb{R}_{++}^S$ such that $q_1^\nu = \tilde{\pi}^\nu V$. Note that the sequence $(\tilde{\pi}^\nu)_{\nu \in \mathbb{N}}$ might not be bounded. Since $(\pi^\nu)_{\nu \in \mathbb{N}}$ is bounded (in any given norm) by, say, $M > 0$, for all $\nu \in \mathbb{N}$, there exists a convex combination $\hat{\pi}^\nu$ of $\tilde{\pi}^\nu$ and π^ν that is bounded by $2M$, such that $\hat{\pi}^\nu \in \mathbb{R}_{++}^S$. Since $(\hat{\pi}^\nu)_{\nu \in \mathbb{N}}$ is bounded there exists a convergent subsequence with limit, say, $\bar{\pi}$, that without loss of generality we take to be the sequence itself. Clearly, $\bar{q} = \bar{\pi}V$ and $\bar{\pi} \in \mathbb{R}_+^S$.

Furthermore, when $\bar{q}_0 > 0$, $\bar{\pi} \in \partial \mathbb{R}_+^S$, since if $\bar{\pi} \in \mathbb{R}_{++}^S$, there would be a full-dimensional ball around $\bar{\pi}$ in the interior of $\mathbb{R}_+^S$. This ball would be mapped in a ball of full dimension around $\bar{q}_1$, which contradicts $\bar{q} \in \partial \bar{Q}$ when $\bar{q}_0 > 0$. □

The following lemma concerns the boundary behaviour of the excess demand function.

LEMMA 10.3 *Let* $(q^\nu)_{\nu \in \mathbb{N}}$ *be a sequence in Q with* $\lim_{\nu \to \infty} q^\nu = \bar{q} \in \partial \bar{Q} \backslash \{0\}$. *Under Assumptions 10.1–10.3 it holds that*

$$f_0(q^\nu) + e^\top V f_1(q^\nu) \to \infty.$$

Proof. Suppose not. Then

$$\exists_{M>0} \forall_{\nu \in \mathbb{N}} : f_0(q^\nu) + e^\top V f_1(q^\nu) \le M.$$

Since $(f_0, V f_1)$ is bounded from below, this implies that $(f_0(q_\nu), V f_1(q_\nu))_{\nu \in \mathbb{IN}}$ is bounded and has a convergent sequence (w.l.o.g. we assume it is the sequence itself) with limit, say, $\bar{f} = (\bar{f}_0, V \bar{f}_1)$.

For all $\nu \in \mathbb{N}$, let $\pi^\nu \in \mathbb{R}_{++}^S$ be a supporting vector, i.e. $q_1^\nu = \pi^\nu V$. By Lemma 10.2 we can choose π^ν, $\nu \in \mathbb{N}$, such that $(\pi^\nu)_{\nu \in \mathbb{N}}$ has a convergent subsequence with $\lim_{\nu \to \infty} \pi^\nu = \bar{\pi} \in \mathbb{R}_+^S$, satisfying $\bar{q}_1 = \bar{\pi}V$.

We consider three cases. First, consider the case where $\bar{q}_0 > 0$ and $\bar{q}_1 \neq 0$. Let $\mathcal{S} = \{s | \bar{\pi}_s = 0\}$ and $\mathcal{S}^c = \{s | \bar{\pi}_s > 0\}$. Since $\bar{q}_1 \neq 0$ and since by Lemma 10.2, $\bar{\pi} \in \partial \mathbb{R}_+^S$, both sets are non-empty. Take $s^c \in \mathcal{S}^c$. Since $\omega_{s^c} > 0$, there exists an $i^c \in \{1, \dots, I\}$ with $\omega_{s^c}^{i^c} > 0$. For $q \in Q$, this consumer has excess demand defined by

$$f^{i^c}(q) = \left(x_0^{i^c}(q) - \omega_0^{i^c}, z^{i^c}(q)\right).$$

Since $(f_0(q^\nu), V f_1(q^\nu))_{\nu \in \mathbb{N}}$ is bounded from above and $(f_0^{i^c}(q^\nu), V f_1^{i^c}(q^\nu))_{\nu \in \mathbb{N}}$ is bounded from below by $-\omega^{i^c}$ the sequence $(f_0^{i^c}(q^\nu), V f_1^{i^c}(q^\nu))_{\nu \in \mathbb{N}}$ is bounded and therefore there is a convergent subsequence with limit $\bar{f}^{i^c} = (\bar{f}_0^{i^c}, V\bar{f}_1^{i^c})$. Let $\bar{x}^{i^c} = (\bar{f}_0^{i^c} + \omega_0^{i^c}, V\bar{f}_1^{i^c} + \omega_1^{i^c})$. Note that for all $q \in Q$ with supporting vector $\pi \in \mathbb{R}_{++}^S$ we have

$$B^{i^c}(q) = \{x \in \mathbb{R}_+^{S+1} | q_0 x_0 + \pi x_1 \leq q_0 \omega_0^{i^c} + \pi \omega_1^{i^c}\}.$$

Hence, $\bar{q}_0 \bar{x}_0^{i^c} + \bar{\pi} \bar{x}_1^{i^c} = \bar{q}_0 \omega_0^{i^c} + \bar{\pi} \omega_1^{i^c}$ since u^{i^c} is continuous and strictly monotonic. Consider the bundle $\tilde{x}^{i^c} = \bar{x}^{i^c} + e(s)$ for some $s \in \mathcal{S}$, where $e(s) \in \mathbb{R}^{S+1}$ is the s-th unit vector. Because of strict monotonicity it holds that $u^{i^c}(\tilde{x}^{i^c}) > u^{i^c}(\bar{x}^{i^c})$. However, since $\bar{\pi}_s = 0$ we have

$$\bar{q}_0 \tilde{x}_0^{i^c} + \bar{\pi} \tilde{x}_1^{i^c} = \bar{q}_0 \bar{x}_0^{i^c} + \bar{\pi} \bar{x}_1^{i^c} = \bar{q}_0 \omega_0^{i^c} + \bar{\pi} \omega_1^{i^c}.$$

Since $\bar{\pi}_{s^c} > 0$ and $\omega_{s^c}^{i^c} > 0$ it holds that $\bar{\pi} \omega_1^{i^c} > 0$ and hence $\bar{q}_0 \tilde{x}_0^{i^c} + \bar{\pi} \tilde{x}_1^{i^c} > 0$. So there exists $s^* \in \mathcal{S}^c$ satisfying $\bar{q}_0 \tilde{x}_0^{i^c} + \bar{\pi}_{s^*} \tilde{x}_{s^*}^{i^c} > 0$ and thus $\tilde{x}_0^{i^c} > 0$ or $\tilde{x}_{s^*}^{i^c} > 0$. Suppose first that $\tilde{x}_{s^*}^{i^c} > 0$. Since $u^{i^c}(\tilde{x}^{i^c}) > u^{i^c}(\bar{x}^{i^c})$ and u^{i^c} is continuous, it holds that

$$\exists_{\delta > 0} : u^{i^c}(\tilde{x}^{i^c} - \delta e(s^*)) > u^{i^c}(\bar{x}^{i^c}).$$

However,

$$\begin{aligned} \bar{q}_0 \tilde{x}_0^{i^c} + \bar{\pi}(\tilde{x}_1^{i^c} - \delta e_1(s^*)) &= \bar{q}_0 \tilde{x}_0^{i^c} + \bar{\pi} \tilde{x}^{i^c} - \bar{\pi}_{s^*} \delta \\ &= \bar{q}_0 \omega_0^{i^c} + \bar{\pi} \omega_1^{i^c} - \bar{\pi}_{s^*} \delta \\ &< \bar{q}_0 \omega_0^{i^c} + \bar{\pi} \omega_1^{i^c}. \end{aligned}$$

Since $q_0^\nu \to \bar{q}_0$ and $\pi^\nu \to \bar{\pi}$ we also have

$$\exists_{\nu_1 \in \mathbb{N}} \forall_{\nu > \nu_1} : q_0^\nu \tilde{x}_0^{i^c} + \pi^\nu(\tilde{x}_1^{i^c} - \delta e_1(s^*)) \leq q_0^\nu \omega_0^{i^c} + \pi^\nu \omega_1^{i^c}.$$

Moreover, since $x^{i^c}(q^\nu) \to \bar{x}^{i^c}$ and u^{i^c} is continuous,

$$\exists_{\nu_2 \in \mathbb{N}} \forall_{\nu > \nu_2} : u^{i^c}(\tilde{x}^{i^c} - \delta e(s^*)) > u^{i^c}(x^{i^c}(q^\nu)).$$

So, for all $\nu > \max\{\nu_1, \nu_2\}$ we have $\tilde{x}^{i^c} - \delta e(s^*) \in B^{i^c}(q^\nu)$ and $u^{i^c}(\tilde{x}^{i^c} - \delta e(s^*)) > u^{i^c}(x^{i^c}(q^\nu))$, which contradicts $x^{i^c}(q^\nu)$ being a best element in $B^{i^c}(q^\nu)$. Suppose now that $\tilde{x}_0^{i^c} > 0$. Using a similar reasoning as above we can show that there exists a $\delta > 0$ such that

$$\exists_{\nu_1 \in \mathbb{N}} \forall_{\nu > \nu_1} : q_0^\nu(\tilde{x}_0^{i^c} - \delta) + \pi^\nu \tilde{x}_1^{i^c} \leq q_0^\nu \omega_0^{i^c} + \pi^\nu \omega_1^{i^c},$$

and

$$\exists_{\nu_2 \in \mathbb{N}} \forall_{\nu > \nu_2} : u^{i^c}(\tilde{x}^{i^c} - \delta e(0)) > u^{i^c}(x^{i^c}(q^\nu)).$$

So, for all $\nu > \max\{\nu_1, \nu_2\}$ we have $\tilde{x}^{i^c} - \delta e(0) \in B^{i^c}(q^\nu)$ and $u^{i^c}(\tilde{x}^{i^c} - \delta e(0)) > u^{i^c}(x^{i^c}(q^\nu))$, which contradicts $x^{i^c}(q^\nu)$ being a best element in $B^{i^c}(q^\nu)$.

If $\bar{q}_0 = 0$, there exists an $i^c \in \{1, \ldots, I\}$ with $\omega_0^{i^c} > 0$. Now the proof follows along the same lines as above with some $s^* \in \mathcal{S}^c$ satisfying $\bar{\pi}_{s^*} \tilde{x}_{s^*}^{i^c} > 0$.

If $\bar{q}_1 = 0$, the set $\mathcal{S}^c$ is empty and $\bar{q}_0 \tilde{x}_0^{i^c} > 0$. We can now look at the proof of the first case and continue in a similar way as before.   □

Since $0 \in \partial \bar{Q}$ there is a tangent hyperplane at 0, i.e. there exists $\tilde{z} \in \mathbb{R}^{J+1} \backslash \{0\}$ such that $q\tilde{z} \geq 0$ for all $q \in \bar{Q}$. Since $\bar{Q}$ is full-dimensional, it holds that $q\tilde{z} > 0$ for all $q \in Q$. We show existence of FME by normalising asset prices to $q\tilde{z} = 1$, i.e. on a hyperplane parallel to the tangent hyperplane in 0. One possible choice for $\tilde{z}$ is the market portfolio z_M which is defined in the following way (cf. Herings and Kubler (2003)). Decompose the vector of total initial endowments in $\omega = \omega_M + \omega_\perp$, where $\omega_M \in \langle V \rangle$ and $\omega_\perp \in \langle V \rangle^\perp$, the null-space of $\langle V \rangle$. The market portfolio z_M is defined to be the unique portfolio satisfying $Vz = \omega_M$. If $\omega_M >> 0$ this implies $qz_M \geq 0$ for all no-arbitrage prices $q \in \bar{Q}$.

In the remainder, we fix $\tilde{z} \in \mathbb{R}^{J+1} \backslash \{0\}$ such that $q\tilde{z} \geq 0$ for all $q \in \bar{Q}$. Denote the set of normalised prices by $\tilde{Q}$, i.e.

$$\tilde{Q} = \{q \in \bar{Q} | q\tilde{z} = 1\}.$$

Note that $\tilde{Q}$ can contain half-spaces and is hence not necessarily bounded. Based on the previous lemma, however, one can show that $f_0 + e^\top V f_1$ becomes arbitrarily large by moving to the boundary of $\tilde{Q}$ or by taking $\|q\|_\infty$ large enough. In the following, let $d(q, A)$ denote the distance from $q \in \bar{Q}$ to $A \subset \bar{Q}$, i.e. $d(q, A) = \inf\{\delta | \exists_{a \in A} : \|a - q\| = \delta\}$.

LEMMA 10.4 *Under Assumptions 10.1–10.3 it holds that for all $M > 0$ there exists $\varepsilon > 0$ and $N > 0$ such that for all $q \in \tilde{Q}$,*

1 $d(q, \partial \tilde{Q}) \leq \varepsilon \Rightarrow f_0(q) + e^\top V f_1(q) > M$;

2 $\|q\|_\infty \geq N \Rightarrow f_0(q) + e^\top V f_1(q) > M$.

Proof. Suppose that 1) does not hold. Therefore, there exists an $\bar{M} > 0$ such that for all $\varepsilon > 0$ there exists a $q^\varepsilon \in \tilde{Q}$ with $d(q^\varepsilon, \partial \tilde{Q}) \leq \varepsilon$ such that $f_0(q^\varepsilon) + e^\top V f_1(q^\varepsilon) \leq \bar{M}$. Let $(q^\nu)_{\nu \in \mathbb{N}}$ be the sequence in $\tilde{Q}$ such that $\varepsilon = \frac{1}{\nu}$ and $q^\nu = q^\varepsilon$ for all $\nu \in \mathbb{N}$.

In case $(q^\nu)_{\nu \in \mathbb{N}}$ is bounded it has a convergent subsequence. Without loss of generality, $\lim_{\nu \to \infty} q^\nu = \tilde{q}$. Since $d(q^\nu, \partial \tilde{Q}) \leq \frac{1}{\nu}$ and $0 \notin \partial \tilde{Q}$ we have that $\tilde{q} \in \partial \tilde{Q} \backslash \{0\}$. From Lemma 10.3 it follows that $f_0(q^\nu) +$

$e^\top V f_1(q^\nu) \to \infty$. This implies that there exists an $\nu_{\bar{M}} \in \mathbb{N}$ such that for all $\nu > \nu_{\bar{M}}$ it holds that $f_0(q^\nu) + e^\top V f_1(q^\nu) > M$, which gives a contradiction.

In case $(q^\nu)_{\nu \in \mathbb{N}}$ is unbounded we are in case 2) with $\|q^\nu\|_\infty \to \infty$. So, suppose $f_0(q^\nu) + e^\top V f_1(q^\nu) \leq M$ for all $\nu \in \mathbb{N}$ with $\|q^\nu\|_\infty \to \infty$. For all $\nu \in \mathbb{N}$ define $\tilde{q}^\nu = \frac{q^\nu}{\|q^\nu\|_\infty}$. Then

$$\tilde{q}^\nu \tilde{z} = \frac{q^\nu \tilde{z}}{\|q^\nu\|_\infty} = \frac{1}{\|q^\nu\|_\infty} \to 0.$$

Moreover, for all $\nu \in \mathbb{N}$ it holds that $\|\tilde{q}^\nu\|_\infty = 1$. Hence, $(\tilde{q}^\nu)_{\nu \in \mathbb{N}}$ is bounded and therefore has a convergent subsequence with limit, say, $\tilde{q}$. Then $\tilde{q}\tilde{z} = \lim_{\nu \to \infty} \tilde{q}^\nu \tilde{z} = 0$, i.e. $\tilde{q} \in \partial \bar{Q}$. Furthermore, $\|\tilde{q}\|_\infty = 1$ and hence $\tilde{q} \neq 0$. From Lemma 10.3 we know that $f_0(\tilde{q}^\nu) + e^\top V f_1(\tilde{q}^\nu) \to \infty$. Since the budget correspondence is homogeneous of degree 0, we also get $f_0(q^\nu) + e^\top V f_1(q^\nu) \to \infty$, which gives a contradiction. □

With these lemmas in place, existence of an FME can be proved by using a direct approach as opposed to the indirect proof of e.g. Magill and Quinzii (1996).

THEOREM 10.2 *Let $\mathcal{E}$ be a finance economy satisfying Assumptions 10.1– 10.3. Then there exists an FME with asset price vector $\bar{q} \in Q$.*

Proof. A vector of prices $\bar{q} \in Q$ gives rise to an FME if and only if $f(\bar{q}) = 0$. Take $M > 0$. According to Lemma 10.4 there exists $\varepsilon > 0$ and $N > 0$ such that $d(q, \partial \tilde{Q}) \leq \varepsilon \Rightarrow f_0(q) + e^\top V f_1(q) > M$ and $\|q\|_\infty \geq N \Rightarrow f_0(q) + e^\top V f_1(q) > M$. Define the set of asset prices

$$\tilde{Q}' = conv\Big(\{q \in \tilde{Q} \,|\, d(q, \partial \tilde{Q}) \geq \varepsilon, \|q\|_\infty \leq N\}\Big),$$

where $conv(\cdot)$ denotes the convex hull. Obviously, $\tilde{Q}' \subset Q$ is compact and convex. Since the excess demand function f is continuous on $\tilde{Q}'$ there exists a stationary point, i.e.

$$\exists_{\bar{q} \in \tilde{Q}'} \forall_{q \in \tilde{Q}'} : q f(\bar{q}) \leq \bar{q} f(\bar{q}).$$

Note that for all $q \in \tilde{Q}'$ one obtains

$$q f(\bar{q}) \leq \bar{q} f(\bar{q}) = 0,$$

because of Walras' law.

It is easy to see that $\bar{q} \in \tilde{Q}' \backslash \partial \tilde{Q}'$. For suppose $\bar{q} \in \partial Q'$ and take $(q_0, q_1) = \frac{(1, e^\top V)}{\tilde{z}_0 + e^\top V \tilde{z}_1} \in \tilde{Q}'.$[2] Then Lemma 10.4 shows that

$$q_0 f_0(\bar{q}) + q_1 f_1(\bar{q}) = \frac{f_0(\bar{q}) + e^\top V f_1(\bar{q})}{\tilde{z}_0 + e^\top V \tilde{z}_1} \geq \frac{M}{\tilde{z}_0 + e^\top V \tilde{z}_1} > 0,$$

which contradicts $\bar{q}$ being a stationary point. Hence, $\bar{q} \in int(\tilde{Q}') \subset Q$.

Since $\bar{q}$ is a stationary point it solves the linear programming problem $\max\{qf(\bar{q})\}$ such that q satisfies $q\tilde{z} = 1$. The dual of this problem is $\min\{\lambda\}$ such that λ satisfies $\lambda \tilde{z} = f(\bar{q})$. Using Walras' law we obtain,

$$0 = \bar{q}f(\bar{q}) = \lambda \bar{q}\tilde{z} = \lambda$$
$$\Longleftrightarrow \lambda = 0.$$

Hence, $f(\bar{q}) = 0$. $\qquad\qquad\qquad\qquad\qquad\qquad\qquad\qquad\qquad\square$

4. A Boundedly Rational Path Towards Equilibrium

In this section we present a boundedly rational explanation for a path of points in $\tilde{Q}$ from an arbitrary starting point in $\tilde{Q}$ to an FME. First, we prove the existence of such a path. Note that the set of prices $\tilde{Q}$ is a (possibly unbounded) polyhedron generated by vertices $\{v^1, \ldots, v^n\}$ and directions $\{q^1, \ldots, q^m\}$. The recession cone of $\tilde{Q}$ is given by

$$re(\tilde{Q}) = \left\{ q \in \mathbb{R}^{J+1} \middle| q = \sum_{k=1}^m \mu_k q^k, \mu \geq 0 \right\}.$$

Let $q^0 \in \tilde{Q}$ be an arbitrary starting point in $\tilde{Q}$ and denote

$$\tilde{Q}_1 = conv(\{v^1, \ldots, v^n\}),$$

i.e. $\tilde{Q}_1$ is the convex hull of the vertices of $\tilde{Q}$. It is assumed without loss of generality that the directions $\{q^1, \ldots, q^m\}$ are such that $q^0 + q^k \notin \tilde{Q}_1$, for all $k = 1, \ldots, m$. Define the polytope

$$\tilde{Q}(1) = \left\{ q \in \tilde{Q} \middle| q = \sum_{h=1}^n \mu_h(v^h - q^0) + \sum_{k=1}^m \mu_{n+k} q^k + q^0, \mu_k \geq 0, \sum_{k=1}^{n+m} \mu_k \leq 1 \right\},$$

---

[2] We can take ε and N such that $\frac{(1, e^\top V)}{\tilde{z}_0 + e^\top V \tilde{z}_1} \in \tilde{Q}'.$

and the set

$$K = \Big\{ q \in re(\tilde{Q}) \Big| q = \sum_{k=1}^{m} \mu_k q^k, \mu_k \geq 0, \sum_{k=1}^{m} \mu_k \leq 1 \Big\}.$$

For simplicity we assume $q^0 \in int(\tilde{Q}(1))$. We can now define the expanding set $\tilde{Q}(\lambda)$,

$$\tilde{Q}(\lambda) = \begin{cases} (1-\lambda)\{q^0\} + \lambda \tilde{Q}(1) & \text{if } 0 \leq \lambda \leq 1; \\ \tilde{Q}(1) + (\lambda - 1)K & \text{if } \lambda \geq 1. \end{cases}$$

Note that for all $\lambda \geq 0$ the set $\tilde{Q}(\lambda)$ is a polytope and that $\lim_{\lambda \to \infty} \tilde{Q}(\lambda) = \tilde{Q}$. In Figure 10.1 some of these sets are depicted.

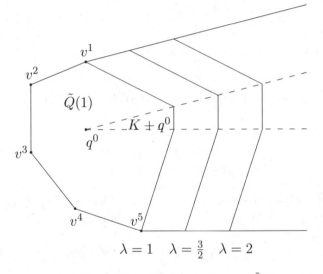

Figure 10.1.   The expanding set $\tilde{Q}(\lambda)$.

By Lemma 10.4 we know that for all $M > 0$ there exists an $N > 0$ such that

$$\|q\|_\infty \geq N \Rightarrow f_0(q) + e^\top V f_1(q) > M.$$

This implies that there exists a $\lambda^0 > 0$ such that for all stationary points $\bar{q}$ of f on $\tilde{Q}$ it holds that $\bar{q} \in \tilde{Q}(\lambda^0)$. Recall that all stationary points of f on $\tilde{Q}$ are FMEs. Let $\lambda^* = \max\{1, \lambda^0\}$ and define the homotopy $h : [0, \lambda^*] \times \tilde{Q}(\lambda^*) \to \tilde{Q}(\lambda^*)$ by

$$h(\lambda, q) = \begin{cases} proj_{\tilde{Q}(\lambda)}\big(q + f(q)\big) & \text{if } q \in \tilde{Q}(\lambda); \\ proj_{\tilde{Q}(\lambda)}\Big(proj_{\tilde{Q}(\lambda)}(q) + f(proj_{\tilde{Q}(\lambda)}(q))\Big) & \text{if } q \notin \tilde{Q}(\lambda), \end{cases}$$

where $proj_A(q)$ is the projection of q in $\|\cdot\|_2$ on the set A. An important property of this homotopy is stated in the following proposition, where $(\lambda, q) \in [0, \lambda^*] \times \tilde{Q}(\lambda^*)$ is a fixed point of h if $h(\lambda, q) = q$.

PROPOSITION 10.2 *Let $\lambda \in [0, \lambda^*]$. If (λ, q) is a fixed point of the homotopy h, then q is a stationary point of f on $\tilde{Q}(\lambda)$ and q is an FME if $q \notin \partial\tilde{Q}(\lambda)$. Moreover, if (λ^*, q) is a fixed point of h, then $q \notin \partial\tilde{Q}(\lambda^*)$, i.e. q is an FME.*

Proof. Note that if $q \notin \tilde{Q}(\lambda)$, q cannot be a fixed point of h. We therefore consider two cases. Firstly, if $q \in \tilde{Q}(\lambda)$ and $q + f(q) \in \tilde{Q}(\lambda)$, then $f(q) = 0$, i.e. q is an FME and hence a stationary point.

Secondly, if $q \in \tilde{Q}(\lambda)$ and $q + f(q) \notin \tilde{Q}(\lambda)$, then $q \in \partial\tilde{Q}(\lambda)$ and the orthogonal projection

$$\min_{q' \in \tilde{Q}(\lambda)} (q' - q - f(q))^\top (q' - q - f(q)),$$

is solved by q since q is a fixed point of h. Hence, for all $q' \in \tilde{Q}(\lambda)$ we have that

$$(q' - q - f(q))^\top (q' - q - f(q)) \geq f(q)^\top f(q),$$

and so

$$(q' - q)^\top (q' - q) \geq 2(q' - q)f(q).$$

Take $\hat{q} = \mu q^0 + (1 - \mu)q$ for any μ, $0 < \mu \leq 1$. Since $\tilde{Q}(\lambda)$ is convex we have $\hat{q} \in \tilde{Q}(\lambda)$ and so for all $0 < \mu \leq 1$ it holds that

$$\mu^2 (q' - q)^\top (q' - q) \geq 2\mu(q' - q)f(q),$$

and so

$$\tfrac{1}{2}\mu(q' - q)^\top (q' - q) \geq (q' - q)f(q).$$

Let $\mu \downarrow 0$. Then $0 \geq (q' - q)f(q)$, i.e.

$$q'f(q) \leq qf(q).$$

So, q is a stationary point of f on $\tilde{Q}(\lambda)$. Furthermore, if $q \notin \partial\tilde{Q}(\lambda)$ Walras' law implies that $f(q) = 0$ and, hence, that q is an FME.   □

By Browder's fixed point theorem (see Browder (1960)) it now follows that there is a path C of fixed points of h such that $C \cap \{0\} \times \tilde{Q}(\lambda) \neq \emptyset$ and $C \cap \{1\} \times \tilde{Q}(\lambda^*) \neq \emptyset$. Proposition 10.2 then implies that there is a connected set in $\tilde{Q}(\lambda^*)$ of stationary points of f connecting q^0 with an FME $\bar{q}$.

The path starts in the price vector q^0 that can be interpreted as the current financial market equilibrium. Suppose that a structural change takes place in the economy, e.g. preferences, initial endowments or asset payoffs change. The resulting environment is the situation where $\lambda = 0$ and the set of possible prices equals $\tilde{Q}(0) = \{q^0\}$. If one interprets $t = 0$ as the start of a trading day and $t = 1$ to be the end, then the price vector q^0 can also be interpreted as the starting prices of assets on the stock exchange, like for example the outcome of the call auction on the NYSE that takes place at the start of each trading day.

In many financial markets, the market maker takes a position in trade and is hence also dealer. In some financial markets, the market maker buys from the sellers and sells to the buyers. In that case he wants to maximise the value of excess demand, since this determines his profit. Therefore, the market maker will start quoting prices in the direction that maximises the value of excess demand. In response the investors give asks and bids to the market maker. This continues until the asks and bids are such that prices in another direction give a higher value of excess demand. In this way, the set of prices expands, shrinks and expands again until an equilibrium price vector has been found.

Since the market maker is unaware of the preferences of the agents it cannot simply quote the equilibrium prices. Therefore, it takes the myopic approach to quote prices that maximise excess demand. Along the adjustment path, the market maker learns about preferences and initial endowments while λ moves from 0 to 1. It need not be the case, however, that there is a one-to-one mapping between λ and time. It can happen that the market maker finds out that he has been moving prices in the wrong direction. As a reaction he shrinks the set $Q(\lambda)$ by decreasing λ and starts moving in another direction.

5.   The Algorithm

There are simplicial algorithms to follow the path of stationary points of f from q^0 to $\bar{q}$. The algorithm of Talman and Yamamoto (1989) results in a path that can be interpreted as a boundedly rational path to equilibrium. The algorithm should first be applied to $\tilde{Q}(1)$. If the algorithm terminates in $\bar{q} \in \tilde{Q}(1) \backslash \partial \tilde{Q}(1)$, an FME has been found. If it terminates at $q \in \partial \tilde{Q}(1)$, we extend the algorithm to $\tilde{Q}(\lambda)$, $\lambda \geq 1$. This procedure is repeated until an FME has been found.

The algorithm generates a path of piece-wise linear approximations to the excess demand function. The set $\tilde{Q}(1)$ is a J-dimensional polytope and can be written as

$$\tilde{Q}(1) = \{q \in \mathbb{R}^{J+1} | q\tilde{z} = 1, a^i q \le b_i, i = 1, \ldots, l\},$$

for some $a^i \in \mathbb{R}^{J+1} \setminus \{0\}$ and $b_i \in \mathbb{R}$, $i = 1, \ldots, l$.

Let $I \subset \{1, \ldots, l\}$. Then $F(I)$ is defined by

$$F(I) = \{q \in \tilde{Q}(1) | a^i q = b_i, i \in I\}.$$

The set $\mathcal{I} = \{I \subset \{1, \ldots, m\} | F(I) \ne \emptyset\}$ is the set of all index sets I for which $F(I)$ is a $(J - |I|)$-dimensional face of $\tilde{Q}(1)$. Let $q^0 \in int(\tilde{Q}(1))$ be the starting point. For any $I \in \mathcal{I}$ define

$$vF(I) = conv(\{q^0\}, F(I)).$$

Now $\tilde{Q}$ is triangulated into simplices in such a way that every $vF(I)$ is triangulated into $(J - |I| + 1)$-dimensional simplices.

Suppose that the algorithm is in $q^* \in vF(I)$, then q^* lies in some t-dimensional simplex $\sigma(q^1, \ldots, q^{t+1})$, with vertices the affinely independent points $q^1, \ldots, q^{t+1}$, where $t = J - |I| + 1$ and $q^i \in vF(I)$ for all $i = 1, \ldots, t+1$. There exist unique $\lambda_1^*, \ldots, \lambda_{t+1}^* \ge 0$, with $\sum_{i=1}^{\tau+1} \lambda_i^* = 1$, such that $q^* = \sum_{j=1}^{t+1} \lambda_j^* q^j$. The piece-wise linear approximation of $f(\cdot)$ at q^* is then given by

$$\bar{f}(q^*) = \sum_{j=1}^{t+1} \lambda_j^* f(q^j).$$

Let λ, $0 \le \lambda \le 1$, be such that $q^* \in \partial \tilde{Q}(\lambda)$. Then $q^* = (1 - \lambda)q^0 + \lambda q'$, for some $q' \in F(I)$. For all $1 = 1, \ldots, m$, define $b_i(\lambda) = (1 - \lambda)a^i q^0 + \lambda b_i$. The point q^* is such that it is a stationary point of $\bar{f}$ on $\tilde{Q}(\lambda)$, i.e. q^* is a solution to the linear program

$$\max\{q\bar{f}(q^*) | a^i q \le b_i(\lambda), i = 1, \ldots, m, q\tilde{z} = 1\}.$$

The dual problem is given by

$$\min\left\{ \sum_{i=1}^m \mu_i b_i(\lambda) + \beta \,\Big|\, \sum_{i=1}^m \mu_i a^i + \beta\tilde{z} = \bar{f}(q^*), \mu \ge 0, \beta \in \mathbb{R} \right\}.$$

This gives a solution μ^*, β^*. Using the complementary slackness condition we get the following:

$$\begin{aligned} I : &= \{i | a^i q^* = b_i(\lambda)\} \\ &= \{i | a^i q' = b_i\} \\ &= \{i | \mu_i^* > 0\}. \end{aligned}$$

Hence,

$$\sum_{j=1}^{t+1} \lambda_j^* f(q^j) = \sum_{i \in I} \mu_i^* a^i + \beta^* \tilde{z},$$

$\sum_{j=1}^{t+1} \lambda_j^* = 1$, and $\mu_i^* \geq 0$, for all $i \in I$. In vector notation this system reads

$$\sum_{j=1}^{t+1} \lambda_j^* \begin{bmatrix} -f(q^j) \\ 1 \end{bmatrix} + \sum_{i \in I} \mu_i^* \begin{bmatrix} a^i \\ 0 \end{bmatrix} + \beta^* \begin{bmatrix} \tilde{z} \\ 0 \end{bmatrix} = \begin{bmatrix} 0 \\ 1 \end{bmatrix}. \tag{10.3}$$

This system has $J + 2$ equations and $J + 3$ variables. The value β^* is a measure for how much the solution for the piecewise linear approximation deviates from Walras' law.

In each step of the algorithm a variable enters the basis. This is achieved by making a linear programming pivot step in (10.3). Given that due to the pivot step a variable leaves the basis, the question is how to determine which variable enters the basis. First, suppose that λ_k leaves the basis. This implies that q^* can be written as

$$q^* = \sum_{j=1, j \neq k}^{t+1} \lambda_j q^j.$$

Assuming non-degeneracy, q^* then lies in the interior of the facet τ of the simplex $\sigma(q^1, \ldots, q^{t+1})$ opposite to the vertex q^k. Now there are three possibilities. First, suppose that $\tau \in \partial v F(I)$ and $\tau \notin \partial \tilde{Q}(1)$. This happens if and only if $\tau \subset v F(I \cup \{i\})$ for some $i \notin I$. So, we increase the dual dimension with one and μ_i enters the basis via a pivot step in (10.3). The second case comprises $\tau \subset \partial \tilde{Q}(1)$. Then the algorithm continues in $\tilde{Q}(2)$. The set τ is a facet of exactly one t-simplex σ' in the extension of $v(F(I))$ in $\tilde{Q}(2)$. The vertex opposite to τ of σ' is, say, q^k. The variable λ_k then enters the basis. Finally, it can be that $\tau \notin \partial v F(I)$. Then there is a unique simplex σ' in $v F(I)$ with vertex, say q^k, opposite to the facet τ. The variable λ_k then enters the basis.

The second possibility is that μ_i leaves the basis for some $i \in I$. So, the dual dimension is decreased with one, i.e. the set I becomes $I \setminus \{i\}$. Now there are two possibilities. If $I \setminus \{i\} = \emptyset$ then $\bar{f}(q^*) = \beta^* \tilde{z}$ and the algorithm terminates. The vector q^* is an approximate equilibrium and the algorithm can be restarted at q^* with a smaller mesh in order to improve the accuracy of the approximation. Otherwise, if $I \setminus \{i\} \neq \emptyset$, then define $I' = I \setminus \{i\}$. Since the primal dimension is increased with one there exists a unique simplex σ' in $v F(I')$ having σ as a facet. The vertex opposite to σ is, say, q^k. The algorithm continues with entering λ_k in the basis by means of a pivot step in (10.3).

The first step of the algorithm consists of solving the linear program

$$\max\{qf(q^0)|a^iq \le b_i, i = 1, \ldots, m, q\tilde{z} = 1\}.$$

Its dual program is given by

$$\min\left\{\sum_{i=1}^{m}\mu_i b_i + \beta \bigg| \sum_{i=1}^{m}\mu_i a^i + \beta\tilde{z} = f(q^0)\right\}.$$

This gives as solution μ^0 and β^0. The set $F(I_0)$ is a vertex of $\tilde{Q}(1)$, where $I_0 = \{i \in \{1, \ldots, m\}|\mu_i^0 > 0\}$. There is a unique one-dimensional simplex $\sigma(w^1, w^2)$ in $vF(I_0)$ with vertices $w^1 = q^0$ and $w^2 \ne w^1$. Then λ_2 enters the basis by means of a pivot step in system (10.3).

As an example of this procedure consider the finance economy $\mathcal{E}(u, \omega, V)$ with two consumers, two assets and three states of nature. The utility functions are given by

$$u^1(x^1) = (x_0^1)^3 x_1^1 x_2^1 x_3^1$$

and

$$u^2(x^2) = x_0^2 x_1^2 x_2^2 (x_3^2)^2,$$

and the initial endowments equal $\omega^1 = (1, 3, 3, 3)$ and $\omega^2 = (4, 1, 1, 1)$, respectively. On the financial markets, two assets are traded, namely a riskless bond and a contingent contract for state 3. That is,

$$V = \begin{bmatrix} 1 & 0 \\ 1 & 0 \\ 1 & 1 \end{bmatrix}.$$

It is easy to see that the set of no-arbitrage prices, Q, is given by

$$Q = \{(q_0, q_1, q_2)|q_0 > 0, q_2 > 0, q_1 > q_2\}.$$

Taking $\tilde{z} = (1, 1, 1)$, we get that

$$\tilde{Q} = \{q \in \mathbb{R}^3|a^iq \le 0, i = 1, 2, 3, q\tilde{z} = 1\},$$

where $a^1 = (-1, 0, 0)$, $a^2 = (0, 0, -1)$, and $a^3 = (0, -1, 1)$. Since $\tilde{Q}$ is a polytope one can set $\tilde{Q}(1) = \tilde{Q}$. The set $\tilde{Q}$ is the convex hull of the points $(1, 0, 0)$, $(0, 1, 0)$, and $(0, 1/2, 1/2)$.

We start the algorithm at the price vector $q^0 = (\frac{5}{8}, \frac{1}{4}, \frac{1}{8})$. The grid size of the simplicial subdivision is taken to be $\frac{1}{8}$. Define the matrix

$A = [a^1 \quad a^2 \quad a^3 \quad \iota]$, where ι denotes the vector of ones. In the first step of the algorithm we solve the linear program

$$\min\{\beta|A(\mu_1, \mu_2, \mu_3, \beta) = f(q^0), \mu_i \geq 0, i = 1, 2, 3\},$$

where $f(q^0) = (-3.02, 8.4667, -1.8333)$. This gives as solution $\mu^0 = (11.4867, 10.3, 0)$ and $\beta^0 = 8.4667$. This implies that $I^0 = \{1, 2\}$. The basic variables are λ_1, μ_1, μ_2, and β. The coefficient matrix corresponding to (10.3) equals

$$B = \begin{bmatrix} 3.02 & -1 & 0 & 1 \\ -8.4667 & 0 & 0 & 1 \\ 1.8333 & 0 & -1 & 1 \\ 1 & 0 & 0 & 0 \end{bmatrix}.$$

The first one-dimensional simplex that is generated is the simplex $\sigma(w^1, w^2) \in vF(I^0)$, where $w^1 = q^0$ and $w^2 = \frac{1}{64}(35, 22, 7)$. The algorithm proceeds by letting λ_2 enter the basis by means of a linear programming pivot step of $(-f(w^2), 1)$ into the matrix B^{-1}. This means, the algorithm leaves q^0 into the direction $vF(I^0) - q^0$ towards $vF(I^0) = (0, 1, 0)$. By doing so one finds that μ_2 leaves the basis. This implies that the dimension of the dual space is reduced and a two-dimensional simplex is generated in $vF(\{1\})$, namely $\sigma(w^1, w^2, w^3)$, where $w^3 = \frac{1}{64}(35, 20, 9)$. One proceeds by entering λ_3 into the basis by performing a pivot step in B^{-1}. In this way one obtains a sequence of two-dimensional adjacent simplices in $vF(\{1\})$ until the algorithm terminates when μ_1 leaves the basis. This happens after, in total, 12 iterations. The path of the algorithm is depicted in Figure 10.2.

The basic variables in the final simplex are $\lambda_2, \lambda_3, \lambda_1$, and β. The corresponding simplex is given by $\sigma(w^1, w^2, w^3)$, where $w^1 = \frac{1}{16}(5, 8, 3)$, $w^2 = \frac{1}{64}(15, 34, 15)$, and $w^3 = \frac{1}{64}(15, 36, 11)$. The corresponding values for λ are given by $\lambda_1 = 0.1223$, $\lambda_2 = 0.8460$, and $\lambda_3 = 0.0316$. This yields as an approximate FME the price vector

$$\bar{q} = \sum_{i=1}^{3} \lambda_i w^i = (0.2439, 0.5284, 0.2267).$$

The value of the excess demand function in $\bar{q}$ is given by $f(\bar{q}) = (-0.0174, 0.0145, -0.0151)$. The approximate equilibrium values for consumption at $t = 0$ and the demand for assets are given by $\bar{x}_0^1 = 3.7494$, $\bar{x}_0^2 = 1.2332$, $\bar{z}^1 = (-0.9794, -0.6756)$, and $\bar{z}^2 = (0.9939, 0.6605)$, respectively. The accuracy of approximation can be improved by restarting the algorithm in $\bar{q}$ and taking a smaller grid size for the simplicial subdivision of $\tilde{Q}$.

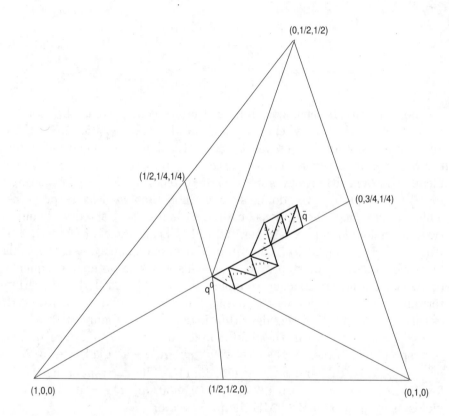

Figure 10.2.   The path of prices (dotted line) generated by the algorithm.

References

Aghion, P. and P. Howitt (1992). A Model of Growth through Creative Destruction. *Econometrica*, **60**, 323–351.

Aghion, P. and P. Howitt (1998). *Endogenous Growth Theory*. MIT Press, Cambridge, Mass.

Akerlof, G.A. (1970). The Market for Lemons: Qualitative Uncertainty and the Market Mechanism. *Quarterly Journal of Economics*, **84**, 488–500.

Alchian, A.A. (1950). Uncertainty, Evolution, and Economic Theory. *Journal of Political Economy*, **58**, 211–221.

Allais, M. (1953). Fondements d'une théorie positive des choix comportant un risque et critique des postulats et axiomes de l'école Américaine. *Colloques internationaux du Centre National de la Recherche Scientifique*, **40**, 257–332.

Alós-Ferrer, C. , A.B. Ania, and F. Vega-Redondo (1999). An Evolutionary Model of Market Structure. In P.J.J. Herings, G. van der Laan, and A.J.J. Talman (Eds.), *The Theory of Markets*, pp. 139–163. North-Holland, Amsterdam, The Netherlands.

Alvarez, L.H.R. and R. Stenbacka (2001). Adoption of Uncertain Multi-Stage Technology Projects: A Real Options Approach. *Journal of Mathematical Economics*, **35**, 71–97.

Ando, A. and F.M. Fisher (1963). Near-Decomposability, Partition and Aggregation, and the Relevance of Stability Discussions. *International Economic Review*, **4**, 53–67.

Arrow, K.J. (1953). Le role des valeurs boursières pour la répartition la meilleure des risques. *Économétrie, Colloques Internationaux du Centre National de la Recherche Scientifique*, **40**, 41–47.

Arrow, K.J. (1962). Economic Welfare and the Allocation of Resources for Inventions. In R.R. Nelson (Ed.), *The Rate and Direction of Incentive Activity*, pp. 609–625. Princeton University Press, Princeton, NJ.

Arrow, K.J. and G. Debreu (1954). Existence of an Equilibrium for a Competitive Economy. *Econometrica*, **22**, 265–292.

Aumann, R.J. (1997). Introductory Remarks. In S. Hart and A. Mas-Colell (Eds.), *Cooperation: Game-Theoretic Approaches*. Springer Verlag, Berlin, Germany.

Axelrod, R. (1984). *The Evolution of Cooperation*. Basic Books, New York, NY.

Bauer, F.L. , E. Deutsch, and J. Stoer (1969). Abschätzungen für die Eigenwerte positiver linearer Operatoren. *Linear Algebra and Applications*, **2**, 275–301.

Benoit, J.P. and V. Krishna (1985). Finitely Repeated Games. *Econometrica*, **53**, 890–904.

Berger, J.O. (1985). *Statistical Decision Theory and Bayesian Analysis* (Second ed.). Springer-Verlag, New York, NY.

Bester, H. and W. Güth (1998). Is Altruism Evolutionary Stable? *Journal of Economic Behavior and Organization*, **34**, 193–209.

Billingsley, P. (1995). *Probability and Measure* (Third ed.). John Wiley & Sons, New York, NY.

Binmore, K.G. (1987). Bargaining and Coalitions. In K.G. Binmore and P. Dasgupta (Eds.), *The Economics of Bargaining*, pp. 61–76. Blackwell, Oxford, UK.

Binmore, K.G. (1994). *Game Theory and the Social Contract, volume 1: Playing Fair*. MIT-press, Cambridge, Mass.

Binmore, K.G. (1998). *Game Theory and the Social Contract, volume 2: Just Playing*. MIT-press, Cambridge, Mass.

Bird, C. (1976). On Cost Allocation for a Spanning Tree: A Game Theoretic Approach. *Networks*, **6**, 335–350.

Björnstedt, B.J. and J. Weibull (1996). Nash Equilibrium and Evolution by Imitation. In K. Arrow and E. Colombatto (Eds.), *The Rational Foundations of Economic Behaviour*, pp. 155–171. Macmillan, New York, NY.

Bloch, F. (1996). Sequential Formation of Coalitions in Games with Externalities and Fixed Payoff Division. *Games and Economic Behavior*, **14**, 90–123.

Bolt, W. and H. Houba (2002). *Credible Threats in Negotiations: A Game-Theoretic Approach*. Number 32 in Theory and Decision Library C: Game Theory, Mathematical Programming and Operations Research. Kluwer Academic Publishers, Dordrecht, The Netherlands.

Bomfim, A.N. and F.X. Diebold (1997). Bounded Rationality and Strategic Complementarity in a Macroeconomic Model: Policy Effects, Persistence and Multipliers. *The Economic Journal*, **107**, 1358–1374.

Bondareva, O. (1993). Some Applications of Linear Programming Methods to the Theory of Cooperative Games. *Problemy Kibernet*, **10**, 119–139. In Russian.

Boone, J. (2000). Competition. CentER, DP 2000-104, Tilburg University, Tilburg, The Netherlands.

Borm, P.E.M. , H.J.M. Hamers, and R.L.P. Hendrickx (2001). Operations Research Games: A Survey. *Sociedad de Estadística e Investigación Operativa Top*, **9**, 139–216.

Bowley, A. (1924). *The Mathematical Groundwork of the Economics*. Oxford University Press, Oxford, UK.

Boyer, M. , P. Lasserre, T. Mariotti, and M. Moreaux (2001). Real Options, Preemption, and the Dynamics of Industry Investments. *Mimeo*, Université du Québec à Montréal, Montreal, Canada.

Brock, W.A. and C.H. Hommes (1997). A Rational Route to Randomness. *Econometrica*, **65**, 1059–1095.

Brouwer, L.E.J. (1912). Über Abbildung von Mannigfaltigkeiten. *Mathematische Annalen*, **71**, 313–327.

Browder, F.E. (1960). On Continuity of Fixed Points under Deformations of Continuous Mappings. *Summa Brasiliensis Mathematicae*, **4**, 183–191.

Chander, P. and H. Tulkens (1997). The Core of an Economy with Multilateral Environmental Externalities. *International Journal of Game Theory*, **26**, 379–402.

Claus, A. and D. Kleitman (1973). Cost Allocation for a Spanning Tree. *Networks*, **3**, 289–304.

Compte, O. (1998). Communication in Repeated Games with Imperfect Private Monitoring. *Econometrica*, **66**, 597–626.

Conlisk, J. (1996). Bounded Rationality and Market Fluctuations. *Journal of Economic Behavior and Organization*, **29**, 233–250.

Cournot, A. (1838). *Recherches sur les principes mathématiques de la théorie de la richesses*. L. Hachette, Paris, France. Edition used: published in 1974 by Calmann-Levy.

Courtois, P.J. (1977). *Decomposability, Queueing and Computer System Applications*. ACM monograph series. Academic Press, New York, NY.

Crampton, P. and T. Palfrey (1990). Cartel Enforcement with Uncertainty about Costs. *International Economic Review*, **31**, 1.

Crawford, V.P. (1989). Learning and Mixed-Strategy Equilibria in Evolutionary Games. *Journal of Theoretical Biology*, **140**, 537–550.

Dai, Y. , G. van der Laan, A.J.J. Talman, and Y. Yamamoto (1991). A Simplicial Algorithm for the Nonlinear Stationary Point Problem on an Unbounded Polyhedron. *SIAM Journal of Optimization*, **1**, 151–165.

Dai, Y. and A.J.J. Talman (1993). Linear Stationary Point Problems. *Mathematics of Operations Research*, **18**, 635–644.

Damme, E.E.C. van (1991). *Stability and Perfection of Nash Equilibria* (Second ed.). Springer-Verlag, Berlin, Germany.

Damme, E.E.C. van (1994). Evolutionary Game Theory. *European Economic Review*, **38**, 847–858.

Dana, R-A and M. Jeanblanc (2003). *Financial Markets in Continuous Time*. Springer-Verlag, Berlin, Germany.

Dasgupta, P. and J. Stiglitz (1980). Uncertainty, Industrial Structure, and the Speed of R&D. *Bell Journal of Economics*, **11**, 1–28.

Debreu, G. (1959). *Theory of Value*. Number 17 in Cowles Foundation Monographs. Yale University press, New Haven.

Décamps, J-P and T. Mariotti (2000). Irreversible Investment and Learning Externalities. Forthcoming in: *Journal of Economic Theory*.

Diamond, P.A. (1967). The Role of a Stock Market in a General Equilibrium Model with Technological Uncertainty. *American Economic Review*, **57**, 759–776.

Dixit, A.K. (1980). The Role of Investment in Entry Deterrence. *The Economic Journal*, **90**, 95–106.

Dixit, A.K. (1993). *The Art of Smooth Pasting*, Volume 55 of *Fundamentals of Pure and Applied Economics*. Harwood Academic Publishers, Chur, Switzerland.

Dixit, A.K. and R.S. Pindyck (1996). *Investment under Uncertainty*. Princeton University Press, Princeton, NJ. Second printing.

Droste, E.J.R. and J. Tuinstra (1998). Evolutionary Selection of Behavioral Rules in a Cournot Model. CentER DP no. 9886, CentER, Tilburg University, Tilburg, The Netherlands.

Dutta, P.K. , S. Lach, and A. Rustichini (1995). Better Late than Early. *Journal of Economics and Management Strategy*, **4**, 563–589.

Dutta, P.K. and A. Rustichini (1995). (s, S) Equilibria in Stochastic Games. *Journal of Economic Theory*, **67**, 1–39.

Eaves, B.C. (1971). On the Basic Theory of Complementarity. *Mathematical Programming*, **1**, 68–75.

Ellsberg, D. (1961). Risk, Ambiguity and the Savage Axioms. *Quarterly Journal of Economics*, **75**, 643–669.

Elzen, A.H. van den and A.J.J. Talman (1991). A Procedure for Finding Nash Equilibria in Bi-Matrix Games. *ZOR–Methods and Models of Operations Research*, **35**, 27–43.

Feller, W. (1971). *An Introduction to Probability Theory and Its Applications, volume II* (Second ed.). John Wiley & Sons, New York, NY.

Fisher, I. (1930). *The Theory of Interest*. MacMillan, New York, NY.

Foster, D.P. and H.P. Young (1990). Stochastic Evolutionary Game Dynamics. *Theoretical Population Biology*, **38**, 219–232.

Frayssé, J. and M. Moreau (1985). Collusive Equilibria in Oligopolies with Long but Finite Lives. *European Economic Review*, **27**, 45–55.

Freidlin, M.I. and A.D. Wentzell (1984). *Random Perturbations of Dynamical Systems*. Springer-Verlag, Berlin, Germany.

Friedman, J.W. (1967). An Experimental Study of Cooperative Duopoly. *Econometrica*, **35**, 379–397.

Friedman, J.W. (1971). A Noncooperative Equilibrium for Supergames. *Review of Economic Studies*, **38**, 1–12.

Friedman, J.W. (1985). Cooperative Equilibria in Finite Horizon Noncooperative Supergames. *Journal of Economic Theory*, **35**, 390–398.

Friedman, J.W. and C. Mezzetti (2002). Bounded Rationality, Dynamic Oligopoly, and Conjectural Variations. *Journal of Economic Behavior & Organization*, **49**, 287–306.

Fudenberg, D. and D.K. Levine (1998). *The Theory of Learning in Games*. MIT-press, Cambridge, Mass.

Fudenberg, D. and E. Maskin (1986). The Folk Theorem in Repeated Games with Discounting and Incomplete Information. *Econometrica*, **54**, 533–554.

Fudenberg, D. and J. Tirole (1985). Preemption and Rent Equalization in the Adoption of New Technology. *The Review of Economic Studies*, **52**, 383–401.

Fudenberg, D. and J. Tirole (1991). *Game Theory*. MIT-press, Cambridge, Mass.

Gale, J. , K.G. Binmore, and L. Samuelson (1995). Learning to be Imperfect: The Ultimatum Game. *Games and Economic Behavior*, **8**, 56–90.

Geanakoplos, J.D. and H.M. Polemarchakis (1986). Existence, Regularity, and Constrained Suboptimality of Competitive Allocations when the Asset Market is Incomplete. In W.P. Heller, R.M. Starr, and D.A. Starrett (Eds.), *Uncertainty, Information and Communication: Essays in Honor of K.J. Arrow, Vol. III*, pp. 65–96. Cambridge University Press, Cambridge, UK.

Gigerenzer, G. and D.G. Goldstein (1996). Reasoning the Fast and Frugal Way: Models of Bounded Rationality. *Psychological Review*, **103**, 650–669.

Gilboa, I. and D. Schmeidler (2001). *A Theory of Case-Based Decisions*. Cambridge University Press, Cambridge, UK.

Giovanni, J. di (2004). What Drives Capital Flows? The Determinants of Cross-Border M&A Activity. Forthcoming in: *Journal of International Economics*.

Grenadier, S.R. (1996). The Strategic Exercise of Options: Development Cascades and Overbuilding in Real Estate Markets. *The Journal of Finance*, **51**, 1653–1679.

Grenadier, S.R. (2000). *Game Choices: The Intersection of Real Options and Game Theory*. Risk Books, London, UK.

Güth, W. and M. Yaari (1992). An Evolutionary Approach to Explain Reciprocal Behavior in a Simple Strategic Game. In U. Witt (Ed.), *Explaining Process and Change - Approaches to Evolutionary Economics*. The University of Michigan Press, Ann Arbor, Mich.

Hanoch, Y. (2002). "Neither an Angel nor an Ant": Emotion as an Aid to Bounded Rationality. *Journal of Economic Psychology*, **23**, 1–25.

Harsanyi, J. and R. Selten (1988). *A General Theory of Equilibrium Selection in Games*. MIT-press, Cambridge, Mass.

Hendricks, K. , A. Weiss, and C. Wilson (1988). The War of Attrition in Continuous Time with Complete Information. *International Economic Review*, **29**, 663–680.

Hens, T. (1991). *Structure of General Equilibrium Models with Incomplete Markets*. Ph. D. thesis, University of Bonn, Bonn, Germany.

Herings, P.J.J. (1996). *Static and Dynamic Aspects of General Disequilibrium Theory*. Number 13 in Theory and Decision Library C: Game Theory, Mathematical Programming and Operations Research. Kluwer Academic Publishers, Dordrecht, The Netherlands.

Herings, P.J.J. and F. Kubler (2002). Computing Equilibria in Finance Economies. *Mathematics of Operations Research*, **27**, 637–646.

Herings, P.J.J. and F. Kubler (2003). Approximate CAPM when Preferences are CRRA. METEOR Research Memorandum 03/040, Maastricht University, Maastricht, The Netherlands.

Hermann-Pillath, C. (2001). On the Ontological Foundations of Evolutionary Economics. In K. Dopfer (Ed.), *Evolutionary Economics: Program and Scope*. Kluwer Academic Publishers, Boston, Mass.

Hertz, N. (2002). *The Silent Takeover: Global Capitalism and the Death of Democracy*. Free Press.

Hicks, J.R. (1939). *Value and Capital*. Clarendon Press, Oxford, UK.

Hildenbrand, W. and A.P. Kirman (1988). *Equilibrium Analysis*. North-Holland, Amsterdam, The Netherlands.

Hirsch, M. , M. Magill, and A. Mas-Colell (1990). A Geometric Approach to a Class of Equilibrium Existence Theorems. *Journal of Mathematical Economics*, **19**, 95–106.

Hofstede, G. (1984). *Culture's Consequences*. Sage, Beverly Hills, Cal.

Hoppe, H.C. (2000). Second-mover Advantages in the Strategic Adoption of New Technology under Uncertainty. *International Journal of Industrial Organization*, **18**, 315–338.

Huisman, K.J.M. (2001). *Technology Investment: A Game Theoretic Real Options Approach*. Number 28 in Theory and Decision Library C: Game Theory, Mathematical Programming and Operations Research. Kluwer Academic Publishers, Dordrecht, The Netherlands.

Huisman, K.J.M. and P.M. Kort (1999). Effects of Strategic Interactions on the Option Value of Waiting. CentER DP no. 9992, Tilburg University, Tilburg, The Netherlands.

Huisman, K.J.M. , P.M. Kort, G. Pawlina, and J.J.J. Thijssen (2004). Strategic Investment under Uncertainty: Merging Real Options with Game Theory. Forthcoming in: *Zeitschrift für Betriebswissenschaft*.

Jänich, K. (1984). *Topology*. Springer-Verlag, New York, NY.

Jensen, R. (1982). Adoption and Diffusion of an Innovation of Uncertain Profitability. *Journal of Economic Theory*, **27**, 182–193.

Jensen, R. (1992a). Dynamic Patent Licensing. *International Journal of Industrial Organization*, **10**, 349–368.

Jensen, R. (1992b). Innovation Adoption and Welfare under Uncertainty. *The Journal of Industrial Economics*, **40**, 173–180.

Kaarbøe, O.M. and A.F. Tieman (1999). Equilibrium Selection in Supermodular Games with Simultaneous Play. *Mimeo*, Dept. of Economics, University of Bergen, Bergen, Norway.

Kalai, E. and W. Stanford (1985). Conjectural Variations in Accelerated Cournot Games. *International Journal of Industrial Organization*, **3**, 133–152.

Kamyia, K. (1990). A Globally Stable Price Adjustment Process. *Econometrica*, **58**, 1481–1485.

Kandori, M. , G.J. Mailath, and R. Rob (1993). Learning, Mutation, and Long Run Equilibria in Games. *Econometrica*, **61**, 29–56.

Kandori, M. and H. Matsushima (1998). Private Observation, Communication and Collusion. *Econometrica*, **66**, 627–652.

Karatzas, I. and S.E. Shreve (1991). *Brownian Motion and Stochastic Calculus*. Springer, New York, NY.

Kihlstrom, R. and X. Vives (1989). Collusion by Asymmetrically Informed Duopolists. *European Journal of Political Economy*, **5**, 371–402.

Kihlstrom, R. and X. Vives (1992). Collusion by Asymmetrically Informed Firms. *Journal of Economics and Management Strategy*, **1**, 371–396.

Klein, N. (1999). *No Logo*. Knopf, New York, NY.

Kohlberg, E. and J-F Mertens (1986). On the Strategic Stability of Equilibria. *Econometrica*, **54**, 1003–1038.

Kosfeld, M. (1999). *Individual Decision-Making and Social Interaction*. Ph. D. thesis, CentER for Economic Research, Tilburg University, Tilburg, The Netherlands.

Laan, G. van der and A.J.J. Talman (1987). Adjustment Processes for Finding Economic Equilibrium Problems on the Unit Simplex. *Economics Letters*, **23**, 119–123.

Lambrecht, B.M. (2004). The Timing and Terms of Mergers Motivated by Economies of Scale. Forthcoming in: *Journal of Financial Economics*.

Lambrecht, B.M. and W. Perraudin (2003). Real Options and Preemption under Incomplete Information. *Journal of Economic Dynamics and Control*, **27**, 619–643.

Lancaster, P. and M. Tismentetsky (1985). *The Theory of Matrices*. Academic Press, Orlando, Fla.

Laville, F. (2000). Should We Abandon Optimization Theory? The Need for Bounded Rationality. *Journal of Economic Methodology*, **7**, 395–426.

Lee, T. and L. Wilde (1980). Market Structure and Innovation: A Reformulation. *Quarterly Journal of Economics*, **194**, 429–436.

Loury, G.C. (1979). Market Structure and Innovation. *Quarterly Journal of Economics*, **93**, 395–410.

Magill, M. and M. Quinzii (1996). *Theory of Incomplete Markets*. MIT Press, Cambridge, Mass.

Mailath, G.J. (1992). Introduction: Symposium on Evolutionary Game Theory. *Journal of Economic Theory*, **57**, 259–277.

Maksimovic, V. and G. Philips (2001). The Market for Corporate Assets: Who Engages in Mergers and Asset Sales and are there Efficiency Gains? *Journal of Finance*, **56**, 2019–2065.

Malueg, D.A. and S.O. Tsutsui (1997). Dynamic R&D Competition with Learning. *RAND Journal of Economics*, **28**, 751–772.

Mamer, J.W. and K.F. McCardle (1987). Uncertainty, Competition and the Adoption of New Technology. *Management Science*, **33**, 161–177.

Mankiw, N.G. and M.D. Whinston (1986). Free Entry and Social Inefficiency. *Rand Journal of Economics*, **17**, 48–58.

Mas–Colell, A. , M.D. Whinston, and J.R. Green (1995). *Microeconomic Theory*. Oxford University Press, New York, NY.

Matsui, A. (1992). Best Response Dynamics and Socially Stable Strategies. *Journal of Economic Theory*, **57**, 343–362.

Maynard Smith, J. (1974). The Theory of Games and Evolution in Animal Conflict. *Journal of Theoretical Biology*, **47**, 209–221.

Maynard Smith, J. (1982). *Evolution and the Theory of Games*. Cambridge University Press, Cambridge, UK.

Maynard Smith, J. and G.R. Price (1973). The Logic of Animal Conflict. *Nature*, **246**, 15–18.

McDonald, R. and D. Siegel (1986). The Value of Waiting to Invest. *Quarterly Journal of Economics*, **101**, 707–728.

Merton, R.C. (1990). *Continuous Time Finance*. Blackwell Publishers, Malden, Mass.

Milgrom, P. and J. Roberts (1991). Adaptive and Sophisticated Learning in Normal Form Games. *Games and Economic Behavior*, **3**, 82–100.

Montero, M. (2000). *Endogenous Coalition Formation and Bargaining.* Ph. D. thesis, CentER for Economic Research, Tilburg University, Tilburg, The Netherlands.

Moscarini, G. and L. Smith (2001). The Optimal Level of Experimentation. *Econometrica*, **69**, 1629–1644.

Mount, K.R. and S. Reiter (2002). *Computation and Complexity in Economic Behavior and Complexity.* Cambridge University Press, Cambridge, UK.

Munkres, J.R. (1975). *Topology, A First Course.* Prentice-Hall, Englewood Cliffs, NJ.

Murto, P. (1999). *On Investment, Uncertainty, and Strategic Interaction with Applications in Energy Markets.* Ph. D. thesis, Helsinki University of Technology, Helsinki, Finland.

Nash, J.F. (1950a). The Bargaining Problem. *Econometrica*, **18**, 155–162.

Nash, J.F. (1950b). Equilibrium Points in *N*-Person Games. *Proceedings of the National Academy of Sciences of the United States of America*, **36**, 48–49.

Neumann, J. von and O. Morgenstern (1944). *Theory of Games and Economic Behavior.* Princeton University Press, Princeton, NJ.

Nielsen, M.J. (2002). Competition and Irreversible Investments. *International Journal of Industrial Organization*, **20**, 731–743.

Offerman, T. , J. Potters, and J. Sonnemans (2002). Imitation and Belief Learning in an Oligopoly Experiment. *Review of Economic Studies*, **69**, 973–997.

Ok, E.A. and F. Vega-Redondo (2001). On the Evolution of Individualistic Preferences: Complete versus Incomplete Information Scenarios. *Journal of Economic Theory*, **97**, 231–254.

Øksendal, B. (2000). *Stochastic Differential Equations* (Fifth ed.). Springer-Verlag, Berlin, Germany.

Osborne, M.J. and A. Rubinstein (1994). *A Course in Game Theory.* MIT Press, Cambridge, Mass.

Pawlina, G. (2003). *Corporate Investment under Uncertainty and Competition: A Real Options Approach.* Ph. D. thesis, CentER for Economic Research, Tilburg University, Tilburg, The Netherlands.

Pawlina, G. and P.M. Kort (2001). Real Options in an Asymmetric Duopoly: Who Benefits from Your Competitive Disadvantage. CentER DP no. 2001-95, Tilburg University, Tilburg, The Netherlands.

Peleg, B. and P. Sudhölter (2003). *Introduction to the Theory of Cooperative Games.* Number 34 in Theory and Decision Library C: Game Theory, Mathematical Programming and Operations Research. Kluwer Academic Publishers, Dordrecht, The Netherlands.

Pennings, H.P.G. (1998). *Real Options and Managerial Decision Making.* Ph. D. thesis, Erasmus University, Rotterdam Institute for Business Economic Studies, Rotterdam, The Netherlands.

Possajennikov, A. (2000). On the Evolutionary Stability of Altruistic and Spiteful Preferences. *Journal of Economic Behavior and Organization*, **42**, 125–129.

Protter, P. (1995). *Stochastic Integration and Differential Equations.* Springer-Verlag, Berlin, Germany.

Radner, R. (1972). Existence of Equilibrium of Plans, Prices, Price Expectations in a Sequence of Markets. *Econometrica*, **40**, 289–304.

Radner, R. (1980). Collusive Behavior in Non-Cooperative Epsilon Equilibria of Oligopolies with Long but Finite Lives. *Journal of Economic Theory*, **22**, 121–157.

Radner, R. (1996). Bounded Rationality, Indeterminacy, and the Theory of the Firm. *The Economic Journal*, **106**, 1360–1373.

Reinganum, J.F. (1981). Dynamic Games of Innovation. *Journal of Economic Theory*, **25**, 21–41.

Reinganum, J.F. (1982). A Dynamic Game of R&D: Patent Protection and Competitive Behaviour. *Econometrica*, **50**, 671–688.

Rijt, J.W. van der (2000). Een alternatief model voor coalitievorming in de politiek. Master's thesis (in Dutch), Department of Econometrics & Operations Research, Tilburg University, Tilburg, The Netherlands.

Roberts, K. (1983). Self-agreed Cartel Rules. IMSSS Technical Report 427. Stanford University.

Roberts, K. (1985). Cartel Behavior and Adverse Selection. *Journal of Industrial Economics*, **33**, 401–413.

Rockafellar, R.T. (1970). *Convex Analysis*. Princeton University Press, Princeton, NJ.

Rousseau, J–J (1762). *Du contrat social*. Edition used: published in 1996 by Booking International, Paris, France.

Rubinstein, A. (1982). Perfect Equilibrium in a Bargaining Model. *Econometrica*, **50**, 97–108.

Rubinstein, A. (1998). *Modeling Bounded Rationality*. MIT Press, Cambridge, Mass.

Samuelson, L. (1996). Bounded Rationality and Game Theory. *The Quarterly Journal of Economics and Finance*, **36**, 17–35.

Samuelson, L. (1997). *Games and Equilibrium Selection*. MIT Press, Cambridge, Mass.

Samuelson, L. and J. Zhang (1992). Evolutionary Stability in Asymmetric Games. *Journal of Economic Theory*, **57**, 363–391.

Sargent, T.J. (1993). *Bounded Rationality in Macroeconomics*. Oxford University Press, Oxford, UK.

Savage, L.J. (1954). *The Foundations of Statistics*. John Wiley and Sons, New York, NY.

Schenk-Hoppé, K.R. (2000). The Evolution of Walrasian Behavior in Oligopolies. *Journal of Mathematical Economics*, **33**, 35–55.

Schipper, B.C. (2003). Imitators and Optimizers in Cournot Oligopoly. *Mimeo*, University of Bonn, Bonn, Germany.

Schlag, K.H. (1998). Why Imitate and If So, How? *Journal of Economic Theory*, **78**, 130–156.

Schumpeter, J.A. (1942). *Capitalism, Socialism and Democracy*. Harper and Brothers, New York, NY. Edition used: published in 1976 by George Allen & Unwin, London, UK.

Shapley, L. (1953). A Value for n-Person Games. In H. Kuhn and A. Tucker (Eds.), *Contributions to the Theory of Games II*. Princeton University Press, Princeton, NJ.

Shapley, L. (1967). On Balanced Sets and Cores. *Naval Research Logistics Quarterly*, **14**, 453–460.

Sherer, F.M. and D. Ross (1990). *Industrial Market Structure and Economic Performance* (Third ed.). Houghton Mifflin, Boston, Mass.

Shiryaev, A.N. (1978). *Optimal Stopping Rules*. Springer-Verlag, Berlin, Germany.

Simon, H.A. (1957). *Models of Man*. Wiley, New York, NY.

Simon, H.A. and A. Ando (1961). Aggregation of Variables in Dynamic Systems. *Econometrica*, **29**, 111–138.

Simon, L.K. (1987a). Basic Timing Games. Working Paper 8745, University of California at Berkeley, Department of Economics, Berkeley, Ca.

Simon, L.K. (1987b). A Multistage Duel in Continuous Time. Working Paper 8757, University of California at Berkeley, Department of Economics, Berkeley, Ca.

Simon, L.K. and M.B. Stinchcombe (1989). Extensive Form Games in Continuous Time: Pure Strategies. *Econometrica*, **57**, 1171–1214.

Smets, F. (1991). Exporting versus FDI: The Effect of Uncertainty, Irreversibilities and Strategic Interactions. Working Paper, Yale University, New Haven, Conn.

Solow, R. (1957). Technical Change and the Aggregate Production Function. *Review of Economics and Statistics*, **39**, 312–320.

Stenbacka, R. and M.M. Tombak (1994). Strategic Timing of Adoption of New Technologies under Uncertainty. *International Journal of Industrial Organization*, **12**, 387–411.

Talman, A.J.J. and J.J.J. Thijssen (2003). Existence of Equilibrium and Price Adjustments in a Fiance Economy with Incomplete Markets. CentER DP 2003–79, Tilburg University, Tilburg, The Netherlands.

Talman, A.J.J. and Y. Yamamoto (1989). A Simplicial Algorithm for Stationary Point Problems on Polytopes. *Mathematics of Operations Research*, **14**, 383–399.

Taylor, P. and L. Jonker (1978). Evolutionary Stable Strategies and Game Dynamics. *Mathematical Biosciences*, **40**, 145–156.

Thijssen, J.J.J. (2001). Stochastic Stability of Cooperative and Competitive Behaviour in Cournot Oligopoly. CentER DP 2001–19, Tilburg University, Tilburg, The Netherlands.

Thijssen, J.J.J. (2003). Evolution of Conjectures in Cournot Oligopoly. Trinity Economic Paper No. 2003–16, Trinity College Dublin, Dublin, Ireland.

Thijssen, J.J.J. (2004). The Optimal and Strategic Timing of Mergers under Uncertainty. *Mimeo*, Department of Economics, Trinity College Dublin, Dublin, Ireland.

Thijssen, J.J.J. , R.L.P. Hendrickx, and P.E.M. Borm (2002). Spillovers and Strategic Cooperative Behaviour. CentER DP 2002–70, Tilburg University, Tilburg, The Netherlands.

Thijssen, J.J.J. , K.J.M. Huisman, and P.M. Kort (2002). Symmetric Equilibrium Strategies in Game Theoretic Real Option Models. CentER DP 2002–81, Tilburg University, Tilburg, The Netherlands.

Thijssen, J.J.J. , K.J.M. Huisman, and P.M. Kort (2003). The Effects of Information on Strategic Investment and Welfare. Trinity Economic Paper No. 2003–10, Trinity College Dublin, Dublin, Ireland.

Thijssen, J.J.J. , K.J.M. Huisman, and P.M. Kort (2004). The Effect of Information Streams on Capital Budgeting Decisions. Forthcoming in: *European Journal of Operational Research*.

Tijms, H.C. (1994). *Stochastic Models: An Algorithmic Approach*. Wiley & Sons, Chichester, UK.

Tijs, S.H. (1981). Bounds for the Core of a Game and the τ-Value. In O. Moeschlin and D. Pallaschke (Eds.), *Game Theory and Mathematical Economics*, pp. 123–132. North Holland, Amsterdam, The Netherlands.

Tijs, S.H. (1987). An Axiomatization of the τ-Value. *Mathematical Social Sciences*, **13**.

Tirole, J. (1988). *The Theory of Industrial Organization*. MIT-press, Cambridge, Mass.

Trigeorgis, L. (1996). *Real Options: Managerial Flexibility and Strategy in Resource Allocation*. MIT Press, Cambridge, Mass.

Tversky, A. and D. Kahneman (1981). The Framing of Decisions and the Psychology of Choice. *Science*, **211**, 453–458.

Vega–Redondo, F. (1996). *Evolution, Games, and Economic Behaviour.* Oxford University Press, Oxford, UK.

Vega–Redondo, F. (1997). The Evolution of Walrasian Behavior. *Econometrica,* **65**, 375–384.

Vives, X. (1999). *Oligopoly Pricing, Old Ideas and New Tools.* MIT-press, Cambridge, Mass.

Wald, A. (1947). *Sequential Analysis.* Wiley & Sons, New York, NY.

Walras, L. (1874). *Eléments d'économie pure.* Corbaz, Lausanne, Switzerland.

Weeds, H.F. (2002). Strategic Delay in a Real Options Model of R&D Competition. *Review of Economic Studies,* **69**, 729–747.

Weibull, J. (1995). *Evolutionary Game Theory.* MIT-press, Cambridge, Mass.

Williams, D. (1991). *Probability with Martingales.* Cambridge University Press, Cambridge, UK.

Yang, Z. (1999). *Computing Equilibria and Fixed Points: The Solution of Nonlinear Inequalities.* Number 21 in Theory and Decision Library C: Game Theory, Mathematical Programming and Operations Research. Kluwer Academic Publishers, Dordrecht, The Netherlands.

Yi, S. (1997). Stable Coalition Structures with Externalities. *Games and Economic Behavior,* **20**, 201–237.

Young, H.P. (1993). The Evolution of Conventions. *Econometrica,* **61**, 57–84.

Young, H.P. (1998). *Individual Strategy and Social Structure.* Princeton University Press, Princeton, NJ.

Zingales, L. (2000). In Search of New Foundations. *The Journal of Finance,* **55**, 1623–1654.

Author Index

Subject Index

maximum degree of coupling, 40
regular perturbed, 37
spectral density decomposition, 40
minimum right vector, 31, 159, 169
monomorphic state, 187, 210
mutation, 15, 183, 185, 203–204

Nash program, 11
nearly-complete decomposability, 17, 43,
181, 200, 210
Net Present Value, 64, 68
no-arbitrage prices, 221, 234

piece-wise linear approximation, 26, 231
polyhedron, 24, 228
polytope, 24, 228
preemption, 9, 77, 79
coordination problem, 77–78, 103, 123
price-adjustment process, 217
prior belief, 58

recession cone, 25, 228
reflection principle, 48
rent equalisation, 7, 89
replicator dynamics, 14

second mover advantage, 9, 112, 116
semimartingale, 46, 80
Shapley value, 30, 155, 158
signals, 56
h-, 58, 118
l-, 58, 118
costly, 72
quality of, 60, 130
quantity of, 60, 130
simplex, 25
diameter of, 26

face of, 25
facet of, 25
vertex of, 25
simplicial algorithm, 217, 231
smooth pasting, 51
spillover
coalitional, 12, 143, 146, 166
information, 112
stationary point, 23, 136, 227
-theorem, 23
stochastic differential equation, 47, 80
stochastic potential, 38
stochastic process, 44
cadlag, 44, 80
diffusion, 49
geometric Brownian motion, 49, 80, 93,
167
Ito, 49
Poisson process, 48, 59, 118
Wiener process, 48
stochastic stability, 15, 38, 180, 190, 198
stopping time, 44, 88, 121, 123
strategy
closed-loop, 87, 89, 104, 123, 126, 134
mixed, 28
simple, 81

tree, 37, 188, 212
triangulation, 25

utopia vector, 31, 159

value function, 63
value matching, 51

Walras' law, 222, 228, 233
war of attrition, 9
welfare measure, 102, 129

About the Author

Dr. Jacco J.J. Thijssen graduated in Econometrics from Tilburg University, Tilburg, The Netherlands in 1999. In the same year he also completed the Master's Program in Economics from CentER at the same university. After that, he carried out his Ph.D. research at the Department of Econometrics & Operations Research, and CentER at Tilburg University. Since September 2003 he is affiliated as a Lecturer in Economics with the Department of Economics at Trinity College Dublin, Dublin, Ireland.